CIRCLE FORWARD

WHAT EDUCATORS ARE SAYING ABOUT *CIRCLE FORWARD*

In this time of great opportunity within our schools, Dreams are coming true . . . my first gaze at *Circle Forward* began a wave of chills . . . have you ever wondered how to bring more SOUL into our schools? Depth, Purpose, and Connection . . . wonder no more. . . this book is sacred and brings us to a holy place . . . we are seen and heard in Peacemaking Circles . . . slowly we Trust . . . *Circle Forward* creates the feeling of being Home! An absolutely amazing, loving GIFT to us all . . . deep gratitude to Kay and Carolyn for this incredible Labor of Love.

— **Jamie Williams,** The Restorative Way: Circle Training for Schools, Minneapolis, Minnesota

It takes skill to author a book that is both inspiring and practical. Kay and Carolyn provide a strong theoretical foundation for Circles and include extensive information about how teachers might utilize Circles in their schools and classrooms. The modules containing models for various types of Circles are extremely helpful and the appendix contains so many valuable resources. As a teacher educator looking to assist teachers as they develop both the knowledge and skills needed to effectively facilitate Circle processes, I am so excited about this book.

— **Kathy Evans,** Assistant Professor of Education, Eastern Mennonite University, active in furthering Restorative Justice in Education (RJE), Harrisonburg, Virginia

As a former schoolteacher and school administrator, I see this book adding positively to literature being written on this topic. You have given our teachers practical methods for using Circles in their classrooms and for creating an Ecosystem of Care in schools. Thank you for sharing your wisdom with our educators!

— **Robert Spicer,** Restorative Justice Consultant and Community Activist: Restorative Strategies, Chicago, Illinois

Across a range of social institutions, people are looking for new ways forward to address growing concerns, such as bullying and alienation, within institutional cultures. *Circle Forward* offers a framework and process to address these concerns within schools, based on a relational paradigm nested in the human need for belonging, power, and respect. This book offers practical guidelines for building community, teaching social and emotional learning, and facilitating difficult conversations for all members of the school community—administrators, teachers, staff, students, and parents. It offers clear hope for all to find a place to belong within their own school community.

— **Brenda Morrison,** Director of the Centre for Restorative Justice at Simon Fraser University and Professor of Criminology, Burnaby Mountain, British Columbia

Carolyn Boyes-Watson and Kay Pranis, leading voices in the Circle practice, have combined their expertise and resources to publish a book that is practical, accessible and inspiring for anyone, whether lay or professional, who wants a better understanding of the Circle process, especially in the school environment.

This guide provides a succinct, step-by-step description of how to facilitate many different kinds of Circles, ranging from friendship and bereavement to gratitude and team-building Circles. Rich and succinct, these model Circles provide just enough detail to grasp the concept, but not too much to be overwhelming.

The authors emphasize the importance of strong peer-to-peer and student-adult relationships built in Circles within the school community to help curb disciplinary issues. When things do go wrong, however, they offer comprehensive, restorative Circle templates for addressing the harm that has been caused and restoring harmony to those involved within and outside the school environment.

An added bonus are the appendices, which are filled with additional prompting questions for deep discussions; opening and closing readings and activities; inspirational quotes and stories; and meditation and movement exercises.

This book—the most authoritative on the market today—is a must-read for those who are already in the field facilitating Circles, those who want to begin this journey, and those who are just curious. Its style of presentation and writing establishes the reverent tone of the Circle—one grounded in compassion and understanding—which leaves the reader with an uplifted spirit, knowing that change is possible when people care.

— **Ann Schumacher,** Ph.D., Circle Keeper and Mediator, Detroit, Michigan

I am very grateful to Kay and Carolyn for their commitment to creating healthy communities for all young people, for their wisdom, and for their generosity. I cannot wait to share this wisdom with our schools—the teachers, administrators, students and their families, student support staff, educational assistants, volunteers, cooks, janitors, bus drivers, and school board members. This book is such a gift!

— **Nancy Riestenberg,** author of *Circle in the Square,* School Climate Specialist, Minnesota Department of Education

Living Justice Press

INSTITUTE for RESTORATIVE INITIATIVES

Circle Forward

BUILDING A RESTORATIVE SCHOOL COMMUNITY

Carolyn Boyes-Watson & Kay Pranis
Foreword by Nancy Riestenberg

Copyright © 2015 by Carolyn Boyes-Watson and Kay Pranis

To obtain copies of *Circle Forward,* please contact either of the co-publishers:

Living Justice Press
2093 Juliet Ave.
St. Paul, MN 55105
http://www.livingjusticepress.org
ljpress@aol.com
(651) 695-1008

Institute for Restorative Initiatives
100 Pacific Street
Cambridge, MA 02139
http://www.instituteforrestorativeinitiatives.org/

Library of Congress Cataloging-in-Publication Data
Boyes-Watson, Carolyn.
Circle forward : building a restorative school community / Carolyn Boyes-Watson & Kay Pranis ; foreword by Nancy Riestenberg.
    pages   cm
    ISBN 978-1-937141-19-6 (spiral bound) — ISBN 978-1-937141-20-2 (ebook)
1. School improvement programs. 2. Classroom management. 3. School environment. 4. Community and school. 5. Inclusive education. 6. Healing circles. I. Pranis, Kay. II. Title.
    LB2822.8.B66   2015
    371.2´07—dc23
                                                            2014028504

20 19 18 17 16 15   5 4 3 2 1

Cover and interior design by Wendy Holdman
Printed by Sheridan Books, Inc., Ann Arbor, Michigan, on recycled paper

Contents

Foreword: Safety and Pies by Nancy Riestenberg — xv
Acknowledgments — xxi
Notes — xxii

PART I: THE BASICS

Introduction — 3
The Theoretical Foundation for Circle Practice in Schools — 6
Our Seven Core Assumptions — 9
Thinking about Healthy Relationships in Schools — 17
The Power and Challenge of Circles in Schools — 23
How Circles Work — 27
The Model Circles in This Book — 38

PART II: BUILDING A POSITIVE SCHOOL CLIMATE

Module 1: Establishing a Circle Practice — 45
1.1 Introducing the Circle to the Staff — 47
1.2 Introducing Circles in Schools — 49
1.3 Introducing the Talking Piece — 51
1.4 Circle for Making a Talking Piece — 52
1.5 Practicing the Use of the Talking Piece Circle — 54
1.6 Building Our Circle Skills Circle — 56

Module 2: Establishing and Affirming Community Norms — 57
2.1 Creating a Safe and Happy Classroom Circle — 59
2.2 Circle for Designing Our Classroom Community to Meet Our Needs — 60
2.3 Exploring Our Values-in-Action Circles — 62
2.4 Coming to Consensus on Classroom Agreements Circle — 63
2.5 Checking-In with Guidelines Circle I: Setting Our Intentions — 65
2.6 Checking-In with Guidelines Circle II: Taking the Temperature on the Classroom Climate — 66
2.7 Understanding and Living with School Rules Circle — 68

Module 3: Teaching and Learning in Circle — 69

- 3.1 Finding Out What Students Already Know Circle — 71
- 3.2 Checking for Understanding Circle — 72
- 3.3 Building Vocabulary Circle — 73
- 3.4 Sharing Student Writing in a "Read-Around" Circle — 75
- 3.5 Practicing a Foreign Language Circle: Beginner to Intermediate — 79
- 3.6 Sharing Reflections Circle — 81
- 3.7 Using Storybooks to Teach Values Circle — 83
- 3.8 Talking about Homework/Studying Circle — 85
- 3.9 Three-Minute Focus Circle — 87

Module 4: Building Connection and Community — 89

- 4.1 Check-In Circle: Practices for Building Relationships — 91
- 4.2 Celebration Circle — 92
- 4.3 Showing Gratitude and Appreciation Circle — 94
- 4.4 Sticking Together Circle — 96
- 4.5 What Is Friendship? Circle — 97
- 4.6 Picturing My Future Circle — 99
- 4.7 What Does Success Mean? Circle — 100
- 4.8 Relationship Building Circle — 101
- 4.9 Exploring Dimensions of Our Identity Circle — 103
- 4.10 The Gender Box Circle — 106
- 4.11 Elements of a Healthy Relationship Circle — 109
- 4.12 Choosing Trustworthy Friends Circle — 111
- 4.13 Sports Team-Building: Relationship Circle — 113
- 4.14 Sports Team-Building: Deepening Relationships Circle — 115
- 4.15 Reflecting on Winning and Losing Circle — 116
- 4.16 Reflection after a Game Circle — 118
- 4.17 Welcome Back after Classroom Absence Circle — 119

Module 5: Social and Emotional Learning — 121

- 5.1 Listening to the Silence Circle — 123
- 5.2 Who and What Make Us Feel Good? Circle — 125
- 5.3 Dealing with Inside and Outside Hurts Circle — 126
- 5.4 What Triggers Your Anger? Circle — 128
- 5.5 What Are You Worried About? Circle — 129
- 5.6 Daily Emotional Weather Report Circle — 131
- 5.7 Who Am I Really? Circle — 135
- 5.8 Safe Space Circle — 138
- 5.9 Managing Mountains Circle — 140

Module 6: Important but Difficult Conversations — 143

6.1	What Motivates You? Circle	145
6.2	Being Left Out Circle	147
6.3	Let's Talk about Bullying Circle	148
6.4	The Impact of Gossip Circle	149
6.5	Bereavement Circle	151
6.6	Responding to Community Trauma Circle	153
6.7	Dealing with Losses Circle	155
6.8	Masking Grief Circle	160
6.9	Understanding Trauma Circle	163
6.10	Witnessing Violence Circle	165
6.11	Roots of Youth Violence Circle	169
6.12	The Impact of Social Hierarchies on Me Circle	172
6.13	Talking about Structural Inequality: Privilege and Oppression Circle	175
6.14	What Do We Know about Race? Circle	179
6.15	What Difference Does Race Make? Circle	182
6.16	Exploring Our Feelings about Race Circle	184
6.17	Exploring White Privilege Circle	186
6.18	Exploring the Impact of Social Inequality Circle	190
6.19	Thinking about Gender and Violence Circle	193
6.20	Thinking about Gender Inequality Circle	196
6.21	Thinking and Talking about OUR Boundaries Circle (For Girls)	198
6.22	Sexual Harassment and Bystander Circle	200
6.23	Love and Marriage Circle	203
6.24	When We're Different or At-Odds with Society Circle	205

Module 7: Working Together as Staff — 207

7.1	Establishing Guidelines for Staff Circle	209
7.2	Staff Weekly Reflection Circle	211
7.3	Staff Team-Building Circle	212
7.4	Why Relationships Matter in Schools Circle	214
7.5	Sustaining Ourselves When the Work Is Difficult Circle	216
7.6	Self-Care Circle	218
7.7	Student and Teacher Class Assessment Circle	220
7.8	Parent–Teacher Conference Circle	222
7.9	How Are the Children? Circle	224
7.10	Exploring Our Core Assumptions Circle	226
7.11	Assessing Our Progress in Moving toward a Restorative School Culture Circle	231
7.12	Challenge of Change Circle	233

Module 8: Engaging Parents and the Wider Community — 235

8.1	Parent Circle: Introduction to the Circle Process	237
8.2	Parent Circle: Building Support in Small Groups	240
8.3	Parent Circle: Feedback to the School	242
8.4	Family–School Engagement Circle	244
8.5	Looking at Our Own Relationship to School Circle	246
8.6	Community–School Partnership Circle	248
8.7	Building Bridges to a New Immigrant Community Circle	250
8.8	IEP (Individualized Education Program) Circle	252

Module 9: Youth-Led and Peer-to-Peer Circles — 255

9.1	What Do Adults Need to Understand about Our Lives? Circle	257
9.2	Visioning a Good Life Circle	259
9.3	Circle for Student Focus Groups on a School Issue or Policy	261
9.4	Exploring Cultural Responsiveness in the School Circle	263

Module 10: Circles for Intensive Support — 265

10.1	Intensive Support: Building Relationships Circle	267
10.2	Intensive Support: Map of Resources Circle	270
10.3	Intensive Support: Making a Plan Circle	272
10.4	Intensive Support: Check-In Circles	274
10.5	Intensive Support: Celebration Circle	276
10.6	What Went Right in Your Family Circle	278
10.7	Identifying Sources of Support Circle	280

PART III: USING CIRCLES WHEN THINGS GO WRONG

Restorative Discipline — 285

Module 11: Learning Restorative Discipline — 289

11.1	Understanding the Restorative Justice Framework for Addressing Harm Circle I	290
11.2	Understanding the Restorative Justice Framework for Addressing Harm Circle II	292
11.3	What Will Make It Right? Circle	294

Doing Restorative Discipline in Circle — 297

Module 12: Restorative Discipline and Conflict Circles — 301

12.1 Template for a Restorative Discipline Circle — 302
12.2 Template for a Circle about a Conflict — 304
12.3 Template for a Silent Circle Responding to Conflict Immediately — 306
12.4 Classroom Circle for Responding to Harm without Focusing on the Wrongdoer — 308
12.5 Welcome Back after Suspension Circle — 310
12.6 The Class That Ate the Sub Circle — 312

Module 13: Complex and Multi-Process Circles for Serious Incidents of Harm — 315

The Importance of Pre-Work and Preparation — 315
Follow-Up Circles — 317
Celebration Circles — 317
Multi-Circle Processes for Serious Harm — 317
Using Circles for Incidents of Bullying — 318
What Bullying Is and What Bullying Is Not — 319
Suggested Possible Circles That Can Be Useful in Bullying Cases — 320

APPENDICES

Appendix 1: Sample Prompting Questions/Topics for Circles — 323

Exploring values — 323
Getting acquainted — 324
Storytelling from our lives to share who we are and what has shaped us — 324
Taking responsibility — 325
Community — 325
Exploring relationships — 326
Hopes and dreams — 327
Toward the end of a Circle — 327

Appendix 2: Openings & Closings — 329

I. Readings Organized by Themes — 329

Circles — 329
Unity & interconnectedness — 333
Listening — 336
Speaking from the heart — 340
Storytelling — 341
Belonging — 342
Respect — 343
Self-love & discovering our true selves — 343
Learning — 346

Self-determination & empowerment	349
Changing the world . . . starting with ourselves	351
Inclusion & exclusion	353
Power	354
Anti-bullying	355
Dealing with conflicts, hurts, & harms	356
Race	358
Love	360
Forgiveness	361
Support for one another	363
Children & ancestors	365
Working together for a better world	368
Hope	372
Healthy sexuality	373
Happiness	373
Strength & resilience	374
Perseverance	376
Life's trials	376

II. Meditations & Visualizations — 377

Basic meditation	377
Big sky meditation	378
Mountain meditation	379
Present moment, wonderful moment meditation	380
Sanctuary: A place of acceptance for who you are	381
Sitting in silence	381
Inner strength visualization	382
A good life visualization	382
Family connections visualization	383
Relaxation exercise	383

III. Affirmation & Group-Building Exercises — 384

Guidelines web activity	384
Making the world a better place for someone	384
Self-affirmations	384
Pass the strengths on and on	385
Gratitude	385
Medicine Wheel Self-Love Collage	385
Respect	385
Role-model ribbon exercise	386

Embodied values	386
Encouragement ribbon exercise	386
The talking piece: The importance of listening and speaking	386
Circle energy	387
Affirming others in the Circle	387
Creating a group story	387
Circle of people	387
We are kitchen implements	388
I can choose . . .	388

IV. Movement Exercises — 389

Name, motion, and remember	389
Name wave	389
Rainstorm activity	389
Group juggle	390
Showing emotions with our bodies	390
Human sculpture	391
Body stretch & shake	391
Yoga, Tai Chi, or Chi Quong	391

V. Music & Songs — 392

Drumming circle	392
Songs about mutual support & creating a better world	392
Songs about resilience & self-confidence	392
Songs related to sexual education	393
Songs about family-life challenges	393
Songs about historical, cultural trauma and healing	393
Other singer-songwriters to consider	393

Appendix 3: Theoretical Essay on Why Circles Are Important in Schools — 395

Educating the whole child	395
Educating the whole child means caring for the whole child	397
The whole school approach: The importance of school climate and connectedness	399
Caring for the whole child also involves disciplining the child	401
The unintended harms of zero tolerance	402
Disciplining with respect: Restorative practices in schools	404
The problem of bullying	406
Addressing trauma in schools	407
The added benefit of mindfulness	410
References	411

Appendix 4: Resources   **417**
   I. Resources on Restorative Justice, the Circle Process, Schools, and Youth   417
   II. Resources for Circle Openings and Closings   422

Appendix 5: A Level Guide to the Circles   **425**

   About the Authors   428
   Institute for Restorative Initiatives (IRIS)   431
   Other Books on Circles and Education from Living Justice Press   432
   Books on Addressing Harms between Peoples from Living Justice Press   433
   Notes   434

Foreword
Safety and Pies

Early in my tenure at the Minnesota Department of Education, I had the opportunity to provide technical assistance to a principal—the principal of my son's school. A student, a 6th grader, had brought a handgun to school, waived it around on the playground, and then when the bell rang at the end of recess, he put it in his coat pocket and hung the coat up in his locker. Not only had this happened while my son was in the school, it had affected a friend's family, because her son was on the playground, saw the gun, and, with a buddy, reported the incident to the principal.

The boy was arrested at school. Neither the principal, the social worker, the arresting officer, nor his mother could induce him to talk—to explain to everyone, who were all so scared, why he had the weapon in the first place, how he got it, or why he took it out on the playground.

The wheels of the systems turned; the boy was expelled, he was charged, and there was a court hearing that my friend and her son attended. She was so frustrated. In all these proceedings, the boy never said a thing.

In an attempt to help the principal and my friend, I contacted the restorative justice (RJ) specialist at county court services, but the boy's case was not referred for a family group conference. I tried to see if Kay Pranis, who was working at the Minnesota Department of Corrections at the time, could help. We could not move the systems, but she did offer an explanation for the boy's silence: "Children will speak," she observed, "when they feel safe." This boy obviously did not feel safe and thought that a handgun would offer safety. His sense of safety must have spiraled out of reach when he was caught. What happened to him that he had access to and took up a gun?

"Children will talk when they feel safe." This is such a simple observation, but one that has profound implications for schools. Some students who don't feel safe will end up in the office because they got into a fight. Some will elect to flee and start skipping classes or whole days. And some will just freeze. They are in the seat, but due to fear, no information goes to the pre-frontal cortex, and there is no "conscience thought" or learning.[1] Cultivating a sense of safety is important not only for an orderly school but for learning itself.

The question of safety in schools is not just about preventing extreme forms of violence, fights, or bullying. It is also about shrinking the achievement gap, since the way a school disciplines the students will either help or hurt academic achievement. Russell Skiba and Jeffrey Sprague succinctly note, "*time spent* learning is the single *best predictor* of positive academic outcomes."[2] Suspensions and expulsions are time spent out of the classroom. As the research of Dr. Skiba and others has shown, using exclusionary practices to keep a well-mannered school has proven to be costly, harmful, and unfair; neither does it bring about the stated goal of safety or improved achievement for all students.[3]

In 2014, the U.S. Secretary of Education and the U.S. Attorney General highlighted the need for alternatives to exclusionary discipline as well as the importance of a positive school climate in a "Dear Colleague" letter to all superintendents of schools in the United States. In that letter, they cite the data that shows that students of color and students with disabilities are more likely to be suspended or expelled, and they state that this disproportionality may be a violation of civil rights laws. In the evidence-based recommendations for remediation, they list restorative justice practices.[4]

This is good news for those of us who have learned the principles and practices of restorative justice and adapted them to schools. We have seen the positive outcomes: reduced suspensions; reduced repeat suspensions; increased connection to school and learning; better relationships between parents and school administration and staff; and better relationships between children and their parents.[5] But we also know that implementing a philosophy involves more than teaching a set of practices. Implementing restorative practices calls for a paradigm shift—a change in the head and the heart.

In Kay and Carolyn's excellent manual, *Circle Forward,* the authors make the case for cultivating not only safety but also a humane, compassionate school. Such a school recognizes the contributions of all members of the school—the students, of course, and the teachers, but also the entire staff, the parents, and the wider community. Through practicing the Circle process regularly, a school can create a climate of care and connection. These school-wide practices enhance the school's capacities for problem solving and community building under almost any circumstance.

This book is comprehensive: just about every aspect of a school's day could be done in Circle—or, more importantly, with the values and principles of the Circle process. Drawing upon restorative justice principles and the Indigenous wisdom of the Circle, the authors clearly articulate the philosophy and practices of a restorative school. They summarize theory and research in the beginning and expand upon it in the theoretical essay in Appendix 3. By providing Circle outline after Circle outline, they make using the process as clear and applicable to every aspect of school life as possible. There are outlines for Circles to build relationships and community and to teach social emotional skills; there are Circles for developing staff buy-in, cohesion, and self-care; and there are Circles that engage parents and community members. Of course, there are Circles to repair harm, even the harm of bullying. After reading the entire manual, one can grasp the interconnectedness of practices that help create a caring school climate: everyone and every aspect of school are part of the mix of a positive school climate.

Several excellent frameworks articulate school climate elements. I recently came across a particularly clear and succinct description: to build a positive community in a school, all students (and I would say all adults, as well) need to feel a sense of *belonging* and *significance*. Graeme George, an Australian teacher and consultant, elaborates:

> One of the key aims of any school is the building of a sense of community among its students, and between students and the adults in the school. For such cooperative relationships to best develop, according to Tyler and Blader (2000), individuals need to feel a high level of pride in membership of the group and a high level of respect within the group. ... [T]he descriptors for these key needs... [are] *belonging* and *significance*. For students to feel part of the school community they must feel that they belong (i.e., they are interested in being part of the group) and that they are significant (i.e., they feel that others are interested in them being part of the group).[6]

How can all students in a school feel belonging and significance? That is the challenge of creating a safe, healthy school. The word 'all' has compelled me to pursue restorative practices and the Circle in particular. I was a "good kid" in school: I liked school, I felt I belonged there, and I was significant. As an extrovert, I raised my hand and was called on, and I felt that I was seen by teachers and peers alike. But many students were not seen. As a teacher, I remember having students whose voices I rarely, if ever, heard. I can't say that I "saw" them in any honest way. They occupied seats to be checked only for attendance. I have heard students say, in effect, that it is so easy to disappear in a school.

To belong, one has to be seen. To be significant, one has to contribute. In its profound simplicity and deep complexity, the Circle process provides the means for everyone to belong and to be significant under any circumstance: as a student learning a world language; as a member of the classroom reviewing for a test; as a teacher, sharing his highs and lows; as a principal, sharing her favorite dessert; as a member of a team, learning winning and losing; as a kid who caused harm, helping to fix things; as a youth who has been hurt, helping others to fix things; or as a parent, working with the school to support the education of all children. The Circle, for a while, flattens the hierarchy between cliques and cliques, between adults and students, and between the book-learned educator and the experience-learned parent. Everyone has a place.

The Circle comes from an oral tradition. People have learned it as part of a larger culture. How do we teach and use this practice in settings outside of the cultures it is part of? How do we ensure that, in the context of the school, both the spirit of the Circle and the principles of restorative justice are implemented with fidelity? How does one maintain fidelity for a process that is so flexible? Conducting a Circle with fidelity is more than setting up chairs in a circle and asking a question.

The practice is taught mostly by doing: sitting around a fire, a dinner table, a lodge, or a set of chairs in a room. Over the last two decades, the Circle process has been taught through participation at workshops and three- and four-day trainings. Books have been written on the theory, and more stories have been told to teach the spirit and the values of the process. Now with *Circle Forward*, the theory and the stories become the practice, the daily gathering, "arranging everyone in a circle of chairs with no other furniture."

The book spans the spectrum of Circle applications and offers several Circle outlines for each kind. Each section of the book has elements of great delight for me. In addition to using the Circle for social-emotional learning, community building, and teaching, I was delighted to see Circle outlines for staff development—developing staff connections. I was delighted to see Circles for parents and community, not just for Individual Education Program (IEP) planning meetings or to repair harm, but for parent-teacher conferences, school planning and improvement, and discussing the values of the family regarding education. I was delighted to read the outlines for student-led Circles. And I was delighted with the examples of the continuum of Circles for repairing harm.

Not every inappropriate behavior in a school rises to the level of "Go to the office!" I once helped to review grant applications for RJ programming in community organizations, correctional facilities, and schools. One reviewer exclaimed, "This school cannot be doing Circles to repair harm to fidelity. They claim they held 200 Circles last school year alone. They can't have done pre-meetings for all of them!" I pointed out that this was an elementary school that used the Circle as a daily practice. They were counting all the Circles that were held to repair harm, and this included ten-minute Circles in which a student keeper passed the purple dinosaur to address taking turns on the swings. Not all Circles in a school are held for a fight.

Circle Forward provides an outline for short Circles, class-repair-of-harm Circles, Circles to address harm when no one is sure who caused the harm, Circles that require pre-meeting preparation, as well as Circles for including many people to provide support. Module 13 gives an excellent discussion of the preparation needed to use Circles to address bullying. Here, the Circle provides great promise, for bullying is a relationship problem, as Debra J. Pepler and Wendy Craig note, and a relationship problem requires relationship solutions.[7] As *Circle Forward* repeats throughout, we are beings who want to be in good relationship with each other.

We know that bullying happens often in the presence of others—whether in person or online. By carefully engaging the person who bullies, the person who was bullied, and the bystanders, we can effectively help people change behaviors—far more than a suspension, an agreement not to talk to each other, or a forced apology can. But preparation is key, from training the keeper to conduct a Circle to repair harm, to holding pre-meetings, to arranging Circles of support and, of course, to coming together in celebration Circles after the agreements have been met.

I was also delighted with the section about setting up ongoing Circles of support. Some students come to school with neural pathways for behaviors that are most useful for survival in a toxic-stress home or community, but these same survival behaviors can be most disruptive in the classroom. In order to choose different behaviors, the student must first learn new ones. Learning anything new takes time. "How do I get to Carnegie Hall?" the young man asks. "Practice, my dear boy, practice!" is the reply. Some students need support from people who show explicitly that they care and who model caring support over a period of time. Building new neural pathways that are strong for new behaviors can take up to six months (for some of us, even longer).

All of this is wonderful, but the part that I am particularly glad for is the section of Circles for staff to explore implementing restorative measures. These three Circles provide that essential first step in implementing any whole-school process: buy-in. Restorative Practices, like Positive Behavior Interventions and Supports and Social and Emotional Learning, represent a paradigm shift for many people. The shift is away from shame, blame, and punishment and toward support and relationship. The idea is to "teach the behaviors we want to see"—to work with, not do to or for. How can we respect the whole child, instead of siloing academics away from the social, emotional, and physical needs of the students?

A paradigm shift requires movement within the head and the heart. Having the staff start with talking about who they are as people and what they value can help them build interest and excitement in making change. Using the Circle process for their own development, the adults can, perhaps, come to consensus about how to help the whole school move forward.

Circle Forward is like a good cookbook. It provides directions for the new baker and ideas and suggestions for the seasoned cook. Starting any new practice can be both frightening and exciting. People will more likely try something new if they feel safe. *Circle Forward* offers that sense of safety for the novice and the experienced Circle keeper. The appendices of openings and closings, of Circle questions, and of the theory that supports it all, combined with the Circle templates, make holding a Circle as easy as pie. There is a recipe, but keepers also apply their own care and intuition. Take a page, add people, and stir with a talking piece!

I am very grateful to Kay and Carolyn for their commitment to creating healthy communities for all young people, for their wisdom, and for their generosity. I cannot wait to share this wisdom with our schools—the teachers, administrators, students and their families, student support staff, educational assistants, volunteers, cooks, janitors, bus drivers, and school board members. This book is such a gift!

Nancy Riestenberg
School Climate Specialist, Minnesota Department of Education
Roseville, Minnesota, July 2014

NOTES

1. The Hawn Foundation, (2011). *The mind-up curriculum: Brain-focused strategies for learning—and living.* Scholastic Teaching Resources, 35.

2. Skiba, R., & Sprague, R. (2008). Safety without suspensions. *Educational Leadership,* 66(1), 38–43. http://www.loudoun.k12.va.us/cms/lib4/VA01000195/Centricity/Domain/63/PBS/Safety_Without_Suspensions_Sept_2008.pdf.

3. For research on outcomes of exclusion, go to the Institute of Educational Sciences' Education Resource Information Center (ERIC): http://eric.ed.gov/?. Also, Dignity in Schools, http://www.dignityinschools.org/content/dignity-schools-campaign-fact-sheets as well Appendices 3 and 4 in this book.

4. "Dear Colleague" Letter on School Climate and Discipline: http://www2.ed.gov/policy/gen/guid/school-discipline/index.html?utm_source=E-News%3A+School+Discipline%2C+Hillary+Clinton%2C+and+Early+Ed&utm_campaign=enews+1%2F15%2F14&utm_medium=email.

5. McMorris, B. J., Beckman, K. J., Shea, G., Baumgartner, J., & Eggert, R. C. (2013). Applying restorative justice practices to Minneapolis public schools students recommended for possible expulsion: A pilot program evaluation of the family and youth restorative conference program. School of Nursing, Healthy Youth Development Prevention Research Center, Department of Pediatrics, University of Minnesota, Minneapolis, MN, the Legal Rights Center, Minneapolis, MN, and Minneapolis Public Schools.

6. Kelly, V. C., Jr., & Thorsborne, M. (2014). Affect and emotion in a restorative school. In V. C. Kelly, Jr., & M. Thorsborne (Eds.), *The psychology of emotion in restorative practice: How affect script psychology explains how and why restorative practice works.* London: Jessica Kingsley Publishers, 212.

7. Pepler, D. J., & Craig, W. (1988, 2000). Making a difference in bullying. Report #60. LaMarsh Centre for Research on Violence and Conflict Resolution, York University, and Department of Psychology, Queen's University.

Acknowledgments

This book has been a labor of love and of generosity. We are deeply indebted to many, many people for guidance and wisdom in our Circle journeys in general and in the journey of this book in particular. We wish to honor our original Circle teachers Barry Stuart, Harold Gatensby, and Mark Wedge. We also wish to acknowledge the pioneers in using Circles in schools in Minnesota: Mary Ticiu, Jack Mangan, Cindy Zwicky, Jamie Williams, and Oscar Reed. These practitioners laid the groundwork for the development of Circle practice in schools.

We wish to recognize the influence of Robin and Beth Casarjian, authors of *Power Source*, for the infusion of mindfulness in the Circles in this book. Their work informed in a significant way our earlier book, *Heart of Hope*, and this book is modeled after that one.

Along the path of putting this book together, we benefited from the experience of many dedicated educators and Circle practitioners, including Rita Renjitham Alfred, Marg Armstrong, Erica Bronstein, Jeanne Carlivati, Janet Connors, Adina Davison, Kati Delahanty, Brenda Hopkins, Marna MacMillian, Bonnie Massey, Kris Miner, Brenda Morrison, Sayra Owen-Pinto, Tracy Roberts, Linda Soloman-Key, Marg Thorsborne, and Dorothy Vandering.

In addition to the individuals noted above, we are grateful to organizations whose support for the development of Circle practice in schools has advanced the practice and informed our work. These include the Minnesota Department of Education, Restorative Justice for Oakland Youth, Oakland Unified School District, Charles Town High School, Partners in Restorative Initiatives, Community Justice for Youth Institute.

We have a very special debt to Nancy Riestenberg, who provided inspiration, guidance, feedback and, very importantly, humor throughout the process of planning and writing this book. The scope and depth of Nancy's experience and conceptual ability contributed enormously to this work.

This book could not have come to fruition without Living Justice Press and the incredible commitment of Mary Joy Breton, Loretta Draths, Deb Feeny, and the LJP Board, who dedicate countless unpaid hours to bring books about Circles and Restorative Justice between Peoples to those who are working to make this a more equitable and loving world. But most of all, our debt is to Denise Breton, editor extraordinaire and passionate promoter of Circles and Restorative Justice. Words are not adequate to describe the work she has done to make this book possible. When we were distracted with other responsibilities, Denise kept the book moving. Her attention to detail, her research to check information and resources, her keen sense of Circle and social justice issues, her gift with words, and her loving patience around our shortcomings have been nothing short of heroic.

We also wish to acknowledge the ancient roots of Circles and the ancient practitioners of Circles. We are their descendants, working to bring our innate human capacities to bear on our complex modern world in a good way.

We humbly give thanks to all these and to those whose gifts to us are so much a part of who we are that we have not noticed them as separate from ourselves.

Notes

The term "keeper" is used to refer to the Circle facilitator. Both terms—keeper and facilitator—are used in this guide.

We are following the convention used by many First Nations as well as other cultures of capitalizing a term that has special or sacred significance. Referring to the peacemaking process, the term "Circle" embodies many dimensions of meaning beyond the spatial or geometric, including sacred meanings, so we have chosen to capitalize it.

PART I
The Basics

Introduction

Circle Forward is a resource guide designed to help teachers, administrators, students, and parents incorporate the practice of Circle into the everyday life of the school community. This resource guide offers comprehensive step-by-step instructions for how to plan, facilitate, and implement the Circle for a variety of purposes. The purpose of the guide is to help school communities use Circles in a number of different contexts within the school environment.

The Circle is a simple structured process of communication that helps participants reconnect with a joyous appreciation of themselves and others. It is designed to create a safe space for all voices and to encourage each participant to step in the direction of their best self. Circles are relevant for all age groups. While the language may vary to be developmentally appropriate, holding certain conversations in Circle is equally beneficial for all members of the school community, from the youngest to the eldest. We believe that the practice of Circles is helpful for building and maintaining a healthy community in which all members feel connected and respected.

The *Circle Forward* manual is neither a curriculum nor a specialized program. It is a guide for learning to bring the Circle practice into the school community. This resource manual provides the foundation of Circle practice by describing the basic process, essential elements, and a step-by-step guide for how to organize, plan, and lead Circles. It also provides over one hundred specific lesson plans and ideas for applying Circles in different contexts and for different purposes. These may be either followed as they are written or modified by the user. We encourage the creative adaptation of any Circle lesson plan. We believe that any caring and responsible individual can learn to use Circle practices safely, creatively, and effectively.

There is no single way to integrate Circles within the school community: each community should incorporate the Circle in its own way to meet its own unique needs. We encourage users to view this resource guide and the model Circles somewhat like recipes in a cookbook. Choose what appeals to you and to those with whom you will be sharing the Circle. You are ultimately the judge of what makes sense for your classroom and school community. We also recognize that it is possible to substitute one ingredient for another, so we encourage users to be creative in adapting specific activities to meet one's own needs. At the same time, not all elements are expendable. Just as oven temperature and cooking time are critical to the success of any recipe, we are clear about what is important not to change.

> The practice of Circles is helpful for building and maintaining a healthy community in which all members feel connected and respected.

WHY BRING CIRCLES TO SCHOOLS?

There is a good reason democratic societies see public education as the foundation for their highest aspirations. Public education is a collective commitment to a vision of a society that affords each individual the opportunity to pursue a meaningful life. For public education to serve as the great equalizer in our society, it is essential that success be possible for all children, including those from the bottom of the social scale as well as those in the middle and top.

It is no secret that within the past twenty years, our schools have been criticized for failing to meet the needs of many of our nation's children and families. There is pressure on schools to ensure U.S. global competitiveness and at the same time to redress social inequality. This is happening at a time when worsening social and economic conditions in many communities result in more children coming to school sorely in need of adult support and guidance. It is no surprise that teachers and school administrators feel overwhelmed by the tasks assigned to them.

We believe the outcry over failing schools masks much more important underlying questions. Howard Gardner suggests that we need to reflect deeply on the "minds" or intelligences we are seeking to cultivate within our educational institutions. This is not a matter of science but a question of values and priorities. As a society, we clearly need experts—those who delve deeply into a particular field and acquire the disciplined knowledge associated with it. But we also need other kinds of "minds": people who create and imagine; those with the ability to sort, synthesize, and distill information; those able to communicate and relate to others; and individuals with the ethical and moral skills to see the connections between our actions and our values and to lead based on that understanding.

Nel Noddings asks us to think deeply about the purpose of public schools within our communities. Rather than seeing schools as businesses designed to manufacture successful workers, she urges us to see schools as special places where our children are cared for everyday. Outside of the family, schools are the single publicly funded social institution where children grow up in the company of adults. In her view, the most important goal of schools is not academic instruction but the development of children as healthy, competent, and moral people. Schools care for all our children—those who are academically gifted and those who are not. Intellectual development is important, but it is not the first priority of schools. The first priority of schools is to care for students. For this reason, above all, schools need to be centers of stability, continuity and community.

This guide is in deep alignment with this understanding of the sacred purpose of public education. In the long run, the measure of our public schools is the measure of our moral commitment to our children. In 1902, John Dewey wrote that what we should want for our schools is what the best and wisest parents would want for their own children. We may disagree about educational philosophy, curriculum,

> Above all, schools need to be centers of stability, continuity and community.

and teaching styles, but all parents want their children to be cared for and treated with respect.

In the end, our schools are a reflection of our values as a society: the schools we create mirror the society we create for ourselves. Within school, the relationships that develop between adults and children mirror the relationships adults have with one another. If adults feel respected, safe, and supported, these values will be replicated in their relationships with the children. Attending to the needs of adults and to the relationships among the adults is equally important to attending to relationships with and among the children. Ultimately, the question of how to build a healthy school community opens the larger question of how to build a healthy community within our society.

We believe that the regular and routine use of the Circle practice is a key infrastructure of a healthy school community. Because schools are the one universal developmental institution outside of the home, they are the one place where children are in regular ongoing relationship with adults. The quality of learning and growth that takes place within school depends on healthy relationships between adults and children as well as among adults and children. Circles support individual learning and growth, and at the same time they contribute to the development of a healthy positive school community for all. While Circles are neither a panacea nor a silver bullet, we strongly believe that an integrated Circle practice within any school community will help to develop relationships that support and foster learning and nurture healthy emotional and social development for both children and adults.

The Theoretical Foundation for Circle Practice in Schools

There are six groups of theories relevant to understanding the power of the Circle in schools. We briefly review them here and later provide an in-depth discussion of these ideas. Readers interested in the full discussion of these theoretical foundations and the sources with citations should turn to Appendix 3 (pages 395–416).

1. THE WHOLE-CHILD APPROACH

The first set of theories is the "whole child approach," which draws attention to the importance of social emotional learning. Insights from what is now termed "positive psychology" have added much to our understanding of the role of character and emotion in academic achievement, resilience in the face of adverse life events, and successful transition to healthy adulthood. It turns out that non-cognitive factors are as important or even more important than cognitive ones. Emotional habits such as persistence, optimism, grit, focus, and curiosity appear to be more influential than intelligence in predicting which individuals will "make it" through college and transition into a healthy satisfied adult life.

> What we refer to as "inner strength" or "resilience" can be developed, and, like the strength of our musculature, will grow stronger with repeated use.

The Circle is a process that intentionally seeks to attend to the whole person and to provide space for emotional, social, and moral development alongside the mental and physical. Emotional habits and attitudes are not simply inborn traits fixed by our genetic code but traits cultivated through interaction with others. Like our muscles, what we refer to as "inner strength" or "resilience" can be developed, and, like the strength of our musculature, will grow stronger with repeated use. Research confirms that emotional skills of empathy, patience, and emotional self-management can be learned and nurtured within the classroom and school community.

2. THE IMPORTANCE OF RELATIONSHIPS IN DEVELOPMENT AND LEARNING

The second set of theories focuses on the importance of relationships in human development and in the process of cognitive and social learning. Attachment theory within psychology; choice theory within education; an ethic of care within moral philosophy; and social control theory within sociology: these are among the relevant theories that identify the quality of the bond between adults and children as a key to learning and healthy human development. The Circle is, above all, a process for building relationships. We believe that the use of the Circle will strengthen trusting and caring relationships between adults and children, as well as among adults and among children, in a way that is highly beneficial to lifelong cognitive and social learning.

3. A WHOLE-SCHOOL APPROACH

The third set of theories falls under the umbrella of a whole school approach highlighting the importance of a positive school climate, a sense of belonging, and a connectedness among students and adults to the school community. "School connectedness" is a term that encompasses the sense of attachment that a student feels to the school community. Building a strong community for both adults and students is key to fostering a sense of connectedness among students.

School climate refers to the level of civility and consideration among the members of the community. It refers to how students routinely treat one another on the playground, on the bus, in class, and in the halls; how adults treat each other in their staff meetings; as well as the tone and quality of interactions between adults and students. The Circle process is a space designed to promote a sense of belonging; to cultivate awareness and consideration of others; and to ensure respectful democratic participation of all members of the community. Because the Circle process is structured to cultivate and support positive behavior inside, and most importantly, outside of the Circle, we believe it is an extremely helpful in generating a positive school climate.

4. POSITIVE DISCIPLINE

The fourth set of theories relevant to the use of Circles in school is the field of positive discipline, particularly the use of restorative practices based on the theory of restorative justice. The Circle is a useful structure for generating and articulating shared values and translating these into a set of common and explicit behavioral norms for conduct within the school community. It is also an effective process for conducting positive discipline—a structured process for addressing harm that meets the needs of those harmed while promoting accountability and responsibility for wrongdoers. Restorative discipline seeks to build a stronger community by involving the whole school community in the positive resolution of wrongdoing and by using conflict as an opportunity to strengthen positive relationships.

> Restorative discipline seeks to build a stronger community by involving the whole school community in the positive resolution of wrongdoing and by using conflict as an opportunity to strengthen positive relationships.

5. A TRAUMA-SENSITIVE LEARNING ENVIRONMENT

The fifth set of theories relevant for the use of Circles within schools comes from the understanding of trauma or adverse childhood experiences and their impact on learning and human development. Like it or not, schools deal with many children who have been neglected, abused, and/or exposed to chronic stress within their home and neighborhoods. These children are growing up under conditions in which they are chronically unsupported by adults in their home and community. Yet the need for adult guidance, safety, and support—both emotional and physical—is far greater than what even the most well funded therapeutic system could possibly provide. We believe that trauma theory helps to reframe academic challenges and student misbehavior, so educators and other support staff can offer support and guidance rather than punishment as a response to student misconduct.

A trauma-sensitive learning environment is one in which a child feels appreciated and cared for by adults at school; the classroom and school environment is emotionally and physically safe; and clearly articulated standards for behavior are reinforced through positive interventions and relationships with adults and peers. We believe that healing from trauma comes from the reliable and repeated experience of supportive and healthy relationships. There is untapped potential in the capacity of schools to be sanctuaries in the lives of stressed children and adults by creating the space for ongoing relational connection. It is simple, cost-effective, and transformative.

> Being in positive relationship—the feeling of being recognized, heard, respected, and valued—is itself a form of healing.

Being in positive relationship—the feeling of being recognized, heard, respected, and valued—is itself a form of healing. A Circle process can also offer the opportunity to gain self-awareness through the connection with others and to learn constructive ways to meet one's needs from one's community. Most importantly, this is a practice that benefits all children—those who are emotionally healthy and those who are struggling. It is a way to cultivate the healing benefits of a healthy community that holds the strength to support and nurture all its members through the good times and bad.

6. MINDFULNESS PRACTICE

> The Circle process encourages participants to slow down and be present with themselves and others.

The final foundation of this guide is the incorporation of the practice of mindfulness within the structure of the Circle itself. Like the Circle process itself, mindfulness is a wellness technique with a long tradition within human societies. The Circle process itself is a mindfulness practice because it encourages participants to slow down and be present with themselves and others. In this guide, we introduce simple meditation and breathing exercises as part of the structure of many Circles. Scientific research confirms what thousands of years of human wisdom and practice has long affirmed: the regular use of simple mindfulness practice enhances mental, physical, emotional, and spiritual well-being. Like regular exercise, the routine use of meditation practice has been shown to have many beneficial effects for all age groups. Research on mindfulness within schools shows that simple techniques can improve the quality of attentiveness and calm focus within a classroom.

Our 7 Core Assumptions
What we believe to be true

In this section, we present our assumptions about human beings. These are basic ideas that we believe to be true about human nature and our relationships to the world. It is important to be aware of one's core assumptions, because what we believe to be true shapes what we see. Our beliefs form the prism through which we see ourselves and others in the world.

For example, when you look at this image, what do you see?

Most likely, you will see a picture of a vase shaped something like a Grecian urn. Yet, take another look. Can you also see the image of two white faces? Both images are there, but what our mind tells us to expect shapes what our eyes are able to see. Your assumption about what is there shapes what you see!

The core assumptions that we are about to present are not unique to this resource guide. They are principles that can be found in wisdom and cultural traditions from around the world. We invite each person who uses this guide to reflect on these assumptions as well as to take time to examine his or her own.

1 The True Self in Everyone Is Good, Wise, & Powerful...

We believe that everyone has a self that is good, wise, powerful, and always there, always present. In this resource guide, we refer to this as the "core" or "true" self. The core self is in everyone. It is in you, your students, and the adults you work with everyday. The nature of the core self is wise, kind, just, good, and powerful. The core self cannot be destroyed. No matter what someone has done in the past and no matter what has happened to him or her in the past, the core self remains as good, wise, and powerful as the day they were born.

This model of the self distinguishes between doing and being. What we do is not the whole of who we are. We often get confused about this. We mistake the roles we play or the emotions we feel for our core self. But how we behave or feel is the not the same as who we are. Our core selves are not always reflected in our actions or feelings. But beneath the acts and masks we humans adopt is a deeper, healthier self. Helping students and all members of the school community tune into the goodness and wisdom of their true self is the first step toward realigning their behavior in the world with this deeper self.

To use a metaphor, the outer shell of the oyster is rough, mottled with lots of bumps and crevices. Some might say that it is ugly. Yet inside, at the center, is a magnificent, smooth, infinitely beautiful pearl. This is how we think of the core self.

The World is Profoundly Interconnected...

> *A human being is part of the whole, called by us the "Universe," a part limited in time and space. He experiences himself, his thoughts and feelings as something separate from the rest—a kind of optical delusion of his consciousness. This delusion is a kind of prison for us, restricting us to our personal desires and to affection for a few persons nearest to us. Our task must be to free ourselves from this prison by widening our circle of compassion to embrace all living creatures and the whole of nature in its beauty.*
>
> — Albert Einstein

According to chaos theory, when a butterfly flaps its wings in South America, the wind changes in North America. This points to the interconnectedness of natural forces around the globe. Climate change is another visible reminder of interconnectedness within nature. We may not always be aware of the impact of our actions on our environment, but we must eventually realize that our actions have consequences. American folk wisdom expresses the same idea in the common phrase, "What goes around, comes around." The Bible, too, says, "As ye sow, so shall ye reap."

In our human relationships, we are every bit as profoundly interconnected. When Native peoples say, "We are all related," they mean that human beings are connected to all living creatures and are part of the natural world. Traditional African society uses the term "ubuntu" to express the idea that each of us is fundamentally a part of the whole. It translates: "I am because we are."

We believe this principle reminds us that there are no throw-away kids or people. We cannot drop out, kick out, or get rid of anything without literally throwing away a part of ourselves. By excluding someone, we harm ourselves as well as the fabric of our community: every suspension and expulsion reverberates through a web of interconnected relationships with unintended harmful consequences. Because we are connected, what we do to others, we also do to ourselves, although we may not always realize that this is happening. The wonderful news is that even the smallest positive actions, the words of support, moments of understanding, and intentional kindnesses are likewise amplified through the interconnected web of relationships. Many wisdom traditions counsel us to act with this understanding in mind. The Buddha said,

> *Do not overlook negative actions merely because they are small; however small a spark may be, it can burn down a haystack as big as a mountain... Do not overlook tiny good actions, thinking they are of no benefit; even tiny drops of water in the end will fill a huge vessel.*

All Human Beings have a Deep Desire to be in a Good Relationship...

We believe that all people want to love and be loved and that all people want to be respected. This may not be what they show in their behavior, particularly when they have not been loved and respected by others. But at our core, we all desire to be in good relationship with others. Nel Noddings reminds us that children "listen to people who matter to them and to whom they matter."

We must stop thinking of human nature as a problem. As Meg Wheatley teaches, human nature is the blessing, not the problem. In our culture, we have a tendency to focus on the bad sides of human conduct. While human greed, anger, fear, and envy are strong human emotions responsible for a great deal of human suffering, this is only half of the human story. In our culture today, we have a great need to remember the overwhelming fact of human goodness.

There is much suffering in the world—physical, material, mental... But the greatest suffering is being lonely, feeling unloved, having no one. I have come more and more to realize that it is being unwanted that is the worst disease that any human being can ever experience.

— *Mother Teresa*

When students feel supported and successful in the classroom, they rarely act out.
When teachers feel supported and successful in school, they rarely burn out.
— *Esther Wright*

All Humans Have Gifts, & Everyone Is Needed for What They Bring . . .

According to some Indigenous teachings, each child is born with four unique gifts from Mother Earth. It is the responsibility of the adults to recognize these four unique gifts and help youth cultivate them, so the child may grow up to realize his or her individual purpose in life and use these gifts to help others. According to a Swahili proverb, the greatest gift we can give each other is not to share our riches with others but to reveal the others' own riches to themselves. All of us need to feel we have something valuable to contribute to others.

We believe that, in human societies, all gifts are indispensable to the well-being of the whole. Within nature, diversity is the source of strength. Interdependence is essential for survival. It is the way of nature. Every cell in our body is differentiated to perform a specialized function that contributes to the whole. This is as true for families as it is for organizations. Different people are needed, because different people see and do things differently. We require the contribution of diverse talents, personalities, and perspectives to find creative and innovative solutions to meeting our needs.

It takes a sense of humility—realizing that each of us alone does not have all the answers—and a sense of gratitude for us to be open to the gifts that others bring.

We must be actively engaged in the setting free of every other person to be who she or he is intended: someone different from who we are, someone who will see the world from another perspective, someone who will not agree with us.
— Caroline A. Westerhoff

Everything
We Need to Make Positive Change
Is Already Here . . .

Gather yourselves.
Banish the word 'struggle' from your vocabulary.
All that we do now must be done in a sacred manner and in celebration.
We are the ones we have been waiting for.
— *Hopi Elders, 2001*

This resource guide is a strength-based model. We believe that everything we need to make positive change within our school community is already here. This is because human creativity and human commitment are our greatest treasure and greatest hope. A deficit model identifies what is missing in order to create change. It is easy to slip into the belief that the resources we need to meet our common needs as human beings are scarce and dwindling. However, what we too often assume to be a lack of resources is, in fact, a question of values and priorities.

We believe school communities hold rich reservoirs of talent and wisdom that are waiting to be accessed. If we fail to see ourselves as creators of our school culture, we deny the power to change it. We need to learn how to tap into the wisdom and creative energy of all our human resources: students, teachers, parents, extended families, administrators, secretaries, custodial staff, school resource officers and many more who are present within our community. Meg Wheatley reminds us to look around ourselves and see who is here, because when a living system is struggling, it needs to start talking to itself and especially "to those it didn't know were even part of itself." By doing this, we liberate the potential of our collective power to create the world we desire. We *are* the ones we have been waiting for.

Human Beings are Holistic...

In the English language, the words "health" and "whole" come from the same root. Our minds, bodies, emotions, and spirits are in all that we do. These are equally important parts of us as human beings—each provides ways of knowing and sources of both knowledge and wisdom.

Learning is a holistic process engaging body, heart, and spirit as well as the mind in an integrated process. How we use our bodies affects the sharpness of our mental processes. No child can learn if they are hungry, tired, cold, or sick. The quality of how we feel about others affects learning. Modern brain research tells us that information with emotional content is more deeply etched in our memory than information without emotional content, and it is often said that children don't care what you know until they know you care. We know too that the absence of emotional and physical safety within the classroom creates stressful feelings, such as fear and dread, that interrupts cognition and prevents learning.

In this approach to creating healthy schools, we seek to engage all parts of ourselves: our intellect, emotions, spirit, and body. We seek to attend to the needs of each of these parts of ourselves so that we can nurture the multiple intelligences that are a part of the human capacities.

The connections made by good teachers are held not in their methods but in their hearts . . .
the place where intellect and emotion and spirit and will converge.
— Parker Palmer

We Need Practices to Build Habits of Living from the Core Self . . .

> *A Grandfather from the Cherokee nation was talking to his grandson.*
> *"A fight is going on inside me," he tells the boy.*
> *It is a terrible fight between two wolves.*
> *One wolf is evil and ugly.*
> *He is anger, envy, war, greed, self-pity, sorrow, regret, guilt, resentment, inferiority, lies, false pride, superiority, selfishness, and arrogance.*
> *The other wolf is beautiful and good: he is friendly, joyful, peaceful, loving, hopeful, serene, humble, kind, just, and compassionate.*
> *This same fight is going on inside of you and inside of every human being.*
> *"But Grandfather!" cries the grandson, "which wolf will win?"*
> *The elder looked at his grandson, "The one you feed."*

We believe we need practices that help us connect with our core self, so we can live aligned with our values and build healthy relationships in classrooms and school communities. The kind of relationships among students and adults within a school community is a matter of intention: if we choose to nurture positive relationships, they will flourish.

Many of our current practices within schools reinforce the walls around the core self and increase our sense of disconnection from our own self and others. Our practices encourage us to assert power over others and to be fearful and distrustful of the wolves that lurk within. We have developed habits of closing our hearts and minds to the feelings of others as well as to our own selves.

The Circles in this guide offer many time-tested means for reconnecting with our healthy core self and to nurture positive relationships within the school environment. The peacemaking Circle has a natural affinity with practices that feed and nurture "the good wolf" in all of us. The magic of Circle is in the *practice* of Circle.

Thinking about Healthy Relationships in Schools

LET'S TALK ABOUT POWER

Healthy power in one's own life is a fundamental human need. As noted in our core assumptions, the core self is good, wise, and *powerful*. Personal power directed by the core self is healthy power; it does not operate at the expense of someone else. If we are able to help others connect with their core selves, they are less likely to try to access power in hurtful ways.

Our exercise of power affects others. We have a responsibility to pay attention to the impact of our use of power. This includes seeking feedback about how others experience our power. The basic human desire to be in good relationships with others suggests that people will be willing to exchange "power over" for "power with." This shift opens us to experiencing the joy of good relationships with others.

We all possess gifts. Our gifts offer a place to feel positive power that is "power with." There are many opportunities within the school environment to nurture and honor the gifts of each child: the more schools work to open the possibility for all students to shine and to have their contribution recognized, the more all students will feel a healthy sense of personal power as a member of the school community.

The practices in this guide help us become more aware of our feelings around power: where we feel empowered and where we feel powerless. This awareness helps us make choices—and assist others in making choices—that fulfill our natural human need for personal power in ways that do not harm others. We already have the power we need within us, both individually and collectively. Our healthy personal power is enough. We do not need power over others to make change; neither do we have to steal power from others to meet our needs.

The way power operates in our society has caused a great deal of harm, because our society is structured in hierarchies. Those at upper levels of the hierarchy have power over those at lower levels. These hierarchies rank worthiness based on standing in the hierarchy. A person with more power is assumed to be more worthy as a human being and is treated accordingly.

These one-up, one-down structures operate in our homes, our schools, our faith communities, our social services, our workplaces, and our government. Issues of power permeate human interaction in the personal, community, and public parts of life. Though power dynamics profoundly shape our interactions, these dynamics frequently go unexamined.

> The more schools work to open the possibility for all students to shine, the more all students will feel a healthy sense of personal power as a member of the school community.

The paradox of influence and control: power in schools

Within schools, as well as in all communities, there is a need for order. Teachers and adults, in general, possess authority. Their authority is a form of power used to direct the behavior of children in the interest of the larger community that necessitates children cooperate with this authority. Learning to respect legitimate authority and cooperate with it is a basic task of growing into healthy adulthood.

Yet there is a paradox associated with the power of authority. If individuals feel that the authority held is legitimate and fair, they will accept and respect that power; when they feel that it is unjustified, they will resent it and typically resist it. The paradox is that, in order for authority to be seen as legitimate, it is necessary that individuals feel their own personal power is still respected by those in authority. Efforts by adults to use authority to control the behavior of young people frequently backfire because young people resist actions they perceive to be a denial of their personal power. As the saying goes, rules without relationship build rebellion. When adults and youth are in healthy relationship, the exercise of authority is rooted in a sense of mutual respect that does not threaten the basic human need for personal power.

Under conditions of respectful and trusting relationships, adults have enormous *influence* over the behavior of young people who have a deep desire to remain in positive relationships with important people in their lives. The more adults cultivate a foundation of good relationship with young people, the more adult authority will be respected. Paradoxically, the less adults use power to control the behavior of young people, the greater is their influence to shape that behavior through the cultivation of a healthy respect for authority.

Power is neither inherently good nor inherently bad. The exercise of power can be healthy and constructive, or it can be imbalanced and harmful. Power in hierarchies is generally exercised over others. "Power-over" relationships often have serious harmful effects. Those in the power-under role feel less worthy, less capable, and less in control of their own destinies. Those with power over others often don't notice when that power is operating. And because they may feel that their intentions are good, they may completely miss the potential for harm in how they are using their power. Teachers function in a hierarchal structure that gives them power over the youth and families they work with. Youth often experience school as a place of powerlessness, as do parents who do not have a middle-class background.

Because worthiness is attached to power, humans in our society often seek power to validate their sense of worthiness. If they cannot gain a sense of power in socially legitimized ways, they will often seek power in other ways. Many of the inappropriate behaviors that cause disruption in schools are attempts by people who feel powerless to gain power in their lives. The need for power is deep in the makeup of human beings. The drive for self-determination and self-actualization—both requiring a healthy, natural exercise of power—is an innate human need. Thwarting this need

> Paradoxically, the less adults use power to control the behavior of young people, the greater is their influence to shape that behavior through the cultivation of a healthy respect for authority.

triggers deep emotions. Feelings of powerlessness feed anger, depression, hurt, and hopelessness.

The Circle process helps individuals and the group experience healthy power in the presence of each other. Each person has voice; each person is valued; no one is more important than anyone else in the Circle. Individual power in Circle is self-determining—having voice, choosing whether to speak. Collective power in the Circle is "power with"—decisions made by a consensus that does not privilege any point of view or position.

LET'S ALSO TALK ABOUT JUSTICE

All human beings have a strong, innate sense of justice. When we are treated in ways that we judge as unfair or disrespectful, we feel we have been treated unjustly. Justice is not something that is defined by law: human beings view every relationship in their lives as either just or unjust. Relationships that are felt to be unjust elicit negative emotions, such as anger, resentment, distrust and humiliation that often motivate people to take action to correct the imbalance or injustice. Relationships that are felt to be fair and just promote a sense of harmony, peace, stability, and satisfaction.

As we noted, youth often perceive their relationship with adults to be unjust when adults exercise their power in ways that do not respect the personal power of youth. Young people respect the authority of adults who, in turn, are respectful of their personal power to exercise meaningful choices. Within the school environment, establishing a sense of collaboration rests on a genuine respect for the participation of young people in regulating themselves and their community. This does not suggest that adults and youth have equal power. Rather, they are afforded equal respect and given the right to exercise power appropriate for their age and role within the community.

In any community, when someone treats another person unjustly, there is a need to restore the sense of justice by having an individual participate in a process that acknowledges the wrong and makes repair through sincere apologies and meaningful reparations. The direct participation of the individuals who feel unjustly treated and those responsible for harming others is essential in repairing the positive relationship between these members of the community, so that future relationships are no longer tainted by a continuing sense of injustice.

Restorative discipline is based on an understanding that restoring a relationship to one in which both parties feel there is equity and mutual respect is the most important goal for the future well-being of the parties and the community as a whole. This is especially important for a school community where all parties to a conflict must continue to be in relationship with one another. Resolving conflict so that all parties feel that the outcome is just and fair is fundamental to maintaining a positive and healthy school culture. Justice is a very personal experience and cannot be delivered by third parties. Circles provide a process for a direct experience of justice when injustice has occurred.

> Justice is not something that is defined by law: human beings view every relationship in their lives as either just or unjust.

> Resolving conflict so that all parties feel that the outcome is just and fair is fundamental to maintaining a positive and healthy school culture.

WE NEED TO TALK ABOUT BELONGING

The need for belonging is not just a result of our socialization. It is deeply imprinted in our genetic make-up. The need to belong is so central to our sense of self that we will do whatever is necessary to meet that need, including violating our values and disconnecting from the core self. If we cannot meet the need for belonging in healthy ways, we will resort to unhealthy ways.

If we want people to act from the core self, we need to provide healthy ways of meeting the need to belong. Belonging to a nuclear family is an essential foundation, but it is not sufficient to meet that need. As we grow, we need to belong to something bigger than our family. Extended family and well-defined villages, tribes, or clans formerly filled this need. In modern society, an extended family and village are often not available to meet the need for belonging beyond the immediate family.

Children are required to go to school, and in school, children are in ongoing relationships with one another and with adults in that school. For better or worse, schools are communities where students experience either belonging or not belonging to that community. The status of belonging or not belonging has a very significant impact on their lives. If they feel they do not belong within the school community, then they will seek some other place to belong that is beyond family. Belonging to something beyond family is a particularly strong developmental imperative in the middle years of schooling.

Belonging means being accepted and valued. It means being seen and appreciated. Belonging also carries with it responsibility and obligation—accepting and valuing others who belong to the group. Sometimes belonging is based on action: our collective work of some kind (what we do) is valued. Sometimes it is based on our being: our collective identity or shared values and vision (who we are) is valued. Both forms of belonging are important for healthy human development.

Schools can provide opportunities for experiencing both kinds of belonging in healthy ways. A sense of belonging in a healthy community promotes learning, cooperative functions, and personal growth, all of which are important elements of success in school. When we belong, we have an investment in the success of the group and in the well-being of all of its members. Empathy and compassion are more readily engaged when we feel we belong. The need to belong is in natural tension with our need for autonomy. Both are important, and they are sometimes in conflict inside us. Achieving healthy balance between our need to belong and our need to act independently requires skills that we work on all our lives.

It is important for schools to nurture a sense of belonging in every student. The pain and fear of not belonging is at the root of much violence and harm in our schools. Living together as if everyone belongs might be the biggest violence prevention measure we could ever devise. The practice of peacemaking Circles helps us live as if everyone belongs. Circles offer a way to create and continually enhance that sense of

> For better or worse, schools are communities where students experience either belonging or not belonging to that community.

> Living together as if everyone belongs might be the biggest violence prevention measure we could ever devise.

belonging. In a Circle, everyone belongs. Even if a participant chooses not to speak, that participant belongs and is valued. In a Circle, the talking piece conveys a message of belonging. "If you are in this Circle, the talking piece will come to you. You belong. We see you."

WE NEED TO TALK ABOUT JOY

It seems so obvious that we would want joy in our lives and that we would naturally be maximizing the possibilities for joy all the time. After all, as human beings we are born with the capacity to experience joy. Every baby, regardless of cultural origins, responds with wriggling delight to a smiling face: this universal reaction reflects an inborn human capacity for joy. The Sufi poet Rumi reminds us that this capacity for joy is our birthright when he writes,

> Keep knocking, and the joy inside
> will eventually open a window
> and look out to see who's there.[1]

Joy is a powerful positive emotion. It brings energy and opens the heart center for connection with others. It reduces defensiveness and isolation and increases confidence in self and others. It increases our capacity to think and speak clearly: mental work is more effective if it is done with joy, whether we are a student or an adult. Our bodies too respond positively to joy. Holistically, our mental, physical, emotional, and spiritual well-being is enhanced by joy. Put simply, joy is an antidote to stress.

As adults, especially when we are confronting difficult challenges or even just the ordinary stresses and weariness of everyday life, we must be intentional about nurturing joy within our own self as well as others. Learning is an experience fraught with frustration, disappointment, and hardship; it requires support, encouragement and the reward of joyous satisfaction that comes from achieving small milestones and victories along the journey. Remembering to celebrate accomplishments, however small and incremental, is key to continuing to nurture the positive effects of joy that support lifelong learning.

The ability to access joy even in difficult circumstances is a quality of resilience. This sometimes feels contradictory, but it is, in fact, paradoxical. The ability to feel emotional pain—anger, fear and sadness—along with positive feelings of joy and pleasure is an intrinsic part of our biological emotional hardware. Choosing to nurture joy does not mean turning a blind eye to pain or difficulty or injustice. It means holding positive possibilities while looking deeply into pain. Deep truth about what is and recognizing joy can exist side by side.

> All of us—children and adults—are better able to learn, teach, and grow when we experience a sense of joyous well-being within our environment.

---

[1] Coleman Barks with John Moyne, translators, *The Essential Rumi* (San Francisco, CA: HarperSanFrancisco, 1995), 101.

Joy is contagious. If we bring joy into our classrooms and schools, we influence others to be more joyful. Homes that are warm and inviting trigger our sense of joy and contentment; schools that are physically, socially, and culturally warm and inviting do the same. All of us—children and adults—are better able to learn, teach, and grow when we experience a sense of joyous well-being within our environment.

Cultivating joy is a practice—one that is self-reinforcing as it grows—but it initially requires intentional choice and energy. The Circle is a space where we connect with a joyous appreciation of our self and others. Circles are one way to consciously cultivate a joyous school environment.

> Circles are one way to consciously cultivate a joyous school environment.

The Power and Challenge of Circles in Schools

WHY CIRCLES ARE SUCH A POWERFUL TOOL FOR BUILDING A POSITIVE SCHOOL CLIMATE

Schools are intense, dynamic communities, continuously working out how participants are going to be together. How well participants are able to be together impacts all aspects of the success of a school. The Circle is a highly structured intentional space designed to promote connection, understanding and dialogue in a group. The Circle is a powerful tool for that basic community function of working out how we are going to be together, which includes building relationships, establishing norms, and working through differences. The Circle fulfills that basic community function: it holds a healthy balance between individual needs and group needs.

The more Circle is practiced, the more the students and adults in a school can carry that underlying philosophy into their interactions when they are not in Circle. When we are using Circle as a regular practice in the community, we are not just building relationships or solving conflicts. *We are practicing basic ways of being that are fundamental to being successful together.*

Much more is going on than just putting chairs in a circle.

Exactly WHAT is being practiced in Circles?

Respect

In Circle, each voice is given an opportunity to speak, and each person is listened to with focused attentiveness.

In a Circle, every perspective is valued as meaningful to that person.

Equality

In Circle, no one is more important or has more rights or power than anyone else; even if they choose not to speak, no one is invisible.

In Circle, the expectations are the same for the adults as they are for the students.

Empathy and emotional literacy

In Circle, we are nurturing and developing our capacity for empathy—our capacity to connect to and mirror others.

In Circle, there is greater opportunity to reflect on what you are feeling and to talk about your feelings than in normal conversations.

Problem solving

The practice of Circle carries an assumption that every participant has something to offer and that the presence of every participant is important for the good of the whole.

In Circle, we are operating from a place of confidence in the innate capacity of humans as a collective to work our way through difficult places without expert help.

Responsibility

Circles are a space for practicing responsibility with both words and actions. The physical structure of a Circle encompasses a non-verbal kind of accountability.

There is no hiding behind the desk, and no one is behind anyone else's back.

Self-regulation and self-awareness

Participants must wait to speak, listen without responding immediately, and delay their own need to speak. This is not our usual way of talking. It takes a lot of self-discipline.

Each participant is exercising self-control to make the Circle possible.

Shared leadership

The Circle allows the gathering of differences, holds space for multiple perspectives, and recognizes the existence of multiple truths. Every member is a leader, and every member owns the decisions of the Circle.

The Circle is a practice of fundamental democracy in which all voices are heard and all interests must be treated with dignity.

WHY CIRCLES ARE SO HARD

> When we sit in Circle, we are "swimming against the current" of unconscious routines built into the very structure of the school day.

Circles are about a way of being together that is dramatically different from the routine habits of our culture. When we sit in Circle, we are "swimming against the current" of unconscious routines built into the very structure of the school day. These routines embody many unspoken rules and assumptions about how to behave and what is important in schools. Becoming aware of these unconscious assumptions will help us understand why the Circle practice, which is so simple to practice in kindergarten, is so challenging when we try and practice it elsewhere. This awareness also helps to reduce anxieties and natural resistances to Circle practice that often arise in the beginning of implementation, especially among adults.

Circles ask us to slow down and be present for the Circle

In Circle, we experience a big slow down in the usual pace of interaction—no rushing or jumping to a conclusion—because every voice needs to be heard in full. Our usual interactions are rushed: we are always in a hurry and have no time to listen to each other (or ourselves) deeply. In our culture, we are rarely fully present in the moment, because we believe we must be doing many things quickly in order to meet expectations placed upon us.

In Circle, each participant's full presence is required—no multi-tasking, no texting, just full attention to the Circle. This is an exercise in patience and self-control for young people, but it also represents a significant change for adults. It is especially hard for adults who are charged with attending to multiple demands and believe they are rarely able to give their full attention to any one single conversation.

> In our culture, we are rarely fully present in the moment, because we believe we must be doing many things quickly in order to meet expectations placed upon us.

The equality of Circles is in tension with hierarchies

Our relationships mirror the structure of power in our society that is operating all the time. Schools are organized as strong hierarchies. The Circle is non-hierarchical. It is a space of equality. Circles challenge practices around power. An authority figure cannot control the process but must instead share power with all the participants. Circles only work if everyone in the Circle cooperates without the power-based intervention of the authority figure. This shift in responsibility takes some practice and challenges the strong need felt by authority figures, such as teachers and principals, to control the process, outcome, and the participants.

Circles ask for everyone to behave towards one another in an equally respectful manner. This means that adults in the Circle comply with the same guidelines as young people. Adults must sit in the Circle just as youth do. The adults cannot leave the room and then come back in. They must stay throughout the conversation and listen just as much as they are listened to.

Circles invite us to speak from the heart and deal with emotions

In our culture, we are socialized to keep conversation at a safe, impersonal level, especially in professional roles within the school environment. We often do not feel it is appropriate or safe to share our personal experience, thoughts, or feelings. Some adults in schools are uncomfortable with emotions. They may feel inadequate at responding to the emotions or may feel that they must fix any negative emotions.

The general privileging in our society of the mental over the emotional and spiritual has resulted in people feeling awkward, fearful, and embarrassed when speaking and listening about personal experiences, beliefs, and feelings. However, personal experiences, beliefs, and feelings impact everything we do, including our relationships with students. Sharing those can help students understand why we do what we do. Adults feel. Adults hurt. Adults have wisdom from their life stories.

Adults in Circle are expected to share from their hearts and from life experiences. This is a different relationship from what the adults normally have with the students and with colleagues, and it takes practice. Some adults find it hard to share personal experiences in ways that maintain the boundaries of their role. It is important to remember that, although the Circle process asks each to speak from his or her own experience, the process allows each person to decide the depth of sharing that he or she is comfortable with. Sitting as an equal in Circle does not mean giving up responsibility for being an adult: the sharing of one's experience is a healthy part of the relationship between adults and students. Adults are expected to be honest but also to share their emotions and experiences in a responsible way that protects the well-being of children.

Emotions in a Circle are accepted as what they are: a reality for that individual, but not necessarily the responsibility of anyone else in the Circle. Emotions are heard with respect and may be responded to with empathy, but they do not require the adult or anyone else to fix them. Other students are often highly skilled at responding to the emotions of their peers.

Circles ask us to prioritize building good relationships

Our culture prioritizes achievement over connection—acts of doing over the act of being in relationship with others, our own selves, or nature. In schools, this translates into an environment where time is scarce and must be dedicated to a demanding set of tasks associated with learning. In many schools, a rigid testing regime enforces the demand to stay focused on the priorities of mastering specific skills and content.

The time it takes to build quality relationships is low on the priority scale of most schools for very understandable reasons. Yet many of the recurring difficulties in school, which in the long run demand much time and resources, arise from the absence of positive relationships. Often trust is not present in schools. Youth don't trust adults; school staff may not trust administrators and visa versa. The greater the level of trust in a group, the more effective the Circle, yet building trust takes time. It is true that an ounce of prevention is worth a pound of cure. Though building trust takes time, in the long run, it is worth the investment, because academic performance depends upon the safety and trust of relationships.

How Circles Work

LEARNING THE CIRCLE PROCESS

What is the Circle?

The Circle is a carefully constructed, intentional dialogue space. The process is rooted in a distinct philosophy, which manifests through structural elements that organize the interaction for maximum understanding, empowerment and connection among the participants. The Circle welcomes difficult emotions and difficult realities, while maintaining a sense of positive possibilities.

The roots: Values and Indigenous teachings

The philosophical foundation of the Circle has two components: 1) values that nurture good relationships, and 2) key teachings common among Indigenous communities. Together, relationship-supportive values and ancient teachings create an environment in which participants begin to connect with the core self and see the core self in others. The values and teachings become the touchstone for the Circle to return to whenever tensions arise or the Circle goes out of balance.

To build the values component of the Circle's foundation, participants identify values that they feel are important for a healthy process and good outcomes for all. The exact words vary with each group, but the values generated by Circles across a wide variety of contexts are consistent in their essence. The values describe who we want to be in our best self. Though the specifics of the process draw from Indigenous traditions, these values are common across most spiritual traditions, East and West. They are the values we learn in kindergarten.

Because these values are so important to the process, the Circle does not take them for granted, nor does the facilitator impose them. The Circle engages participants at the beginning of the process in a conscious conversation about the values they wish to hold in the collective space. Discussing values is a critical part of the Circle process. This conversation about values can be lengthy or quite brief, depending upon the context of the Circle. Typically, people identify values such as honesty, respect, openness, caring, courage, patience, and humility as the basis for the process.

Having the conversation about values before discussing difficult issues can dramatically change the way people interact when it comes time to engage the more challenging concerns. Because the values express our best self, they give us a glimpse of what our core self is like. We experience ourselves acting from our core self more than we would do if we did not talk about values first. The Circle space is designed to help us move in the direction of our best self or core self—*from wherever we are. In Circle, we are accepted as we are and supported as we move toward our best self.*

The Indigenous origins of the Circle process are the source of key teachings that are foundational to the process. These teachings often build on the Circle image as a metaphor for how the universe operates. For many Indigenous people, the Circle is a symbolic expression of a worldview—a way of understanding how the world works. The following teachings are an integral part both of that worldview and of the space that Circles create.

> The Circle space is designed to help us move in the direction of our best self.

- Everything is interconnected.
- Though everything is connected, there are distinct parts, and it is important for them to be in balance.
- Every part of the universe contributes to the whole and is equally valuable.
- In the cyclical nature of life, there is always another chance.

These Indigenous teachings, which are part of the Circle's foundation, include many of the concepts that we have identified as our Core Assumptions.

ESSENTIAL ELEMENTS OF CONSTRUCTING THE CIRCLE

The visible structure of the Circle is built on the foundation that the values and Indigenous teachings establish. These structural elements organize the interaction within the Circle to support participants, so that they embody the values and Indigenous teachings as they interact with one another. The Circle's structure creates the space to encourage all participants to speak their truth respectfully to one another on an equal basis and to seek a deeper understanding of themselves and others. These structural elements include:

Seating all the participants in a circle (preferably without any tables)
Mindfulness moment
Opening ceremony
Centerpiece
Talking piece
Identifying values
Generating guidelines based on the values
Guiding questions
Agreements (if the Circle is making decisions)
Closing ceremony

Seating all the participants in a circle

Geometry matters! It is very important to seat everyone in a circle. This seating arrangement allows everyone to see everyone else and to be accountable to one another face to face. It also creates a sense of focus on a common concern without creating a sense of "sides." The circle form emphasizes equality and connectedness. Having no furniture in the center encourages complete presence and openness to one another. It also increases accountability, because all body language is obvious to everyone.

> Having no furniture in the center encourages complete presence and openness to one another.

Mindfulness moment

A short, distinct moment of stillness at the beginning disconnects participants from external distractions and makes the transition to the Circle space easier for most people. Brief focused breathing or a brief pleasant sound or tone can be used to create this stillness. Ringing a bell or making a sound tone with instructions to listen for the very last vibration and then to raise a hand creates a stillness. Focusing on the tone helps participants disconnect from other stimuli.

Opening ceremony

Circles use openings and closings to mark the Circle as a sacred space. From the time of the opening ceremony until the closing ceremony, participants learn that they can be present with themselves and one another in a way that is different from an ordinary meeting or group. Clearly marking the beginning and end of the Circle is very important. The Circle invites participants to drop the ordinary masks and protections they may wear that create distance from their core self and the core self of others. Openings help participants center themselves, slow down, be more reflective, bring themselves into full presence in the space, recognize interconnectedness, release unrelated distractions, and be mindful of the values of the core self. Openings can be quite simple, using breathing techniques or silence or short inspirational readings. Sometimes it is useful to incorporate movement in the opening to release energy before expecting students to sit attentively in Circle. Openings are always chosen to fit the particular nature of the group and the Circle purpose. Once students are familiar with the Circle, they can create and lead openings.

Centerpiece

Circle keepers often use a centerpiece to create a focal point that supports speaking from the heart and listening from the heart. The centerpiece is usually placed on the floor in the center of the open space inside the circle of chairs. Typically, a cloth or mat serves as the base. The centerpiece may include items representing the values of the core self, the foundational principles of the process, or a shared vision of the group. Centerpieces often emphasize inclusion by incorporating symbols of individual Circle members as well as the cultures represented in the Circle. Whatever is included in the center should convey a sense of warmth, hospitality, and inclusion. The centerpiece should also reinforce the values that undergird the process. Keepers must pay careful attention when they choose objects to place in the center, so that they do not inadvertently include something that alienates a member of the Circle. It is important to explain the meaning of any objects placed in the center by the keeper.

As time goes on, centerpieces can be collectively built with more and more representations of the group and the individuals in the Circle. For example, the Circle might start with a cloth and a bowl of flowers. Participants might be asked before the Circle to bring an object that represents an important aspect of their lives. During the values discussion, participants might write a value on a paper plate and place that in the center. In a subsequent round, participants might be asked to introduce themselves, to share the object they brought and what it means to them, and then to place the object in the center. The center will now have the original cloth and bowl of flowers and the values and all the objects brought by the participants. A centerpiece that includes something from every participant is a powerful symbol both of connectedness and common ground and of the richness of diversity.

Talking piece

Circles use a talking piece to regulate the dialogue of the participants. The talking piece is passed from person to person around the rim of the circle. Only the person holding the talking piece may speak. The talking piece allows the holder to speak without interruption and allows the listeners to focus on listening and not be distracted by thinking about a response to the speaker. The use of the talking piece allows for full expression of emotions, thoughtful reflection, and an unhurried pace.

The talking piece is a powerful equalizer. It gives every participant an equal opportunity to speak and carries an implicit assumption that every participant has something important to offer the group. As it passes physically from hand to hand, the talking piece weaves a connecting thread among the members of the Circle. Participants are *never* required to speak and may simply pass the talking piece without speaking. They may also choose to hold it for a moment of silence before passing it.

The talking piece lifts the burden of control off the keeper and instead distributes control of the process among all the participants. The keeper may speak without the talking piece but will do so only when necessary to maintain the integrity of the process. Whenever possible, the talking piece represents something important to the group. The more meaning the talking piece has (consistent with the values of Circle), the more powerful it is for engendering respect for the process and aligning speakers with the core self. The meaning or story of the talking piece is shared with the group when it is introduced.

The talking piece always goes in order around the Circle and does not bounce around the Circle. In Circle, adults must also honor the expectation that one can speak only when holding the talking piece.

Identifying values

As mentioned above the participants in the Circle name the values they want for the Circle. A common practice is to have each person write a value on a paper plate or piece of paper. With a pass of the talking piece, each person shares the value and explains why it is important. After sharing, each person places the value in the center of the circle.

Generating guidelines based on the values identified by the Circle

Participants in a Circle play a major role in designing their own space in two ways. First, by discussing the values that are important to them and that they want to bring to the dialogue, they lay the foundation of the Circle space in values. Second, participants work together to define the guidelines or community standards for their discussion.

The guidelines articulate the agreements among participants about how they will conduct themselves in the Circle dialogue in an effort to be in alignment with the values they have identified. The guidelines describe the behaviors that the participants feel will make the space safe for them to speak their truth. Guidelines are not rigid constraints but supportive reminders of the behavioral expectations that the participants in the Circle share. They are not imposed on the participants but rather are adopted by the consensus of the Circle. Participants work out the guidelines together, agree to them together, and then support each other in sticking to the guidelines.

When time allows, the participants generate the guidelines for the group by using the talking piece and finding consensus. When time is short, the keeper may suggest several basic guidelines and ask the participants if they accept those guidelines and if they want to add any other guidelines. Typical basic guidelines are:

- Respect the talking piece;
- Speak from the heart;
- Listen from the heart;
- Personal information shared in the Circle is confidential except where safety is at risk;
- Remain in Circle.

Guiding questions

Circles use prompting questions or themes at the beginning of each round of the talking piece to stimulate conversation or reflection by the Circle. Every member of the Circle has an opportunity to respond to the prompting question or theme of each round. Guiding questions are carefully constructed to build relationships, explore issues or concerns, and generate ideas for moving forward, depending on the phase of the Circle. The questions are intentionally designed to facilitate a discussion that goes beyond surface responses. Effective questions are framed to:

- encourage participants to speak from their own lived experiences;
- invite participants to share stories from their lives;
- focus on feelings and impacts rather than on facts;
- help participants transition from discussing difficult or painful events to discussing what can be done now to make things better.

Questions should never invite attacks on another individual or group. Asking participants to respond using "I" statements rather than "you" statements is sometimes helpful. Appendix 1: "Sample Prompting Questions/Topics for Circles" offers ideas for developing guiding questions for a Circle.

Agreements (if the Circle is making decisions)

Decisions in the Circle are made by consensus. The standard of consensus in a Circle requires the decision to be one that every participant can live with. Agreements are typically recorded for clarity and for future reference. All Circle members are responsible for the successful implementation of the agreement.

Closing ceremony

Closings acknowledge the efforts of the Circle. They affirm the interconnectedness of those present. They convey a sense of hope for the future, and they prepare participants to return to the ordinary space of their lives. Openings and closings are designed to fit the nature of the particular group. For example, they provide opportunities for cultural expression. The closing ceremony may be simply a moment of quiet breathing or a simple reading. In an ongoing group, participants may be involved in conducting openings and closings or may design the opening and closing for the group.

The role of the keeper

The facilitator of the Circle, often called a keeper, assists the group in creating and maintaining a collective space in which each participant feels safe enough to speak honestly and openly without disrespecting anyone. The keeper does this by leading the group through the process of identifying their values and guidelines and by supporting proper use of the talking piece. Through questions or topic suggestions, the keeper stimulates the reflections of the group, all the while monitoring the quality of the collective space. The keeper does not control the issues raised by the group or try to move the group toward a particular outcome. The keeper's role is to initiate a space that is respectful and safe and to engage participants in sharing responsibility for the space and for their shared work. The keeper is in a relationship of caring about the well-being of every member of the Circle. Keepers do this not from a place of detachment but as an equal participant in the Circle.

> The keeper is in a relationship of caring about the well-being of every member of the Circle.

Circles are never about persuasion. They are a process of exploring meaning from each perspective in the Circle. Through that exploration, participants may find common ground or they may understand more clearly why another person sees something differently. The more diverse the perspectives in a Circle, the richer the dialogue and the opportunities for new insights will be. The keeper does not control this process but helps the Circle work through uncomfortable moments. Keepers do this by maintaining the use of the talking piece going in order around the Circle and by engaging the Circle in reflecting on its own process when needed.

The keeper organizes the Circle logistics, mindful of the needs and interests of all Circle members. This includes setting the time and place, extending invitations, preparing all the parties, selecting the talking piece and centerpiece, planning the opening and closing ceremonies, and formulating some guiding questions. The keeper may involve participants in choosing the physical elements of the Circle by:

- inviting someone to bring a talking piece;
- providing an array of talking pieces for Circle members to chose from;
- inviting one or more participants to do an opening or closing ceremony;
- inviting Circle members to bring or create items for the center.

The importance of relationship building in Circles

The Circle's commitment to building relationships before discussing the core issues is a very intentional and important strategy of the Circle process. Circles deliberately delay the dialogue about sensitive issues until the group has done some work on building relationships. An introduction round with a question invites people to share something about themselves. Rounds follow that identify the values that participants want to bring to the dialogue and the guidelines they need in place for the space to feel safe.

> Circles deliberately delay the dialogue about sensitive issues until the group has done some work on building relationships.

A storytelling round on a topic tangentially related to the key issue also precedes the discussion of the difficult issues when those are the focus of the Circle.

These relationship-building parts of the Circle generate a deeper awareness of connection among Circle participants. They discover how their human journeys, different as they may have been, have nonetheless included similar experiences, expectations, fears, dreams, and hopes. The opening movements of the Circle present participants to one another in unexpected ways, gently challenging assumptions they may have made about one another.

Creating guidelines together provides an opportunity for the group to experience finding common ground in spite of differences. A Circle intentionally does *not* "get right to the issues." Taking time to create experiences of shared space and connection in the group increases the level of emotional safety. It allows for deeper truth telling, enhanced self-exploration, and greater opportunities for learning from each other. It also promotes a mutual awareness of the humanity of all the participants.

BALANCE IN THE PROCESS

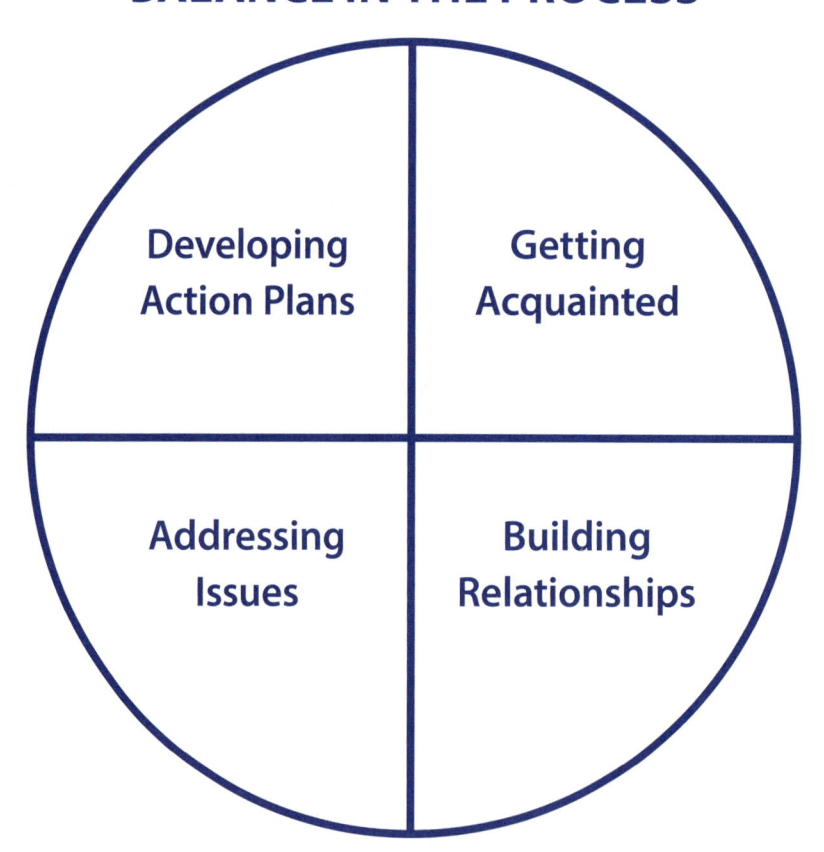

Developing Action Plans	Getting Acquainted
Addressing Issues	Building Relationships

This diagram shows the importance of building relationships in Circles. The Circle process is divided into four equal parts based on the framework of the Medicine Wheel, which is widely used by Native Peoples. One of the lessons of the Medicine Wheel is that the four parts must operate in balance. In Circle dialogue, this means that, overall, as much time is spent on getting acquainted and building relationships as is spent on exploring the issues and developing plans.

In a school setting, getting acquainted and relationship building occur over time in many smaller Circles. One Circle may establish values and guidelines. Another Circle may be sharing stories. And another Circle may be discussing a difficulty in the classroom. The balance of the Medicine Wheel may be over time rather than in each Circle. The critical understanding is that, without relationship building, Circles for difficult issues will be less successful.

Preparation

Because Circles are an intentional space, preparation is important. The time required for preparation varies with the purpose, but all Circles require some preparation. In simpler Circles, the preparation just involves determining logistics and the physical elements of the Circle. In Circles for conflict or difficult conversations, preparation may involve individual meetings with key parties before the Circle. (For a more detailed discussion, see Part III.)

PLANNING THE SPECIFICS OF THE CIRCLE

The keeper puts together a plan for the Circle by answering the following questions:

- Who will be part of the Circle?
- What time?
- Where?
- What will be the talking piece?
- What will be in the center?
- What opening ceremony will be used?
- What question will be used to generate values for the Circle? (If the Circle does not already have values from previous Circles.)
- What question will be used to develop the guidelines for the Circle? (If the Circle does not already have guidelines from previous Circles.)
- What question will be used for an introduction or check-in round?
- Is there a need for further relationship building before getting into the issues? If so, how will that be done?
- What question(s) will be used to begin the dialogue about the key issues?
- What further questions might be useful if the group is not getting deeply enough into the issues?
- What questions will be used to begin crafting an agreement if that is necessary in the situation?
- What closing ceremony will be used?

To help educators get started in Circle practice, this resource guide presents a number of model Circles. These model Circles include specific answers to the questions in the second half of this list.

Self-preparation

As we discussed earlier, Circles involve a way of being together that is different from many of the routine habits of our culture. Becoming an effective Circle keeper requires self-awareness and self-care in order to overcome those habits. The space of Circle calls for intentional behavior that is aligned with the values of the best self as much as possible. That is not easy to do in the context of high-pressure jobs and personal lives.

The journey of self-awareness is an ongoing one. Personal practices of centering, quieting the mind, and noticing our own emotions are important for cultivating a capacity to facilitate Circles without trying to control the process. The ability of the keeper to sit with difficult emotions without rushing to fix or suppress the feelings allows participants to feel safe in expressing their emotions. That ability grows with practice and with increasing self-awareness. In schools, the adults' awareness of their body language, facial expressions, and affect are critical for creating spaces in which children feel safe. Seeking feedback and listening deeply are strategies for increasing awareness of how others read us. Regular debriefing with colleagues on the same journey is very helpful.

Self-care—taking time to rest properly, eat properly, exercise, and find joy—supports the possibility of being present in the Circle in a good way. The journey of self-awareness intensifies the need for self-care, because it requires us to look at ourselves honestly without getting defensive. Some of what we see in the mirror will make us proud and some will not. In those moments, we will need to offer ourselves empathy and acceptance, just as we offer it to every other member of the Circle. Habits of self-care give us more patience, resilience, and strength to accept ourselves as less than perfect as well as to accept others.

> Self-care—taking time to rest properly, eat properly, exercise, and find joy—supports the possibility of being present in the Circle in a good way.

Combining the Circle with other formats

Circles can be used with many other forms of dialogue or activities. If you want to combine Circles with other techniques, we have found it most effective to "surround" the other dialogue with the Circle process. By that, we mean to use the Circle process as a frame for the other technique.

Specifically, establish the Circle frame with an opening, a check-in round, and some dialogue with the talking piece. You can then suspend the talking piece for open dialogue or facilitator-directed dialogue. Or, you can suspend the talking piece and engage the group in journaling, art, music, movement, or a variety of exercises.

At the conclusion of the open dialogue or activity, use the talking piece again in Circle to share reactions to what has come up. Also, use the talking piece for a final closing round. Many of the model Circles in this guide offer this combination of a non-Circle exercise embedded within a Circle.

In most groups, a small number of people dominate open discussion. *If the talking piece is suspended for open dialogue for too long, this dynamic will emerge, and the experience will no longer be a Circle.* The talking piece effectively engages everyone in taking responsibility for the process. Without the talking piece, the facilitator must take more control of the dialogue, and this reduces the degree of self-responsibility of the members of the group.

How is a Circle different from a group?

In most group processes, the facilitator controls the process and is responsible for its effectiveness. By contrast, several characteristics of the Circle reduce the power of the facilitator and make the facilitator more of a participant on an equal footing with other members of the Circle. This naturally shifts power and responsibility to the participants for how the process goes. Circles minimize the power of the facilitator in several ways.

- Most obviously, the talking piece regulates the dialogue by determining who speaks and when. This in itself dramatically reduces the responsibility of the facilitator for managing the flow of the discussion.
- Because the participants collectively create the guidelines, the Circle members own the guidelines. This, too, reduces the role of the facilitator as the enforcer of the guidelines.
- The facilitator or "keeper" participates as another member of the Circle. He or she shares experiences and perspectives from his/her own life when the talking piece comes to him or her and engages in the activities of the Circle, such as arts or journaling. The facilitator does not try to maintain a detached, "above it all" role.
- Circles are not about performance, neither are participants judged for the quality or content of their participation. By contrast, the facilitators of many groups with youth must evaluate the participants' performance.
- Circles do not try to direct participants toward a pre-determined outcome. Circles are constrained by values, but not by specific outcomes.

Circles require a shift in power dynamics and relationships between adults and students. If that shift in power is not appropriate, Circle is not a good choice of process.

The Model Circles in This Book

THE CIRCLE OUTLINE

We provide the details in the following outline to offer concrete examples and to stimulate creative thinking. We do not intend our descriptions to be prescriptive. The Circle is not a rigid process. It is always important to be responsive in the moment. The needs of the Circle participants may not follow the outline you may have planned beforehand. Nonetheless, it can be useful to have an outline to guide you as a keeper. This outline describes a Circle incorporating all the elements and phases of the Circle. Some applications of the Circle process in schools use parts of the Circle but not the full process. Adjust this outline to fit your use of the Circle. For instance, once the basic values and guidelines are developed for a classroom the process of identifying group values and guidelines does not need to be repeated in every Circle. On the other hand, there might be occasions of conflict or difficult conversations where you will deliberately return to a discussion of values and guidelines before discussing the core issue.

WELCOME Welcome everyone to the Circle. Thank them for coming. Express appreciation for the willingness to work together in a shared space.

MINDFULNESS MOMENT Use a bell or other sound tone or a brief period of silence or focus on breath to create a moment of stillness.

OPENING Openings mark the time and space of the Circle as distinct from everyday life. Lead the group in whatever opening ceremony you have chosen. In Appendix 2, we have listed some sample opening and closing ceremonies that we have found effective.

EXPLAIN THE CENTERPIECE If you have created a centerpiece, identify the items in the center and why you chose to place them there.

EXPLAIN THE TALKING PIECE Explain that the talking piece is a critical element of the Circle process. Its use creates a space in which all participants can both speak and listen from a deep place of truth. The person holding the talking piece has the opportunity to speak without interruption, while everyone else has the opportunity to listen without the need to respond. The talking piece will be passed around the Circle from person to person. Only the person holding the talking piece may speak. It is always okay to pass the talking piece without speaking. The keeper may speak without the talking piece if necessary to facilitate the process. If the specific talking piece was chosen because of a particular meaning, be sure to explain that.

STATE THE PURPOSE Remind participants of the purpose of the Circle.

INTRODUCTION/CHECK-IN ROUND Invite participants to introduce themselves if they are not already acquainted. If participants already know each other, do some form of check-in. We suggest that, in this first round, the keeper share first. Sometimes it is useful to pose a question in this round that invites participants to share about themselves, so the participants can get to know one another better. In Appendix 1: Sample Prompting Questions, we offer some possible questions under Getting Acquainted.

GENERATING VALUES Before the Circle starts, place a paper plate or half sheet of paper and a marker at each seat. Ask participants to think of a value they feel would be important in order to feel safe to speak from the heart and listen from the heart. Ask them to write the value on the paper plate or sheet of paper. Pass the talking piece and ask them to share the value they chose, explain why it is important, and place their value in the center of the Circle. Here again, it is helpful if the keeper goes first and models a response. If literacy is a challenge for the group, the keeper may write the values when participants name them and then have the participant place the value in the center.

DEVELOPING GUIDELINES After establishing values, the next step is to develop guidelines for the Circle.

Pass the talking piece and ask participants to name one agreement important to their participation in Circle. Some guidelines might include "Speak only for yourself" or "Keep body language respectful." Write down the suggested guidelines on a sheet of paper or flip chart. When the talking piece has gone all the way around, read the list. Pass the talking piece again and ask participants to indicate whether they accept these guidelines and can commit to them. If anyone has objections, explore both the objections and the original purpose of the person who proposed that guideline. Work to find wording that is acceptable to everyone. Do not allow the discussion of guidelines to become a process of persuasion. Circles are never about persuasion. If the Circle does not agree on a suggested guideline, then it is not a consensus guideline. Acknowledge that this guideline is important to some but not everyone can commit to it. Emphasize that the remaining guidelines that everyone agrees on are sufficient to hold a good space together.

Extensive conversation about the guidelines can be good practice for working through a difference in opinion or perspective in a respectful way. In an ongoing Circle group, the values and guidelines generated at the first Circle continue to hold in subsequent Circles unless the Circle agrees to change them. Often keepers place the paper plates on which the values are written around the centerpiece and post the guidelines where everyone can see them as a continual reminder of the quality of space they are trying to create together.

STORYTELLING ROUND In community building Circles and any Circles about conflict or difficulty, it is crucial to take the time for people to share stories from their own lives, so they can increase their understanding of one another and build empathy. Stories often shatter stereotypes or assumptions that participants may have about each another. This greater understanding or sense of connection makes it possible for them to hear one another more clearly when they discuss sensitive issues later on in the Circle. We provide ideas for storytelling in Appendix 1: Sample Prompting Questions. The keeper generally goes first in a storytelling round as well.

EXPLORING THE TOPIC OF THE CIRCLE To begin to explore the issue or topic that is the purpose of the Circle, keepers pose a pertinent question and then pass the talking piece. In these rounds, keepers generally go last. Appendix 1: Sample Prompting Questions can help keepers develop questions that can open the dialogue.

Alternatively, keepers might direct participants to engage in an activity that helps them connect with their thoughts and feelings on the topic. Follow the exercise with multiple rounds to draw out reflections about what they just experienced as well as reflections about the topic. Thank participants for the wisdom shared in the process. Acknowledge the courage that it takes to speak and listen from the heart.

Three parts of the Circle relevant in conflict or decision-making Circles:

1. GENERATING PLANS FOR A POSITIVE FUTURE Pass the talking piece and ask participants what they think can be done to repair any harm or to create a positive future. On a further pass, ask each participant what s/he can offer to help make a positive future a reality. (For possible questions see Appendix 1: Sample Prompting Questions.)

2. MAKING AGREEMENTS Determine any plans or commitments that are important to the Circle and everyone agrees on. Write those down.

3. CLARIFYING EXPECTATIONS Pass the talking piece to ask how people will know that the Circle has been helpful and what sort of follow up they want to ensure the integrity of the process.

CHECK-OUT ROUND To close the Circle, invite participants to share their thoughts about the Circle, and then pass the talking piece. Alternatively, if time is short, you might ask participants for one word that sums up how they are feeling right now as the Circle comes to a close. We suggest that the keeper go last on this round.

CLOSING Lead the Circle in a closing ceremony. In Appendix 2, we offer some sample opening and closing ceremonies. Incorporating a mindfulness moment such as focused breathing, listening to a sound or a moment of silence may be a short but powerful way to mark the ending of the Circle.

THANKS Thank everyone for coming and participating. Also, thank them for their efforts to understand themselves and others in a way that allows everyone to be at peace with themselves.

HOW TO USE THE MODEL CIRCLES

The model Circles are designed to be a springboard from which you can launch your own practice of Circles. They are not meant to be prescriptive (what you "should" or "ought" to do) but to stimulate your own imagination and intuition. You may wish to change opening or closing ceremonies or the questions you pose before a round. You may also combine activities from different Circles. Or you may wish to follow a completely different thread of discussion that emerges from the group as the Circle progresses. The Circle process offers enormous flexibility for adapting the process to the specific group and situation.

However, the Circle process has fixed pillars that support this flexibility. These pillars should not be changed. They include:

- a commitment to treating everyone with dignity and respect no matter what happens;
- the use of opening and closing ceremonies or mindfulness moments to mark the Circle space;
- the use of the talking piece going in order around the Circle;
- the participation by the keeper as a member of the Circle.

Appendices to aid Circle practice

Appendix 1 includes sample prompting questions for rounds. Appendix 2 offers a wide range of ideas for opening and closing ceremonies that might be used in the model Circles. Appendix 4, Section II, provides a list of resources for the openings and closings given in Appendix 2. All of these samples and options are, of course, only a start: the options for asking questions and opening and closing a Circle, as well as the resources, are endless. We encourage you to create your own according to the subject and needs of a Circle. Appendix 5 lists all the Circles with a guide to the grade levels for which they are most appropriate without much adaptation.

PART II
Building a Positive School Climate

MODULE 1

Establishing a Circle Practice

Establishing a Circle practice with students in the classroom begins with the classroom teacher's commitment to create a caring and respectful classroom culture. The Circle is a means to foster this climate. Because the Circle practice is different from most of our routine ways of meeting together, it takes time for students of all ages to become accustomed to the Circle. Sitting in a Circle facing other students can be an unsettling experience; using the talking piece requires practice to listen patiently and resist the temptation to interrupt or comment on what is being said; speaking in Circle with all eyes fixed on the speaker may also be an unfamiliar experience for students.

Learning to be in Circle takes practice. It takes time for students to become familiar with the ritual of the talking piece; to learn how to speak their own truth; to listen attentively; and to honor and value the process. According to Marg Armstrong, a leading Circle practitioner in Australia, it typically takes six to eight weeks for a Circle practice to become well established within a classroom. The most important quality is the attitude of the classroom teacher. If he/she believes that this process is a healthy one and believes that all students can learn to sit in Circle, this will happen.

Some teachers committed to establishing a Circle practice within the classroom begin the first day by putting students in a Circle just to have them get used to sitting facing one another without desks, coats, or backpacks. Some teachers mark a Circle with masking tape and ask students to place their chairs with the front legs on the tape to create the Circle. Over time, the transition to the physical space of Circle will become routine, but at first it is a good idea to provide simple guidance to get things started in a good way.

One high school English teacher uses Circles in her classroom everyday. But on the first day of the new school year, she only arranges the chairs in a Circle and has the class sit in the space as they talk about the format of the class for the coming year. She does not do any further Circle practice at that time. In her experience, sitting in a Circle facing a group of new students without all the usual desks, notebooks, and backpacks is itself a significant departure from the usual classroom environment. By sitting in a physical Circle on the first day, without saying a word, she signals to the students that, in this class, relationships will be different. This teacher begins building a trusting Circle-based classroom climate one step at a time. On subsequent days, she introduces the talking piece, a mindfulness moment, and other structural elements of the Circle.

> The most important quality is the attitude of the classroom teacher. If he/she believes that this process is a healthy one and believes that all students can learn to sit in Circle, this will happen.

We also suggest that teachers familiarize students with the use of the talking piece by practicing rounds with the talking piece to introduce their names and their favorite food, music, or movie. In younger grades, children can get accustomed to the practice of turn-taking by passing around smiles, winks, a good morning greeting, handshakes, or funny faces. In all these ways, students can begin to get comfortable with the structure and rhythm of the Circle.

Establishing a robust Circle practice means involving everyone in the room in the Circle. There are no observers of a Circle. It also means everyone, including adults, participate in answering the question or doing the activity of the Circle. When the adults model full presence and full engagement in the Circle, their behavior sets the foundation for establishing a strong Circle practice among the students.

CIRCLES TO INTRODUCE CIRCLES

The templates in this module offer lesson plans for introducing Circles to staff and for introducing them within the classroom for elementary school, middle school and high school age students. The goal of these Circles is a simple introduction to the format, especially practicing the use of the talking piece. All the classroom Circles use simple and engaging questions to familiarize students with the use of the talking piece.

Many schools begin their experience with Circle by holding Circles for staff before introducing them to students. Understandably, many teachers prefer to experience a process before deciding to use it within the classroom. And the best way to learn about the Circle is to participate in one. The most common use of Circles for staff is to use the Circle as an opportunity to do team building or shared support on teaching practice. The first template in this module offers a Circle plan for reflecting on teaching.

Introducing the Circle to the Staff

1.1

PURPOSES To create an opportunity for a direct experience of being in Circle for staff; to introduce basic elements of the Circle; and to build relationships among staff.

MATERIALS Talking piece, bells, Circle center, paper plates, markers.

PREPARATION Arrange a circle of chairs with no furniture in the middle. Before the Circle begins, place one paper plate and one marker under each chair.

WELCOME EVERYONE TO THE SPACE OF THE CIRCLE.

MINDFULNESS MOMENT *Pause, breathe, and listen to the sound.*

OPENING See Appendix 2 or create your own.

INTRODUCE THE TALKING PIECE Explain how the talking piece works and introduce the talking piece, explaining its story or meaning.

INTRODUCE A "ROUND" A "round" is a pass of the talking piece around the Circle. The keeper poses a question and, as a participant, may answer first. The keeper then passes the talking piece to the person to his/her left or right, indicating which direction the talking piece will continue to move around the Circle. On the first round, participants are invited to say their name as well as respond to the question. Remember, it is always okay for a participant to pass.

CHECK-IN ROUND *How are you doing today?*

MAIN ACTIVITY Experience a Simple Relationship-Building Circle

ROUND *Tell us who you are, how long you have been an educator, and why you chose to become an educator.*

Ask each participant to think of a value they bring to their work as educators and want to model for their students as they grow into whole human beings. Ask each person to write this value on a paper plate, using the markers provided.

ROUND *Please share with us what value you chose and what it means to you.*

The keeper begins the round with his/her own sharing and places his/her paper plate in the center.

Explain that the discussion of values is a very important part of the Circle process. The values discussion encourages us to be more self-aware of how we want to show up and consequently encourages us to be more intentional about showing up that way.

ROUND *Tell us about a proud moment in your career as an educator.*

The keeper might make note of any connections between the values and the stories of proud moments.

ROUND *Pass the talking piece again, inviting any responses or reflections about the stories they shared about their proud moments.*

CHECK-OUT ROUND *How did it feel to share these experiences and thoughts in this Circle?*

CLOSING Explain the importance and purpose of a closing.

See Appendix 2 for a closing or create your own.

Thank everyone for coming here today!

Introducing Circles in Schools

1.2

PURPOSES To introduce the talking piece, to begin practicing using a talking piece, and to explore the concept of a Circle.

MATERIALS Talking piece, paper, and markers (one for each person in the Circle).

PREPARATION Arrange everyone in a circle of chairs with no other furniture. (Everyone can also sit on the floor if this is comfortable for everyone.)

Welcome to the space of the Circle.

MINDFULNESS MOMENT *Pause, breathe, and listen to the sound.*

OPENING See Appendix 2 or create your own.

INTRODUCE "ROUNDS" A "round" is a pass of the talking piece around the Circle. The keeper poses a question and, as a participant, may answer first. The keeper then passes the talking piece to the person to his/her left or right. On the first round, participants are invited to say their name as well as respond to the question. Remember, it is always okay for a participant to pass.

MAIN ACTIVITY Students' First Circle Experience

Explain that we are going to practice a new way of being together and of talking to one another. It is a way that will be helpful from time to time. We would not always talk this way but will discover together the times we all feel that talking this way is important.

Introduce the idea of the talking piece—explain how it works and its purpose. Some possible ideas to share are that the talking piece is here to make sure each of you gets a chance to speak; to make sure others listen carefully when you speak; to make sure you are finished before someone else speaks; and to help all of us talk from our hearts.

ROUND *What do you think it means to speak from your heart?*

ROUND *Can you think of other times when you sit in a Circle either at home or with your friends? Can you tell us about these times?*

Note that people often sit in Circle (e.g. dinner table), and this process is similar but also has some things that are different and special for this way of talking.

ROUND Ask students to draw a Circle and then to notice something that is special about the shape of a Circle.

What do you notice that is special about the Circle?

ROUND Reflect on the ideas and observations shared by students and make connections to the process of talking in Circle where appropriate.

How did it feel to you to use the talking piece and sit in Circle?

CLOSING See Appendix 2 or create your own. Consider doing a stretching-standing closing for participants new to Circle.

Thank everyone for participating in the Circle!

Introducing the Talking Piece

1.3

PURPOSE To introduce and practice using the talking piece.

MATERIALS The talking piece.

PREPARATION Arrange everyone in a circle of chairs with no other furniture.

Welcome to the space of the Circle.

MINDFULNESS MOMENT *Pause, breathe, and listen to the sound.*

OPENING See Appendix 2 or create your own.

INTRODUCE "ROUNDS" A "round" is a pass of the talking piece around the Circle. The keeper poses a question and, as a participant, may answer first. The keeper then passes the talking piece to the person to his/her left or right. On the first round, participants are invited to say their name as well as respond to the question. Remember, it is always okay for a participant to pass.

MAIN ACTIVITY A First Experience of Using the Talking Piece

Explain that, *Circle is a new way of talking and that sometimes we will do it this way in this classroom. Today we are learning how it works by using the talking piece.* Consider having students suggest questions for these rounds.

ROUND *Share something or someone that always makes you laugh and tell us why you think it is funny.*

ROUND *Tell us your favorite song or movie or artist and why this is your favorite.*

ROUND *Tell us your perfect dinner—what would you have for your main meal, drink, and dessert?*

ROUND Explain that, *Now you have had practice using the talking piece; you have had a chance to see how the talking piece works.*

   What do you notice about how the talking piece works?

   What do you notice that is different when you are using a talking piece?

CHECK-OUT ROUND *Share one word about how you are feeling at this moment.*

CLOSING Choose from Appendix 2 or create your own.

Thank everyone for participating in the Circle!

1.4 Circle for Making a Talking Piece

PURPOSE To connect participants physically to the practice of the Circle and to increase their understanding of the role and importance of the talking piece.

MATERIALS Talking piece; a wide selection of materials to construct a talking piece, for example feathers, pieces of driftwood or small branches, ribbon, yarn, buttons, shells, beads, rocks, markers, popsicle sticks, strips of felt or leather, glue etc.

PREPARATION Arrange everyone present in a circle of chairs without tables in the middle and place materials on a table or two outside the circle of chairs.

Welcome to the space of the Circle.

MINDFULNESS MOMENT Pause, breathe, and listen to the sound.

OPENING See Appendix 2 or create your own.

CHECK-IN ROUND If you were a kind of weather today, what kind would you be?

MAIN ACTIVITY Creating a Talking Piece with Personal Meaning

EXPLAIN TO THE GROUP You know from our previous Circles that the talking piece is a very important part of how the Circle works. Today we are going to each make our own talking piece. A symbol is an object that can stand for more than one thing—it can have many meanings. A talking piece is like that. It can be an object, or it can also represent other things not as tangible, not as specific. The apple is a piece of fruit, but it can also symbolize all fruit, or it can symbolize health, or the apple can symbolize education. Your talking piece can symbolize something about who you are as an individual. We can talk about who we are by telling the story of our talking piece, and what the parts mean.

We have a variety of materials on the tables over there that you can use to make a talking piece that you like or that represents you. Remember that the talking piece goes around the Circle, so it must be sturdy enough to be handled by many people.

You will have 20 minutes to work on making your talking piece, and then we will return to the Circle to share the talking pieces we have created. At the end of the allotted time, call everyone back to Circle.

ROUND Now, let's explain our talking pieces. What did you use to make your piece, and why did you choose those things, those ribbons or beads or colors or sticks, those elements? What does this talking piece say about you? What did you use, why did you choose those things, and how is your talking piece expressing something about you?

ROUND *What ideas do you have for using these talking pieces and for using the Circle in our classroom or anywhere else?*

CHECK-OUT ROUND *Share one word about how you are feeling at this moment.*

CLOSING Choose from Appendix 2 or create your own.

Thank everyone for participating in the Circle today!

Adapted from Nancy Riestenberg, Minnesota Department of Education.

1.5 Practicing the Use of the Talking Piece Circle

PURPOSE To practice talking with the talking piece and reflecting on how different it is; to suggest ideas for possible talking pieces for the group.

MATERIALS Talking piece.

PREPARATION Arrange everyone in a circle of chairs with no furniture.

Welcome to the space of the Circle.

MINDFULNESS MOMENT *Pause, breathe, and listen to the sound.*

OPENING See Appendix 2 or create your own.

INTRODUCE "ROUNDS" A "round" is a pass of the talking piece around the Circle. The keeper poses a question and, as a participant, usually answers first. The keeper then passes the talking piece to the person to his/her left or right. On the first round, participants are invited to say their name as well as respond to the question. Remember, it is always okay for a participant to pass.

MAIN ACTIVITY More Experience with Using the Talking Piece

INTRODUCE THE TALKING PIECE Introduce the talking piece by explaining that it helps us to speak and listen to one another. Remind students again how talking piece works and explain why you chose the particular talking piece you are using today.

ROUND *What is your favorite food to have for dinner?*

Follow with similar rounds—*What is your favorite dessert, your favorite movie and why, your favorite game and why?*—to practice using the talking piece.

ROUND *Now I want to ask you to tell us what you notice about using the talking piece: What is different about this way of talking from how we usually talk together?*

ROUND *If you could choose a talking piece for our class, what would it be? Why?*

The teacher may suggest an occasion to use the talking pieces that the students chose; or the teacher might invite students to create talking pieces in class; or the teacher might give each student in the class an opportunity to bring the talking piece for when he/she holds a Circle.

ROUND *What do you like about this way of talking?*

CLOSING Choose from Appendix 2 or create your own.

Thank everyone for participating in the Circle!

1.6 Building Our Circle Skills Circle

PURPOSE To build the students' and teacher's skills of listening and speaking from the heart.

MATERIALS Talking piece, bells.

PREPARATION Arrange everyone in a circle of chairs with no other furniture.

Welcome to the space of the Circle.

MINDFULNESS MOMENT Pause, breathe, and listen to the sound.

OPENING See Appendix 2 or create your own.

INTRODUCE "ROUNDS" A "round" is a pass of the talking piece around the Circle. The keeper poses a question and, as a participant, usually answers first. The keeper then passes the talking piece to the person to his/her left or right. On the first round, participants are invited to say their name as well as respond to the question. Remember, it is always okay for a participant to pass.

> **MAIN ACTIVITY** Reflecting on What It Means to Listen and Speak from the Heart

EXPLAIN In the Circle, we try very hard to listen from the heart and speak from the heart. We are not always able to do that, but we keep trying.

ROUND What does it mean to listen from the heart?

ROUND Who do you know who is good at listening from the heart?

ROUND What does it mean to speak from the heart?

ROUND Who do you know who is good at speaking from the heart?

ROUND Who is someone you can talk to from your heart?

ROUND When is it difficult to listen from the heart and speak from the heart?

ROUND What helps us listen from the heart and speak from the heart?

CHECK-OUT ROUND How did you like the Circle today?

CLOSING Choose from Appendix 2 or create your own.

Thank everyone for participating in the Circle!

MODULE 2

Establishing and Affirming Community Norms

This section of model Circles is designed to help classrooms as well as whole school communities explore, articulate, and establish the expectations and standards for conduct for all members of the community. One of the powerful insights of positive discipline is the importance of shifting attention away from negative behaviors—those behaviors we do not wish to see in our community—to an explicit focus on the behaviors we do wish to see within our community. How do we want people—students and adults—to act towards one another? The more we are concrete, clear, and explicit about our expectations for positive behavior, the more we nurture, nourish, and promote that behavior within our culture.

> The more we are concrete, clear, and explicit about our expectations for positive behavior, the more we nurture, nourish, and promote that behavior within our culture.

The purpose of these Circles is to intentionally work together as a community to answer the all-important question: How do we want to treat one another and why? In the model Circles in this section, the community answers this question together, as they explore what each person needs in order to feel a sense of belonging and safety within the classroom and school community. It always begins with a discussion of our values rooted in our desire to be in good relationship with one another. The values discussion is followed by a series of discussions about what those values look like when they are put into action. Out of these Circles emerge the behavioral norms that are important to the group. We refer to these norms as "guidelines" or "agreements." They are the positive standards for conduct arising from a shared vision for a positive classroom and school environment.

In this guide, we differentiate between guidelines or agreements that arise from the consensus of the group and "rules" established and enforced by an authority figure. We believe it is important that the positive standards for behavior that we call guidelines be co-created, so that all members of the community feel they have been involved in establishing these agreements. A positive school climate cannot be simply created and enforced by an external authority. For students to treat each other well on the playground, in the hallways, or when the teacher's back is turned must arise from a shared commitment to these values; individuals across the community must have internalized them. Students must choose to behave and uphold these standards. This insight reflects a fundamental truth about the Circle process: in order to successfully practice the Circle itself, individuals must choose to respect the talking piece, speak from their heart, and honor the guidelines.

As we noted in our discussion about power, all of us need to feel that our personal power is respected; at the same time, we all must learn to cooperate and respect the needs of the wider collective. For our children, becoming aware of the impact of their behavior on others is part of developing the capacity to be a self-determining adult. Experiencing respect for their own needs and voices is part of learning how to respect the needs and voices of others. By establishing guidelines together, children experience a sense of mutual respect and shared power. Once these guidelines exist within the community, they become a powerful resource to draw on when difficulties arise, reminding the community of its highest and best aspirations.

In addition to "agreements" that arise from the desire of the group to be in good relationship with one another, there are also "rules" that are imposed by others and that are generally in place for sound reasons beyond the needs of a particular classroom or set of individuals. All schools and classrooms have rules. Some teachers refer to these as nonnegotiable, because they are not open to modification. Yet we believe it is important to have a discussion about these rules nonetheless to develop a shared understanding about the purpose behind them, to fully hear everyone's feelings and concerns about the rules, and to construct a set of agreements for how to live with the rules in a positive way. We include a model Circle to discuss how to make agreements for complying with school rules.

Finally, we include here two model Circles for checking in with the guidelines and to monitor how well the community is doing with these agreements. Because a positive school climate is a shared accomplishment and always a work in progress, it is essential that community agreements are continually revisited, revised, and renewed in order to remain a vital force helping to shape the climate. Although the work of establishing community norms is generally done at the start of the school year, schools must continually check in—at least monthly—and reaffirm these norms to keep them fresh in the minds and hearts of the community.

> By establishing guidelines together, children experience a sense of mutual respect and shared power.

Creating a Safe and Happy Classroom Circle

2.1

PURPOSE To explore the values and behaviors that help to create a safe learning environment for everyone.

MATERIALS Talking piece; centerpiece items; classroom values/guidelines; small stuffed animals—one per child, a bell or sound maker.

PREPARATION Arrange everyone in a circle of chairs with no other furniture. Everyone can also sit on the floor if this is comfortable for everyone.

Welcome to the space of the Circle.

MINDFULNESS MOMENT *Pause, breathe, and listen to the sound.*

OPENING See Appendix 2 or create your own.

INTRODUCE "ROUNDS" A "round" is a pass of the talking piece around the Circle. The keeper poses a question and, as a participant, usually answers first. The keeper then passes the talking piece to the person to his/her left or right. On the first round, participants are invited to say their name as well as respond to the question. Remember, it is always okay for a participant to pass.

MAIN ACTIVITY Exploring What Makes Students Feel Safe and Happy

Distribute the soft animals, one to each child, including one for the teacher. Tell the children that this is the animal's first day coming to school, and he/she is a little worried that he won't be happy in school because others might not be nice to him/her.

ROUND *Can you tell us something that you can do for your animal friend that would help him/her feel happy and safe in this classroom?*

The teacher writes down their suggestions on a flipchart or board.

ROUND *Which of these things make you feel safe and happy in the classroom?*

ROUND *Do you think we should try and treat each other this way in the classroom?*

CHECK-OUT ROUND *How did you like the Circle today?*

CLOSING Choose from Appendix 2 or create your own.

Thank everyone for participating in the Circle!

2.2 Circle for Designing Our Classroom Community to Meet Our Needs

PURPOSE To explore the values and behaviors which help to create a safe learning environment for everyone.

MATERIALS Paper, large strip of paper with three sections on it "From Teacher," "From Students," "From Self"; lots of markers.

PREPARATION Arrange everyone in a circle of chairs with no other furniture.

Welcome to the space of the Circle.

MINDFULNESS MOMENT *Pause, breathe, and listen to the sound.*

OPENING See Appendix 2 or create your own.

INTRODUCE "ROUNDS" A "round" is a pass of the talking piece around the Circle. The keeper poses a question and, as a participant, usually answers first. The keeper then passes the talking piece to the person to his/her left or right. On the first round, participants are invited to say their name as well as respond to the question. Remember, it is always okay for a participant to pass.

CHECK-IN ROUND *How are you doing?*

MAIN ACTIVITY Expressing Needs and Helping to Meet Them

ROUND *All of us need support and help from others to do our best work. The purpose of this Circle is to talk about what we need from others and ourselves so we can be our best here. For me as a teacher, to do my best I need . . .*

EXPLAIN *As the keeper, I model for students by identifying what I need to do for myself, what I need from my students; and what I need from my colleagues in order to be the best teacher possible.*

Hand out paper and ask each student to write down one way they need to be treated by the teacher, by fellow students, and by themselves in order to do their best work. Explain to students when they are finished to come up and write it on the big sheet of paper.

Post the paper on the wall. The keeper reads through comments under each section.

ROUND *Can you name at least one thing identified on the wall that you feel you could do to help your fellow students do their best? Can you name one thing you could do to help yourself do your best?*

ROUND *What did you learn about yourself, other students, and your teacher from doing this exercise?*

CHECK-OUT ROUND *How did you like the Circle today?*

CLOSING Choose from Appendix 2 or create your own.

Thank everyone for participating in the Circle!

2.3 Exploring Our Values-in-Action Circles

PURPOSE To understand how values are expressed in behavior in order to create an intentionally safe school classroom.

MATERIALS Paper plates, markers, and a talking piece.

PREPARATION Arrange everyone in a circle of chairs with no other furniture.

Welcome to the space of the Circle.

MINDFULNESS MOMENT Pause, breathe, and listen to the sound.

OPENING See Appendix 2 or create your own.

INTRODUCE "ROUNDS" A "round" is a pass of the talking piece around the Circle. The keeper poses a question and, as a participant, usually answers first. The keeper then passes the talking piece to the person to his/her left or right. On the first round, participants are invited to say their name as well as respond to the question. Remember, it is always okay for a participant to pass.

CHECK-IN ROUND How are you doing?

> **Main Activity** Naming Positive Values and the Behavior that Goes with Them

Distribute the paper plates and markers to the participants. Ask students to choose a value that is important to them and the way they want to be treated in school. Write that value on the outer rim of the paper plate.

ROUND Share the value you wrote and explain what it means to you and why you chose it.

Ask each student to write in the center of the plate one behavior or action in the classroom that would express that value.

ROUND Explain how the behavior you wrote embodies the value that is most important to you.

The teacher gathers the paper plates and develops a list of values and actions that are important to the group. This list can later be used in the "Coming to Consensus on Classroom Agreements Circle" (2.4).

CHECK-OUT ROUND How do you feel about the Circle today?

CLOSING Choose from Appendix 2 or create your own.

Thank everyone for participating in the Circle!

Coming to Consensus on Classroom Agreements Circle

2.4

PURPOSE To develop agreements about how classroom members will regularly treat each other and interact with each other.

MATERIALS Talking piece, hand-shaped cutouts; flip chart with huge Circle on it; markers and crayons.

PREPARATION Arrange everyone in a circle of chairs with no other furniture.

Welcome to the space of the Circle.

MINDFULNESS MOMENT *Pause, breathe, and listen to the sound.*

OPENING See Appendix 2 or create your own.

INTRODUCE "ROUNDS" A "round" is a pass of the talking piece around the Circle. The keeper poses a question and, as a participant, usually answers first. The keeper then passes the talking piece to the person to his/her left or right. On the first round, participants are invited to say their name as well as respond to the question. Remember, it is always okay for a participant to pass.

CHECK-IN ROUND *How are you doing?*

Main Activity Forming Agreements (Guidelines) Based on Values and Qualities

Use a flip chart to draw large Circle. Each participant takes a hand-shaped cutout. On each finger, each participant writes a quality or value, such as honesty, respect, or sharing, that they express when they feel they are at their best.

ROUND After sharing what you wrote on your own hand cutout, invite the participants to do so as well: *Please share what you wrote on your hand and then place the hand in the center.*

ROUND *What agreements do you need from yourself or others in order to be at your best here in this classroom?*

The keeper writes these down in the center of the Circle on the flip chart.

ROUND *Ask people if they can agree to try to do what is written in the Circle. Are there some of these agreements that you are not willing to try to keep?*

Explain that agreements or guidelines are not the same as rules. Agreements or guidelines are reminders of the kind of behaviors we want from others and ourselves. They are not imposed by others on the group but are decided on together. Everyone agrees to try to honor them and help support each other in sticking to the guidelines.

ROUND *Which of these agreements would be easiest for you to honor? Which one would be the most difficult or challenging for you?*

CHECK-OUT ROUND *How do you feel about the Circle today?*

CLOSING Choose from Appendix 2 or create your own.

Thank everyone for participating in the Circle!

Checking-In with Guidelines Circle (I)
Setting Our Intentions

2.5

PURPOSE To periodically check-in on the effectiveness of the guidelines in everyday life in the classroom; to encourage participants to reflect on their behavior and its alignment with the shared agreements in the classroom.

MATERIALS Talking piece; pen and paper; list of classroom agreements/values.

PREPARATION Arrange everyone in a circle of chairs with no other furniture.

Welcome to the space of the Circle.

MINDFULNESS MOMENT *Pause, breathe, and listen to the sound.*

OPENING *See Appendix 2 or create your own.*

CHECK-IN ROUND *Please say your name and tell us, how are you doing? Is there anything particular on your mind that is important for us to know and that you feel comfortable sharing with the group?*

MAIN ACTIVITY Aligning Actions with Intentions

Remind the group of the values and guidelines they have created in previous Circles. Review the list of classroom values and agreements. Ask each student to write down a single value and/or agreement that they really need to practice and honor today.

ROUND *Please share your value and explain why you chose it.*

ROUND *Can you describe an action or behavior that you can do that will help you practice your value?*

ROUND *Can you think of anything your fellow classmates could do to help you practice that value?*

CHECK-OUT ROUND *How do you feel about the Circle today?*

CLOSING *Choose from Appendix 2 or create your own.*

Thank everyone for participating in the Circle!

2.6 Checking-In with Guidelines Circle II
Taking the Temperature on the Classroom Climate

PURPOSE To reflect on the success of the group in following the class agreements; to see if there are any changes needed in those agreements; and to help the group recommit to those agreements.

MATERIALS Talking piece, flip chart, journals, pen/pencils.

PREPARATION Arrange everyone in a circle of chairs with no other furniture. Post the guidelines where everyone can see them.

Welcome to the space of the Circle.

MINDFULNESS MOMENT *Pause, breathe, and listen to the sound.*

OPENING See Appendix 2 or create your own.

INTRODUCE "ROUNDS" A "round" is a pass of the talking piece around the Circle. The keeper poses a question and, as a participant, usually answers first. The keeper then passes the talking piece to the person to his/her left or right. On the first round, participants are invited to say their name as well as respond to the question. Remember, it is always okay for a participant to pass.

CHECK-IN ROUND *How are you doing? Is there anything particular on your mind that is important for us to know and that you feel comfortable sharing with the group?*

> **MAIN ACTIVITY** Reflecting on How Well the Group Is Following the Guidelines

Ask each person to look at the guidelines and think about how well the class as a whole is doing in honoring these guidelines in everyday interactions together. Emphasize that this is not about identifying any individuals or particular incidents. Ask each person to take notes in his/her journal, give a "grade" for the group, and then write why they gave that grade. Then ask each person to write in the journal one value or guideline that he or she believes the class is doing well on and one value or guideline that they observe people struggling with.

ROUND *What is your overall 'grade' for our class on honoring the guidelines? Can you tell us why you chose that grade?*

ROUND *Now can you share the guideline you think we are doing well on? What makes you feel that way?*

ROUND *Please share with us the value or guideline you think the class is struggling with the most. What makes you feel that way?*

ROUND *What do you think might help the class practice the guidelines better? Are there any changes in the guidelines you would like to make? Any guidelines you would want to add?*

ROUND Pass the talking piece and ask if everyone is satisfied with the agreements and will agree to try to practice them to the best of their ability. Remind everyone that guidelines are there to help us be our best selves everyday. As long as we are willing to try, we are honoring the guidelines.

CHECK-OUT ROUND *How do you feel about the Circle today?*

CLOSING Choose from Appendix 2 or create your own.

Thank everyone for participating in the Circle!

2.7 Understanding and Living with School Rules Circle

PURPOSE To help students reflect and understand the reasoning behind "non-negotiable" school rules and to decide together how to comply with those rules in a positive way.

MATERIALS Talking piece, school rule(s) posted on a flipchart or whiteboard.

PREPARATION Arrange everyone in a circle of chairs with no other furniture.

Welcome to the space of the Circle.

MINDFULNESS MOMENT Pause, breathe, and listen to the sound.

OPENING See Appendix 2 or create your own.

INTRODUCE "ROUNDS" A "round" is a pass of the talking piece around the Circle. The keeper poses a question and, as a participant, usually answers first. The keeper then passes the talking piece to the person to his/her left or right. On the first round, participants are invited to say their name as well as respond to the question. Remember, it is always okay for a participant to pass.

Remind the group of classroom values and guidelines.

CHECK-IN ROUND How are you doing? Is there anything important on your mind that you feel comfortable sharing with the group?

MAIN ACTIVITY Becoming More Intentional about Following School Rules

Choose a specific school policy or rule that is set by the administration that all students and teachers must conform to. Examples would include cell phone policy; school dress code; attendance policy; language; etc. Place the policy where everyone can see it.

ROUND What do you think is the reason for this rule? What do you see as the benefits of having this rule in your school community? What do you see as the burden of having this rule in your school community?

ROUND For you, what is the hardest thing about following this rule?

ROUND What would help you personally comply with this rule? What do you think would help others comply with this rule? Are there things you can do to help others follow this rule?

CHECK-OUT ROUND How was the Circle today?

CLOSING Choose from Appendix 2 or create your own.

Thank everyone for participating in the Circle!

MODULE 3

Teaching and Learning in Circle

Once established as a practice within the classroom, the Circle helps teachers create a safe space for learning. Learning is a risky business. Students need to feel safe with their teacher and with their peers in order to ask questions, admit confusions, and try new skills. Creating a safe classroom and school environment is a foundation for academic achievement.

Circles are also an excellent venue for developing student voice: for articulating one's ideas, for critical thinking, and for sharing one's views. For the outgoing student who enjoys speaking in class, the Circle offers practice in listening and learning from what others have to say. For the quiet student who is more reflective or reticent, the Circle offers a predictable and reliable structure within which they can begin to develop their voice. Many teachers find that over time the Circle fosters participation by all members of the classroom. The right to pass reduces the fear and stress that may block higher brain functioning, making it more possible to participate constructively. Ironically, the genuine choice to say "no" encourages students to engage—provided the questions are real and meaningful and the opportunity to participate is always present.

> Ironically, the genuine choice to say "no" encourages students to engage

The value of Circle as a pedagogical tool is nearly limitless. In this module, we offer a set of templates for using the Circle to:

- prepare students for learning;
- check for student understanding;
- practice skills such as foreign language;
- learn new vocabulary;
- share reflections on literature;
- present and give feedback on student writing;
- identify areas of strengths and weaknesses in a given subject in order to seek and offer help with peers;
- reflect on struggles;
- develop tips and strategies in doing homework, so students support and learn from one another.

We acknowledge that this is only a fraction of what is possible for using Circles for teaching and learning, and we strongly encourage you to apply the Circle creatively to promote learning.

As much as we value the Circle as a tool for pedagogy, it is extremely important that teachers not use the Circle when this format is not suited to their pedagogical needs. If a teacher does not want to give the student the right to pass, then the Circle is not the right pedagogical forum for that lesson. In Circle, it is essential that students exercise honest choice. If they are going to be penalized for their lack of participation, then it is not appropriate to use the Circle. Circles should also not be used for assessment purposes. Additionally, Circles should not be used if the teacher wants to be able to respond or react immediately to what a student is saying without waiting for the talking piece. Circles work best within the community when they are used appropriately and with integrity.

Experienced teachers implement additional strategies that support the Circle process. For example, one teacher displays the questions to be posed within the Circle on a power point, so students can read it as well as hear it. Others give students the questions ahead of time, so they can gather their thoughts prior to the Circle. It is also effective to combine the Circle with journal writing. Some teachers provide clipboards, so students can write on their laps during the Circle. One teacher asks high school students to write a reflection about the comments they have heard within Circle in an online classroom blog. One model Circle is a practice developed by a music teacher to foster focus and attention as students cycled through her classroom in short 25-minute periods throughout the day. The creative possibilities for the use of Circles for learning are endless.

> If a teacher does not want to give the student the right to pass, then the Circle is not the right pedagogical forum for that lesson.

Finding Out What Students Already Know Circle

3.1

PURPOSE To generate excitement and curiosity about a new topic/unit by checking in with students on what they already think or know about a topic.

MATERIALS Talking piece; any visual presentation that instructor thinks is necessary to introduce a topic to students a word, image, or object.

PREPARATION Arrange everyone in a circle of chairs with no other furniture.

Welcome to the space of the Circle.

MINDFULNESS MOMENT *Pause, breathe, and listen to the sound.*

OPENING See Appendix 2 or create your own.

INTRODUCE "ROUNDS" A "round" is a pass of the talking piece around the Circle. The keeper poses a question and, as a participant, usually answers first. The keeper then passes the talking piece to the person to his/her left or right. On the first round, participants are invited to say their name as well as respond to the question. Remember, it is always okay for a participant to pass.

Remind the group of classroom values and guidelines.

CHECK-IN ROUND *How are you doing? Is there anything particular on your mind that is important for us to know today?*

MAIN ACTIVITY Sharing What You Know and Want to Learn

ROUND *We are about to start to learn about _____. Today we are having the Circle to hear about what each of you may already think or know about this topic. You may have learned about it before, or you may have just heard about it from others, or you may just want to share what you think it is about. So please share with us whatever you think or know about this topic or what you think this topic is about.*

ROUND *After listening to what others have said, what are some things about this topic that you hope you will learn or know how to do?*

ROUND *Do you have any concerns or worries about learning this topic? What do you think would be helpful for you?*

CHECK-OUT ROUND *How was the Circle today?*

CLOSING Choose from Appendix 2 or create your own.

Thank everyone for participating in the Circle!

3.2 Checking for Understanding Circle

PURPOSE To encourage a classroom climate in which students are forthcoming about areas of confusion or misunderstanding and develop a positive habit of asking for help.

MATERIALS Talking piece.

PREPARATION Arrange everyone in a circle of chairs with no other furniture.

Welcome to the space of the Circle.

MINDFULNESS MOMENT Pause, breathe, and listen to the sound.

OPENING See Appendix 2 or create your own.

INTRODUCE "ROUNDS" A "round" is a pass of the talking piece around the Circle. The keeper poses a question and, as a participant, usually answers first. The keeper then passes the talking piece to the person to his/her left or right. On the first round, participants are invited to say their name as well as respond to the question. Remember, it is always okay for a participant to pass.

Remind the group of classroom values and guidelines.

MAIN ACTIVITY Gaining Students' Self-Assessment of What They Understand

ROUND We are going to do a quick check-in round to assess how well you feel you understand the material we have been studying. If you put up all your fingers—a full hand—you feel completely clear on pretty much everything we have covered so far. No fingers or your fist means just the opposite: you are feeling really lost and confused. One finger means you still have lots and lots of questions; two means fewer questions, and so forth. So, when I pass the talking piece, just do a show of your hand.

ROUND Now we are going to go a bit deeper. If you put your full hand up, can you tell us what you think you understand best? If you kept some or all of your fingers down, can you share what you feel most unclear or confused by?

ROUND What do you think would help you personally to get a full hand of understanding? What do you think we can do as a class to have all students have a better understanding of this unit?

CHECK-OUT ROUND How was the Circle today?

CLOSING Choose from Appendix 2 or create your own.

Thank everyone for participating in the Circle!

Building Vocabulary Circle

PURPOSE To prepare students for reading a short story or article with challenging or unfamiliar vocabulary.

MATERIALS Flash cards with words from the article/short story; paper/pen and clipboards or journals; or a prepared PowerPoint of vocabulary words.

PREPARATION Arrange everyone in a circle of chairs with no other furniture.

Welcome to the space of the Circle.

MINDFULNESS MOMENT *Pause, breathe, and listen to the sound.*

OPENING See Appendix 2 or create your own.

INTRODUCE "ROUNDS" A "round" is a pass of the talking piece around the Circle. The keeper poses a question and, as a participant, usually answers first. The keeper then passes the talking piece to the person to his/her left or right. On the first round, participants are invited to say their name as well as respond to the question. Remember, it is always okay for a participant to pass.

Remind the group of classroom values and guidelines.

CHECK-IN ROUND *How are you doing? Is there anything important on your mind that you feel comfortable sharing with the group?*

MAIN ACTIVITY Learning the Meaning of Words

Show flash cards or PowerPoint slides or flip chart with vocabulary words. Ask each person to write down a definition of what he or she thinks each word means. Encourage them to make their best guess, even if they are unsure or have no idea.

ROUND *Please share your guess of the word. After sharing your guess, say if you think someone else's is the correct definition instead of yours.*

Continue around the Circle.

The teacher shares the definition/meaning with the PowerPoint slide.

Continue doing **rounds** for all the vocabulary words.

ROUND *Now that you've heard the meaning of these words, do you have a sense or can you guess what the story/poem/article we are going to read is about?*

CHECK-OUT ROUND *How was the Circle today?*

CLOSING Choose from Appendix 2 or create your own.

Thank everyone for participating in the Circle!

Sharing Student Writing in a "Read-Around" Circle

3.4

PURPOSE To share student writing and help to build a climate of trust and constructive feedback among students.

MATERIALS Talking piece; copies of student work, so each person has a copy of the work being shared; clipboards; pens; and Rosanne Bane's article, "Seven Levels of Writing Feedback."

PREPARATION Arrange everyone in a circle of chairs with no other furniture.

Welcome to the space of the Circle.

MINDFULNESS MOMENT Pause, breathe, and listen to the sound.

OPENING See Appendix 2 or create your own.

INTRODUCE "ROUNDS" A "round" is a pass of the talking piece around the Circle. The keeper poses a question and, as a participant, usually answers first. The keeper then passes the talking piece to the person to his/her left or right. On the first round, participants are invited to say their name as well as respond to the question. Remember, it is always okay for a participant to pass.

Remind the group of classroom values and guidelines.

CHECK-IN ROUND *How are you doing? Is there anything particular on your mind that is important for us to know?*

MAIN ACTIVITY Reading Written Pieces and Giving Feedback on Them

Introduce students to the different levels of feedback by reading Rosanne Bane's article, "Seven Levels of Writing Feedback." Or simply remind them of these levels in subsequent classes.

Ask for a student to volunteer to share his or her writing and hand the student the talking piece. The student tells the group which level of feedback he/she is looking for. The student then reads the piece aloud, while students take notes on the copy of the work.

ROUND *As writers, we all can gain insights by listening to the feedback from our audience, but it is always important to remember that, as the author, you are the one to make use of it in a way that makes sense to you. _____ has asked for this kind of feedback, so if you have something to share that fulfills that need, please share when the talking piece comes to you.*

The talking piece continues around until it comes back to the writer/student, who is free to respond or thank others. The talking piece then passes to the next author to share his or her work.

Continue until all the students have shared their work. If time is short, the Circle should be closed at the allotted time period and re-opened the next opportunity to hear all the written work.

CHECK-OUT ROUND *How did you like the Circle today?*

CLOSING Choose from Appendix 2 or create your own.

Thank everyone for participating in the Circle!

This activity is adapted from Angela Wilcox, "Teaching Writing in Circle," in Riestenberg, *Circle in the Square,* pp. 128–35.

Seven Levels of Writing Feedback

by Rosanne Bane

Use these seven levels as a starting point in a discussion of how your writer's group or class will define feedback.

LEVEL 1

Respondents should always begin by offering congratulations for bringing the piece to the current state of completion. Let's not forget how much work writing is, and let's not be skimpy in our praise. One of the thrills of writing is finding an appreciative audience. Kudos are always in order.

LEVEL 2

Next, respondents identify what they most noticed. Because respondents use what therapists call "I language" (e.g. "I was struck by the sensory details," or "I really understood and resonated with the dialogue in this section" or "I felt the character's grief"), there is no judgment implied about the writing. Readers share their observations and responses to the writing; they do not evaluate the writing.

LEVEL 3

Respondents ask questions and let the writer know where they want more information or details. Sincere questions about a character's background or motivation, for example, may help the writer develop that character.

Thinly disguised criticism such as "Do you intend to have your character's dialogue sound stilted?" is obviously out-of-bounds. "Why did the character do that?" could be a sincere question or disguised criticism, depending on the intention and the tone of voice.

LEVEL 4

To highlight the strongest elements, respondents identify what they thought was particularly effective. Readers are encouraged to both repeat others' responses to give greater emphasis and to disagree to reveal divergent opinions.

LEVEL 5

Respondents indicate the areas they think need refinement. "I think you need to improve the dialogue, especially in the third scene," is legitimate at this level of feedback. Again, the use of "I language" makes it clear that these are opinions, not statements of fact. So, "Your dialogue is stilted," is still out-of-bounds.

Respondents do not offer suggestions for how to revise in Level 5; they only identify what they think needs more attention.

LEVEL 6

Respondents are invited to make rewrite suggestions. These are most helpful when phrased as "What if?" questions. "What if you move the third scene to the beginning?"

Exercise care here. The most exciting writing conversations often occur at level 6. Our imaginations get sparked, and we start wondering how we'd tackle the challenge. Telling someone else how to write gives us all the satisfaction of solving the challenge without any of the hard work, so of course we want to do that. But we need to remember whose piece it is and rein in any tendency to take charge of another writer's work.

LEVEL 7

Respondents are asked to read carefully and make line edits using standard proofreaders' marks.

BUILDING LAYERS

It is important to note that the seven levels are cumulative layers, not either-or choices. All feedback should begin with the Level 1, then continue through Level 2 and so on to the level requested.

If, for example, you're ready to hear feedback about where your readers think the writing needs refinement (Level 5), respondents first offer congratulations (Level 1), tell you what they noticed and how they responded (Level 2), ask questions (Level 3), and highlight what they thought was effective (Level 4), before detailing where they think the writing needs work. And since you have not asked for Levels 6 or 7, they should not offer rewrite suggestions or provide line edits.

Who have you received good feedback from? Who would you never ask for feedback again?

From Rosanne Bane's blog, *The Bane of Your Resistance*, © Rosanne Bane. Reprinted with permission. Available online at: http://baneofyourresistance.com/2013/04/16/seven-levels-of-writing-feedback/.

Practicing a Foreign Language Circle
Beginner to Intermediate

3.5

PURPOSE To practice speaking and translating a foreign language by telling a collective story.

MATERIALS Talking piece; flipchart.

PREPARATION Arrange everyone in a circle of chairs with no other furniture.

Welcome to the space of the Circle.

MINDFULNESS MOMENT *Pause, breathe, and listen to the sound.*

OPENING See Appendix 2 or create your own.

INTRODUCE "ROUNDS" A "round" is a pass of the talking piece around the Circle. The keeper poses a question and, as a participant, usually answers first. The keeper then passes the talking piece to the person to his/her left or right. On the first round, participants are invited to say their name as well as respond to the question. Remember, it is always okay for a participant to pass.

Remind the group of classroom values and guidelines.

CHECK-IN ROUND *How are you doing? Is there anything particular on your mind that is important for us to know?*

MAIN ACTIVITY Translating and Speaking a Foreign Language

Beginner Foreign Language: Sharing about Ourselves in a Foreign Language

The teacher introduces him/herself in a foreign language and shares something about him/herself (how many people are in your family, your number of brothers/sisters, if you have a pet).

ROUND *Please first translate into English what you have heard about the person to your right and then share the same about yourself in _____ (language) and hand the talking piece to the next person to translate into English.*

Continue around full Circle.

Intermediate Language Arts: Writing a collective story

ROUND The teacher begins in a foreign language, *One morning a ten-year-old boy we had never seen before knocked on our front door.* The teacher hands the talking piece to the next person, who translates the sentence into English and adds his or her own sentence to the story in the foreign language. Continue around full Circle.

The teacher should write each sentence on the flipchart, and at the end, read the entire story in the foreign language and then ask for a volunteer to translate it into English.

CHECK-OUT ROUND *How did you like the Circle today?*

CLOSING Choose from Appendix 2 or create your own.

Thank everyone for participating in the Circle!

Adapted from Riestenberg, *Circle in the Square*, p. 138.

Sharing Reflections Circle

3.6

PURPOSE To encourage students to reflect and share their responses to a particular work such as a short story/novel/article/film/poem and to listen to the responses of their classmates.

MATERIALS Talking piece, (optional) journal.

PREPARATION Arrange everyone in a circle of chairs with no other furniture. The teacher should prepare two reflective questions about the specific content. These questions are best if they are open-ended, designed to provoke thought and encourage students to express their own opinions about the material. Post questions on the board/PowerPoint/flip chart, and ask students to take time to write their responses. This journaling can be done prior to the Circle when students enter the room as a "Do Now" or as part of the Circle after a check-in.

Welcome to the space of the Circle.

MINDFULNESS MOMENT *Pause, breathe, and listen to the sound.*

OPENING See Appendix 2 or create your own.

INTRODUCE "ROUNDS" A "round" is a pass of the talking piece around the Circle. The keeper poses a question and, as a participant, usually answers first. The keeper then passes the talking piece to the person to his/her left or right. On the first round, participants are invited to say their name as well as respond to the question. Remember, it is always okay for a participant to pass.

Remind the group of classroom values and guidelines.

CHECK-IN ROUND *How are you doing? Is there anything important on your mind that you feel comfortable sharing with the group?*

MAIN ACTIVITY Journaling, Sharing, and Reflecting on What Is Shared

ROUND *I invite you to share all or some of what you have written in your journal. Please feel free to read what you have written or tell us about it. Let's start with . . . (first question).*

ROUND *Now that you have heard each person share their thoughts, is there anything you would like to say about what you have heard others say? Do any new thoughts or ideas come up for you about this work after listening to everyone? Please feel free to share more about what you wrote or think as well.*

ROUND Repeat with second reflection question.

CHECK-OUT ROUND *How did you like the Circle today?*

CLOSING Choose from Appendix 2 or create your own.

Thank everyone for participating in the Circle!

Using Storybooks to Teach Values Circle

3.7

● ● ● ● ●

PURPOSE To engage students in reflecting about values, especially as they apply to difficult situations; to engage students in identifying constructive interventions in and responses to difficult situations.

MATERIALS Talking piece, center items, storybook.

PREPARATION Arrange everyone present in a circle of chairs no other furniture. Choose a storybook about a particular socially harmful behavior (teasing, leaving someone out, making fun of someone, etc.).

Welcome everyone to the space of the Circle.

MINDFULNESS MOMENT *Pause, breathe, and listen to the sound.*

OPENING See Appendix 2 or create your own.

INTRODUCE "ROUNDS" A "round" is a pass of the talking piece around the Circle. The keeper poses a question and, as a participant, usually answers first. The keeper then passes the talking piece to the person to his/her left or right. On the first round, participants are invited to say their name as well as respond to the question. Remember, it is always okay for a participant to pass.

Remind the group of classroom values and guidelines.

CHECK-IN ROUND *How are you doing? Is there anything important on your mind that you feel comfortable sharing with the group?*

> **MAIN ACTIVITY Reading a Book to Reflect on Values and How They Help Us Address Problems**

Read the storybook out loud.

ROUND Ask a **general** question that relates to a key value in the book (e.g., *What does it mean to tease someone?*).

ROUND Ask a **personal** question (e.g., *Tell us about a time when someone teased you. How did that make you feel?*).

ROUND Challenge the students to brainstorm solutions to the problem being discussed. For example, "What are we going to do to make this teasing problem go away?"

ROUND Discuss the solutions proposed and ask students how they plan to put these new behaviors into practice.

CLOSING ROUND *How did you like the Circle today?*

CLOSING Choose from Appendix 2 or create your own.

Thank everyone for participating in the Circle!

This Circle template comes from Jack Mangan's website under the heading, "Using Storybooks to Teach Moral Values": http://restorative.tripod.com/page0009.html. On his website, he provides an extensive list of children's storybooks for elementary grades and identifies the value or skill that each book conveys.

Talking About Homework/ Studying Circle

3.8

PURPOSE To provide support and invite students to talk about their challenges/ strategies for doing school work at home and studying for tests at home; to share ideas and help identify difficulties students are having and help them discover successful strategies that work for them.

MATERIALS Talking piece, paper, flip chart/white board with questions below.

PREPARATION Arrange everyone in a circle of chairs with no other furniture; ask students to journal before Circle; or include journaling time inside the Circle.

Welcome to the space of the Circle.

MINDFULNESS MOMENT *Pause, breathe, and listen to the sound.*

OPENING See Appendix 2 or create your own.

INTRODUCE "ROUNDS" A "round" is a pass of the talking piece around the Circle. The keeper poses a question and, as a participant, usually answers first. The keeper then passes the talking piece to the person to his/her left or right. On the first round, participants are invited to say their name as well as respond to the question. Remember, it is always okay for a participant to pass.

Remind the group of classroom values and guidelines.

CHECK-IN ROUND *How are you doing? Is there anything particular on your mind that is important for us to know?*

MAIN ACTIVITY Identifying Helpful and Distracting Study Habits

Post the following on a whiteboard or flip chart and ask students to make a list on their own piece of paper.

> *Name three habits or strategies that help you to focus on your homework or studying when you are at home.*
>
> *Name three habits or strategies that distract you from homework or studying when you are at home.*

Ask students to get together in pairs to share their lists: *Which are the most important habits or strategies for focusing on homework, and which are the most distracting habits and strategies? Can you narrow it down to one habit for each?*

ROUND *What did you and your partner decide is the most helpful habit or strategy and which is the most distracting habit or strategy?*

> Then ask the second partner: *Can you explain why you chose these as the most helpful and the most distracting?*
>
> The teacher scribes the list on a flipchart: Helpful/Distracting.

ROUND *For you personally, of these on the list, which of these habits and strategies do you practice at home?*

ROUND *What is the one thing you could to do to improve your focus on homework and reduce distractions?*

ROUND *What is one thing you could do to help others improve their focus and reduce distractions?*

CHECK-OUT ROUND *How did you like the Circle today?*

CLOSING Choose from Appendix 2 or create your own.

Thank everyone for participating in the Circle!

Three-Minute Focus Circle

3.9

PURPOSE To help students clear their minds from distractions arising from their interactions in the hallway or from a previous class, so they are able to be present and are ready to focus on the current class.

MATERIALS Talking piece; timer with a harmonious ringer.

PREPARATION Arrange everyone in a circle of chairs with no other furniture.

Welcome everyone to the space of the Circle.

To increase your focus on the coming class, please close your eyes and listen quietly to the sound and feel of your own breath for one minute.

Set the timer for one minute.

ROUND *Please share one word that describes how you are feeling today.*

Begin class!

This Circle is adapted from a Circle format that a music teacher uses to focus the class at the beginning of the class period. See Riestenberg, *Circle in the Square*, pp. 145–46.

MODULE 4

Building Connection and Community

This chapter will provide lesson plans for using Circles to build and strengthen relationships among members of the school community on an ongoing basis. The practice of using Circles to deepen and strengthen relationships when there is not a problem prevents many conflicts from erupting. It also makes it possible to bring people together in Circle more quickly and constructively when something does go wrong in the relationship.

As we discussed earlier, the quality of the relationships within the school community affects the quality of the learning that takes place within that school. A positive school climate, a strong sense of community, and a sense of attachment to the community have all been shown to increase academic achievement. Conversely, research also confirms that a negative school climate, a lack of sense of community, and detachment from the community are all associated with poor academic outcomes for individuals and the school as a whole.

Because of the pressure on schools to focus on achievement, however, relationship and community building are often a neglected activity. Too often, many students and teachers feel adrift from the school community. Parents, staff, and other members of the school can also feel as if they are invisible and not personally valued within the school community. We believe there are profound benefits to investing in intentional time to build relationships that foster connection and create a sense of belonging within the school community. All Circles, whatever their purpose, build connection.

The Circles in this module are designed for use in many places within the school community: the classroom, staff room, advisory sessions, after-school activities, sports teams, and extra-curricular groups and activities. Although the guide offers specific Circles in later modules for engaging with staff and parents, many of these Module 4 can also be adapted for building relationships among adults.

One common feature of Circles is the check-in round. This pass of the talking piece is designed to allow participants to share the feelings they are bringing to the Circle at that particular moment before the group launches into any given conversation or activity. The purpose of the check-in is to acknowledge that each of us has a complex life that extends beyond our time in school. Each of us may be carrying burdens and

> The purpose of the check-in is to acknowledge that each of us has a complex life that extends beyond our time in school.

stresses as well as assets and gifts from events earlier in the day or from situations in our lives that influence how present we are able to be within the Circle and the classroom.

A check-in round allows participants to briefly share those feelings and acknowledge this reality, which, in turn, greatly enhances the ability to let go and focus on the topic at hand. The check-in round also allows other members of the community to know what is going on in the lives of their fellow students and co-workers, so they may lend support or simply extend their compassionate understanding. Check-in practices can communicate someone's internal state quickly with a show of fingers, or the round can take more time by sharing the highs and lows of the previous week or weekend. The first model Circle offers several different forms of "check-in" that are routinely used within the Circle.

Community building Circles are sometimes simply "check-in Circles." They allow participants to share with each other at length the highs and lows of their week or weekend. It is a common practice in schools to hold a check-in Circle at the end of the week on Friday. Holding regular Circles on Monday as well can help students transition back to school from the weekend. Doing check-ins on a routine basis creates a reliable and predictable space for students to share important events that are going on in their lives that affect their learning.

The remaining Circles within this module focus on community building through sharing our experiences in our families, with friends, and other important relationships, sharing our understandings of success, and sharing our goals and vision for the future. We also offer model Circles for celebrating positive achievements or milestones for individuals and the group, as well as Circles for expressing gratitude and affirmations. Additionally, we offer model Circles that sports teams can use to build positive connections and to reflect on the meaning of winning and losing.

Check-In Circle: Practices for Building Relationships

4.1

PURPOSE To build a sense of connection among those in the classroom by sharing moods, feelings and moments of joy and pain; increase awareness of what is going on for others in the classroom; create space to acknowledge and release tensions related to external situations that may otherwise be distracting;

MATERIALS Talking piece, bells, Circle center, classroom values and guidelines.

PREPARATION Arrange students and adults who are present in a Circle.

Welcome everyone to the space of the Circle.

MINDFULNESS MOMENT *Pause, breathe, and listen to the sound.*

OPENING See Appendix 2 or create your own.

MAIN ACTIVITY Checking-In

Explain to students that the check-in Circle is an opportunity to talk about what is going for them or what might be on their mind or heart.

ROUND Pass the talking piece with one of the following check-in questions or prompts:

- *Tell us about a high point and a low point in your life since our last check-in (e.g., within the past week, over the last weekend, in the last month, in the last year, over the summer, etc.).*
- *Hold up your hand with fingers raised to reflect how you are feeling this morning (today; this afternoon; right now). The scale goes from 5 fingers = "Terrific—I am feeling great and am available to help out anyone," to 1 finger = "I am struggling."*
- *What are the roses and thorns in your life in the past week?*
- *What do others need to know about how you are feeling today?*
- *What is something you are looking forward to today or this week?*
- *What's really on your mind this morning?*

ROUND Pass the talking piece again for students to respond to one another or make additional comments.

CHECK-OUT ROUND *How did you like the Circle today?*

CLOSING Choose from Appendix 2 or create your own.

Thank everyone for participating in the Circle!

4.2 Celebration Circle

PURPOSE To build and strengthen relationships by focusing shared energy on happy occasions and positive accomplishments. These Circles also help students practice affirming their peers.

MATERIALS Talking piece, bells, Circle centerpiece.

PREPARATION Arrange everyone in a circle of chairs with no other furniture.

Welcome to the space of the Circle.

MINDFULNESS MOMENT *Pause, breathe, and listen to the sound.*

OPENING See Appendix 2 or create your own.

INTRODUCE "ROUNDS" A "round" is a pass of the talking piece around the Circle. The keeper poses a question and, as a participant, usually answers first. The keeper then passes the talking piece to the person to his/her left or right. On the first round, participants are invited to say their name as well as respond to the question. Remember, it is always okay for a participant to pass.

Remind the group of classroom values and guidelines.

CHECK-IN ROUND *How are you doing? Is there anything particular on your mind that is important for us to know and that you feel comfortable sharing with the group?*

> **MAIN ACTIVITY Celebrating a Person or Achievement and Those Who Helped**

Celebration Circles can be used for honoring an individual, a group, or an entire classroom. A celebration Circle could be used for a birthday, the completion of a unit or class project, the successful performance of a play or concert, or any occasion that warrants recognition and affirmation.

If a birthday is being celebrated, invite participants to offer a "word present" to that person.

Explain the occasion of the celebration or honoring.

ROUND *I invite you to share your feelings about this event/achievement/person and to share any good wishes or positive thoughts you have.*

ROUND *No achievement is made by one person alone. We all get help somewhere along the way. So today, as we celebrate _____ , whom would you like to thank for helping you/us along the way?*

ROUND *Is there anything people would like to add to what has been said?*

CHECK-OUT ROUND *How did you feel about today's Circle?*

CLOSING Choose from Appendix 2 or create your own.

Thank everyone for participating in the Circle!

4.3 Showing Gratitude and Appreciation Circle

PURPOSE To build relationships through positive recognition; increase skills in giving compliments; increase awareness of strengths.

MATERIALS Talking piece, bells, Circle center, classroom values and guidelines.

PREPARATION Arrange everyone in a circle of chairs with no other furniture.

Welcome to the space of the Circle.

MINDFULNESS MOMENT *Pause, breathe, and listen to the sound.*

OPENING See Appendix 2 or create your own.

INTRODUCE "ROUNDS" A "round" is a pass of the talking piece around the Circle. The keeper poses a question and, as a participant, usually answers first. The keeper then passes the talking piece to the person to his/her left or right. On the first round, participants are invited to say their name as well as respond to the question. Remember, it is always okay for a participant to pass.

Remind the group of classroom values and guidelines.

CHECK-IN ROUND *How are you doing? Is there anything important on your mind that you feel comfortable sharing with the group?*

MAIN ACTIVITY Expressing Gratitude and Appreciation for Others

Choose one of the following to focus the round or pass of the talking piece:

ROUND OPTIONS

Tell us about a good characteristic you see in one of your classmates.

　　　or

Tell us one thing you feel grateful for today/this week.

　　　or

Today we want to express our appreciation for (name of person). What do you appreciate about (name of person)? (A variation is to put the names of everyone in the Circle on a piece of paper in a basket and let people pick a paper and express something positive about that person.)

or

When you have the talking piece, turn to the person on your left and tell that person one thing you appreciate about him or her.

or

What is something you appreciate about yourself today?

CHECK-OUT ROUND *How did you feel about today's Circle?*

CLOSING Choose from Appendix 2 or create your own.

Thank everyone for participating in the Circle!

4.4

Sticking Together Circle

PURPOSE To encourage thoughtful reflection about loyalty, to build connections by sharing perspectives, and to increase self-awareness.

MATERIALS Talking piece, bells, Circle center, classroom values and guidelines.

PREPARATION Arrange everyone in a circle of chairs with no other furniture.

Welcome to the space of the Circle.

MINDFULNESS MOMENT Pause, breathe, and listen to the sound.

OPENING See Appendix 2 or create your own.

INTRODUCE "ROUNDS" A "round" is a pass of the talking piece around the Circle. The keeper poses a question and, as a participant, usually answers first. The keeper then passes the talking piece to the person to his/her left or right. On the first round, participants are invited to say their name as well as respond to the question. Remember, it is always okay for a participant to pass.

Remind the group of classroom values and guidelines.

CHECK-IN ROUND How are you doing? Is there anything particular on your mind that is important for us to know?

> **MAIN ACTIVITY Reflecting on Sticking Together—Good and Not So Good**

ROUND What does it mean to you when people stick together?

ROUND Can you share an experience in your life when sticking together was a good decision that helped you in some way?

ROUND Can you share an experience in your life when sticking together was not a good decision?

ROUND Based on your own experiences and from listening to others, what have you learned about being loyal and sticking together?

CHECK-OUT ROUND How did you feel about today's Circle?

CLOSING Choose from Appendix 2 or create your own.

Thank everyone for participating in the Circle!

What Is Friendship? Circle

4.5

PURPOSE To encourage thoughtful reflection about friendship and to increase understanding and connection among participants by sharing perspectives on an important aspect of their lives.

MATERIALS Talking piece, bells, Circle center, classroom values and guidelines, drawing materials.

PREPARATION Arrange everyone in a circle of chairs with no other furniture.

Welcome to the space of the Circle.

MINDFULNESS MOMENT *Pause, breathe, and listen to the sound.*

OPENING See Appendix 2 or create your own.

INTRODUCE "ROUNDS" A "round" is a pass of the talking piece around the Circle. The keeper poses a question and, as a participant, usually answers first. The keeper then passes the talking piece to the person to his/her left or right. On the first round, participants are invited to say their name as well as respond to the question. Remember, it is always okay for a participant to pass.

Remind the group of classroom values and guidelines.

CHECK-IN ROUND *How are you doing? Is there anything important on your mind that you feel comfortable sharing with the group?*

MAIN ACTIVITY Reflecting on Friendship

Invite students to use the drawing materials to create an image that represents "friendship" to them. Allow 10–15 minutes for drawing.

ROUND *I invite you each to share your drawing and tell us what it means to you.*

ROUND *Why are friends important to you?*

ROUND *What do you value most in a friend?*

ROUND *What is hard about friendship for you?*

ROUND *What do you do when you are being a "good friend" to someone?*

ROUND *After listening to everyone today, is there anything you learned about friendship that is new for you?*

CHECK-OUT ROUND *How did you feel about today's Circle?*

CLOSING Choose from Appendix 2 or create your own.

Thank everyone for participating in the Circle!

Picturing My Future Circle

4.6

PURPOSE To encourage awareness of possibilities in the future and to build connection through sharing dreams and aspirations.

MATERIALS Talking piece, bells, Circle center, classroom values and guidelines, drawing materials.

PREPARATION Arrange everyone in a circle of chairs with no other furniture.

Welcome to the space of the Circle.

MINDFULNESS MOMENT *Pause, breathe, and listen to the sound.*

OPENING See Appendix 2 or create your own.

INTRODUCE "ROUNDS" A "round" is a pass of the talking piece around the Circle. The keeper poses a question and, as a participant, usually answers first. The keeper then passes the talking piece to the person to his/her left or right. On the first round, participants are invited to say their name as well as respond to the question. Remember, it is always okay for a participant to pass.

Remind the group of classroom values and guidelines.

CHECK-IN ROUND *How are you doing? Is there anything particular on your mind that is important for us to know?*

MAIN ACTIVITY Drawing "Me in the Future" and Reflecting on That Person

Invite students to create a drawing representing the person they would like to be five or ten years from now. Allow 10–15 minutes for the drawing.

ROUND *I invite you to share your drawing and tell us what you have depicted about the person you would like to be in five or ten years.*

ROUND *Do you feel that person inside you now? What part of you is already like that person? What part of you do you need to develop to be that person?*

CHECK-OUT ROUND *How did it feel to do this Circle?*

CLOSING Choose from Appendix 2 or create your own.

Thank everyone for participating in the Circle!

4.7 What Does Success Mean? Circle

PURPOSE To encourage thoughtful reflection about the meaning of success and to build connections by sharing perspectives.

MATERIALS Talking piece, bells, Circle center, classroom values and guidelines.

PREPARATION Arrange everyone in a circle of chairs with no other furniture.

Welcome to the space of the Circle.

MINDFULNESS MOMENT *Pause, breathe, and listen to the sound.*

OPENING See Appendix 2 or create your own.

INTRODUCE "ROUNDS" A "round" is a pass of the talking piece around the Circle. The keeper poses a question and, as a participant, usually answers first. The keeper then passes the talking piece to the person to his/her left or right. On the first round, participants are invited to say their name as well as respond to the question. Remember, it is always okay for a participant to pass.

Remind the group of classroom values and guidelines.

CHECK-IN ROUND *How are you doing? Is there anything important on your mind that you feel comfortable sharing with the group?*

MAIN ACTIVITY Sharing Stories of Success and Their Meaning

ROUND *Tell us about a time in your life where you felt you were successful.*

ROUND *What was the most important about that success to you?*

ROUND *In your experience, are success and happiness the same experience?*

ROUND *In your experience, has success ever caused you to feel unhappy?*

CHECK-OUT ROUND *How did it feel to do this Circle?*

CLOSING Choose from Appendix 2 or create your own.

Thank everyone for participating in the Circle!

Relationship Building Circle

PURPOSE To help Circle members know each other better and to build trust.

MATERIALS Talking piece, centerpiece items, drawing paper, markers, crayons, etc.

PREPARATION Arrange everyone in a circle of chairs with no other furniture.

Welcome to the space of the Circle.

MINDFULNESS MOMENT *Pause, breathe, and listen to the sound.*

OPENING See Appendix 2 or create your own.

INTRODUCE "ROUNDS" A "round" is a pass of the talking piece around the Circle. The keeper poses a question and, as a participant, usually answers first. The keeper then passes the talking piece to the person to his/her left or right. On the first round, participants are invited to say their name as well as respond to the question. Remember, it is always okay for a participant to pass.

Remind the group of classroom values and guidelines.

CHECK-IN ROUND *How are you doing? Is there anything particular on your mind that is important for us to know and that you feel comfortable sharing with the group?*

MAIN ACTIVITY Sharing Self-Images and Learning about Others

Invite participants to draw what they would like others to know about themselves. Ask people to pair up with the person sitting next to them and share their pictures with their partners. Allow 5–10 minutes for this sharing.

ROUND When participants have finished sharing one-on-one with their partners, pass the talking piece around and invite people to share their picture with everyone in the Circle: *I invite you to share your drawing and tell us what it says about you.*

The keeper should model by going first. After sharing the story of your picture, place it in the center of the Circle and invite others to put their pictures in as well after speaking.

ROUND *What is something you value about your family (community, neighborhood, school or culture) that helps shape who you are today?*

ROUND *What is something you learned about others that interested or surprised you?*

CHECK-OUT ROUND *Share one word that sums up how you are feeling right now.*

CLOSING Choose from Appendix 2 or create your own.

Thank everyone for coming and being in the Circle together.

This Circle is adapted from Boyes-Watson and Pranis, *Heart of Hope,* pp. 70–72.

Exploring Dimensions of Our Identity Circle

4.9

PURPOSE To raise awareness of aspects of ourselves that are universal, those parts of ourselves that are shared with others but are not universal; and those aspects of ourselves that are unique to us as an individual. One purpose of this Circle is to recognize ways that assumptions might be made based on a group identity that are not accurate for individuals within that group.

MATERIALS Talking piece, centerpiece items, worksheet with pyramid or large construction paper, pens, or markers with a narrow point, copies of a closing poem or poem written on large sheet or board in the room.

PREPARATION Arrange everyone in a circle of chairs with no other furniture.

Welcome to the space of the Circle.

MINDFULNESS MOMENT *Pause, breathe, and listen to the sound.*

OPENING See Appendix 2 or create your own.

INTRODUCE "ROUNDS" A "round" is a pass of the talking piece around the Circle. The keeper poses a question and, as a participant, usually answers first. The keeper then passes the talking piece to the person to his/her left or right. On the first round, participants are invited to say their name as well as respond to the question. Remember, it is always okay for a participant to pass.

Remind the group of classroom values and guidelines.

CHECK-IN ROUND *How are you doing? Is there anything important on your mind that you feel comfortable sharing with the group?*

> **MAIN ACTIVITY Sorting Out Universal, Collective (Group), and Personal Characteristics**

Distribute the pyramid worksheet or have participants draw a similarly divided pyramid figure on a large sheet of colored paper (the teacher/keeper does this as well). In the bottom layer of the pyramid, ask participants to list words to describe themselves that they think are true for all people. Then ask them to identify a group or culture that they feel a part of (ethnicity, male/female, youth, etc.) and write that group name next to the second level of the pyramid. Then, in that second layer of the pyramid, ask them to list words to describe themselves that are not true for all people but are generally true for the culture or group they identify with. Then, in the top layer of the pyramid, ask them to list words to describe themselves that they think are unique to themselves: no one else is just like that.

ROUND *I invite you to share what you wrote about yourself in each layer of the pyramid. The keeper goes first.*

ROUND *How does it feel to look at yourself in this way? Do you see yourself differently or understand yourself differently after doing this activity?*

Ask participants to return to their pyramid and look closely at the second layer—the group or culture that they belong to. Ask them to list on the side of the figure several describing words that other people associate with that group but which are not true for them. Give an example from your own pyramid.

ROUND *Can you share any words you wrote that are associated with a group you belong to but are not particularly true for you personally? How does it feel when people assume this is true about you when, in fact, it is not?*

ROUND *What other thoughts and ideas have come to you while filling out this pyramid and hearing what others share about their pyramids?*

CHECK-OUT ROUND *Share one word that sums up how you are feeling right now.*

CLOSING Choose from Appendix 2 or create your own.

Thank everyone for coming and being in the Circle together.

This Circle is adapted from Boyes-Watson and Pranis, *Heart of Hope,* pp. 172–76. The "Identity Pyramid" worksheet is adapted from a design by the Ibis Consulting Group, Inc. Online at: www.ibisconsultinggroup.com.

IDENTITY PYRAMID

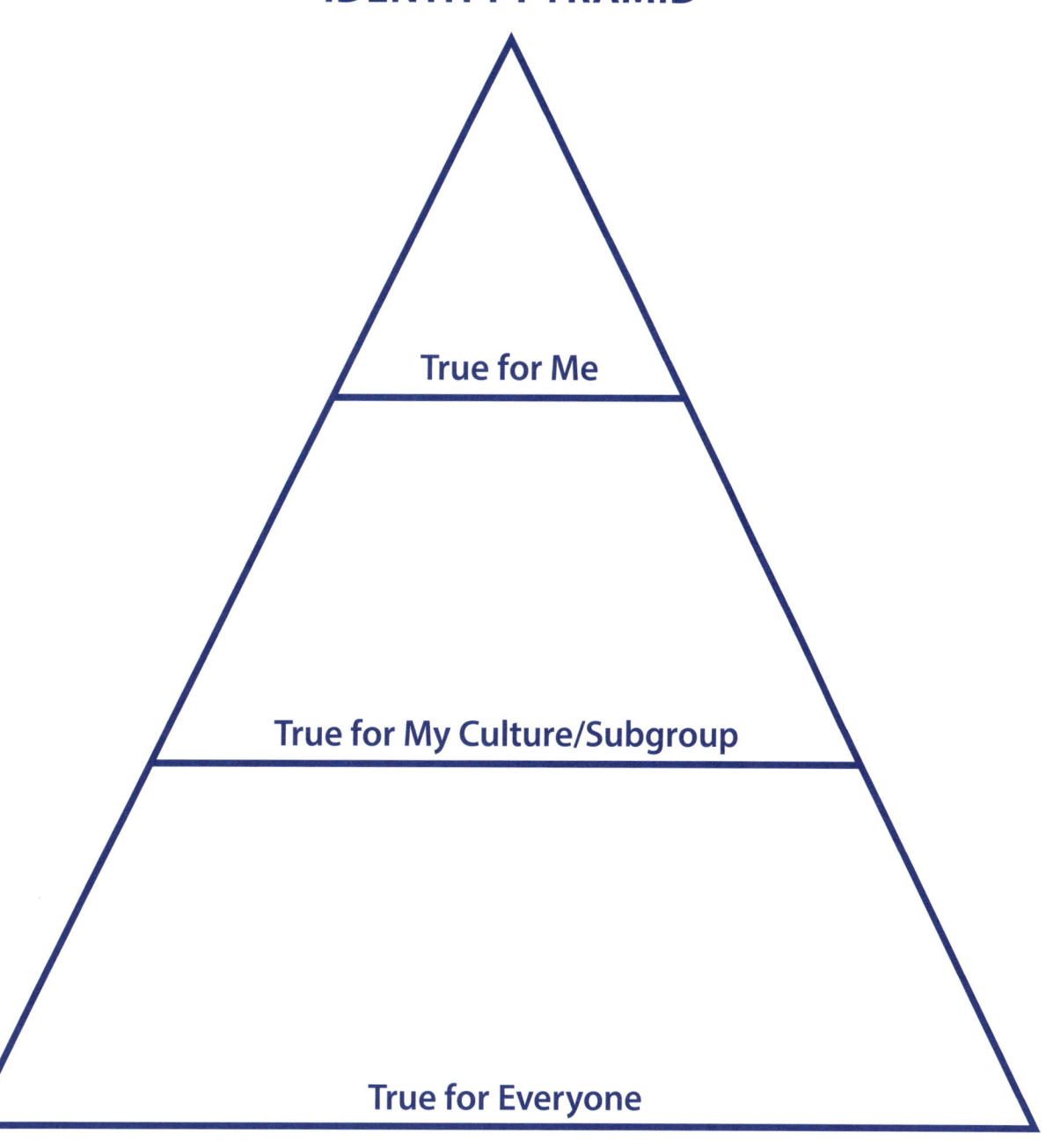

- True for Me
- True for My Culture/Subgroup
- True for Everyone

4.10

The Gender Box Circle

PURPOSE To explore male and female stereotypes and the pressures from these societal messages on one's sense of self.

MATERIALS Talking piece, centerpiece items, gender box worksheet; pen for each participant.

PREPARATION Arrange everyone in a circle of chairs with no other furniture.

Welcome to the space of the Circle.

MINDFULNESS MOMENT *Pause, breathe, and listen to the sound.*

OPENING See Appendix 2 or create your own.

INTRODUCE "ROUNDS" A "round" is a pass of the talking piece around the Circle. The keeper poses a question and, as a participant, usually answers first. The keeper then passes the talking piece to the person to his/her left or right. On the first round, participants are invited to say their name as well as respond to the question. Remember, it is always okay for a participant to pass.

Remind the group of classroom values and guidelines.

CHECK-IN ROUND *How are you doing? Is there anything important on your mind that you feel comfortable sharing with the group?*

> **MAIN ACTIVITY** Naming What Is Inside and Outside the Box for Each Gender

Give each participant a copy of the Gender Box worksheet. Each participant should work alone first. Ask participants to fill inside the male and female boxes all the characteristics or traits that they believe society tells boys or girls to be or do.

On the outside of the box, participants should list characteristics or traits that they believe are "outside the box" for each gender.

Ask participants to think about where they think these messages have come from. Did they hear them from their parents? From movies, television, or music? Friends?

ROUND *I invite you to share what you wrote in your gender box that is "expected" for males and females and then the characteristics that are "out of the box" for males and females.*

ROUND *Can you think of where you heard messages about what males and females should be like? Your parents? Movies? TV? Music? Friends? School?*

Ask participants to look at their Gender Diagram and reflect on what they believe to be true about themselves that is inside the box and the parts of themselves that are outside the box. They can circle parts of themselves that are both inside and outside the "gender" box.

Or ask participants to write in a journal for ten minutes. Are there parts of themselves that are out of the box for their gender? Do they ever feel pressure not to express things outside the box for their gender? How do they respond to that pressure or deal with it?

ROUND *Do you see parts of yourself that are both inside and outside the societal gender box?*

CHECK-OUT ROUND *Share one word that sums up how you are feeling right now.*

CLOSING Choose from Appendix 2 or create your own.

Thank everyone for coming and being in the Circle together.

This Circle is adapted from Boyes-Watson and Pranis, *Heart of Hope,* pp. 188–91. The Gender Boxes exercise was originally created by the Oakland Men's Project; see Paul Kivel, "The Oakland Men's Project," http://paulkivel.com/resources/articles/item/70-the-oaklands-men-project.

Ouside the box traits for males	Inside the box traits for males	Inside the box traits for females	Outside the box traits for females

Elements of a Healthy Relationship Circle

4.11

PURPOSE To help participants think about the elements of relationships that bring them positive benefits in their lives.

MATERIALS Talking piece, centerpiece items, flipchart.

PREPARATION Arrange everyone in a circle of chairs with no other furniture.

Welcome to the space of the Circle.

MINDFULNESS MOMENT *Pause, breathe, and listen to the sound.*

OPENING See Appendix 2 or create your own.

INTRODUCE "ROUNDS" A "round" is a pass of the talking piece around the Circle. The keeper poses a question and, as a participant, usually answers first. The keeper then passes the talking piece to the person to his/her left or right. On the first round, participants are invited to say their name as well as respond to the question. Remember, it is always okay for a participant to pass.

Remind the group of classroom values and guidelines.

CHECK-IN ROUND *How are you doing? Is there anything particular on your mind that is important for us to know and that you feel comfortable sharing with the group?*

MAIN ACTIVITY Identifying Behaviors That Makes You and Others Feel Positive

Ask each person to brainstorm for five minutes about the following two questions:

What do you do in your relationships with other people in your life that makes them happy, peaceful, and joyful?

What do other people do for you that makes you happy, peaceful, and joyful?

When all the participants have finished making their lists, ask them to get together in pairs to make a list of the important ingredients of healthy relationships. Gather the lists on a flip chart for the whole group.

ROUND *Looking at this list of important ingredients for healthy relationships, do you think this is the same for all kinds of relationships? Is it different for a romantic relationship? How about the relationship between a parent and child? Friends? Co-workers?*

ROUND *Can you describe to us one relationship in your life that you consider to be a healthy relationship?*

ROUND *Can you identify the most important ingredient you feel you bring into that relationship?*

CHECK-OUT ROUND *How did you like the Circle today?*

CLOSING Choose from Appendix 2 or create your own.

Thank everyone for coming and being in the Circle together.

This Circle is adapted from Boyes-Watson and Pranis, *Heart of Hope,* pp. 214–18.

Choosing Trustworthy Friends Circle

4.12

PURPOSE To think about how to choose friends who are trustworthy and will be a positive influence on your lives.

MATERIALS Talking piece, centerpiece items, piece of paper or journal for participants, pens/markers.

PREPARATION Arrange everyone in a circle of chairs with no other furniture.

Welcome to the space of the Circle.

MINDFULNESS MOMENT *Pause, breathe, and listen to the sound.*

OPENING See Appendix 2 or create your own.

INTRODUCE "ROUNDS" A "round" is a pass of the talking piece around the Circle. The keeper poses a question and, as a participant, usually answers first. The keeper then passes the talking piece to the person to his/her left or right. On the first round, participants are invited to say their name as well as respond to the question. Remember, it is always okay for a participant to pass.

Remind the group of classroom values and guidelines.

CHECK-IN ROUND *How are you doing? Is there anything particular on your mind that is important for us to know?*

MAIN ACTIVITY Assessing Signs of Trustworthiness and Untrustworthiness

Suspend talking piece for a brainstorming activity.

First, ask the students to brainstorm the meaning of the word "trust" for themselves. *What does "trust" mean to you?* Give participants five minutes to write down what they think it means.

Gather all the meanings of the word on a flip chart for the group to see. There is no need to come to agreement on this list. Just record all the meanings the group offers for the word 'trust.'

Second, ask participants to think about why trust is important. Now ask each participant to list at least three benefits you get from trusting your friends.

Gather these on the flip chart.

Third, ask people to think about how they can tell or judge if someone they are friends with or a boyfriend/girlfriend is someone they can trust. *What are some of the small signs that tell us that someone is trustworthy? What are some of the signals or small signs that tell us that someone is untrustworthy?*

As the facilitator, offer some examples, such as, Does a person show up when he or she says he/she will? Or, does the person pay you back if he or she borrows some money? Signs that someone is untrustworthy might be that the person promises to call but doesn't or is untruthful about where he or she is or what he or she is doing.

Gather the signs on a flipchart:

> Small Signs That Someone Is Trustworthy
>
> Small Signs That Someone Is Untrustworthy

Resume the use of the talking piece.

ROUND *In our lives, we don't choose our family, but we do choose our friends and our partners. Would any of these "signs" that we have gathered here today help you decide if you want to be friends with someone or begin dating someone?*

ROUND *Do you think you should form a relationship with someone who gives you signs that they may be untrustworthy?*

ROUND *Are there things you can do to make yourself more trustworthy as a friend or a partner?*

ROUND *Based on your own experiences, what is the most important lesson about choosing trustworthy friends that you would share with others?*

CHECK-OUT ROUND *How did you feel about the Circle today?*

CLOSING Choose from Appendix 2 or create your own.

Thank everyone for coming and being in the Circle together.

This Circle is adapted from Boyes-Watson and Pranis, *Heart of Hope*, pp. 220–23.

Sports Team-Building
Relationship Circle

4.13

PURPOSE To increase a sense of connection among teammates, to increase awareness of the diverse experiences and perspectives of teammates, and to build relationships.

MATERIALS Talking piece and center items related to the sport, standard guidelines, paper plates, markers.

PREPARATION Arrange everyone in a circle of chairs with no other furniture.

Welcome to the space of the Circle.

MINDFULNESS MOMENT Pause, breathe, and listen to the sound.

OPENING See Appendix 2 or create your own.

INTRODUCE "ROUNDS" A "round" is a pass of the talking piece around the Circle. The keeper poses a question and, as a participant, usually answers first. The keeper then passes the talking piece to the person to his/her left or right. On the first round, participants are invited to say their name as well as respond to the question. Remember, it is always okay for a participant to pass.

Remind the group of values and guidelines.

CHECK-IN ROUND *How are you doing? Is there anything particular on your mind that is important for us to know and that you feel comfortable sharing with the group?*

> **MAIN ACTIVITY** Reflecting on Values, on Doing a Sport, and on Being on a Team

Ask participants to write a value that is important to them as a member of the team on the paper plate.

ROUND *Can you share with us the value you wrote and what it means to you?*

ROUND *When and why did you start playing this sport?*

ROUND *Why are you still involved in this sport?*

ROUND *Tell us about a proud moment in your career in this sport.*

ROUND *What skill have you learned doing this sport that helps you in other parts of your life?*

ROUND *What do you appreciate about your team?*

ROUND *Pick one of the values we have in the center and tell us about a time when you saw a teammate demonstrate that value.*

CHECK-OUT ROUND *How do you feel about today's Circle?*

CLOSING Choose from Appendix 2 or create your own.

Thank everyone for participating in the Circle today!

Sports Team-Building
Deepening Relationships Circle

4.14

PURPOSE To get to know one another on the team and to share more about ourselves outside of the sport.

MATERIALS Talking piece and center items related to the sport, values from previous Circle, and standard guidelines.

PREPARATION Arrange everyone in a circle of chairs with no other furniture.

Welcome to the space of the Circle.

MINDFULNESS MOMENT Pause, breathe, and listen to the sound.

OPENING See Appendix 2 or create your own.

INTRODUCE "ROUNDS" A "round" is a pass of the talking piece around the Circle. The keeper poses a question and, as a participant, usually answers first. The keeper then passes the talking piece to the person to his/her left or right. On the first round, participants are invited to say their name as well as respond to the question. Remember, it is always okay for a participant to pass.

Remind the group of values and guidelines.

CHECK-IN ROUND How are you doing? Is there anything important on your mind that you feel comfortable sharing with the group?

MAIN ACTIVITY Getting to Know Team Members More Fully

ROUND What does it mean to you to be on a team?

ROUND How important is it to know one another outside of the sport? Do you feel you know your teammates outside of the sport?

ROUND Can you tell your teammates something about yourself that they probably don't know and you would like them to know?

ROUND Did you hear anything about a teammate that surprised you?

ROUND What could you do to get to know your teammates better?

CHECK-OUT ROUND How did you feel about the Circle today?

CLOSING Choose from Appendix 2 or create your own.

Thank everyone for coming and being in the Circle today!

4.15 Reflecting on Winning and Losing Circle

PURPOSE To increase an emotional understanding of winning and losing and to increase resilience in the face of setbacks and/or adversity.

MATERIALS Talking piece and center items related to the sport, standard guidelines, values from a previous Circle.

PREPARATION Arrange everyone in a circle of chairs with no other furniture.

Welcome to the space of the Circle.

MINDFULNESS MOMENT *Pause, breathe, and listen to the sound.*

OPENING See Appendix 2 or create your own.

INTRODUCE "ROUNDS" A "round" is a pass of the talking piece around the Circle. The keeper poses a question and, as a participant, usually answers first. The keeper then passes the talking piece to the person to his/her left or right. On the first round, participants are invited to say their name as well as respond to the question. Remember, it is always okay for a participant to pass.

Remind the group of classroom values and guidelines.

CHECK-IN ROUND *How are you doing? Is there anything particular on your mind that is important for us to know and that you feel comfortable sharing with the group?*

MAIN ACTIVITY Sharing Experiences with Winning and Losing

ROUND *What does it mean to you to win? How does it feel to you when you win?*

ROUND *What does it mean to you to lose? How does it feel to you when you lose?*

ROUND *Can you share a time when you had a difficult experience of losing?*

ROUND *Can you share a time when you lost but felt good about yourself?*

ROUND *What responsibilities come with winning?*

ROUND *At the end of a game, what feeling do you want to go away with regardless of whether you won or lost?*

ROUND *Who is a good role model for you in how that person handles winning and losing?*

CHECK-OUT ROUND *What have you learned about winning and losing from this Circle today?*

CLOSING Choose from Appendix 2 or create your own.

Thank you for participating in the Circle today!

4.16 Reflection after a Game Circle

PURPOSE To reflect on what individuals did well or could do better, to reflect on what the team did well or could do better, and to recognize and appreciate efforts and skills of the other team.

MATERIALS Talking piece and center items related to the sport, standard guidelines, and values from a previous Circle.

PREPARATION Arrange everyone in a circle of chairs with no other furniture.

Welcome to the space of the Circle.

MINDFULNESS MOMENT Pause, breathe, and listen to the sound.

OPENING See Appendix 2 or create your own.

INTRODUCE "ROUNDS" A "round" is a pass of the talking piece around the Circle. The keeper poses a question and, as a participant, usually answers first. The keeper then passes the talking piece to the person to his/her left or right. On the first round, participants are invited to say their name as well as respond to the question. Remember, it is always okay for a participant to pass.

Remind the group of classroom values and guidelines.

CHECK-IN ROUND *How are you doing? Is there anything particular on your mind that is important for us to know?*

MAIN ACTIVITY Assessing Strengths and Areas to Be Improved

ROUND *What did you feel that you did well in today's game?*

ROUND *What do you feel you could do better?*

ROUND *What did you feel the team did well in today's game?*

ROUND *What do you feel the team could do better?*

ROUND *What did you notice that the other team did well today?*

ROUND *What is your commitment for the next practice/game?*

CHECK-OUT ROUND *How do you feel about today's Circle?*

CLOSING Choose from Appendix 2 or create your own.

Thank everyone for participating in the Circle today!

Welcome Back after Classroom Absence Circle

4.17

Any time a member of the community is away for more than a day or two, it can be awkward or uncomfortable to come back. For instance, if a student is ill and misses multiple days of school, that student will likely feel that a great deal has happened while s/he was away and may feel that s/he does not fit in upon returning. A quick Circle to reconnect that student can smooth the transition back and function as a review of material for the entire class.

PURPOSE To integrate a student who has been away back into the community of the classroom and to strengthen relationships.

MATERIALS Talking piece, center, classroom values, and guidelines.

PREPARATION Arrange everyone in a circle of chairs with no other furniture.

Welcome to the space of the Circle.

MINDFULNESS MOMENT *Pause, breathe, and listen to the sound.*

OPENING See Appendix 2 or create your own.

INTRODUCE "ROUNDS" A "round" is a pass of the talking piece around the Circle. The keeper poses a question and, as a participant, usually answers first. The keeper then passes the talking piece to the person to his/her left or right. On the first round, participants are invited to say their name as well as respond to the question. Remember, it is always okay for a participant to pass.

Remind the group of classroom values and guidelines.

CHECK-IN ROUND *How are you doing? Is there anything particular on your mind that is important for us to know and that you feel comfortable sharing with the group?*

MAIN ACTIVITY Welcoming and Updating the Returning Student

We want to welcome (name of student) back to our classroom.

ROUND *Please check in and say HI to (name of student).*

ROUND *Please share with (name of student) something that we did as a class while s/he was gone or something that you learned that it is important for (name of student) to know.*

ROUND *Is there anything else you would like to tell (name of student) to help him/her catch up?*

CHECK-OUT ROUND *How do you feel about today's Circle?*

CLOSING Choose from Appendix 2 or create your own.

Thank everyone for participating in the Circle today!

See also 12.5 Welcome Back After Suspension Circle (page 310), which is designed specifically for a student returning after a suspension.

MODULE 5

Social and Emotional Learning

All Circles are an opportunity to practice social and emotional skills, as participants learn to share their thoughts, feelings, and experiences with one another. Listening deeply to others is an important social and emotional skill developed within the Circle. As students and adults listen, they develop empathy, perspective, and awareness of the needs, feelings, and life experiences of others. The Circles in this module focus on developing social and emotional literacy. We offer nine Circles specifically designed to help participants reflect on and talk about feelings in many different contexts.

Research has shown that social emotional literacy is both a critical faculty for success in life and a set of skills that improve with practice. Fundamental emotional skills include:

- recognizing and managing one's own emotions;
- reading and responding to emotions in others;
- developing empathy and concern for others;
- making responsible decisions; and
- establishing and maintaining healthy positive relationships.

For adolescents, in particular, intentional learning and practice around the important skills of emotional self-regulation and responsible decision-making strengthens developing pathways in the neo-cortex region of the brain. Again, all Circles, whatever the topic, provide this practice, but those presented in this module provide intentional practice designed to help young people become aware of their feelings and learn how to manage them successfully. There are many excellent curricula for developing social emotional learning, and we believe that many of the activities in those curricula can be easily adapted to be shared within the Circle format presented in this guide.

One significant difference between commonly used social emotional curricula and the Circle practice presented in this guide is the active participation of the keeper in all Circles, including those in this module. In many Circles, the keeper intentionally answers the question first to provide a model for the rest of the group. If there is an exercise involving drawing, journaling, or a worksheet as part of the Circle, the keeper should do it as well. It is a sign of respect that the keeper offers his/her feelings and is willing to show vulnerability.

Keepers should never ask a question that they are not willing to answer themselves. Keep in mind that all participants must feel free to share only at the level at which they feel comfortable and are always free to pass. Especially in Circles focused on social and emotional skills, the adult keeper of the Circle is encouraged to share his or her own feelings and to honestly engage with the material, bearing in mind that the process they are keeping is safe for all. Adults need to talk about their own feelings and to model the ability to do so in a responsible and respectful manner. By doing this, adults fulfill their fundamental responsibility to care for the well-being of children by being a positive role model in expressing and managing their feelings.

> Adults need to talk about their own feelings and to model the ability to do so in a responsible and respectful manner.

Listening to the Silence Circle

5.1

PURPOSE Increase emotional literacy by increasing the ability to be still and become aware of the inner state of self.

MATERIALS Talking piece, bells, Circle centerpiece, classroom values and guidelines, drawing materials if you are using the optional activity.

PREPARATION Arrange everyone in a circle of chairs with no other furniture.

Welcome to the space of the Circle.

MINDFULNESS MOMENT *Pause, breathe, and listen to the sound.*

OPENING See Appendix 2 or create your own.

INTRODUCE "ROUNDS" A "round" is a pass of the talking piece around the Circle. The keeper poses a question and, as a participant, usually answers first. The keeper then passes the talking piece to the person to his/her left or right. On the first round, participants are invited to say their name as well as respond to the question. Remember, it is always okay for a participant to pass.

Remind the group of classroom values and guidelines.

CHECK-IN ROUND *How are you doing? Is there anything particular on your mind that is important for us to know?*

MAIN ACTIVITY Listening to Silence and Reflecting on the Experience

Read the following slowly:

We are going to explore the experience of being silent. What do we notice when we listen to the silence of no one talking? Take a deep breath and exhale slowly. When you finish exhaling, close your eyes to focus on your ears. Continue to breathe deeply and focus your attention on your ears. Notice your ears. Put all your attention on your ears. Listen, listen. I will stop talking and we will all be silent for one minute. Notice what you hear even though no one is talking.

One minute of silence.

Now I invite you to open your eyes.

ROUND *What did you notice with your ears when no one was talking?*

Read the following slowly:

This time we will listen to our own body and mind. Close your eyes. Focus your attention on your insides – the inside of your body and the inside of your mind. With your eyes closed notice your heart, feel it beat, notice your lungs, feel them breathe, notice your feelings. I will stop talking for one minute and we will all be silent noticing what is happening inside us.

One minute of silence

Now I invite you to open your eyes.

ROUND What did you notice about your insides when we were all quiet?

OPTIONAL Draw a picture of what you noticed inside your body when we were silent.

ROUND Pass the talking piece and invite participants to share their drawings.

CHECK-OUT ROUND How did it feel to do this Circle?

CLOSING Choose from Appendix 2 or create your own.

Thank everyone for participating in the Circle today!

Who and What Makes Us Feel Good? Circle

5.2

PURPOSE To increase emotional literacy by increasing awareness of what contributes to making one's self and others feel good.

MATERIALS Talking piece, bells, Circle centerpiece, classroom values and guidelines, drawing materials.

PREPARATION Arrange everyone in a circle of chairs with no other furniture.

Welcome to the space of the Circle.

MINDFULNESS MOMENT *Pause, breathe, and listen to the sound.*

OPENING See Appendix 2 or create your own.

INTRODUCE "ROUNDS" A "round" is a pass of the talking piece around the Circle. The keeper poses a question and, as a participant, usually answers first. The keeper then passes the talking piece to the person to his/her left or right. On the first round, participants are invited to say their name as well as respond to the question. Remember, it is always okay for a participant to pass.

Remind the group of classroom values and guidelines.

CHECK-IN ROUND *How are you doing? Is there anything important on your mind that you feel comfortable sharing with the group?*

MAIN ACTIVITY Drawing a Picture of Who Makes Us Feel Good

Take a deep breath, close your eyes, and think about someone who makes you feel good. Notice who it is that makes you feel good. Notice how your body feels, notice how your heart feels. Breathe deeply, and then open your eyes. . . . Now, make a picture of the person who makes you feel good.

Allow sufficient time for drawing.

ROUND *I invite you to share your picture and tell us what this person does to make you feel good.*

ROUND *What do you think you do to help other people feel good?*

CHECK-OUT ROUND *Do you have anything else you would like to say about our Circle today?*

CLOSING Choose from Appendix 2 or create your own.

Thank everyone for participating in the Circle today!

5.3 Dealing with Inside and Outside Hurts Circle

PURPOSE To increase emotional literacy by providing a framework to talk about non-physical hurts.

MATERIALS Talking piece, Circle center, classroom values and guidelines.

PREPARATION Arrange everyone in a circle of chairs with no other furniture.

Welcome to the space of the Circle.

MINDFULNESS MOMENT *Pause, breathe, and listen to the sound.*

OPENING See Appendix 2 or create your own.

INTRODUCE "ROUNDS" A "round" is a pass of the talking piece around the Circle. The keeper poses a question and, as a participant, usually answers first. The keeper then passes the talking piece to the person to his/her left or right. On the first round, participants are invited to say their name as well as respond to the question. Remember, it is always okay for a participant to pass.

Remind the group of classroom values and guidelines.

CHECK-IN ROUND *How are you doing? Is there anything important on your mind that you feel comfortable sharing with the group?*

> **MAIN ACTIVITY** Finding Ways to Help When We Experience Hurts to Our Hearts

EXPLAIN *Different kinds of hurts happen to us. Some hurts are physical, like cuts or bruises or headaches. Some hurts are to our hearts and feelings.*

ROUND *Who do you go to when you feel hurt on the outside? Who do you go to when you feel hurt on the inside?*

ROUND *What kind of hurts cause hurt to our hearts?*

ROUND *What has helped you to feel better when you have experienced a hurt to your heart?*

ROUND *What could you do to help someone who has a hurt to his or her heart?*

COMMENT *Thank you so much for the good ideas you have about helping someone who has a hurt in their heart.*

CHECK-OUT ROUND *Do you have anything else you would like to say about our Circle today?*

CLOSING Choose from Appendix 2 or create your own.

Thank everyone for participating in the Circle today!

5.4 What Triggers Your Anger? Circle

PURPOSE To increase emotional literacy by increasing the ability to recognize and talk about feelings of anger.

MATERIALS Talking piece, bells, Circle center, classroom values and guidelines.

PREPARATION Arrange everyone in a circle of chairs with no other furniture.

Welcome to the space of the Circle.

MINDFULNESS MOMENT *Pause, breathe, and listen to the sound.*

OPENING See Appendix 2 or create your own.

INTRODUCE "ROUNDS" A "round" is a pass of the talking piece around the Circle. The keeper poses a question and, as a participant, usually answers first. The keeper then passes the talking piece to the person to his/her left or right. On the first round, participants are invited to say their name as well as respond to the question. Remember, it is always okay for a participant to pass.

Remind the group of classroom values and guidelines.

CHECK-IN ROUND *How are you doing? Is there anything important on your mind that you feel comfortable sharing with the group?*

> **MAIN ACTIVITY** Exploring Anger and How to Express It in Ways That Help

EXPLAIN *In our Circle today we are going to explore some strong feelings.*

ROUND *What are some situations that cause you to laugh really hard?*

ROUND *What are some situations where you get angry?*

ROUND *What do you do with angry feelings?*

ROUND *In your life, has anger ever been helpful? Has anger ever gotten you in trouble or been unhelpful?*

ROUND *How can you express your anger in a way that does not get you in trouble or make things worse?*

CHECK-OUT ROUND *Do you have anything else you would like to say about our Circle today?*

CLOSING Choose from Appendix 2 or create your own.

Thank everyone for participating in the Circle today!

What Are You Worried About? Circle

5.5

PURPOSE To increase emotional literacy by increasing awareness of anxieties and the ability to talk about them.

MATERIALS Talking piece, bells, Circle center, classroom values and guidelines, journaling materials and/or drawing material.

PREPARATION Arrange everyone in a circle of chairs with no other furniture.

Welcome to the space of the Circle.

MINDFULNESS MOMENT *Pause, breathe, and listen to the sound.*

OPENING See Appendix 2 or create your own.

INTRODUCE "ROUNDS" A "round" is a pass of the talking piece around the Circle. The keeper poses a question and, as a participant, usually answers first. The keeper then passes the talking piece to the person to his/her left or right. On the first round, participants are invited to say their name as well as respond to the question. Remember, it is always okay for a participant to pass.

Remind the group of classroom values and guidelines.

CHECK-IN ROUND *How are you doing? Is there anything important on your mind that you feel comfortable sharing with the group?*

MAIN ACTIVITY Exploring Hope, Worries, and How to Relieve Stress from Worries

EXPLAIN *In this Circle, we are going to explore what gives us hope and what causes us to worry.*

ROUND *What gives you hope?*

Invite participants to use their journals to answer the question: What are you worried about? They may write or draw. Allow sufficient time for writing/drawing.

ROUND *I invite you to share something about your worries from your journal or show us your drawing and explain what it means to you.*

ROUND *How can you tell if you or someone else is worried or very stressed?*

ROUND *What can you do to relieve the stress of your worries?*

Circle *Forward* MODULE 5: SOCIAL AND EMOTIONAL LEARNING

ROUND *Tell us more about what brings you hope, especially when you are worried.*

Thank everyone for their ideas about how to cope with stress or worry.

CHECK-OUT ROUND *Do you have anything else you would like to say about our Circle today?*

CLOSING Choose from Appendix 2 or create your own.

Thank everyone for participating in the Circle today!

Daily Emotional Weather Report Circle

5.6

PURPOSE To assist participants in becoming more aware of the emotions and thoughts that underlie their behavior and to increase participants' ability to recognize, label, and modulate their feelings.

MATERIALS Talking piece, centerpiece items, and copies of the Daily Emotional Weather Report worksheets.

PREPARATION Arrange everyone in a circle of chairs with no other furniture.

Welcome to the space of the Circle.

MINDFULNESS MOMENT *Pause, breathe, and listen to the sound.*

OPENING See Appendix 2 or create your own.

INTRODUCE "ROUNDS" A "round" is a pass of the talking piece around the Circle. The keeper poses a question and, as a participant, usually answers first. The keeper then passes the talking piece to the person to his/her left or right. On the first round, participants are invited to say their name as well as respond to the question. Remember, it is always okay for a participant to pass.

Remind the group of classroom values and guidelines.

CHECK-IN ROUND *How are you doing? Is there anything important on your mind that you feel comfortable sharing with the group?*

> **MAIN ACTIVITY Taking Stock of Feelings, What Triggered Them, and Our Bodies' Responses**

Introduce the following: *Before you even got to the Circle today, you probably dealt with quite a few people. Maybe you had some positive experiences or maybe some unpleasant ones. You might not be in the habit of thinking about or even remembering the feelings you have. It might not be something you think of doing on a day-to-day basis. But a big part of taking control over your behavior is first seeing what feelings are underneath your behavior. To do that, we have come up with something called the Daily Emotional Weather Report.*

Distribute the worksheets (include yourself). Go over the list of emotions and explain the meaning of any words that are not familiar to the participants. Invite participants to complete the worksheet. Allow ample time for them to work on it.

ROUND *What was the experience like for you to fill out the worksheet? Were you able to identify emotions and thoughts related to a particular situation?*

ROUND *On this round, I invite you to share some of the feelings or body sensations you identified on the worksheet.*

ROUND *Has filling out this weather report changed how you think or feel about responding to situations in your life? Is there some way of feeling you would choose to be different?*

CHECK-OUT ROUND *Do you have anything else you would like to say about our Circle today?*

CLOSING Choose from Appendix 2 or create your own.

Thank everyone for participating in the Circle today!

This activity is adapted from Casarjian and Casarjian, *Power Source Facilitator's Manual*, pp. 74–75. (see Appendix 4: Resources, Section I). The activity is also in Boyes-Watson and Pranis, *Heart of Hope*, pp. 108–114.

Daily Emotional Weather Report Worksheet

1. Give a general description of your emotional "weather."

2. What triggered you today? Be specific. List people, places, activities, events, thoughts, weather, anything that you experienced.

3. What feelings got triggered? And what were you feeling below the surface?

Circle or underline the words that describe the range of your feelings.

abandoned	combative	envious	ignored	mad	sad
amused	confused	exasperated	imposed	miserable	scared
angry	contemptuous	excited	upon	nervous	silly
annoyed	concerned	exhausted	impressed	offended	spiteful
anxious	crushed	exuberant	indifferent	outraged	tender
ashamed	defeated	fearful	infuriated	overwhelmed	tense
bitter	delighted	fed	insecure	pained	troubled
blissful	desirous	up	inspired	panicked	unsettled
blue	despairing	foolish	intimidated	persecuted	upset
bored	diminished	frightened	isolated	pleased	vulnerable
burdened	disconnected	glad	jealous	pressured	weary
calm	distraught	guilty	joyous	proud	worried
capable	disturbed	happy	left	rejected	
cheated	eager	helpless	out	relieved	
cheerful	edgy	hopeful	lonely	remorseful	
childish	empty	hurt	low	restless	

continued on next page

continued from previous page

4. What thoughts got triggered?

5. What body sensations or physical signs of stress did you experience?

muscle tension	numbness	insomnia
headache	fatigue	blurred vision
sweating	hyper	watery eyes
difficulty breathing	restless	physical pain
pounding heart	digestive problems	body got hot or cold
tingling	got sick	a sense of blood pressure rising

Did you experience any other sensations?

6. How did you react or respond?

7. In the situation in which you got triggered, what was the real issue?

Complete the following:

The issue is (was) _____

The real issue is (was) _____

The issue is (was) really _____

Keep completing the above sentence until you have no more responses. Be open. Look deeply. And appreciate yourself for having the courage and taking the time to do this.

8. Could you have done anything differently? If so, what?

9. What did you learn from this?

Who Am I Really? Circle

5.7

PURPOSE To promote self-reflection at a level deeper than normally experienced and help increase self-awareness.

MATERIALS Centerpiece items, talking piece, worksheet "Who Am I Really?" for each participant, and pens or pencils for participants.

PREPARATION Arrange everyone in a circle of chairs with no other furniture.

Welcome to the space of the Circle.

MINDFULNESS MOMENT *Pause, breathe, and listen to the sound.*

OPENING See Appendix 2 or create your own.

INTRODUCE "ROUNDS" A "round" is a pass of the talking piece around the Circle. The keeper poses a question and, as a participant, usually answers first. The keeper then passes the talking piece to the person to his/her left or right. On the first round, participants are invited to say their name as well as respond to the question. Remember, it is always okay for a participant to pass.

Remind the group of classroom values and guidelines.

CHECK-IN ROUND *How are you doing? Is there anything particular on your mind that is important for us to know and that you feel comfortable sharing with the group?*

MAIN ACTIVITY Exploring Who We Are

Distribute the worksheet "Who Am I Really?" to all participants, including the keeper(s). Ask participants to complete the worksheet, writing responses for each line. Note that the question is deliberately repeated as a way to help people go beyond their usual answers to see what they find. Ask participants to do this worksheet in silence, so that they can hear their own answers from inside themselves. If you have enough space available, invite them to go to a corner or their own little space to focus on the task. Allow five minutes for participants to complete the worksheet. Bring them back into Circle.

ROUND *How did it feel to do the worksheet?*

ROUND *Share one answer on your worksheet that you think would surprise others and then explain why you think it might surprise them.*

ROUND *Share the one answer on the workshop that you personally feel best about.*

Ask participants to look at their answers and mark which answers are true all the time with an A, and mark those that are true only some of the time with an S.

ROUND *Can you share one answer that you think is always true about you (A) and an answer that is true about you only some of the time (S)?*

ROUND *Have you learned anything about yourself that you did not notice before by doing this exercise?*

CHECK-OUT ROUND *Do you have anything else you would like to say about our Circle today?*

CLOSING *Choose from Appendix 2 or create your own.*

Thank everyone for participating in the Circle today!

This Circle is adapted from Casarjian and Casarjian, *Power Source Facilitator's Manual,* p. 48. Also in Boyes-Watson and Pranis, *Heart of Hope,* pp. 82–86.

Who Am I Really?

If someone asked you to describe yourself, what would you say?

I am _____

I am _____

I am _____

I am _____

I am _____

I am _____

I am _____

I am _____

I am _____

I am _____

I am _____

I am _____

5.8 Safe Space Circle

PURPOSE To identify conditions that help people connect to their best selves.

MATERIALS Talking piece, centerpiece items, drawing paper, markers, crayons, etc.

PREPARATION Arrange everyone in a circle of chairs with no other furniture.

Welcome to the space of the Circle.

MINDFULNESS MOMENT *Pause, breathe, and listen to the sound.*

OPENING See Appendix 2 or create your own.

INTRODUCE "ROUNDS" A "round" is a pass of the talking piece around the Circle. The keeper poses a question and, as a participant, usually answers first. The keeper then passes the talking piece to the person to his/her left or right. On the first round, participants are invited to say their name as well as respond to the question. Remember, it is always okay for a participant to pass.

Remind the group of classroom values and guidelines.

CHECK-IN ROUND *How are you doing? Is there anything particular on your mind that is important for us to know and that you feel comfortable sharing with the group?*

> **MAIN ACTIVITY** Imagining and Drawing A Safe Place and Reflecting on It

Take several deep breaths, notice your breath coming in and going out. Close your eyes if you are comfortable doing that, and imagine a place where you feel completely accepted for who you are—a place where you can most be yourself. Notice who and what are around you. Notice what you see, feel, hear, smell, and taste. . . . When you can see that place in your mind, use the art materials to create something that represents that place.

ROUND *I invite you to share your drawing and explain what it means to you.*

ROUND *Looking at your drawing, what have you learned about yourself and your own needs?*

ROUND *What could you do to create more spaces in your life where you can most fully be yourself?*

CHECK-OUT ROUND *Do you have anything else you would like to say about our Circle today?*

CLOSING *Choose from Appendix 2 or create your own.*

Thank everyone for participating in the Circle today!

This Circle is adapted from Boyes-Watson and Pranis, *Heart of Hope,* pp. 62–65.

5.9 Managing Mountains Circle

PURPOSE To increase emotional literacy by developing the ability to articulate and acknowledge challenges; and to increase self-awareness of strengths to help build resilience in the face of those challenges.

MATERIALS Talking piece, bells, Circle center, classroom values and guidelines, drawing materials.

PREPARATION Arrange everyone in a circle of chairs with no other furniture.

Welcome to the space of the Circle.

MINDFULNESS MOMENT *Pause, breathe, and listen to the sound.*

OPENING See Appendix 2 or create your own.

INTRODUCE "ROUNDS" A "round" is a pass of the talking piece around the Circle. The keeper poses a question and, as a participant, usually answers first. The keeper then passes the talking piece to the person to his/her left or right. On the first round, participants are invited to say their name as well as respond to the question. Remember, it is always okay for a participant to pass.

Remind the group of classroom values and guidelines.

CHECK-IN ROUND *How are you doing? Is there anything particular on your mind that is important for us to know and that you feel comfortable sharing with the group?*

MAIN ACTIVITY Using a Mountain Metaphor to Reflect on Overcoming Challenges

---

EXPLAIN *In this Circle we are going to talk about challenges or hard things that we face in our lives. These challenges or hard things sometimes feel like mountains that are blocking our way. What is the biggest mountain that you feel in front of you? Use the art materials to draw that mountain. Think about what color that mountain is, what shape it is, and what is on that mountain that makes it hard to climb.*

Allow some time for drawing the mountain.

ROUND *What did it feel like for you to draw that mountain?*

NEXT STEP *Now draw yourself getting to the other side of the mountain.*

Allow some time for drawing.

INVITE REFLECTION *Think of two or three things about yourself that helped you get to the other side of that mountain. What qualities in you made you able to overcome the challenge of the mountain? Did you go over it or around it or through the mountain to get to the other side?*

ROUND *I invite you to share your picture of getting to the other side of the mountain. What abilities helped you get to the other side? Who and what helped you get to the other side?*

Thank everyone for the insights and strengths they bring to overcoming challenges in their lives.

CHECK-OUT ROUND *Do you have anything else you would like to say about our Circle today?*

CLOSING Choose from Appendix 2 or create your own.

Thank everyone for participating in the Circle today!

This Circle is inspired by Roffey, *Circle Time for Emotional Literacy,* p. 128.

MODULE 6

Important but Difficult Conversations

This module offers model Circles that are designed to allow us to talk about issues that are extremely important but too frequently avoided because they are hard. Issues of exclusion, unfairness, inequality, poverty, discrimination, oppression, violence, loss, grief, and trauma all have a profound impact on the lives of students and adults within the school community. These issues shape our worldview, behavior, choices, perceptions, and relationships in profound ways, and they are often the source of conflicts, misunderstandings, and negative behaviors within the school community.

Important as they are, these topics are also painful, complex, and difficult to talk about. Many adults feel that they are ill-equipped to talk about sensitive and explosive issues of race, class privilege, gender, sexuality, bullying, and violence. And they are right. Our society struggles to honestly confront the complex issues that underlie many of the problems that affect children and families. Yet when adults remain silent, we fail to provide a safe space for youth to talk about what they see, experience, think, and feel about these realities. Nor do we open space for a shared discussion about how we all cope in healthy and unhealthy ways with these realities in our daily lives.

As a shared space, the Circle is unique in its capacity to hold strong emotions and uncomfortable truths safely. All of the Circles in this module are intended for classrooms, schools, and groups that have had enough experience in Circles to trust the Circle process. The rituals of the Circle remind us of all we share as human beings, especially the fact that we all share the desire to be in good relationship. The Circle encourages us to be our best selves and to see the best selves in others. Within the context of this understanding, we are then able to look more honestly and directly at hard truths about our ability to cause harm to one another.

The need for safety in these Circles is greater than in many of the Circles presented so far in this book. Consequently, it is important to spend more time on values, guidelines, and a meaningful check-in. A well-established practice in the group of honoring the talking piece and respectful listening is essential for honest conversations about these challenging topics. If the group is unable to maintain a respectful space, it is best to calmly, without blame, close the Circle and return to the topic another time when participants are more able to hold a respectful space. Meaningful participation

> Our society struggles to honestly confront the complex issues that underlie many of the problems that affect children and families.

by the Circle keeper—answering the same questions and doing the same activities as the students—enhances the Circle's safety and models respectful engagement on uncomfortable topics. When the round invites vulnerability, it is important for the keeper to go first to model vulnerability. In the Circles in this section, it is often useful to do a second pass of the talking piece on a question. Doing a second round allows participants more reflection time and more opportunity to pull their thoughts together.

Many of the Circles in this module address the unfairness and harm that arise from the unequal nature of the wider society. Students and teachers live with the burdens of inequality based on race, religion, sexual orientation, gender, wealth, and ability, both physical and mental. Those who are privileged carry burdens of guilt, denial, alienation, discomfort, silence, and disconnection from others. We need to find safe spaces to talk about these issues, to look honestly at how these realities impact our relationships with one another, to understand how our behavior is shaped by these realities, and to explore alternative choices for coping if what we are doing now is causing harm to others or ourselves. We need to explore how we can build positive connections based on our choice to see one another as fellow human beings. These model Circles are designed to allow us to hold these important but difficult conversations.

There may be many other important but difficult conversations that you would like to have with other staff, parents, or students. You can design your own Circles about the topics that are most compelling for your school community. These are the conversations that will move us as a culture beyond an intellectual analysis of our difficulties and allow our hearts and spirits to lead us to new places together.

6.1

What Motivates You? Circle

PURPOSE To help students reflect on the struggles and sources of their motivations, especially for long term goals such as going to college. The goal of this Circle is to learn from others' experiences and to help students find ways to ask for the help and support they need.

MATERIALS Talking piece, paper, and pens.

PREPARATION Arrange students and adults who are present in a circle.

Welcome to the space of the Circle.

MINDFULNESS MOMENT *Pause, breathe, and listen to the sound.*

OPENING See Appendix 2 or create your own.

Explain the talking piece.

CHECK-IN ROUND *How are you doing today physically, mentally, and emotionally?*

Remind participants about the values/guidelines that are important to the Circle.

> **MAIN ACTIVITY Identifying What Supports Positive Motivation and How to Get Support**

EXPLAIN The dictionary defines "motivation" as a force or influence that causes someone to do something. Another definition is the reason or reasons one has for acting or behaving in a particular way.

FURTHER EXPLAIN *The purpose of this Circle is to talk about how each of us finds the motivation to do homework or study for a test—as well as other necessary tasks—even though they are difficult or unpleasant. How do we get ourselves to do what we know we need to do when other parts of ourselves would rather sleep, watch TV, play video games, or talk on the phone with our friends?*

Ask participants: *Label one side of a sheet of paper "influences that help and motivate me" and the other side "influences that get in my way." Make a list for both categories for yourself.* Allow time for the participants to make their lists.

Circle *Forward* — MODULE 6: IMPORTANT BUT DIFFICULT CONVERSATIONS — 145

ROUND *Please share with us: What are the forces or influences that help you get your homework done when you would rather do something else? What are some of the forces that get in your way?*

ROUND *Now think about other obligations or goals in your life? How do you "motivate" yourself to do physical things, such as working out or going to the gym? How do you "motivate" yourself to eat healthy foods? Care for your body?*

ROUND *Can you identify what you need that would help you be more motivated? Can you identify what would you need from others? What would you need from yourself?*

ROUND *What are three things you could do to get the support and help you need to stay motivated in school?*

CHECK-OUT ROUND *What can you take away from this Circle today?*

CLOSING Choose from Appendix 2 or create your own.

Thank everyone for participating in the Circle today!

Being Left Out Circle

6.2

PURPOSE To talk about the experience of social exclusion, to develop awareness of the common but hurtful social dynamics of exclusion, and to help the group develop social practices that prevent these dynamics.

MATERIALS The talking piece, centerpiece items, classroom values/guidelines, the children's book *Puppies For Sale* by Dan Clark (see Resources II), bell or sound maker.

PREPARATION Arrange everyone in a circle of chairs with no other furniture.

Welcome to the space of the Circle.

MINDFULNESS MOMENT *Pause, breathe, and listen to the sound.*

OPENING See Appendix 2 or create your own.

INTRODUCE "ROUNDS" A "round" is a pass of the talking piece around the Circle. The keeper poses a question and, as a participant, usually answers first. The keeper then passes the talking piece to the person to his/her left or right. On the first round, participants are invited to say their name as well as respond to the question. Remember, it is always okay for a participant to pass.

Remind the group of classroom values and guidelines.

CHECK-IN ROUND *How are you doing? Is there anything particular on your mind that is important for us to know and that you feel comfortable sharing with the group?*

MAIN ACTIVITY Reflect on Experiences of Being Left Out

Keeper reads the story aloud or has the group read the story aloud.

ROUND *In your experience, what does it feel like to be left out?*

ROUND *Can you share a time when you felt left out?*

ROUND *Can you think of something that you could do next time you see someone being left out?*

CHECK-OUT ROUND *How did you like our Circle today?*

CLOSING Choose from Appendix 2 or create your own.

Thank everyone for participating in the Circle today!

This activity has been adapted from Jack Mangan's work with Circles in schools. See his website, Restorative Measures in Schools, in Appendix 4: Resources, Section I, Websites.

6.3 Let's Talk about Bullying Circle

PURPOSE To increase our understanding of the impact of bullying behaviors; to increase the capacity to recognize bullying; to strengthen bystanders' ability to support targets of bullying.

MATERIALS Talking piece, centerpiece items, bell or sound maker.

PREPARATION Arrange everyone in a circle of chairs with no other furniture.

Welcome to the space of the Circle.

MINDFULNESS MOMENT *Pause, breathe, and listen to the sound.*

OPENING See Appendix 2 or create your own.

VALUES ROUND *Please share a value that for you is connected to **Respect**.* Write a list of those values as participants name them and place the list in the center of the Circle.

Review the basic Circle guidelines.

INTRODUCE "ROUNDS" A round is a pass of the talking piece around the Circle. The keeper poses a question and, as a participant, usually answers first and then passes the talking piece to the person to their left or to their right. On the first round, participants are invited to say their name as well as respond to the question. Remember, it is always okay for a participant to pass.

CHECK-IN ROUND *If you were a kind of weather today, what would the weather be?*

MAIN ACTIVITY Reflecting on Bullying Behavior and Our Options for Responding

ROUND *What does it feel like to be bullied?*

ROUND *What actions make you feel bullied?*

ROUND *Why do you think that a person bullies?*

ROUND *Remember a time when you saw someone else being bullied. How did that feel?*

ROUND *What could you do the next time you see someone being bullied?*

CHECK-OUT ROUND *What are you taking away from this Circle that could help you or someone else in the future?*

CLOSING See Appendix 2 or create your own.

Thank everyone for participating in the Circle today!

The Impact of Gossip Circle

6.4

PURPOSE To increase our understanding of the impact of gossip; to increase our capacity to resist the temptation to gossip; to strengthen relationships.

MATERIALS Talking piece, centerpiece items, bell or sound maker.

PREPARATION Arrange everyone in a circle of chairs with no other furniture.

Welcome to the space of the Circle.

MINDFULNESS MOMENT *Pause, breathe, and listen to the sound.*

OPENING See Appendix 2 or create your own.

VALUES ROUND *Name a value that is important for healthy relationships in a community.* Write a list of those values as participants name them and then place the list in the center.

Review the basic Circle guidelines.

INTRODUCE "ROUNDS" A round is a pass of the talking piece around the Circle. The keeper poses a question and, as a participant, usually answers first and then passes the talking piece to the person to their left or to their right. On the first round, participants are invited to say their name as well as respond to the question. Remember, it is always okay for a participant to pass.

CHECK-IN ROUND *How are you doing today physically, mentally, and emotionally?*

MAIN ACTIVITY Reflecting on Gossip, Its Effects, and How to Opt Out of It

ROUND *Tell us one or two words that come to mind when you hear the word gossip. Record the words on the board.*

Ask participants to think of a time when someone shared gossip about them. Notice the feelings that come up about that. Ask them to write down three to five feeling words about someone gossiping about them.

ROUND *What feelings did you write down? Record the feelings on the board.*

Circle *Forward* — MODULE 6: IMPORTANT BUT DIFFICULT CONVERSATIONS

Ask participants, *Think of a time when you spread gossip about someone else. What feelings do you notice in yourself right now, thinking about that time? Write down several of these feelings.*

ROUND *What feelings did you notice thinking about that time that you spread gossip? Record the feelings on the board.*

ROUND *What forms of gossip do you consider most harmful?*

ROUND *What personal harm have you experienced or observed from gossip?*

ROUND *Are there any benefits to gossip?*

ROUND *When is sharing something that happened or telling a story about someone else not gossip?*

ROUND *What is the hardest thing about someone sharing gossip with you?*

ROUND *What strategies have you developed for getting out of a gossip conversation?*

CHECK-OUT ROUND *What can you take from today's Circle that could be helpful to yourself or others in the future?*

CLOSING Read a short quote by Bernard Gimbel, "Two things are bad for the heart—running uphill and running down people." Or create your own.

Thank everyone for participating in the Circle today!

Bereavement Circle

6.5

PURPOSE To provide a space for the community to come together and share their feelings in the wake of the loss of a member of the community.

MATERIALS Talking piece, centerpiece items related to the situation, Circle values and guidelines, bell or sound maker.

PREPARATION Arrange everyone in a circle of chairs with no other furniture.

Welcome to the space of the Circle.

MINDFULNESS MOMENT *Pause, breathe, and listen to the sound.*

OPENING See Appendix 2 or create your own.

VALUES ROUND *Tell us about an important value you learned from someone you admire.* Write a list of those values as participants name them and place the list in the center.

Review the basic Circle guidelines.

INTRODUCE "ROUNDS" A "round" is a pass of the talking piece around the Circle. The keeper poses a question and, as a participant, usually answers first. The keeper then passes the talking piece to the person to his/her left or right. On the first round, participants are invited to say their name as well as respond to the question. Remember, it is always okay for a participant to pass.

MAIN ACTIVITY Processing the Loss Together

Identify the loss that the Circle is about. Explain that it is very common for people to have many different kinds of feelings when they experience loss. Explain that feelings are personal and may be different for each person.

ROUND *To check in, please share one, two, or three feelings you are having right now in one sentence.*

ROUND *Where were you when you heard the news of (this loss)? How did you feel? Where did you feel it in your body?*

ROUND *What will you miss the most about this person?*

ROUND *Please share with us one positive or funny memory of him or her.*

ROUND *What is one positive thing about this person that you want to carry on in his/her honor?*

CHECK-OUT ROUND *How has this Circle been for you?*

CLOSING Choose from Appendix 2 or create your own.

Thank everyone for participating in the Circle today!

Responding to Community Trauma Circle

6.6

PURPOSE To create a space for acknowledging a community trauma and its impact and for expressing emotions; to access the healing effects of connecting with others to cope with the trauma.

MATERIALS Talking piece, centerpiece items, bell or sound maker.

PREPARATION Arrange everyone in a circle of chairs with no other furniture.

Welcome to the space of the Circle.

MINDFULNESS MOMENT *Pause, breathe, and listen to the sound.*

OPENING See Appendix 2 or create your own.

VALUES ROUND *Name a value that is important to you when you face a difficult situation.* Write a list of those values as participants name them and place the list in the center.

Review the basic Circle guidelines.

INTRODUCE "ROUNDS" A round is a pass of the talking piece around the Circle. The keeper poses a question and, as a participant, usually answers first and then passes the talking piece to the person to their left or to their right. On the first round, participants are invited to say their name as well as respond to the question. Remember, it is always okay for a participant to pass.

CHECK-IN ROUND *What strength do you bring to the Circle today?*

> **MAIN ACTIVITY** Reflecting on a Community Trauma, Its Impact, and What Helps

Identify the community trauma (e.g., shooting death of a young person, family murder/suicide in the community, large fire, school bus accident, tornado, flooding—any local event that has caused disorientation, fear, confusion, anger at a community level).

EXPLAIN *We are going to use the Circle to give us all a chance to talk about how we have been affected by this event and to help each other as we struggle to put our lives back in order.*

ROUND *What are your feelings about what happened?*

ROUND *What has been the hardest thing for you because of what happened?*

ROUND *What fears about the future do you have because of what happened?*

ROUND *Who has helped you feel better when you feel down about this?*

ROUND *What physical activities help you to feel better?*

ROUND *What strengths have you seen in yourself and in others as people get through this situation?*

ROUND *What gives you hope at difficult times?*

Choose the questions that seem most relevant if there is not time for all the questions. Pass the talking piece for a follow-up round on a question if that question feels unfinished.

CHECK-OUT ROUND *How will you take care of yourself as you leave our Circle?*

CLOSING See Appendix 2 or create your own.

Thank everyone for participating in the Circle today!

Dealing with Losses Circle

6.7

PURPOSE To identify losses in the lives of the participants and the impact on their lives.

MATERIALS Talking piece, centerpiece items, drawing materials (paper, markers, crayons, colored pencils), handout of Losses Some Kids Have to Deal With, list of Acting-in and Acting-out Behaviors on chart or handout, Needs Inventory list on a chart or handout, and a bell or sound maker.

PREPARATION Arrange everyone in a circle of chairs with no other furniture.

Welcome to the space of the Circle.

MINDFULNESS MOMENT *Pause, breathe, and listen to the sound.*

OPENING See Appendix 2 or create your own.

VALUES ROUND Share a value that you have been able to practice this week. Write a list of those values as participants name them and place the list in the center.

Review the basic Circle guidelines.

INTRODUCE "ROUNDS" A "round" is a pass of the talking piece around the Circle. The keeper poses a question and, as a participant, usually answers first. The keeper then passes the talking piece to the person to his/her left or right. On the first round, participants are invited to say their name as well as respond to the question. Remember, it is always okay for a participant to pass.

CHECK-IN ROUND *Tell us about something you are grateful for in your life.*

MAIN ACTIVITY Exploring the Needs and Feelings around Losses

Share the handout, "Losses Some Kids Have to Deal With," the "Needs Inventory," and the list of "Acting-in/Acting-out Behaviors." Invite participants to identify a major loss in their lives (it does not have to be on the list) and to draw an image or picture representing that loss.

ROUND *Please share your drawing, explaining the loss in your life and the feelings you have about that loss.*

ROUND *What needs were underneath the feelings you named—needs that were/are not being met?*

ROUND *In your own past, did you rely on any behaviors of "acting out" or "acting in" to deal with your loss?*

ROUND *Can you identify how you might have met your needs in a more healthy way?*

CHECK-OUT ROUND *What can you take away from this Circle today?*

CLOSING Choose from Appendix 2 or create your own.

Thank everyone for participating in the Circle today!

This activity is adapted from Boyes-Watson and Pranis, *Heart of Hope*, pp. 123–26, 140–46. Also adapted from Youth STAR, *When Violence and Trauma Impact Youth: Facilitator's Training Manual*. See the website for the STAR program at the Center for Justice and Peacebuilding, Eastern Mennonite University, Harrisonburg, Virginia.

Needs Inventory

AUTONOMY
- To choose one's dreams, goals, values
- To choose one's plan for fulfilling one's dreams, goals, values

CELEBRATION
- To celebrate the creation of life and dreams fulfilled
- To celebrate losses: loved ones, dreams, etc. (mourning)

INTEGRITY
- Authenticity
- Creativity
- Meaning
- Self-worth

INTERDEPENDENCE
- Acceptance
- Appreciation
- Closeness
- Community
- Consideration
- Contribution to the enrichment of life (to exercise one's power by giving that which contributes to life)
- Emotional Safety
- Empathy
- Honesty (the empowering honesty that enables us to learn from our limitations)
- Love
- Reassurance
- Respect
- Support
- Trust
- Understanding
- Warmth

PHYSICAL NURTURANCE
- Air
- Food
- Movement, exercise
- Protection from life-threatening forms of life: viruses, bacteria, insects, predatory animals (especially human beings)
- Rest
- Sexual expression
- Shelter
- Touch
- Water

PLAY

SPIRITUAL COMMUNION
- Beauty
- Harmony
- Inspiration
- Order
- Peace

Marshall Rosenberg, Center for Nonviolent Communication www.cnvc.org

Losses Some Kids Have to Deal With

- Having a parent abandon you or never knowing your parents

- Having your parents get divorced

- Having a parent die

- Being removed from your home and placed in foster care or adopted

- Suffering an illness that prevents you from participating in the activities that other kids are involved in; this is a loss of health

- Moving from place to place and having to start at new schools and make new friends; this is a loss of stability and safety

- Going to bad or unsafe schools where you could not get the kind of education that would prepare you for your future

- Having a parent get addicted to drugs or alcohol and losing their attention, love, and support

- People who grow up in dangerous neighborhoods may not be able to safely go outside and hang out with friends; this is a loss of freedom

- Having a friend or relative die from violence in your neighborhood

- Being physically abused, sexually assaulted, or molested. This is a loss of personal integrity, meaning your right to have your personal boundaries respected. This can also hurt your self-respect and esteem. You may feel like you are broken, damaged, or have lost your sense of "wholeness."

- Being locked up in a detention center or a residential treatment center. In these places you lose your ability to make many choices for yourself, like when to eat, where to go, even when to bathe.

- Losing your belief or faith that you have a positive and constructive future ahead of you. Losing hope that things can be different from the way they have been in the past

- Having the world not make sense to you or having it suddenly seem unfair or uncaring

Acting-in and Acting-out Behaviors

Adapted from Youth STAR — When Violence and Trauma Impact Youth — Youth Handbook

ACTING IN:
- Alcohol and drug abuse
- Overwork
- Eating disorders
- Depression (sadness, hopelessness)
- Feelings of numbness, anxiety, self-blame, shame
- Pain, headaches, weakness, etc.

ACTING OUT:
- Getting in trouble with the law
- Aggression, blaming, irritability
- Inflexibility, intolerance
- Inability to show empathy to others
- High risk behavior, substance abuse or inappropriate sexual activity
- Bullying
- Repetitive conflicts

6.8

Masking Grief Circle

PURPOSE To raise awareness of the natural emotions of grief and to recognize the ways that masks may hide those feelings.

MATERIALS Talking piece, centerpiece items, bell or sound maker, a copy of "The Masks I Wear" poem by Charles C. Finn (available on Charles C. Finn's website: http://www.poetrybycharlescfinn.com/), copies of "Masks" handout, paper plates, construction paper, light cardboard, markers, yarn, scissors, glue, hole punches, miscellaneous art materials.

PREPARATION Arrange everyone in a circle of chairs with no other furniture.

Welcome to the space of the Circle.

MINDFULNESS MOMENT *Pause, breathe, and listen to the sound.*

OPENING Read the "Masks I Wear" poem or create your own opening.

VALUES ROUND *Name a value that is important to you when you face a difficult situation.* Write a list of those values as participants name them and place the list in the center.

Review the basic Circle guidelines.

INTRODUCE "ROUNDS" A round is a pass of the talking piece around the Circle. The keeper poses a question and, as a participant, usually answers first and then passes the talking piece to the person to their left or to their right. On the first round, participants are invited to say their name as well as respond to the question. Remember, it is always okay for a participant to pass.

CHECK-IN ROUND *Tell us something heavy on your mind today and something light on your mind today.*

> **MAIN ACTIVITY** Reflecting on Grief and the Masks We Use to Hide It

Ask participants to brainstorm what "grief" means. Write answers on a flip chart or board.

ROUND *What feelings are part of grief?* Keep notes, then read the list when the talking piece comes back to you.

EXPLAIN TO PARTICIPANTS *Sometimes we hide our true grief feelings behind emotion masks; we often try to cover our feelings of loss by acting angry, harsh, or tough.*

Distribute the "mask" handout that lists the masks that people sometimes wear.

Ask each participant to choose which kind of mask they think they use to hide grief. They may have a different mask from those on the sheet. Then invite them to create a mask that they use with the art materials. Use the materials to reflect the feelings/attitudes/emotions that they convey when wearing the mask.

When they are finished making the masks, bring them back into Circle.

ROUND *Please tell us about the feelings that go with the mask you use to hide grief, and then tell us what feelings you think are not visible because the mask is covering them up for you.*

ROUND *How do you act when you are wearing that mask?*

ROUND *What would help you take the mask off and show your true emotions underneath?*

CHECK-OUT ROUND *What can you take away from today's Circle that could be helpful to you?*

CLOSING *See from Appendix 2 for ideas and options or create your own.*

Thank everyone for participating in the Circle today!

Masks

Here is a list of masks that people sometimes wear. Masks usually are an attempt to cover a certain kind of feeling we don't want to experience. Do any of the following masks below seem familiar to you?

- Angry Mask
- Know-It All Mask
- I Don't Give A Shit Mask
- Gangster Mask
- Clown Mask
- Druggie Mask
- Bad Boy/Girl Mask
- Loser Mask
- Nothing Bothers Me Mask
- Loner Mask
- Spaced-Out Mask
- Hyper or Out of Control Mask

How do you act when you are wearing this mask?

Understanding Trauma Circle

PURPOSE To uncover and recognize the wisdom of the youth about trauma based on their life experiences or observations of others.

MATERIALS Talking piece, centerpiece items, bell or sound maker, paper or journals, pens or pencils, values/guidelines.

PREPARATION Arrange everyone in a circle of chairs with no other furniture.

Welcome to the space of the Circle.

MINDFULNESS MOMENT *Pause, breathe, and listen to the sound.*

OPENING See Appendix 2 or create your own.

VALUES ROUND *Name a value that is important to you when you are discussing a difficult topic.* Write the values as participants name them and place the list in the center.

Review the basic Circle guidelines.

INTRODUCE "ROUNDS" A "round" is a pass of the talking piece around the Circle. The keeper poses a question and, as a participant, usually answers first. The keeper then passes the talking piece to the person to his/her left or right. On the first round, participants are invited to say their name as well as respond to the question. Remember, it is always okay for a participant to pass.

CHECK-IN ROUND *How are you doing today? Is there anything you wish to share with the Circle as a check-in?*

> **MAIN ACTIVITY Reflecting on Traumatic Experiences and Feelings around Trauma**

Post in a visible place the following definition of trauma. "Trauma is a deep wound that happens when something abnormally shocking, painful, or harmful occurs and leaves us feeling overwhelmed." Read the definition to the Circle participants. Ask for some examples of trauma. Clarify that not every frightening or upsetting event is a trauma. Trauma is not the same as stress. Stress might be taking a test or going to a job interview, but these are normal events.

Ask participants to write down on a piece of paper a time when they or someone they know experienced stress, and then write down on the paper a time when they or someone they know experienced trauma. Ask them to journal about the feelings that resulted from the trauma. *What was it like to experience trauma or to know someone experiencing trauma?*

Allow time for the group to journal.

ROUND *Please share the event that you considered stressful and the event that you considered traumatic.*

ROUND *Please share the feelings you associated with trauma. What is it like to experience trauma?*

ROUND *What are your thoughts about how you or others are impacted by trauma?*

ROUND *We all have wisdom from our own life experience. What wisdom do you have about trauma based on your own life experience that you would want to share with someone younger?*

CHECK-OUT ROUND *What can you take away from this Circle today?*

CLOSING Choose from Appendix 2 or create your own.

Thank everyone for participating in the Circle today!

This activity is adapted from Boyes-Watson and Pranis, *Heart of Hope*, pp. 148–51.

Witnessing Violence Circle

6.10

PURPOSE To share experiences of being a witness to violence and to explore the impact that this exposure to violence has had on participants.

MATERIALS Talking piece, centerpiece items, bell or sound maker, journal, pens, a list of the types of violence (see "Types of Violence Worksheet").

PREPARATION Arrange everyone in a circle of chairs with no other furniture.

Welcome to the space of the Circle.

MINDFULNESS MOMENT *Pause, breathe, and listen to the sound.*

OPENING See Appendix 2 or create your own.

VALUES ROUND *Name a value that is important to you when you are discussing a difficult topic.* Write a list of these values as the participants name them and place the list in the center.

Review the basic Circle guidelines.

INTRODUCE "ROUNDS" A "round" is a pass of the talking piece around the Circle. The keeper poses a question and, as a participant, usually answers first. The keeper then passes the talking piece to the person to his/her left or right. On the first round, participants are invited to say their name as well as respond to the question. Remember, it is always okay for a participant to pass.

CHECK-IN ROUND *What strength do you bring to the Circle today?*

MAIN ACTIVITY Reflecting on Violence Witnessed and on How to Cope

EXPLAIN *There are many kinds of violence within our society, and our exposure to violence depends on many factors.* Review with participants the types of violence on the list.

Ask participants to use their journal to reflect on the types of violence they have witnessed within the past week, past month, and past year of their lives.

Ask them to describe at least one or more incidents in their journal and to reflect on how they felt while they were witnessing that incident.

ROUND *I invite you to share the thoughts and feelings you wrote about based on your experiences of witnessing violence.*

ROUND *Did you take any action in response to the violence you witnessed, and how do you feel about the action you took? If you did not take any action, is there something you wish you could have done?*

ROUND *What strength has helped you get through witnessing violence? How do you handle the stress of violence around you?*

ROUND *What you have learned from today's Circle about the impact of witnessing different kinds of violence and the ways people cope with violence around them?*

ROUND *What advice would you give to someone younger about how to cope with witnessing violence?*

CHECK-OUT ROUND *What gives you hope even when things are difficult?*

CLOSING See Appendix 2 or create your own.

Thank everyone for participating in the Circle today!

Types of Violence Worksheet

Type of violence or abuse	Definition	Examples
Physical violence/abuse	The intentional use of physical force with the potential for causing death, disability, injury, or harm	Scratching, pushing, shoving, throwing, grabbing, biting, choking, shaking, slapping, punching, burning, using a weapon, using restraints or one's body, size, or strength against another person
Sexual violence/abuse	Any sexual act that is perpetrated against someone's will; any unwanted sexual attention, contact, or activity	Rape, unwanted coercive contact, pressure for sex, vulgar comments, unwanted touching/fondling, non-contact sexual abuse or harassment, sexting
Emotional violence/abuse	Words or actions done to make a person feel stupid or worthless	Name calling, blaming, talking down, shaming, insulting, shunning, isolating, humiliating, intimidating, threatening, invading privacy
Psychological/mental violence/abuse	An action or set of actions that directly impairs the psychological integrity of the victim, usually committed through verbal and physical abuse	Playing mind games, twisting things to create an advantage; threatening violence to gain control; stalking/criminal harassment; using undue pressure to make a person act against their desires or interests; treating a competent person like a child or servant; distorting reality so one thinks one is losing one's mind
Spiritual violence/abuse	Using a person's spiritual beliefs to manipulate, dominate, or control	Forcing a spiritual or religious practice on another; making fun of others' spiritual beliefs or practices; not allowing a person to pursue his/her preferred tradition and ways

Type of violence or abuse	Definition	Examples
Cultural/structural violence/abuse	Any use of physical, sexual, or psychological violence against a group of people on the basis of race, sexual orientation, religious background, or cultural beliefs and values	Hate crimes, war, genocide, terrorism, religious persecution, committing "honor" crimes against women; lynching
Verbal abuse	Using language, written or spoken, to cause harm to a person	Yelling, shouting, interrupting, cyber-bullying, insulting, swearing at; ordering around; telling a person he or she is worthless or nothing but trouble; mocking, spreading harmful rumors and gossip about; name calling
Financial/economic abuse	Using power and manipulation to maintain control over another's financial resources; withholding a person's access to money; or forbidding one's attendance at school or employment	Withholding money, denying access to education; controlling a person's choice of occupation; committing fraud and scams; misusing funds through lies and deception; taking funds without permission; shaming a person for how he or she spends money
Neglect	Failing to provide adequate care to a dependent or elder when one has the responsibility to do so	Failing to meet the needs of a person who is unable to meet those needs alone; abandoning, not remaining with a person who needs help
Moral injury	Harm to one's moral compass when someone who holds legitimate authority, including oneself, betrays what is right in a high-stakes situation	Looking the other way on bullying; not acting to right injustices by those (including oneself) who have the power to do so

This worksheet is compiled from information on two websites: (1) Violence Prevention Initiative, Government of Newfoundland and Labrador, "Defining Violence and Abuse" at: http://gov.nl.ca/VPI/types/index.html#1 and (2) Just for Teens: Promoting Alternatives to Violence through Education, "6 Types of Abuse" at: http://www.projectpave.org/6-types-abuse.

Roots of Youth Violence Circle

6.11

PURPOSE To explore together the group's understanding of the underlying causes of youth violence.

MATERIALS Talking piece, centerpiece items, bell or sound maker, "Roots of Violence Worksheet" for participants and larger version of the image on a flip chart.

PREPARATION Arrange everyone in a circle of chairs with no other furniture.

Welcome to the space of the Circle.

MINDFULNESS MOMENT *Pause, breathe, and listen to the sound.*

OPENING See Appendix 2 or create your own.

VALUES ROUND *Name a value that is important to you when you are discussing a difficult topic.* Write a list of those values as the participants name them and place the list in the center.

Review the basic Circle guidelines.

INTRODUCE "ROUNDS" A "round" is a pass of the talking piece around the Circle. The keeper poses a question and, as a participant, usually answers first. The keeper then passes the talking piece to the person to his/her left or right. On the first round, participants are invited to say their name as well as respond to the question. Remember, it is always okay for a participant to pass.

CHECK-IN ROUND *Tell us about a peaceful moment in your life recently.*

> **MAIN ACTIVITY** Tracing Violence to Its Roots and Considering Actions in Response

Ask the participants to think about common kinds of youth violence.

ROUND *Name different kinds of violence.*

Write these kinds of violence in the foliage section of the large tree image on the flip chart.

ROUND *Are there other kinds of violence to add to this tree?* Continue until all forms of violence are within the foliage.

Examples would include: fist fighting; relationship violence; packing a gun or knife; threatening someone with a gun/knife; rape; sexual harassment; a parent hitting a child; youth hitting parents; gang violence; elder abuse.

Divide participants into small groups and ask them together to write on the roots of their trees the underlying or root causes of each kind of violence. Tell them that each root cause may, in turn, have deeper root causes. Continue to fill in the roots with causes until they have listed all possible causes.

ROUND *Please share something that you feel is important to think about from your chart.*

ROUND *What have you learned from your own thoughts and from hearing from others about the causes of violence?*

ROUND *Are there any actions you want to take as a result of seeing these causes of violence?*

CHECK-OUT ROUND *What can you take from this Circle that would reduce violence in your life?*

CLOSING See Appendix 2 or create your own.

Thank everyone for participating in the Circle today!

This activity draws on the "Root Causes" activity designed by The Mikva Challenge, presented in Kaba, Mathew, and Haines, *Something Is Wrong Curriculum*, pp. 39–42.

ROOTS OF VIOLENCE WORKSHEET

6.12 The Impact of Social Hierarchies on Me Circle

PURPOSE To raise awareness of social hierarchies based on aspects of identity; to recognize the harm caused by those hierarchies; to increase awareness that most people experience both being in privilege and out of privilege in different parts of their lives.

MATERIALS Talking piece, centerpiece items, copies of worksheet "Social Identity Wheel," paper or journals, pencils or pens, bell or sound maker.

PREPARATION Arrange everyone in a circle of chairs with no other furniture.

Welcome to the space of the Circle.

MINDFULNESS MOMENT Pause, breathe, and listen to the sound.

OPENING See Appendix 2 or create your own.

INTRODUCE "ROUNDS" A "round" is a pass of the talking piece around the Circle. The keeper poses a question and, as a participant, usually answers first. The keeper then passes the talking piece to the person to his/her left or right. On the first round, participants are invited to say their name as well as respond to the question. Remember, it is always okay for a participant to pass.

Remind the group of classroom values and guidelines.

CHECK-IN ROUND How are you doing? Is there anything particular on your mind that might be important for us to know and that you feel comfortable sharing with the group?

> **MAIN ACTIVITY** Exploring One's Place in the Social Hierarchy and the Feelings that Go with It

REMIND PARTICIPANTS The core self in everyone is good, wise, and strong, no matter what happens in life. Yet despite this core self in everyone, society creates rankings that value some people more than others for aspects of their identity that are not inherently more valuable. This hierarchy of worthiness gives more power and privilege to those ranked as better or more important. Our society has hierarchies related to several aspects of identity, including skin color, gender, age, sexual orientation, income, and religion.

Ask participants, in an open dialogue, to identify which groups have privilege or power regarding skin color and which groups lack privilege or power regarding skin color.

Ask them to identify who has privilege or power regarding gender and who does not. Who has privilege or power regarding socio-economic class and who does not?

Distribute the worksheet "Social Identity Wheel." For each section on the wheel, ask participants to decide whether they are ranked high and have privilege in society in that aspect of who they are, or whether they are ranked low and lack privilege in that aspect. Invite them to mark each section with HI or LO to reflect how society ranks them on that dimension of their identity.

Distribute journaling materials and ask participants to journal about the feelings they have when the social hierarchy devalues them.

ROUND *Identify an aspect of your life where you are ranked low, and share specific experiences where you have been harmed by being in that position in the social hierarchy.*

ROUND *What feelings have you had from the experience of being devalued by society?*

ROUND *Identify an aspect of your life where you are the one with privilege (a section you marked HI on the wheel).*

If participants have trouble identifying an area of privilege, ask them whether they have younger brothers and sisters or children over whom they get to exercise authority: this would be a privilege associated with age.

ROUND *Are these privileges fair?*

ROUND *Share an experience where you didn't like someone because they belonged to a group that is not valued, and then you discovered that the person is someone you really like.*

ROUND *Please share any additional thoughts or responses you have to what others have said.*

CHECK-OUT ROUND *How do you feel about the Circle today?*

CLOSING Choose from Appendix 2 or create your own.

Thank everyone for participating in the Circle today!

This activity is adapted from Boyes-Watson and Pranis, *Heart of Hope,* pp. 178–82.

Social Identity Wheel

Adapted from "Voices of Discovery," Intergroup Relations Center, Arizona State University.

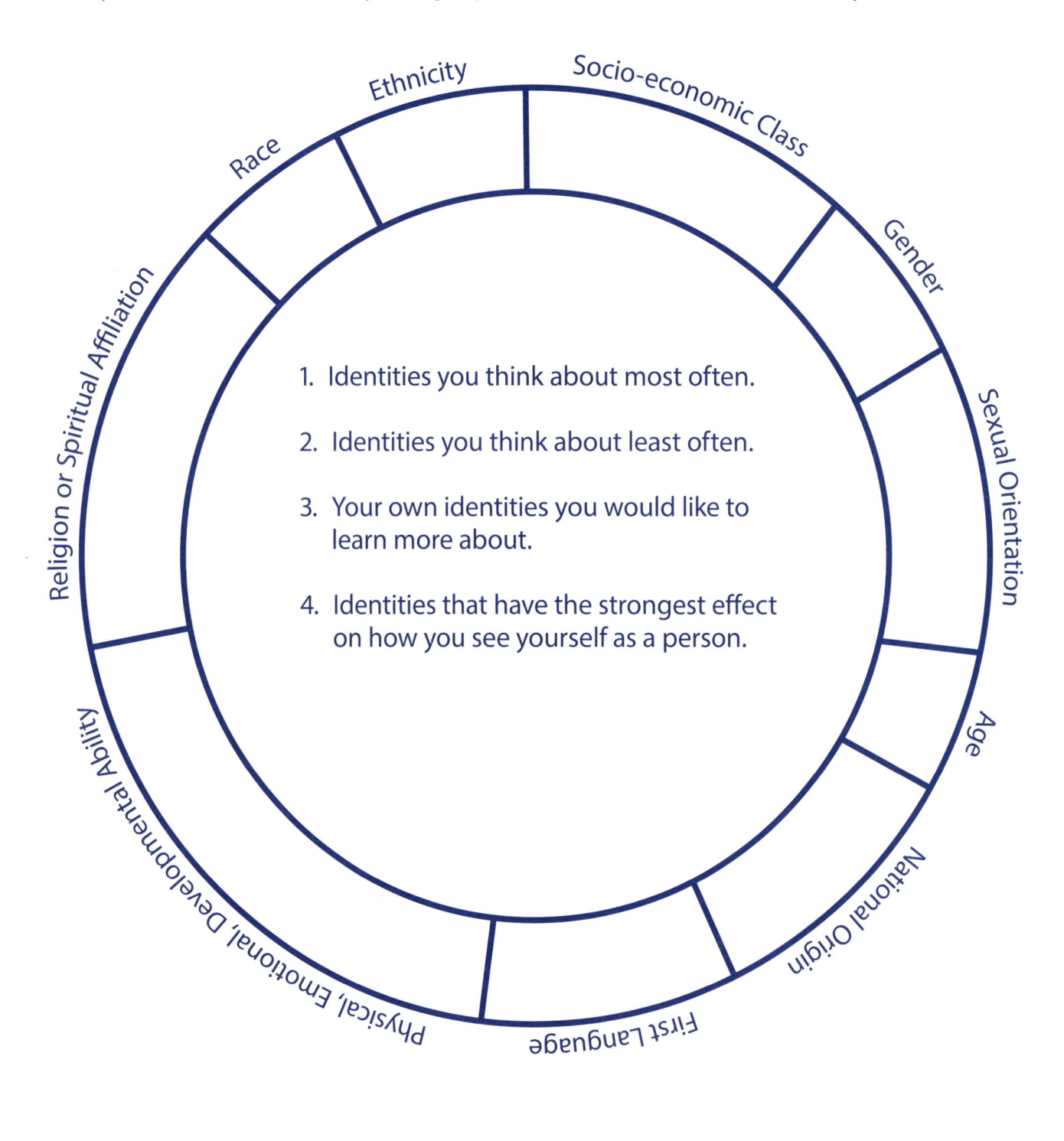

Wheel segments (clockwise from top): Ethnicity, Socio-economic Class, Gender, Sexual Orientation, Age, National Origin, First Language, Physical, Emotional, Developmental Ability, Religion or Spiritual Affiliation, Race.

1. Identities you think about most often.

2. Identities you think about least often.

3. Your own identities you would like to learn more about.

4. Identities that have the strongest effect on how you see yourself as a person.

Reprinted with the permission of Dr. Jesus Trevino, Associate V.P. for Diversity, University of South Dakota, who created this Social Identity Wheel. Online: https://awnastas.expressions.syr.edu/wp-content/uploads/2011/12/Social-Identity-Wheel.pdf.

Talking about Structural Inequality
Privilege and Oppression Circle

6.13

PURPOSE To create a dialogue about the experience of privilege and oppression in the lives of participants and to raise awareness about how structural inequality plays out in the day-to-day lives of all of us.

MATERIALS Talking piece, centerpiece items, bell or sound maker, "Privileged or Oppressed? Worksheet" and "Understanding Oppression Worksheet."

PREPARATION Arrange students and adults who are present in a Circle.

Welcome to the space of the Circle.

MINDFULNESS MOMENT *Pause, breathe, and listen to the sound.*

OPENING See Appendix 2 or create your own.

VALUES ROUND *Name a value that is important to you in how others treat you.* Write a list of those values as participants name them and place the list in the center.

Review the basic Circle guidelines.

INTRODUCE "ROUNDS" A "round" is a pass of the talking piece around the Circle. The keeper poses a question and, as a participant, usually answers first. The keeper then passes the talking piece to the person to his/her left or right. On the first round, participants are invited to say their name as well as respond to the question. Remember, it is always okay for a participant to pass.

CHECK-IN ROUND *How are you doing today physically, mentally, and emotionally?*

MAIN ACTIVITY Naming Privileges and Disadvantages Due to Our Status in Society

EXPLAIN TO PARTICIPANTS *In any society or group with structural inequality, those who are privileged by the society enjoy benefits and advantages that are often taken for granted and are invisible to them, while those with less power and privilege face obstacles and deprivations that are very obvious and painful to them.*

EXPLAIN FURTHER *We derive benefits from being male or white or straight or able-bodied without taking any personal action against a woman, a person of color, a gay/*

lesbian/bisexual person, or a person with a disability. The purpose of this exercise is to raise our awareness, so we can choose to take actions that support social equality.

Distribute the "Privileged or Oppressed? Worksheet." Ask participants to fill out the worksheet by identifying the places where they enjoy privilege and places where their status causes them a lack of privilege.

ROUND *Please share what is on your worksheet. What feelings came up for you as you filled out this sheet?*

Ask participants to turn the worksheet over and to write on the back of the sheet: *Name the privileges that come from being a member of a dominant group, and name the disadvantages or obstacles that come from being a member of an oppressed group.*

ROUND *Please share some of the ideas you wrote down about privileges and disadvantages related to social inequalities.*

ROUND *Where in your daily life do you experience privilege? How does it make your life easier?*

ROUND *What are some of the strengths that come from membership in an oppressed group?*

CHECK-OUT ROUND *What are some of the feelings that have come up for you in this discussion? What have you learned from this exercise today?*

CLOSING See Appendix 2 or create your own.

Thank everyone for participating in the Circle today!

See also Las Caras Lindas, Youth LEAD Institute, *LEAD Core Program Curriculum*, especially pp. 17–19. Available online at: http://www.tandemspring.com/wp-content/uploads/LCL-Core-Program-Curriculum_Full-2013.pdf.

Privileged or Oppressed? Worksheet

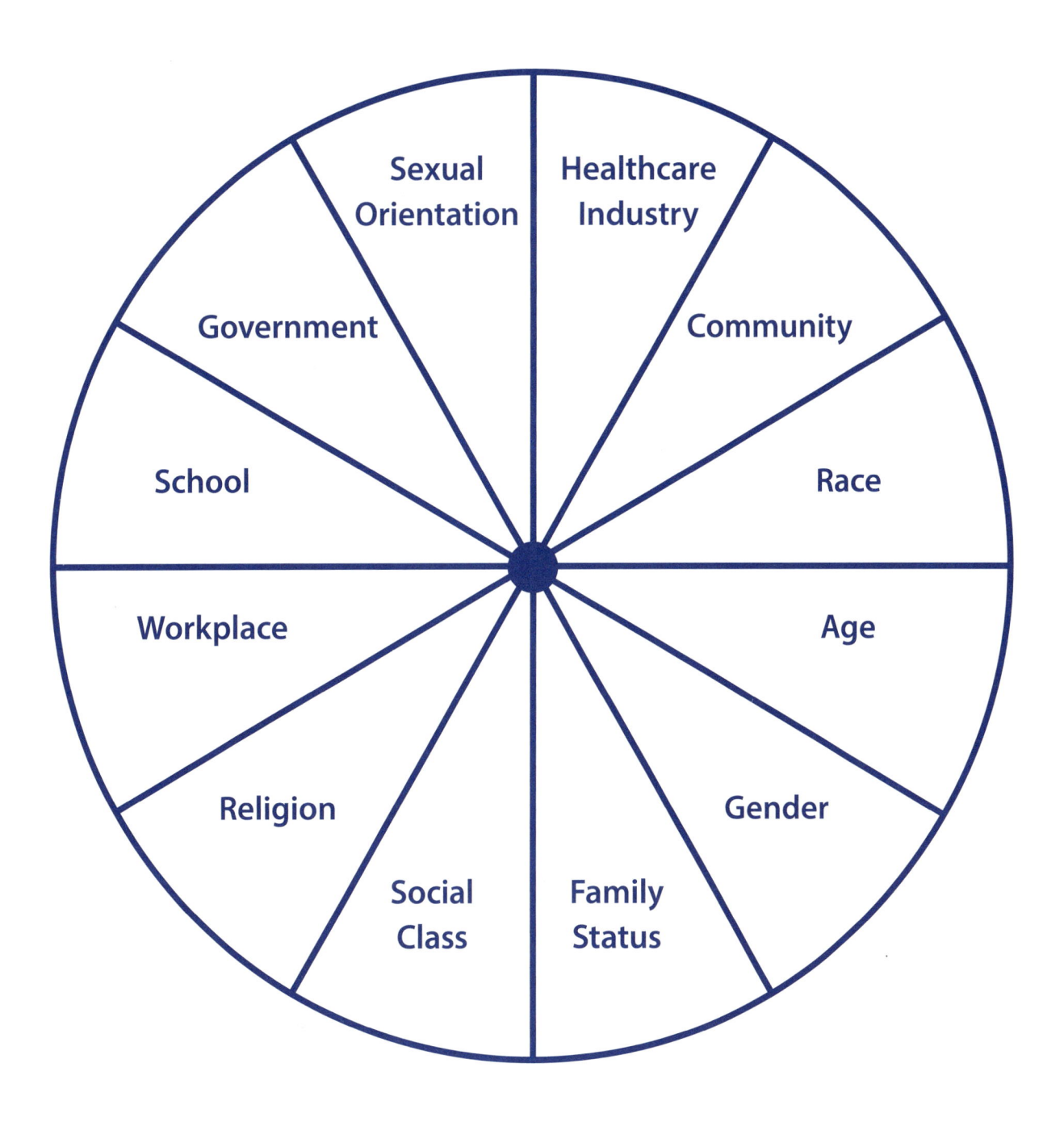

- Sexual Orientation
- Healthcare Industry
- Government
- Community
- School
- Race
- Workplace
- Age
- Religion
- Gender
- Social Class
- Family Status

Circle *Forward* — MODULE 6: IMPORTANT BUT DIFFICULT CONVERSATIONS

Understanding Oppression Worksheet

Types of Oppression	Variable	Non-Target Groups	Target Groups
Racism	Race	White	People of Color (African, Asian, Native, Latino/a)
Sexism	Gender	Men	Women
Classism	Socio-Economic Class	Middle, Upper Class	Poor, Working Class
Elitism	Educational Level Place in Hierarchy	Formally Educated Managers, Exempt, Faculty	Informally Educated Clerical, Non-Exempt, Students
Religious Oppression	Religion	Christians, Protestants	Muslims and Others
Anti-Semitism	Religion	Christians	Jews
Militarism	Military Status	WW I & II, Korean, Gulf War, Operation Iraqi Freedom, Afghan War	Vietnam Veterans
Ageism	Age	Younger Adults	Elders (over 65)
Adultism	Age	Adults	Children/Youth
Heterosexism	Sexual Orientation	Heterosexuals	Gay, Lesbian, Bisexual, Transgender
Ableism	Physical or Mental Ability	Temporarily Able-Bodied	Physically or Mentally Challenged
Xenophobia	Immigrant Status	U.S. Born	Immigrant (documented or undocumented)
Linguistic Oppression	Language	English	English as a second language Non-English
Specieism	Species	Human	Animal/Plants/Flora

From Mariame Kaba, *Something Is Wrong Curriculum,* "Understanding Oppression (longer version)," by Mariame Kaba, with activities adapted from Anne Bishop, 33. Reproduced with permission.

What Do We Know about Race? Circle

6.14

PURPOSE To explore the meaning of race among those in the Circle; to open a dialogue that can introduce new possibilities in understanding the meaning of race.

MATERIALS Talking piece, centerpiece items, bell or sound maker, copies of the reading about race, "Race—The Power of an Illusion, Interview with Alan Goodman," guidelines.

PREPARATION Arrange everyone in a circle of chairs with no other furniture.

Welcome to the space of the Circle.

MINDFULNESS MOMENT *Pause, breathe, and listen to the sound.*

OPENING See Appendix 2 or create your own.

VALUES ROUND *Name a value that helps you participate in a good way when you are discussing a very difficult topic.* Write the values as participants name them and place the list in the center.

Review the basic Circle guidelines.

INTRODUCE "ROUNDS" A "round" is a pass of the talking piece around the Circle. The keeper poses a question and, as a participant, usually answers first. The keeper then passes the talking piece to the person to his/her left or right. On the first round, participants are invited to say their name as well as respond to the question. Remember, it is always okay for a participant to pass.

CHECK-IN ROUND *How are you doing today? What gift do you bring to our Circle today?*

MAIN ACTIVITY Exploring What We Know and Experience of Race

We are starting a journey together of talking about race. Race has a huge presence in our society, but we have very few opportunities to talk with one another about what race means to each of us. It takes courage to talk about race in an honest and respectful way. This is a journey of courage. Thank you for bringing yourself to this journey in the best way you can.

ROUND *What does race mean to you? Is race an important part of your identity on a daily basis?*

ROUND *When are you most conscious of your race? Share an experience of being particularly conscious of your race.*

ROUND *When are you most conscious of the race of others?*

Distribute a copy of the reading about race, "Race—The Power of an Illusion, Interview with Alan Goodman," to every Circle participant and read the text out loud. Allow a minute or two of silence for students to digest the words or to re-read the text to themselves.

ROUND *Is anything in this piece compelling or surprising to you? If so, tell us about what gets your attention and why.*

ROUND *Do you have any additional thoughts about this piece or about what others in the Circle have expressed?*

ROUND *What would you like to learn more about regarding race?*

ROUND *How could you go about learning more?*

CHECK-OUT ROUND *What can you take away from this Circle today?*

CLOSING Invite everyone to stand and shake their bodies all over to shake out the discomfort or tension that may have come up. Then share an appropriate reading from Appendix 2 or create your own.

Thank everyone for participating in the Circle today!

Race—The Power of an Illusion, Interview with Alan Goodman

PBS Online, edited transcript

How difficult is it to jettison the idea of race as biology?

To understand why the idea of race is a biological myth requires a major paradigm shift—an absolute paradigm shift, a shift in perspective. And for me, it's like seeing what it must have been like to understand that the world isn't flat. The world looks flat to our eyes. And perhaps I can invite you to a mountaintop or to a plain, and you can look out the window at the horizon, and see, "Oh, what I thought was flat I can see a curve in now." And that race is not based on biology, but race is rather an idea that we ascribe to biology.

That's quite shocking to a lot of individuals. When you look and you think you see race, to be told that no, you don't see race, you just think you see race, you know, it's based on your cultural lens—that's extremely challenging.

What's heartening is that so many students love it. They feel liberated by beginning to understand that, in fact, whiteness is a cultural construction, that race is a cultural construction, that we really are fundamentally alike. It's our politics, it's political economy, it's an old ideology that tends to separate us out. It's institutions that have been born with the idea of race and racism that tend to separate us out.

Young children today, kids today, in my experience, love it that we can have some common humanity, that we can come together as one, that this idea of biological race is a myth that's separating us. They love the idea that there's really some wall that can be smashed down and help bring us together....

Why is it important to overturn the idea of race as biology?

We live in racial smog. This is a world of racial smog. We can't help but breathe that smog. Everybody breathes it. But what's nice is that you can recognize that you are breathing that smog, and that's the first step.

We all live in a racialized society. And individuals of color are exposed to it more obviously, with more virulence, more force, than anybody is.

But what is important is that race is a very salient social and historical concept, a social and historical idea. It's shaped institutions, it's shaped our legal system, it shapes interactions in law offices and housing offices and in medical schools, in dentist's offices. It shapes that. And I think by stripping the biology from it, by stripping the idea that race is somehow based in biology, we show the emperor to have no clothes, we show race for what it is: it's an idea that's constantly being reinvented, and it's up to us about how we want to invent it and go ahead and reinvent it. But it's up to us to do it.

Alan Goodman, Euro-American, is a professor of biological anthropology at Hampshire College and co-editor of *Genetic Nature / Culture: Anthropology and Science Beyond the Cultural Divide* and *Building a New Bio-Cultural Synthesis*. This interview is available online at: http://www.pbs.org/race/000_About/002_04-background-01-07.htm

RACE—The Power of an Illusion is a 3-episode PBS documentary produced by California Newsreel in 2003. Online at: http://www.pbs.org/race/000_General/000_00-Home.htm

6.15 What Difference Does Race Make? Circle

PURPOSE To create space for an honest conversation about the reality of the social construct of race; to allow young people to reflect on the realities they observe that may not otherwise be acknowledged.

MATERIALS Talking piece, centerpiece items, bell or sound maker, paper or journals, pens or pencils, guidelines.

PREPARATION Arrange everyone in a circle of chairs with no other furniture.

Welcome to the space of the Circle.

MINDFULNESS MOMENT *Pause, breathe, and listen to the sound.*

OPENING See Appendix 2 or create your own.

VALUES ROUND *Name a value that helps you participate in a good way when you are discussing a very difficult topic.* Write the values as participants name them and place the list in the center.

Review the basic Circle guidelines.

INTRODUCE "ROUNDS" A "round" is a pass of the talking piece around the Circle. The keeper poses a question and, as a participant, usually answers first. The keeper then passes the talking piece to the person to his/her left or right. On the first round, participants are invited to say their name as well as respond to the question. Remember, it is always okay for a participant to pass.

CHECK-IN ROUND *How are you doing today? Tell us about something positive you did in the past 24 hours.*

> **MAIN ACTIVITY Reflecting on the Impact of Race in Society and in Our Lives**

ROUND *Please share with us an experience in your life where you felt left out or disrespected and it was very painful.*

We are going to talk now about the role of race in our society—the ways that race leaves people out or offers them opportunities. This may be an emotionally difficult conversation. Despite that challenge, we think it is very important to acknowledge the reality of race in our lives. Each time the talking piece comes to you, you may wish to take one or two deep breaths before speaking to help you take care of yourself in this difficult conversation. And remember that it is always okay to pass.

ROUND *Where does race make a difference in this society?*

ROUND *Where else does race make a difference in this society?*

ROUND *How much do you have to think about the differences that race makes in your daily life?*

ROUND *How do you cope with the difficulties that race creates for you or for others you care about?*

ROUND *Is there anything else you would like to say before we do our closing round in our Circle?*

CHECK-OUT ROUND *What can you take away from this Circle today?*

CLOSING Invite everyone to stand and shake their bodies all over to shake out the discomfort or tension that may have come up, and then share an appropriate reading from Appendix 2 or create your own.

Thank everyone for participating in the Circle today!

6.16 Exploring Our Feelings about Race Circle

PURPOSE To notice and reflect on how our bodies, minds, hearts, and spirits react to the topic of "race"; to raise awareness of the power of what is unspoken around the issue of race.

MATERIALS Talking piece, centerpiece items, bell or sound maker, paper or journals, pens or pencils, guidelines.

PREPARATION Arrange everyone in a circle of chairs with no other furniture.

Welcome to the space of the Circle.

MINDFULNESS MOMENT *Pause, breathe, and listen to the sound.*

OPENING See Appendix 2 or create your own.

VALUES ROUND *Name a value that helps you participate in a good way when you are discussing a very difficult topic.* Write the values as participants name them and place the list in the center.

Review the basic Circle guidelines.

INTRODUCE "ROUNDS" A "round" is a pass of the talking piece around the Circle. The keeper poses a question and, as a participant, usually answers first. The keeper then passes the talking piece to the person to his/her left or right. On the first round, participants are invited to say their name as well as respond to the question. Remember, it is always okay for a participant to pass.

CHECK-IN ROUND *How are you doing today? Is there anything you wish to share with the Circle as a check-in?*

> **MAIN ACTIVITY** Exploring Our Emotions around Race—the Word, an Experience, Feelings, and Wisdom from Experience

Write the word 'RACE' on a board or flip chart in large bold letters.

Invite participants to write 5 to 10 words that come to mind when they see or hear the word 'RACE.'

ROUND *Please share with us some of the words that you wrote.*

Think about a time when race had an impact on your life. Remember for a moment that experience. Now sit silently for one minute (eyes closed or gazing downward), noticing what is going on inside you—in your body, in your mind, in your heart, and in your spirit. I invite you to journal about what you notice. You can write words, phrases, or sentences about what you feel mentally, physically, emotionally, and in your spirit, or you can draw images to reflect the feelings you notice.

ROUND *How do you feel when you remember that experience? How does your body feel? How does your mind feel? How does your spirit feel? How does your heart feel?*

ROUND *Please share any additional thoughts you have about how you feel when you hear the word 'race.'*

ROUND *What is the hardest thing about talking about race?*

ROUND *Are there places in your life where you can talk about the feelings that you have about the topic of race? If so, where are those places?*

ROUND *We all have wisdom from our own life experiences. What wisdom do you have about the topic of race based on your own life experience that you would want the adults in the school to understand?*

ROUND *Is there anything else you would like to say before we do our closing round in our Circle?*

CHECK-OUT ROUND *What can you take away from this Circle today?*

CLOSING Invite everyone to stand and shake their bodies all over to shake out the discomfort or tension that may have come up and then share an appropriate reading from Appendix 2 or create your own.

Thank everyone for participating in the Circle today!

6.17 Exploring White Privilege Circle

PURPOSE To create space for an honest conversation about the reality of the social construct of race; to allow young people to reflect on the realities they observe that may not otherwise be acknowledged.

MATERIALS Talking piece, centerpiece items, bell or sound maker, paper or journals, pens or pencils, two readings by Tim Wise, guidelines.

PREPARATION Arrange everyone in a circle of chairs with no other furniture.

Welcome to the space of the Circle.

MINDFULNESS MOMENT *Pause, breathe, and listen to the sound.*

OPENING See Appendix 2 or create your own.

VALUES ROUND *Name a value that helps you participate in a good way when you are discussing a very difficult topic.* Write the values as participants name them and place the list in the center.

Review the basic Circle guidelines.

INTRODUCE "ROUNDS" A "round" is a pass of the talking piece around the Circle. The keeper poses a question and, as a participant, usually answers first. The keeper then passes the talking piece to the person to his/her left or right. On the first round, participants are invited to say their name as well as respond to the question. Remember, it is always okay for a participant to pass.

CHECK-IN ROUND *How are you doing today? Tell us about something positive you did in the past 24 hours.*

> **MAIN ACTIVITY Identifying White Privilege in Experience and Reflecting on Tim Wise's Words**

ROUND *What does the term white privilege mean to you?*

ROUND *Do you see white privilege in the world around you? If so, can you tell us where you see it?*

Distribute the two readings from the Preface to Tim Wise's book, *White Like Me*. Read them aloud. Allow a minute or two of silence for students to digest the words or to re-read the text to themselves.

ROUND Is anything in this piece compelling or surprising to you? If so, tell us about what gets your attention and why.

ROUND Do you have any additional thoughts about this piece or about what others in the Circle have expressed?

ROUND What is the most important idea in this piece to you?

ROUND What do you think Tim Wise means when he says, "Everything I say I say from a place of love"?

ROUND Is there anything else you would like to say before we do our closing round in our Circle?

CHECK-OUT ROUND What can you take away from this Circle today?

CLOSING Invite everyone to stand and shake their bodies all over to shake out the discomfort or tension that may have come up, and then share an appropriate reading from Appendix 2 or create your own.

Thank everyone for participating in the Circle today!

Tim Wise on Race and Whiteness

"We are all experiencing race"

Being a white man, born and reared in a society that has always bestowed upon me privileges and advantages that it has just as deliberately withheld from people of color, I am not expected to think the way I do, I suppose, let alone to act on those beliefs. After all, to be privileged, to be advantaged, is a coveted position in society, so why, many ask, would I seek to change a set of social conditions that work to my benefit? . . .

Although white Americans often think we've had few first-hand experiences with race—because most of us are so isolated from people of color in our day-to-day lives—the reality is that this isolation *is* our experience with race. We are all experiencing race, because from the beginning of our lives we have been living in a racialized society, where the color of our skin means something, even while it remains a matter of biological and genetic irrelevance. Race may be a scientific fiction, but it is a social fact: one that none of us can escape no matter how much or how little we talk about it. . . .

But despite the fact that white privilege plays out differently for different folks, . . . the fact remains that when all other factors are equal, whiteness matters and carries with it great advantage. So, for example, although whites are often poor, their poverty does not alter the fact that relative to poor and working class persons of color, they typically have a leg up. No one privilege system trumps all the others every time, but no matter the ways in which individual whites may face obstacles on the basis of nonracial factors, our race continues to elevate us over similarly situated persons of color. . . .

Above all else, and this is mostly for my family, but perhaps in a strange way for anyone reading it, please know that everything I say I say from a place of love: true love, which is neither unreflective nor uncritical nor blind, but which is, above all else, honest. Just as you must now deal with my honesty, I am prepared to deal with yours in reaction to it, whatever that might mean.

— Tim Wise, from *White Like Me: Reflections on Race from a Privileged Son,* pp. viii–xi. Tim Wise is a Euro-American anti-racism activist and writer.

"Key lessons about whiteness that I am in the process of learning"

I have divided the book [*White Like Me*] into six sections reflecting the key lessons about whiteness that I am in the process of learning. The first of these is that to be white is to be "born to belonging." This is a term I first heard used by my friend and ally, Mab Segrest; although she used it in a different context, I always thought it captured the essence of whiteness. To be white is to be born into an environment where one's legitimacy is far less likely to be questioned than would be the legitimacy of a person of color, be it in terms of where one lives, where one works, where one goes to school, or pretty much anything else. To be white is, even more, to be born into a system that has been set up for the benefit of people like you, and as such provides a head start to those who can claim membership in this, the dominant club.

Second, to be white not only means that one will typically inherit certain advantages from the past but also means that one will continue to reap the benefits of ongoing racial privilege, which itself is the flipside of discrimination against people of color.

Third, whites can choose to resist a system of racism and unjust privilege, but doing so is never easy. In fact, the fear of alienating friends and family, and the relative lack of role models from whom we can take direction renders resistance rare, and even when practiced, often ineffective, however important it may be.

Fourth, oftentimes even in our resistance, we inadvertently collaborate with racism and reinforce racial domination and subordination—in other words, we must always be on guard against our own screw-ups.

Fifth, whites pay enormous costs in order to access the privileges that come from a system of racism: costs that are intensely personal and collective, and which should inspire us to fight against racism for our own sake.

And finally, in struggle against injustice, against racism, there is the possibility of redemption.... The trick is getting from privilege, collaboration, and loss to resistance and redemption, so that we may begin to belong to a society more just and sustainable than what we have now.

Tim Wise, from the Preface to *White Like Me,* p. xi.

6.18 Exploring the Impact of Social Inequality Circle

PURPOSE To understand the connection between social inequality and adverse outcomes in people's lives, such as poor health, and to raise participant awareness about the cumulative and often hidden impact of social inequality.

MATERIALS Talking piece, copies of "Tommy's Story," journal.

PREPARATION Arrange everyone in a circle of chairs with no other furniture.

Welcome to the space of the Circle.

MINDFULNESS MOMENT *Pause, breathe, and listen to the sound.*

OPENING See Appendix 2 or create your own.

CHECK-IN ROUND *How are you doing today physically, mentally, and emotionally?*

Remind participants about values/guidelines that are important to the Circle.

> **MAIN ACTIVITY** Reading "Tommy's Story" and Reflecting on Why He Died

Pass out copies of "Tommy's Story," and either the facilitator reads it aloud alone or the group reads it together in a round.

Ask participants to answer the following question in their journal: *Who is responsible for Tommy's death?*

Ask respondents to write about the feelings that come up for them as they read this story.

ROUND Pass the talking piece and ask respondents to share what they wrote by reading it or talking about it.

ROUND Pass the talking piece to ask participants what they are taking away from the Circle today.

CHECK-OUT ROUND See Appendix 1 for ideas and options.

CLOSING See Appendix 2 or create your own.

Thank everyone for participating in the Circle today!

This activity is adapted from "Tommy's Story: Understanding the Roots of Violence" by Mariame Kaba, which in turn is based on work by Health Organizing through Popular Education (H.O.P.E.). Presented in Kaba, Mathew, and Haines, *Something Is Wrong Curriculum*, 69–73.

Tommy's Story
Understanding the Roots of Violence

This is the story of a little boy named Tommy J. who died suddenly at age 9 of an asthma attack. He was in his backyard playing when the attack came on quickly and fiercely. Although he had had a slight cold the last few days and had felt at times that an attack could be coming on, he hadn't been paying much attention to the slight wheezing. He tried to ignore it because he didn't want to upset his parents anymore. Things had been so tense in the house with so much yelling and screaming—he just tried to stay out of the way. It seemed that the fighting just made his wheezing worse.

Tommy would say that all the problems started when his dad got laid off at work. Dad had been a sheet metal worker and had worked for an automobile manufacturing company. Sometimes his dad and he would lean over the railing at the highway overpass and watch the cars whiz underneath. His dad would brag about the different models of cars that he had helped to build. Tommy was proud of his dad's strong back and muscular arms that molded those sports cars and family vans. He never thought about the pollution spewing from the vehicles' exhaust pipes. Tommy's mom was a hairdresser who worked at a nearby salon and attended the local state university part-time. She was working towards a degree in business administration and hoped someday to open up her own small business. Tommy was proud of his mom for working so hard to earn a college degree.

But then the automobile manufacturer "downsized" and laid off a couple thousand workers in his town. The company had decided to build these cars in Mexico where the labor was cheaper and the environmental restrictions more relaxed. The factory workers were incensed that the local government officials hadn't offered the auto company some incentives to keep the jobs in the area. Mr. J. was disappointed in the union leadership who said that they had done all they could to avoid the lay-offs.

All of a sudden, Tommy's father's pay stub of $15.65 an hour was gone. Their health insurance, retirement, and other benefits had also disappeared. Severance pay and unemployment benefits kept the family going for a while as Mr. J. looked for another job. But he learned that despite his good health and excellent work record, he had few marketable skills and another job in the industrial sector was hard to find. With just a high school diploma, he was locked out of employment opportunities in any technical field. He thought to enroll himself in a job re-training program, but he couldn't afford the fees and he needed to earn money now to pay the bills.

Mrs. J. cut back on her class load in order to put in more hours at the beauty parlor. Mr. J. found himself working two jobs—both low-paying, both with few or no benefits. In the early morning and late afternoon he drove a school bus for the district. $35.00 a day, no benefits. In between bus routes he worked at a fast-food restaurant. Two jobs, longer hours—and he felt all the time just one step ahead from the collecting agency.

What worried the J. family the most was lack of health insurance. The fast food restaurant offered Mr. J. health benefits, but only for him. He would have to pay the cost of coverage for the rest of the family. But frankly, they couldn't afford it. Besides, they were still trying to pay off a hospital bill from a few months back when Tommy had a particularly bad attack and had required intensive respiratory treatment. So the Js decided to try to stay healthy and utilize community health services as much as possible. They were caught in the middle—too poor for private health insurance, too rich for public assistance.

It was during times like this that Tommy's mother felt regret for not breastfeeding, because she had heard it might have helped Tommy stay healthy. Tommy's first asthmatic attack had occurred when he was just 3 years old. It had frightened the whole family, but Tommy's breathing had relaxed with the first injection given to him in their local ER. Follow up visits with the family care provider were helpful. They learned about asthma, how to handle the disease, what to do to prevent attacks, and what to do when wheezing started.

Tommy's dad managed to stop smoking, and his mom carefully changed her clothes before coming home from the salon for fear of what perfumes and chemicals might be in the hair products she used at work. They moved to an apartment in a newer building. The rent was higher, but there was less concern over molds that are common in older buildings. Tommy still suffered occasional attacks, but for the most part his asthma was under control.

At least it was so until his dad had lost his job at the car factory, and he got so crabby and so tired, and his mom so nervous and so irritable. Tommy's attacks increased in frequency and intensity. They could no longer afford the private pediatrician's fees, and began seeking care at different community clinics and emergency rooms. Different faces, different treatment styles. Some health workers were friendly, some were mean and chewed out Tommy's parents for one thing or another. Like the time they had to wait so long to be attended and Tommy's younger sister started acting up. The clerk yelled at Tommy's mother until she nearly cried. They returned home so frazzled that Tommy's parents swore they would never return to that clinic again. When an attack came on, the Js tried to control it at home as much as possible. But it couldn't always be done.

Life just unraveled. Screaming, yelling, crying, mom and dad working so hard, so little food on the table, no McDonald's, no trips to the mall. The Js couldn't afford the high rent anymore, so they moved into a basement apartment belonging to Mrs. J's boss. The dampness and molds were not good for Tommy. Nor was the stale smoke from his dad's cigarettes as Mr. J. had recently started up smoking again, and he was smoking heavily. Not only that, but the apartment happened to be next to a brown field and a community with a lot of factories. Very often, the atmosphere was full of a hazy smoke.

Maybe it was the foods Tommy was eating that were causing problems. With the house in such turmoil and so little money, it was hard to maintain any sense of nutrition and dietary control. The Food Pantry was helpful, but Mrs. J. had been told once not to serve so much processed packaged food. But then, who can afford fresh fruits and vegetables, chicken, and fish? Tommy had had a few episodes of wheezing, and all of his medication had been used up. The Js were waiting until the next paycheck to buy his meds.

When the attack came on, it was late afternoon and Tommy and his younger sister Ann were alone in the house. Their mother was working at the beauty salon a few blocks away, and their dad was driving the school bus. Ann rushed to the neighbor's house to call their mother, who came running home. Mrs. J. felt helpless.

There was nothing to give Tommy and he was fighting to catch his breath. The neighbor called 911, and thank God, the paramedics came quickly. They attended to Tommy, gave him some oxygen and some meds, stabilized him, and took him to the nearest ER. At the hospital, Tommy was checked. His breathing was calmer, but he needed to be admitted. However, the hospital could not accept Tommy because the Js had no insurance. Tommy was transferred to County Hospital. One the way there, Tommy suffered a severe attack that could not be stopped. He died shortly after arriving at County.

"Tommy's Story," courtesy of Health Organizing Through Popular Education (H.O.P.E.), Chicago, 1996. In Kaba, Mathew, and Haines, *Something Is Wrong Curriculum*, pp. 70–73.

Thinking about Gender and Violence Circle

6.19

PURPOSE To help participants reflect on their own assumptions and values around male privilege, sexual entitlement, and violence against women.

MATERIALS Talking piece, centerpiece items, bell or sound maker, copies of the story, "The Drawbridge," journals, pen.

PREPARATION Arrange everyone in a circle of chairs with no other furniture.

Welcome to the space of the Circle.

MINDFULNESS MOMENT *Pause, breathe, and listen to the sound.*

OPENING See Appendix 2 or create your own.

VALUES ROUND *Name a value that is important to you when you are discussing a difficult topic.*

Write a list of those values as participants name them and place the list in the center.

Review the basic Circle guidelines.

INTRODUCE "ROUNDS" A "round" is a pass of the talking piece around the Circle. The keeper poses a question and, as a participant, usually answers first. The keeper then passes the talking piece to the person to his/her left or right. On the first round, participants are invited to say their name as well as respond to the question. Remember, it is always okay for a participant to pass.

CHECK-IN ROUND *How are you doing today? Is there something on your mind that the Circle should know about and that you feel comfortable sharing with the group?*

> **MAIN ACTIVITY** Reading "The Drawbridge" and Reflecting on Responsibility and Gender

Hand out the story, "The Drawbridge," and read it aloud to participants.

Ask participants to answer the following questions in their journals based on their own moral values:

- *Who do you believe is most responsible for the death of the baroness?*
- *For each of the participants in the story, do you believe they bear any responsibility for the death of the baroness?*

- *How would you rank each of the participants from the most responsible to the least responsible?*

ROUND *Please share your ranking of responsibility and tell us why you ranked them that way, particularly the person you consider most responsible.*

ROUND *What feelings come up for you both in reading the story and in hearing how others think about responsibility in this story?*

ROUND *What have you learned from this exercise about our cultural attitudes about sexuality, gender, and violence against women?*

CHECK-OUT ROUND *How do you feel at the end of this Circle, and is there anything you need as you leave here?*

CLOSING See Appendix 2 or create your own.

Thank everyone for participating in the Circle today!

This activity is adapted from "The Drawbridge" in Katz, *White Awareness*, pp. 70–72.

See also the use and application of the Drawbridge exercise in "Power and Violence" by Mariame Kaba with an activity developed by Sgt. Charles Howard, Fort Lee (Virginia) in Kaba, Mathew, and Haines, *Something Is Wrong Curriculum*, pp. 53–59. Available online at: http://www.project-nia.org/docs/Something_Is_Wrong-Curriculum.pdf.

The Drawbridge

As he left for a visit to his outlying districts, the jealous baron warned his pretty [wife]: "Do not leave the castle while I am gone, or I will punish you severely when I return!"

But as the hours passed, the young baroness grew lonely, and despite her husband's warning, she decided to visit her lover, who lived in the countryside nearby. The castle was situated on an island in a wide, fast-flowing river. A drawbridge linked the island to the mainland at the narrowest point in the river. "Surely my husband will not return before me," she thought, and ordered the servant to lower the drawbridge and leave it down until she returned. After spending several pleasant hours with her lover the baroness returned to the drawbridge. Only to find it blocked by a gatemen wildly waving a long, cruel knife.

"Do not attempt to cross this bridge, Baroness, or I will have to kill you" he cried. "The baron ordered me to do so."

Fearing for her life, the bareness returned to her lover and asked him for help. "Our relationship is only a romantic one," he said. "I will not help." The baroness then sought out a boatman on the river, explained her plight to him, and asked him to take her across the river in his boat.

"I will do it but only if you can pay the fee of five marks."

"But I have no money with me!" the baroness protested.

"That is too bad. No money, no, ride," the boatmen said flatly.

Her fear growing, the baroness ran crying to the home of a friend and, after explaining her desperate situation, begged for enough money to pay the boatman his fee.

"If you had not disobeyed your husband this would not have happened," the friend said. "I will give you no money."

With dawn approaching and her last resource exhausted, the baroness returned to the bridge in desperation, and waited to cross to the castle, and was slain by the gateman.

After reading the scenario, rank the characters from 1-6.

1 = most responsible for the death of the baroness, 6 = least responsible

	Individual Ranking	Group Ranking
Baron		
Baroness		
Gateman		
Boatman		
Friend		
Lover		

Be prepared to explain and discuss your rankings.

"The Drawbridge" in Katz, *White Awareness: Handbook for Anti-Racism Training*, pp. 70–72.

6.20 Thinking about Gender Inequality Circle

PURPOSE To reflect on our cultural attitudes, values, and behavior towards teen pregnancy.

MATERIALS Talking piece, centerpiece items, bell or sound maker, lyrics to Tupac's song "Brenda's Got a Baby" (from the Internet), journals, pens.

PREPARATION Arrange everyone in a circle of chairs with no other furniture.

Welcome to the space of the Circle.

MINDFULNESS MOMENT *Pause, breathe, and listen to the sound.*

OPENING See Appendix 2 or create your own.

VALUES ROUND *Name a value that you would want to pass on to your children if you ever have children.* Write a list of those values as participants name them and place the list in the center.

Review the basic Circle guidelines.

INTRODUCE "ROUNDS" A round is a pass of the talking piece around the Circle. The keeper poses a question and, as a participant, usually answers first and then passes the talking piece to the person to their left or to their right. On the first round, participants are invited to say their name as well as respond to the question. Remember, it is always okay for a participant to pass.

CHECK-IN ROUND *What strength do you bring to the Circle today?*

> **MAIN ACTIVITY** Reading "Brenda's Got a Baby" and Reflecting on Why She Died

Read aloud the lyrics of the song, "Brenda's Got a Baby" by Tupak Shakur (from online) or play the song on a smart phone. Ask participants to answer in their journal the following question: *Why did Brenda die?*

ROUND *Please share your thoughts about why Brenda died.*

ROUND *What are your feelings about this situation?*

ROUND *Do you think this situation has any connection to gender inequality? Why or why not?*

ROUND *What have you learned from our discussion today?*

CHECK-OUT ROUND *How do you feel about today's Circle?*

CLOSING See Appendix 2 or create your own.

Thank everyone for participating in the Circle today!

This activity is adapted "'It's Not Just One Thing'—Young Women's Oppression and Liberation," developed by the Rogers Park Young Women's Action Team with support from the adult ally, Mariame Kaba. Published in Kaba, Mathew, and Haines, *Something Is Wrong Curriculum,* pp. 61–62.

6.21 Thinking and Talking about OUR Boundaries Circle (For Girls)

• • • • • •

PURPOSE To engage adolescent girls in thinking about the kinds of behavior—both physical and non-physical—that cause harm to them because it violates their own sense of safety, dignity, and autonomy; to explore and practice ways to speak out when others cross our boundaries.

MATERIALS A talking piece, centerpiece items, bell or sound maker, journals, pens.

PREPARATION Arrange everyone in a circle of chairs with no other furniture.

Welcome to the space of the Circle.

MINDFULNESS MOMENT *Pause, breathe, and listen to the sound.*

OPENING See Appendix 2 or create your own.

VALUES ROUND *Name a value that you would want to pass on to your daughter if you ever have children.* Write a list of those values as participants name them and place the list in the center.

Review the basic Circle guidelines.

INTRODUCE "ROUNDS" A round is a pass of the talking piece around the Circle. The keeper poses a question and, as a participant, usually answers first and then passes the talking piece to the person to their left or to their right. On the first round, participants are invited to say their name as well as respond to the question. Remember, it is always okay for a participant to pass.

CHECK-IN ROUND *How are you doing today physically, mentally, and emotionally?*

> **MAIN ACTIVITY Explore Our Boundaries and How to Respond When Someone Crosses Them**

ROUND *Let's brainstorm the meaning of the word "boundary." What does it mean to you?*

Write a definition on the flipchart or board: *A boundary is a line that marks the limits of an area or a dividing line. It also refers to limits that define acceptable behavior.*

EXPLAIN Each of us has our own sense of our boundaries—physical, verbal, and emotional—and we may need to articulate to others how we feel when these boundaries are violated.

Put the following scenarios on the flipchart or board (or create this as a worksheet), and ask participants to write in their journals about how they would feel if they were treated this way.

- You are getting on the bus and someone pushes you in order to get past you.
- A student grabs a pencil out of your hand without asking permission.
- A student hugs you without asking permission.
- A student kisses you on the cheek without asking permission.
- A student makes a comment about what you are wearing.
- Someone whistles at you as you walk by.
- Someone puts an arm around you without your permission.
- Someone taps you on your butt without your permission.

ROUND Which of these behaviors violate your sense of personal boundaries? How would it feel if that happens?

ROUND Imagine you feel comfortable speaking out: what would you want to say to the person who violates your personal boundaries?

ROUND What do you think you can do for yourself or for others, so that personal boundaries are respected in your community?

CHECK-OUT ROUND What have you learned from our Circle today that could be useful to you?

CLOSING See Appendix 2 or create your own.

Thank everyone for participating in the Circle today!

This activity is adapted from Pittsburgh Action Against Rape, *Teens and Primary Prevention of Sexual Violence: Where to Start!*

6.22 Sexual Harassment and Bystander Circle

PURPOSE To think about common forms of sexual harassment; to explore how these behaviors affect others; to consider ways students might intervene on behalf of the target.

MATERIALS Talking piece, centerpiece items, bell or sound maker, prepared scenarios on a flip chart, copies of "Choose a Scenario" worksheet so that each participant receives three copies.

PREPARATION Arrange everyone in a circle of chairs with no other furniture.

Welcome to the space of the Circle.

MINDFULNESS MOMENT *Pause, breathe, and listen to the sound.*

OPENING See Appendix 2 or create your own.

VALUES ROUND *Name a value that is important to you when you face a difficult decision.* Write a list of those values as participants name them and place the list in the center.

Review the basic Circle guidelines.

INTRODUCE "ROUNDS" A round is a pass of the talking piece around the Circle. The keeper poses a question and, as a participant, usually answers first and then passes the talking piece to the person to their left or to their right. On the first round, participants are invited to say their name as well as respond to the question. Remember, it is always okay for a participant to pass.

CHECK-IN ROUND *Tell us something heavy on your mind today and something light on your mind today.*

> **MAIN ACTIVITY** Reflecting on Harassment Scenarios and Options for Responding

Read the following scenarios, which you have written on a flip chart or board:

SCENARIO 1 *You are walking down the hall and see someone grab a girl's butt. You can tell the girl is upset but she does nothing.*

SCENARIO 2 *You see a classmate push a younger student into the boys' or girls' bathroom and hold the door shut. You can hear the younger student yelling and kicking the door.*

SCENARIO 3 *Your friends plan to pull up the skirt of a girl they don't like in front of other people.*

SCENARIO 4 *You are sitting with a group of friends. Someone dares another person in the group to pull down another student's pants.*

SCENARIO 5 *Someone sends you a nude photo of a classmate on your cell phone.*

SCENARIO 6 *You hear a sexual rumor about a friend.*

SCENARIO 7 *You saw a sexual comment about a friend on a classmate's Facebook or other social media page.*

Distribute the "Choose a Scenario" worksheet, three copies per participant Ask students to choose three of the scenarios and fill out a "Choose a Scenario" worksheet for each one.

ROUND *Choose a scenario and share how you think the target person felt, how you would feel if you were a bystander observing this, and the options for helping the target person.*

ROUND *Has anything like these scenarios happened to you? Can you share a personal experience when your boundaries were violated? What did you feel? What did you say or do? What did others say or do?*

ROUND *Have you ever witnessed any of these scenarios? What were you feeling? What did you say or do? What did you want to say or do?*

ROUND *Think about the options for helping that have been suggested. Do you believe these options are realistic? What are the obstacles that you see to these options?*

ROUND *What do you need in order to exercise these options as a bystander and to stand up for someone who is being harassed?*

CHECK-OUT ROUND *What can you take away from this Circle to help others?*

CLOSING *See Appendix 2 or create your own.*

Thank everyone for participating in the Circle today!

This activity is adapted from Pittsburgh Action Against Rape, *Teens and Primary Prevention of Sexual Violence: Where to Start!*

Choose a Scenario

Choose a scenario and share how you think the target person felt, how you would feel if you were a bystander observing this, and the options for helping the target person.

Write your scenario in the space below:

How do you think the target person felt?	How would you feel if you were a bystander observing this?	What might you do to help this person?

Love and Marriage Circle

6.23

PURPOSE To explore perspectives on love; to share our views on what marriage means; to explore how our views of marriage impact our belief in marriage equality/gay marriage.

MATERIALS Talking piece, centerpiece items, bell or sound maker, markers, pens/pencils, index cards, string, hole punch.

PREPARATION Arrange everyone in a circle of chairs with no other furniture.

Welcome to the space of the Circle.

MINDFULNESS MOMENT *Pause, breathe, and listen to the sound.*

OPENING See Appendix 2 or create your own.

Review the basic Circle guidelines.

INTRODUCE "ROUNDS" A round is a pass of the talking piece around the Circle. The keeper poses a question and, as a participant, usually answers first and then passes the talking piece to the person to their left or to their right. On the first round, participants are invited to say their name as well as respond to the question. Remember, it is always okay for a participant to pass.

CHECK-IN ROUND *Please share three words that describe your emotional frame of mind today.*

> **MAIN ACTIVITY Exploring Attitudes and Feelings around Marriage and Love**

Explain that there are many different views on marriage and that everyone deserves love. Acknowledge that differences of opinion about marriage are often based on strongly held beliefs. Remind everyone that it is extremely important to respect each other's views on marriage. Respect does not mean agreement. It means a willingness to listen to a different opinion without dismissing the value of the other person as a person.

Invite participants to write on an index card what value they need most today for a conversation about love and marriage. Ask participants to make a necklace with the index card using string and a hole puncher. Ask participants to put the necklace around their necks so others in the Circle can be reminded of the specific value they have chosen.

ROUND *Please share the value you wrote and why you chose that value.*

ROUND *What is love? Are there different kinds of love?*

ROUND *What do you think the relationship should be between marriage and love?*

ROUND *Is marriage important? Why?*

ROUND *What thoughts or feelings come up for you from the following quote:*

> I believe that marriage isn't
> between a man & woman
> but between love and love.
>
> — Frank Ocean, African-American singer, songwriter, and rapper

ROUND *What are your greatest fears about societal attitudes toward marriage?*

ROUND *Do you think marriage is appropriate between two women or two men?*

CHECK-OUT ROUND *Reflect on what you have heard today and tell us why your value was important for this discussion.*

CLOSING Ask everyone in the Circle to join hands and close their eyes for one minute to remember and reflect on the core assumption that everyone is equal. By joining hands, they connect to one another and in that moment are all on the same level, no matter what participants' beliefs are. Or create your own closing.

Thank everyone for participating in the Circle today!

When We're Different or At-Odds with Society Circle

6.24

PURPOSE To talk about how it feels when your identity is at odds with societal expectations; to further understand identities that go against society's norm; to increase the ability to have thoughtful conversations about potentially difficult subjects.

MATERIALS Talking piece, centerpiece items, bell or sound maker, stiff paper to fold lengthwise into a tent for each participant, markers.

PREPARATION Arrange everyone in a circle of chairs with no other furniture.

Welcome to the space of the Circle.

MINDFULNESS MOMENT *Pause, breathe, and listen to the sound.*

SUGGESTED OPENING

> *Never forget what you are, for surely the world will not.*
> *Make it your strength. Then it can never be your weakness.*
> *Armour yourself in it, and it will never be used to hurt you.*
>
>   — George R.R. Martin, Euro-American novelist and short story writer

Review the basic Circle guidelines.

INTRODUCE "ROUNDS" A round is a pass of the talking piece around the Circle. The keeper poses a question and, as a participant, usually answers first and then passes the talking piece to the person to their left or to their right. On the first round, participants are invited to say their name as well as respond to the question. Remember, it is always okay for a participant to pass.

CHECK-IN ROUND *What strength are you bringing to the Circle today?*

> **MAIN ACTIVITY Reflecting on Difference, Expectations, and Tensions between Them**

Distribute paper tents and markers.

ROUND *What value would you like to bring to our conversation about difference? Please write that value on both sides of the paper tent. When the talking piece comes to you, please tell us about your value and why it is important to you. Then place the tent in front of you on the floor.*

ROUND What are some of the ways that people are different from society's expectations?

ROUND Have you ever felt that you were different from society's expectations of you?

ROUND What does it feel like when you do not fit in with the people you are close to (friends and family)? Have you ever felt this way?

ROUND What do you think people need as support when they feel different?

ROUND How do you cope when you feel different?

ROUND How can you help others who may feel different and struggle with their identity?

ROUND When the talking piece comes this time, I invite you to respond to what you heard from others in the Circle. What thoughts or ideas have come to you as you listen to others' experiences with difference?

CHECK-OUT ROUND How do you feel about today's Circle?

CLOSING See Appendix 2 or create your own.

Thank everyone for participating in the Circle today!

MODULE 7

Working Together as Staff

Circles are for everyone. The Circle is an important resource within any community for creating a strong and healthy sense of connection among its members. In all the ways that Circles are valuable for students, they are equally useful for staff. This is about caring for and developing ourselves as human beings. We all need practice speaking from the heart and developing our own social and emotional literacy. We all need to feel a sense of belonging and to feel that others value the gifts we bring. We all need others to care about our problems and to be available to us when we are struggling with the vicissitudes of life. We all sometimes need to engage in difficult but important conversations, so we are able to overcome the harms of the past. We all need one another to help bring our best selves forward.

In many schools, the first Circles practiced are among the staff. As we noted earlier, teachers often want to experience a Circle before deciding if it is appropriate for their classroom. Training to facilitate a Circle also happens through the experience of participating in a Circle. Thus a common approach to bringing Circles into a school community is to hold staff Circles to introduce the practice among adults before holding Circles with students. In Module 1, we have provided a template for an introductory Circle with staff that focuses on the values and challenges of their role as educators.

This module offers twelve additional Circles for use with staff. By staff, we are referring to all the adults employed within the school community. This includes administrative, support, guidance, clerical, janitorial, transportation, and school safety staff as well as teaching staff. The stronger the connections between all adults responsible for the well-being of the children, the stronger the community will be in its capacity to care for them. One of the core assumptions of this guide is that all the resources we need to care well for one another are already present within our community. We strongly believe there are untapped resources within the hearts and minds of all the staff, parents, and students within the community. The more we cultivate the gifts within our midst, the more we unleash our creative potential to meet the needs of all our children.

> The more we cultivate the gifts within our midst, the more we unleash our creative potential to meet the needs of all our children.

The module begins with a Circle for exploring values and creating guidelines. The foundation for a strong community is clarity around core values and an intentional commitment to live those values in action. As adults, we need the time and space to explore our shared values, to prioritize, to understand what our values mean and look like in our daily lives, and to create systems and processes that support our desired action. This is an ongoing creative process of community building, and it is one of the most important activities for a community. It is also one of the most neglected activities within most school communities. Endlessly pushed for time, adults within schools rarely have the luxury of sitting together to build connection, articulate their most heartfelt values, acknowledge the struggles, ask for help, and extend support. The space for this kind of mutuality is hard to find within the typical packed school day and academic calendar.

We propose that making time and space for these kinds of conversations within the Circle on an occasional but routine basis will have a profound impact on the quality of relationships, and this will, in turn, enhance the learning and living for all members. Creating a positive school culture is a collective activity. It cannot be dictated from above or enforced through laws or policy. It is the result of thousands of gestures, words, smiles, acts of kindness, consideration, and care. These gestures, small and larger, arise from countless individual decisions made every second of every day. If the goal is a positive school climate that supports the well-being and belonging for all students, then adults must create and experience this kind of climate as well. We know no better way than to occasionally but routinely sit in Circle to reflect on the all-important questions of how we treat one another within the community.

Ultimately, building a restorative school is about values and intentionally putting those values into action every day. Policies, structures, schedules, and systems must also support and reflect values, so the behavior that is encouraged and rewarded aligns with these priorities. This is hard work, and it is the work of many, not just a few. But Circle reminds us that we all choose how we behave. We are the only ones truly in control of how we choose to behave towards others and ourselves. Children within any community need the adults to remain true to their values and to be clear and intentional about living those values. Our actions teach our children most of all.

> Children within any community need the adults to remain true to their values and to be clear and intentional about living those values.

Establishing Guidelines for Staff Circle

7.1

PURPOSE Develop a set of agreements about how the adults will work together in the school so that they model effective, respectful interactions for students.

MATERIALS Talking piece, centerpiece items, bell or sound maker, slips of paper (five per participant), several longer strips of paper, pens, markers.

PREPARATION Arrange everyone in a circle of chairs with no other furniture.

Welcome to the space of the Circle.

MINDFULNESS MOMENT *Pause, breathe, and listen to the sound.*

OPENING See Appendix 2 or create your own.

INTRODUCE "ROUNDS" A round is a pass of the talking piece around the Circle. The keeper poses a question and, as a participant, usually answers first and then passes the talking piece to the person to their left or to their right. On the first round, participants are invited to say their name as well as respond to the question. Remember, it is always okay for a participant to pass.

VALUES ROUND *Name one value that is important to you in how you relate to students.* Write a list of those values as participants name them and then place the list in the center.

CHECK-IN ROUND *How are you doing? Is there anything particular on your mind that is important for us to know?*

MAIN ACTIVITY Developing Guidelines among Staff

EXPLAIN *In the Circle today, we want to develop a set of guidelines for us as staff. Those will be agreements about how we work together and how we treat one another. Through our commitment to these guidelines, we will model for our students the way we hope they can treat each other and us.*

Provide everyone with 5 strips of paper. Ask participants: *Write five things you need from others to work at your best—one on each strip.*

ROUND *I invite you to read one of your pieces of paper, explain why it is important to you, and lay it on the floor. If the need is similar to one already displayed, place it with similar ones.*

Repeat 5 times around the Circle to share all the needs.

ROUND *What do you notice about the needs that have been expressed? What surprises you?*

Suspend the talking piece briefly to group the needs in clusters of related needs. Identify the theme of each cluster. Break the Circle into smaller groups—one for each cluster of related needs. Ask each small group to turn their cluster of needs into a guideline by completing the statement, "To work at our best when we are together, we will . . ." Instruct them to write their guideline on a long strip of paper.

Bring the group back into Circle. Invite each group to present their guideline and place their strip in the center.

ROUND *Can you agree to these guidelines for us as staff in our daily interactions? We understand that we are human and will make mistakes. The idea of guidelines is that we are willing to be accountable to one another when we fail to honor the guidelines. Can you commit to these guidelines?*

If there are objections to any of the guidelines, pass the talking piece to explore what needs that guideline is trying to meet and what needs make it objectionable. Work with the language being used and the underlying needs to search for common ground to create a guideline acceptable to everyone. A guideline around which there is not consensus may be set aside for future conversation, while the remaining guidelines are adopted.

Thank everyone for the work they have done today to build a positive culture for the students. These guidelines may be revisited at any time if they are not working for us.

ROUND *What are your closing thoughts about this Circle?*

CLOSING See Appendix 2 or create your own.

Thank everyone for participating in the Circle today!

Post the consensus guidelines and bring them to subsequent staff Circles.

Adapted from Vaandering and VanderVennen, "Putting Restorative Justice into Practice."

Staff Weekly Reflection Circle

7.2

PURPOSE To support continuing growth and self-reflection among staff and to build relationships among staff.

MATERIALS Talking piece, bell or sound maker, centerpiece items, values and guidelines from previous Circles.

PREPARATION Arrange everyone in a circle of chairs with no other furniture.

Welcome to the space of the Circle.

MINDFULNESS MOMENT *Pause, breathe, and listen to the sound.*

OPENING See Appendix 2 or create your own.

Remind the group of the values and guidelines they have created in previous Circles.

INTRODUCE "ROUNDS" A round is a pass of the talking piece around the Circle. The keeper poses a question and, as a participant, usually answers first and then passes the talking piece to the person to their left or to their right. On the first round, participants are invited to say their name as well as respond to the question. Remember, it is always okay for a participant to pass.

MAIN ACTIVITY Reflecting on the Week

Choose rounds from the following questions according to available time and current circumstances:

ROUND *What was the best thing about this week?*

ROUND *What was the most challenging thing about this week?*

ROUND *What do you wish you could have done differently?*

ROUND *If you could say something to students/classrooms, what would it be?*

ROUND *Tell us one thing you are grateful for from this week.*

CHECK-OUT ROUND *What is the one thing you are going to do this weekend to take care of yourself so you can start next week new?*

CLOSING See Appendix 2 or create your own.

Thank everyone for participating in the Circle today!

7.3

Staff Team-Building Circle

PURPOSE To strengthen relationships and a sense of shared purpose among staff.

MATERIALS Centerpiece items related to the work of the staff (e.g. mission statement, goals, tools of the work, symbols of the desired outcomes of the work), talking piece, bell or sound maker, ball of yarn or heavy string.

PREPARATION Arrange everyone in a circle of chairs with no other furniture.

Welcome to the space of the Circle.

MINDFULNESS MOMENT *Pause, breathe, and listen to the sound.*

SUGGESTED OPENING One of the ball of yarn web-making exercises, see Appendix 2, Section III, pages 384 and 387.

Remind the group of values and guidelines created in previous Circles.

INTRODUCE "ROUNDS" A round is a pass of the talking piece around the Circle. The keeper poses a question and, as a participant, usually answers first and then passes the talking piece to the person to their left or to their right. On the first round, participants are invited to say their name as well as respond to the question. Remember, it is always okay for a participant to pass.

CHECK-IN ROUND *How are you doing? Is there anything particular on your mind that is important for us to know and that you feel comfortable sharing with the group?*

MAIN ACTIVITY Reflecting on the Work Experience in a Positive Frame

ROUND *I invite you to share why you came to the job you currently have and what that job means to you.*

ROUND *Please share a life experience outside of work that helped prepare you for the work you do.*

ROUND *What do you think the staff/work team does well?*

ROUND *What part of your job is most difficult and what makes it difficult?*

ROUND *What kind of support would you like to help you in doing your job?*

ROUND *What strength or gift can you offer to support others in your team?*

CHECK-OUT ROUND *How do you feel about our Circle today?*

CLOSING See Appendix 2 or create your own.

Thank everyone for participating in the Circle today!

Based on Boyes-Watson & Pranis, *Heart of Hope,* pp. 278–80.

7.4 Why Relationships Matter in Schools Circle

PURPOSE To create a reflective space to explore the importance of relationships for learning; to support staff in taking the time to do the relationship work with students and each other; and to build a culture of valuing relationships.

MATERIALS Talking piece, bell or sound maker, centerpiece items, values and guidelines from previous Circles, paper and pens.

PREPARATION Arrange everyone in a circle of chairs with no other furniture.

Welcome to the space of the Circle.

MINDFULNESS MOMENT *Pause, breathe, and listen to the sound.*

OPENING See Appendix 2 or create your own.

Remind the group of the values and guidelines they have created in previous Circles.

INTRODUCE "ROUNDS" A round is a pass of the talking piece around the Circle. The keeper poses a question and, as a participant, usually answers first and then passes the talking piece to the person to their left or to their right. On the first round, participants are invited to say their name as well as respond to the question. Remember, it is always okay for a participant to pass.

MAIN ACTIVITY Reflecting on Who and What Helps Others and Us

EXPLAIN *The Circle helps us access the collective wisdom of us all. Our own life experience is a source of wisdom and insight into challenges we may face today. We are going to explore our own life experiences about relationships to help us help the children.*

ROUND *Share an experience from your own work as an educator where you were able to encourage and influence someone who wanted to give up.*

ROUND *Who influences you to keep going when you want to give up? Why are you influenced by this person?*

Invite participants to use the paper or a journal to write the names of five role models in their lives. Beside the names, write one or more characteristics they modeled that are important to you.

ROUND *Share the characteristics of your role models. Record the answers on a list.*

ROUND *What do you notice about our list? What seems to be the nature of our connection with our role models? Is the connection physical, emotional, mental, or spiritual?*

ROUND *What is your experience about the importance of relationships in your work—both with students and with colleagues?*

ROUND *What are the most effective strategies you have found for building relationships in a classroom?*

Thank the group for sharing from their own life experiences to help us look at how we can strengthen our school culture for the success of all.

CHECK-OUT ROUND *Do you have anything else you would like to say in closing our Circle today?*

CLOSING *See Appendix 2 or create your own.*

Thank everyone for participating in the Circle today!

7.5 Sustaining Ourselves When the Work Is Difficult Circle

PURPOSE To create a space of support and reflection for school staff and to build resiliency in staff.

MATERIALS Talking piece, bell or sound maker, centerpiece items, values and guidelines from previous Circles, "Who Packed Your Parachute?" reading from Appendix 2, Section I, under the heading "Working together for a better world, pages 370–71.

PREPARATION Arrange everyone in a circle of chairs with no other furniture.

Welcome to the space of the Circle.

MINDFULNESS MOMENT Pause, breathe, and listen to the sound.

OPENING See Appendix 2 or create your own.

Remind the group of the values and guidelines they have created in previous Circles.

INTRODUCE "ROUNDS" A round is a pass of the talking piece around the Circle. The keeper poses a question and, as a participant, usually answers first and then passes the talking piece to the person to their left or to their right. On the first round, participants are invited to say their name as well as respond to the question. Remember, it is always okay for a participant to pass.

> **MAIN ACTIVITY** Reading "Who Packed Your Parachute?" and Reflecting on Support

ROUND How are you doing? Share a high point of this past week.

ROUND What is difficult in your work as an educator right now?

ROUND What inspires you to keep going when the work is discouraging?

ROUND I will send the talking piece around again to add anything or to respond to what you heard from others.

Read aloud "Who Packed Your Parachute?"

ROUND Who packs your parachute?

ROUND *What do you need from colleagues to sustain you in difficult moments?*

ROUND *What can you offer to colleagues to support them in difficult moments?*

CHECK-OUT ROUND *Do you have anything else you would like to say in closing our Circle today?*

CLOSING See Appendix 2 or create your own.

Thank everyone for participating in the Circle today!

7.6 Self-Care Circle

PURPOSE To encourage care of self in all dimensions.

MATERIALS Talking piece, centerpiece items, bell or sound maker, paper (8.5 x 11 or larger), markers, pens.

PREPARATION Arrange everyone in a circle of chairs with no other furniture.

Welcome to the space of the Circle.

MINDFULNESS MOMENT *Pause, breathe, and listen to the sound.*

OPENING See Appendix 2 or create your own.

Remind the group of the values and guidelines they have created in previous Circles.

INTRODUCE "ROUNDS" A round is a pass of the talking piece around the Circle. The keeper poses a question and, as a participant, usually answers first and then passes the talking piece to the person to their left or to their right. On the first round, participants are invited to say their name as well as respond to the question. Remember, it is always okay for a participant to pass.

CHECK-IN ROUND *Please share something that has brought you joy recently.*

MAIN ACTIVITY Assessing the Balance of Self-Care in Our Lives

Invite participants to draw a large Circle on a piece of paper, and then draw lines dividing the Circle into four equal parts and label one section 'mental,' one 'physical,' one 'emotional,' and one 'spiritual.' Ask participants to write in each section what they do to take care of themselves in that dimension of their lives. When participants are finished, ask them to think about whether they would like to be doing more care of self in any of those dimensions. Then invite them to create a goal for further self-care in each quadrant and to write that goal beside the quadrant.

ROUND *Please share your reactions to the process of assessing your self-care in this way as well as your insights or your goals.*

ROUND *I invite you to add any other insights you have from further thought or from listening to others in the Circle.*

ROUND *What is most challenging to you in taking care of yourself?*

CHECK-OUT ROUND *Is there anything you would like to say as we close our Circle?*

CLOSING See Appendix 2 or create your own.

Thank everyone for participating in the Circle today!

This activity is adapted from Boyes-Watson & Pranis, *Heart of Hope,* pp. 202–204.

7.7 Student and Teacher Class Assessment Circle

PURPOSE To strengthen the pedagogical work of the classroom and to model how to engage in assessing the classroom's work and relationships constructively.

MATERIALS Talking piece, bell or sound maker, centerpiece items, values and guidelines from previous Circles.

PREPARATION Arrange everyone in a circle of chairs with no other furniture.

Welcome to the space of the Circle.

MINDFULNESS MOMENT *Pause, breathe, and listen to the sound.*

OPENING See Appendix 2 or create your own.

Remind the group of the values and guidelines they have created in previous Circles.

INTRODUCE "ROUNDS" A round is a pass of the talking piece around the Circle. The keeper poses a question and, as a participant, usually answers first and then passes the talking piece to the person to their left or to their right. On the first round, participants are invited to say their name as well as respond to the question. Remember, it is always okay for a participant to pass.

CHECK-IN ROUND *How are you doing today? Is there anything particular on your mind that you would like the Circle to be aware of?*

> **MAIN ACTIVITY** Assessing What Is Working and What Could Be Improved in the Classroom

ROUND *What is working well in our relationships in this classroom between students and the teacher and among students?*

ROUND *Where do we have challenges in the relationships in this classroom?*

ROUND *What is the teacher doing well in the teaching and learning in this classroom?*

ROUND *What are the students doing well in the teaching and learning in this classroom?*

ROUND *What is confusing or difficult in the teaching and learning in this classroom?*

ROUND *What suggestions do you have to continue to grow in our relationships and our teaching and learning?*

ROUND *What can you do personally to support growth in our relationships and success in the teaching and learning?*

Summarize ideas and any commitments that may have been made.

CHECK-OUT ROUND *How do you feel about our Circle today?*

CLOSING See Appendix 2 or create your own.

Thank everyone for participating in the Circle today!

7.8 Parent–Teacher Conference Circle

PURPOSE To empower parents to sit in the conference process as an equal; to more fully access the wisdom of the parents about the student; to strengthen the relationship between the family and the school.

MATERIALS Talking piece, bell or sound maker.

PREPARATION Arrange everyone in a circle of chairs with no other furniture.

Welcome to the space of the Circle.

MINDFULNESS MOMENT *Pause, breathe, and listen to the sound.*

OPENING See Appendix 2 or create your own.

Introduce the talking piece and the way it works.

INTRODUCE "ROUNDS" A round is a pass of the talking piece around the Circle. The keeper poses a question and, as a participant, usually answers first and then passes the talking piece to the person to their left or to their right. On the first round, participants are invited to say their name as well as respond to the question. Remember, it is always okay for a participant to pass.

CHECK-IN ROUND *How are you feeling right now?*

> **MAIN ACTIVITY Assessing a Student's Strengths, Difficulties, and Options for Support**

ROUND *What are the strengths of (name of child)? What is special about (name of child)?*

ROUND *What do you see going well for (name of child) in school?*

ROUND *Do you have anything to add or want to respond to what others have said?*

ROUND *Is (name of child) having any difficulties in school?*

ROUND *Do you have anything to add or want to respond to what others have said?*

ROUND *What suggestions do you have to increase (name of child)'s success?*

ROUND *Do you have any other ideas to increase his/her success?*

ROUND *Is there anything else we should talk about?*

Clarify the expectations of all parties. Identify any unresolved concerns and how they will be dealt with.

CHECK-OUT ROUND *What do you appreciate about the family and about the school as we work together?*

CLOSING See Appendix 2 or create your own.

Thank everyone for participating in the Circle today!

7.9 How Are the Children? Circle

PURPOSE To stimulate a deep reflection on the state of the children; to engage adults in committing to improving the state of the children.

MATERIALS Talking piece, bell or sound maker, centerpiece items, "How Are the Children?" reading, small stuffed animals for group juggle, values and guidelines from a previous Circle.

PREPARATION Arrange everyone in a circle of chairs with no other furniture.

Welcome to the space of the Circle.

MINDFULNESS MOMENT Pause, breathe, and listen to the sound.

SUGGESTED OPENING Group juggle with small stuffed animals (see Appendix 2, Section IV, page 390).

INTRODUCE "ROUNDS" A round is a pass of the talking piece around the Circle. The keeper poses a question and, as a participant, usually answers first and then passes the talking piece to the person to their left or to their right. On the first round, participants are invited to say their name as well as respond to the question. Remember, it is always okay for a participant to pass.

ROUND What does the group juggle activity bring to mind for you?

OBSERVE As many of you noted, the hectic nature of our lives has us juggling lots of things. We cannot do it alone—we need one another. And play, humor, and laughter are very important for our well-being and the well-being of the children. This activity reminds us of play, which is a critical activity for healthy child and adult development.

Remind the group of values and guidelines they have created in previous Circles.

CHECK-IN ROUND How has your day been so far today?

> **MAIN ACTIVITY Assessing the Collective Well-Being of Children in a Classroom or School**

Read "And How Are the Children?" (see Appendix 2, Section I: Children & Ancestors, page 366).

Allow a few moments of silence to absorb the reading.

ROUND How would you answer the question, "How are the children?" about the children in this school?

ROUND I will pass the talking piece again for you to add to what you said or to respond to what others have said.

ROUND On a scale of 1 to 10—1 means the children are in great danger and 10 means the children are completely well and thriving—what number would you assign to the children of this school or of your classroom?

ROUND What could you do to move that number one notch (e.g., from a 3 to a 4 or from a 6 to a 7) for at least some of the children?

ROUND What can we do as a school community to help keep this question "How are the children?" at the center of our work?

CHECK-OUT ROUND Do you have anything else you would like to say about our Circle today?

CLOSING See Appendix 2 or create your own.

Thank everyone for participating in the Circle today!

7.10 Exploring Our Core Assumptions Circle

PURPOSE To reflect on our deep beliefs; to raise awareness of our underlying beliefs so we can become more intentional about our behaviors; to explore differences in deep beliefs.

MATERIALS Talking piece, bell or sound maker, centerpiece items, values and guidelines from previous Circles, Core Assumptions worksheet for each participant.

BEFORE THE CIRCLE Distribute copies of the Core Assumptions worksheet to the participants, asking them to read and fill out the worksheet before the Circle.

PREPARATION Arrange everyone in a circle of chairs with no other furniture.

Welcome to the space of the Circle.

MINDFULNESS MOMENT *Pause, breathe, and listen to the sound.*

OPENING See Appendix 2 or create your own.

Remind the group of the values and guidelines they have created in previous Circles.

INTRODUCE "ROUNDS" A round is a pass of the talking piece around the Circle. The keeper poses a question and, as a participant, usually answers first and then passes the talking piece to the person to their left or to their right. On the first round, participants are invited to say their name as well as respond to the question. Remember, it is always okay for a participant to pass.

CHECK-IN ROUND *How has your day been going today?*

> **MAIN ACTIVITY** Reflecting on Our Core Assumptions and Their Role in Our Lives

ROUND *In reading and thinking about the Core Assumptions, did you have any physical reaction? Emotional reaction? Mental reaction? Spiritual reaction? How did it feel to work on this?*

ROUND *Choose one of the core assumptions and tell us about your reaction to that assumption. Does it resonate for you or does it not feel like your truth? What images come up for you related to that Core Assumption? What do you want to say about that assumption?*

ROUND *As the talking piece comes this time, I invite you to share additional thoughts or respond to what you are hearing from others.*

ROUND *What other core assumptions, not in this list, are important guideposts for you in your work with children and young people?*

ROUND *Do you find it useful to spend time thinking about core assumptions?*

CHECK-OUT ROUND *Do you have anything you would like to say as we close our Circle?*

CLOSING See Appendix 2 or create your own.

Thank everyone for participating in the Circle today!

Core Assumptions Worksheet

The following are the Core Assumptions of this book, *Circle Forward*. Please read each one and then assess the degree to which it fits your own beliefs or not by ranking the assumption on a scale of 1 to 5: 1 means DO NOT AGREE AT ALL and 5 means COMPLETELY AGREE. At the end, we invite you to identify your own Core Assumptions that might be different from these.

1. The true self in everyone is good, wise, and powerful.

We believe that everyone has a self that is good, wise, powerful, and always there, always present. Everyone has a core self. It is in you, your students, and the adults you work with. The nature of the core self is wise, kind, just, good, and powerful. The core self cannot be destroyed. No matter what someone has done in the past and no matter what has happened to him or her in the past, the core self remains as good, wise, and powerful as the day he or she was born.

This model of the self distinguishes doing and being. What we do is not the whole of who we are. Our core selves are not always reflected in our actions or feelings. But beneath the acts and masks we humans adopt is a deeper healthier self.

1	2	3	4	5
disagree				**agree**

COMMENT _____

_____

2. The world is profoundly interconnected.

According to chaos theory, when a butterfly flaps its wings in South America, the wind patterns change in North America. This points to the interconnectedness of natural forces around the globe. Climate change is another visible reminder of interconnectedness within nature. We may not always be aware of the impact of our actions on our environment, but we must eventually realize that our actions have consequences.

In our human relationships, we are every bit as profoundly interconnected. When Native Peoples say, "we are all related," they mean that human beings are connected to all living creatures and are part of the natural world. Traditional African society uses the term "ubuntu" to express the idea that each of us is fundamentally a part of the whole and hence each other. It translates: "I am because we are."

1	2	3	4	5
disagree				**agree**

COMMENT _____

_____

3. All human beings have a deep desire to be in good relationship.

We believe that all people want to love and be loved and that all people want to be respected. This may not be what they show in their behavior particularly when they have not been loved and respected by others. But, at our core, we all desire to be in good relationship with others. Nel Noddings reminds us that children "listen to people who matter to them and to whom they matter."

1	2	3	4	5
disagree				agree

COMMENT _____
_____

4. All humans have gifts, and everyone is needed for what they bring.

According to some Indigenous teachings, each child is born with four unique gifts from Mother Earth. It is the responsibility of the adults to recognize these four unique gifts and to help youth cultivate them, so the child may grow up to realize his or her individual purpose in life and use these gifts to help others. According to a Swahili proverb, the greatest gift we can give each other is not to share our riches with others but to reveal their own riches to themselves. All of us need to feel we have something valuable to contribute to others.

We believe that, in human societies, all gifts are indispensable to the well-being of the whole. This is as true for families as it is for organizations. Different people are needed because different people see and do things differently. We require the contribution of diverse talents, personalities, and perspectives to find creative and innovative solutions to meeting our needs.

1	2	3	4	5
disagree				agree

COMMENT _____
_____

5. Everything we need to make positive change is already here.

We believe that everything we need to make positive change within our school community is already here. This is because human creativity and human commitment are our greatest treasures and our greatest hope.

We believe school communities hold rich reservoirs of talent and wisdom that are waiting to be accessed. We need to learn how to tap into the wisdom and creative energy of all our human resources: students, teachers, parents, extended families, administrators, secretaries, custodial staff, school resource officers and many more who are present within our community. By doing this, we liberate the potential of our collective power to create the world we desire. We are the ones we have been waiting for.

1	2	3	4	5
disagree				agree

COMMENT _____
_____

6. Human beings are holistic.

In the English language, the words "health" and "whole" come from the same root. Our minds, bodies, emotions, and spirits are in all that we do. These are equally important parts of us as human beings—each part provides ways of knowing and sources of both knowledge and wisdom.

Learning is a holistic process engaging body, heart, and spirit as well as the mind in an integrated process. Modern brain research tells us that information with emotional content is more deeply etched in our memory than information without emotional content. It is often said that children don't care what you know until they know you care.

In this approach to creating healthy schools, we seek to engage all parts of ourselves: our intellect, emotions, spirit, and body. We seek to attend to the needs of each of these parts of ourselves, so that we can nurture the multiple intelligences that are a part of our capacities as humans.

1	2	3	4	5
disagree				agree

COMMENT _____

_____

7. We need practices to build habits of living from the core self.

We believe we need practices that help us connect with our core self, so we can live aligned with our values and build healthy relationships in classrooms and school communities. The quality of the relationships among students and adults within a school community is a matter of intention: if we choose to nurture positive relationships, they will flourish.

The Circles in this guide offer many time-tested means to reconnect with our healthy core self and to nurture positive relationships within the school environment. The peacemaking Circle has a natural affinity with practices that feed and nurture "the good wolf" in all of us. The magic of Circle is in the practice of Circle.

1	2	3	4	5
disagree				agree

COMMENT _____

_____

MY OWN CORE ASSUMPTIONS

1. _____
2. _____
3. _____
4. _____
5. _____

OTHER COMMENTS

_____
_____
_____
_____
_____
_____
_____
_____
_____
_____
_____
_____
_____
_____

Assessing Our Progress in Moving toward a Restorative School Culture Circle

7.11

PURPOSE To reflect on ways that the shift to a restorative culture becomes visible in the school community; to reflect on successes and challenges in moving toward a restorative school culture; to support continuing growth and self-reflection among staff.

MATERIALS Talking piece, bell or sound maker, centerpiece items, values and guidelines from previous Circles.

PREPARATION Arrange everyone in a circle of chairs with no other furniture.

Welcome to the space of the Circle.

MINDFULNESS MOMENT *Pause, breathe, and listen to the sound.*

OPENING See Appendix 2 or create your own.

Remind the group of the values and guidelines they have created in previous Circles.

INTRODUCE "ROUNDS" A round is a pass of the talking piece around the Circle. The keeper poses a question and, as a participant, usually answers first and then passes the talking piece to the person to their left or to their right. On the first round, participants are invited to say their name as well as respond to the question. Remember, it is always okay for a participant to pass.

CHECK-IN ROUND *Share a recent moment of gratifying connection with a student or colleague.*

> **MAIN ACTIVITY Assessing Positive Steps and Addressing Frustrations in Making The Shift**

ROUND *What do you look for in student behavior that indicates that the students are applying a restorative approach in their relationships?*

ROUND *We will do another round to add to what you said before and to give you a chance to respond to what others have said.*

ROUND *What do you look for in adult behavior that indicates that the adults are applying a restorative approach in their relationships?*

ROUND *Where are you seeing some signs of that shift toward a restorative culture in our school? Please share an example or story.*

ROUND *Are there places where you are feeling frustration in trying to implement this shift?*

ROUND *What would be helpful to you in maintaining your energy and commitment to this shift?*

CHECK-OUT ROUND *What can you take from this Circle that is helpful to you?*

CLOSING See Appendix 2 or create your own.

Thank everyone for participating in the Circle today!

Challenge of Change Circle

7.12

PURPOSE To reduce the stress of change; to increase the positive potential of change; to increase resilience in the face of change; to build relationships.

MATERIALS Talking piece, bell or sound maker, centerpiece items, values and guidelines from prior Circles, small stuffed animals for opening.

PREPARATION Arrange everyone in a circle of chairs with no other furniture.

Welcome to the space of the Circle.

MINDFULNESS MOMENT *Pause, breathe, and listen to the sound.*

SUGGESTED OPENING Group Juggle from Appendix 2, Section IV, p. 390, or create your own.

Remind the group of the values and guidelines they have created in previous Circles.

INTRODUCE "ROUNDS" A round is a pass of the talking piece around the Circle. The keeper poses a question and, as a participant, usually answers first and then passes the talking piece to the person to their left or to their right. On the first round, participants are invited to say their name as well as respond to the question. Remember, it is always okay for a participant to pass.

CHECK-IN ROUND *Please share with us a source of joy in your life right now and a source of stress.*

> **MAIN ACTIVITY Reflecting on Change—Its Benefits, Challenges, and Calls for Support**

ROUND *What are the major changes you are experiencing in our school?*

ROUND *What is exciting or energizing about this change?*

ROUND *What are you grieving regarding this change? What loss is there in this change?*

ROUND *When change feels overwhelming, what are your coping strategies?*

ROUND *What can we do as a community to support one another through the process of change?*

On any of these rounds, you might do a second pass for additional thoughts.

CHECK-OUT ROUND *How was this Circle for you?*

CLOSING See Appendix 2 or create your own.

Thank everyone for participating in the Circle today!

MODULE 8

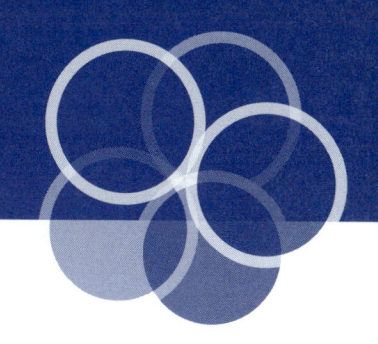

Engaging Parents and the Wider Community

Creating a restorative school culture involves not just the school, but also the families of students and the larger community surrounding the school. Schools operate in the context of these relationships and, as Core Assumption 2 suggests, everything is connected. The quality of these relationships impacts the effectiveness of the school.

A healthy partnership between the school and parents goes a long way toward ensuring school success for the student. Healthy partnerships are relationships of equality based on respect. As noted in our Core Assumption 4, "We believe that, in human societies, all gifts are indispensable to the well-being of the whole. Interdependence is essential for survival." We need everyone's gifts to do this job of nurturing and teaching our children well. No one person or institution can do this alone.

In many schools, there are significant barriers to that family-school partnership. Some parents are struggling daily to meet basic needs and have little time to focus on the partnership. Some families are intimidated by schools because of negative feelings from their own school experiences, which trigger a sense of inadequacy. Many parents underestimate the importance of their wisdom about the child and their influence on the child.

The Circle opens a space for the parent voice that is so often missing in parent-school communication, in spite of great efforts by schools to include that voice. The capacity of Circle for empowerment and voice is profound. Circles create a space for building a healthy relationship between parents and the school and for empowering parents to bring all of their gifts and knowledge to the process of educating their child. Circles also offer a space to build relationships among parents to support them in the very challenging job of raising children.

The school and the wider community also need one another's gifts. Schools have a direct impact on the strength of a community and the quality of life in a community. The community also has a direct impact on the school. Circles allow both the school and community to be more intentional about ensuring that the impact in both directions is a positive one.

> Parents and community members involved in Circles with the school will gain skills that they can use in other parts of their lives.

Engaging both parents and the wider community in Circles reinforces the use of Circles in the school. When students see the process used outside of school and with adults, it conveys a message that this process is a fundamental process for life, not just for schools. Parents and community members involved in Circles with the school will gain skills that they can use in other parts of their lives. The ripple effects in community strengthen the community, which in turn strengthens the school in a cycle of continual learning and growth.

The following Circles are just a beginning for developing a Circle practice among parents and community members. Growth of that practice will likely come from the parents and community identifying their own needs and interests in using Circles.

Parent Circle
Introduction to the Circle Process

8.1

PURPOSE To provide a learning opportunity for parents to experience and understand the Circle process and to build relationships among parents.

MATERIALS Talking piece, bell or sound maker, centerpiece items, paper plates, and markers.

PREPARATION Arrange everyone in a circle of chairs with no other furniture.

Welcome to the space of the Circle.

MINDFULNESS MOMENT *Pause, breathe, and listen to the sound.*

EXPLAIN *Circles always begin with an intentional opening to help us focus on being fully present, to release distractions not related to our purpose here, and to slow down from the hectic pace of life.*

SUGGESTED OPENING *Meditate with deep breathing and relaxation. Now picture each of your children on the day they were born. Remember the feelings you had when you held your child for the first time for each of your children. Breathe slowly, holding the memory. Now bring your focus to this time and place, still feeling the warmth of that moment.*

INTRODUCE THE TALKING PIECE Explain in detail how it works and the meaning of the particular talking piece you are using.

INTRODUCE "ROUNDS" A round is a pass of the talking piece around the Circle. The keeper poses a question and, as a participant, usually answers first and then passes the talking piece to the person to their left or to their right. On the first round, participants are invited to say their name as well as respond to the question. Remember, it is always okay for a participant to pass.

ROUND *Tell us who you are and how you came to choose this school or this community as a place to live.*

Ask participants to think of a value they would like to pass on to their children—a value that is important to them in how they live their lives. Ask them to write the value on the paper plate at their seat with the marker in large letters.

ROUND *Please share the value that you wrote and tell us what it means to you and why it is important to pass this value on to your children. Then place your value in the center so that everyone can see it.*

At the end of the round, thank everyone for sharing their values.

EXPLAIN *These values are the foundation of the Circle process. They help us to be together in a good way for the well-being of our children.*

EXPLAIN *In addition to the values you have brought to the Circle, we would like to offer several guidelines for us:*

1. *Respect the talking piece;*
2. *Speak & listen with respect;*
3. *Speak & listen from the heart;*
4. *Be present; and*
5. *Honor privacy.*

Write these guidelines down on a board or flip chart.

ROUND *Are these guidelines okay with you? Do you want to add anything to our guidelines to help us have a good conversation?*

Add any suggestions to the list and check with the group to see if everyone is okay with the additional guidelines.

EXPLAIN *Each time we meet in Circle, we will bring these values and guidelines back to help us work well together on behalf of the children.*

MAIN ACTIVITY Getting to Know the Children through Their Parents' Reflections about Them

EXPLAIN *The reason we come together is for our children, so we will now have a chance for each of you to introduce your children to the rest of us.*

ROUND *Tell us about your family, how many children you have, their names and ages, and which ones attend this school.*

ROUND *Tell us something special about each of your child(ren)—what is your favorite thing about each of your children?*

ROUND *Tell us about some of the challenges your child(ren) have struggled with as they have developed.*

ROUND *Tell us about a way in which your child(ren) have been teachers to you.*

ROUND *Tell us a funny story about your child(ren).*

THANK EVERYONE *Thank you for introducing all of us to your children. The Circle is a special space for talking about the things that matter most to us. Our children matter deeply to us. It is lovely to get to know your children through your eyes. Circles are a place for deep reflection, for paying attention to our values and for humor. We have had all of that in our Circle today.*

CHECK-OUT ROUND *What are your closing thoughts about this Circle?*

CLOSING See Appendix 2 or create your own.

Thank everyone for participating in the Circle today!

8.2 Parent Circle
Building Support in Small Groups

● ● ● ● ● ●

PURPOSE To create small, ongoing groups of parents who can support one another in and out of Circle; to strengthen parents' ability to engage effectively with the school.

BEFORE THE CIRCLE Recruit parents interested in engaging in a small group process with other parents. Organize those interested in groups of eight or ten. Invite parents who are coming to the Circle to bring an object that symbolizes family to them that will be placed in the center during the Circle.

MATERIALS Talking piece, bell or sound maker, centerpiece items, paper plates, and markers.

PREPARATION Arrange everyone in a circle of chairs with no other furniture.

Welcome to the space of the Circle.

MINDFULNESS MOMENT *Pause, breathe, and listen to the sound.*

OPENING See Appendix 2 or create your own.

INTRODUCE THE TALKING PIECE Explain in detail how it works and the meaning of the particular talking piece you are using.

INTRODUCE "ROUNDS" A round is a pass of the talking piece around the Circle. The keeper poses a question and, as a participant, usually answers first and then passes the talking piece to the person to their left or to their right. On the first round, participants are invited to say their name as well as respond to the question. Remember, it is always okay for a participant to pass.

ROUND *Tell us who you are, how long you have been involved in the school and who are your children (ages, grades)?*

Ask participants to think of a value they would like to have for this group—a value that is important to them in how they relate to others. Ask them to write the value on the paper plate at their seat with the marker in large letters.

ROUND *Please share the value that you wrote and tell us what it means to you and why it is important for the group. Then place your value in the center so that everyone can see it.*

Explain that, in addition to the values they have brought to the Circle, we would like to offer several guidelines for us:

> 1. Respect the talking piece;
> 2. Speak & listen with respect;
> 3. Speak & listen from the heart;
> 4. Be present; and
> 5. Honor privacy.

Write these guidelines down on a board or flip chart.

ROUND *Are these guidelines okay with you? Do you want to add anything to our guidelines to help us have a good conversation?*

Add any suggestions to the list and check with the group to see if everyone is okay with the additional guidelines.

EXPLAIN *Each time we meet in Circle, we will bring these values and guidelines back to help us work well together on behalf of the children.*

MAIN ACTIVITY Reflecting on Parenting and the Support Parents Need

ROUND *If you brought an object that symbolizes family to you, please tell us about that object. If you did not bring an object, can you think of an object and tell us about it?*

ROUND *Tell us about what it means to you to be a parent?*

ROUND *Tell us about ways your children are like you and ways they are different.*

ROUND *Tell us about a time when you supported someone who was struggling as a parent.*

ROUND *Tell us about a time when you needed the support of someone to help you parent well.*

ROUND *In what ways do you think this group of parents might help one another in their role of parent?*

ROUND *What would be the next steps for you as a group?*

Summarize the plans or ideas presented. Clarify expectations about what will happen next.

CHECK-OUT ROUND *What are your closing thoughts about this Circle?*

CLOSING *See Appendix 2 or create your own.*

Thank everyone for participating in the Circle today!

8.3 Parent Circle
Feedback to the School

PURPOSE To enhance parent-school communication; to offer parents an opportunity to provide feedback on the school experience of their children; to build relationships among parents.

MATERIALS Talking piece, bell or sound maker, centerpiece items, ribbon for opening, paper plates, and markers.

PREPARATION Arrange everyone in a Circle with no other furniture. Place ribbons, quarter inch wide, 1 yard long on each chair; put paper plates and markers at each chair.

Welcome to the space of the Circle.

MINDFULNESS MOMENT *Pause, breathe, and listen to the sound.*

SUGGESTED OPENING Role-model ribbon exercise (see Appendix 2, Section III, page 386).

INTRODUCE THE TALKING PIECE How it works and the meaning of the particular talking piece you are using.

INTRODUCE "ROUNDS" A round is a pass of the talking piece around the Circle. The keeper poses a question and, as a participant, usually answers first and then passes the talking piece to the person to their left or to their right. On the first round, participants are invited to say their name as well as respond to the question. Remember, it is always okay for a participant to pass.

ROUND *Tell us who you are, how long you have lived in the community, and who are your children (ages, grades).*

Ask participants to think of a value that they try to teach children by modeling—a value that is important to them in how they relate to children. Ask them to write the value on the paper plate at their seat with the marker in large letters.

ROUND *Please share the value that you wrote and tell us what it means to you and why it is important. Then place your value in the center so that everyone can see it.*

EXPLAIN *In addition to the values you have brought to the Circle, we would like to offer several guidelines for us:*

> 1. Respect the talking piece;
> 2. Speak & listen with respect;
> 3. Speak & listen from the heart;
> 4. Be present; and
> 5. Honor privacy.

Write these guidelines down on a board or flip chart.

ROUND *Are these guidelines okay with you? Do you want to add anything to our guidelines to help us have a good conversation?*

Add any suggestions to the list and check with the group to see if everyone is okay with the additional guidelines.

EXPLAIN *We are here in this Circle on behalf of the children. The mentors we named in our opening are role models for us in how to serve our children. Our values are the light to help us see the way forward in serving our children. Let's talk now about how the children are doing.*

MAIN ACTIVITY Sharing What Is Working and Not Working for the Child(ren)

ROUND *What is working well at school for your child(ren)?*

ROUND *Is there anything you would like to add about what is working well?*

ROUND *What is not working well or is a struggle for your child(ren) at school?*

ROUND *Is there anything you would like to add about what is not working well?*

ROUND *What is one step you would like to take to help your child(ren) in school?*

ROUND *What is one step you would like to see the school take to help your child(ren)?*

CHECK-OUT ROUND *Do you have anything else you would like to say about our Circle today?*

CLOSING See Appendix 2 or create your own.

Thank everyone for participating in the Circle today!

8.4 Family-School Engagement Circle

PURPOSE To support the development of strong school–family relationships to maximize the success of the child(ren) in school; to increase clarity about the roles of family and school staff.

MATERIALS Talking piece, bell or sound maker, centerpiece items, paper plates, and markers.

PREPARATION Arrange everyone in a circle of chairs with no furniture.

Welcome to the space of the Circle.

MINDFULNESS MOMENT *Pause, breathe, and listen to the sound.*

SUGGESTED OPENING Web activity (see Appendix 2, Section III, page 384).

INTRODUCE "ROUNDS" A round is a pass of the talking piece around the Circle. The keeper poses a question and, as a participant, usually answers first and then passes the talking piece to the person to their left or to their right. On the first round, participants are invited to say their name as well as respond to the question. Remember, it is always okay for a participant to pass.

> **MAIN ACTIVITY   Sharing Needs on Both Sides—Parents and School Staff**

ROUND *Tell us who you are, how long you have been associated with the school, and what your hopes for this Circle are.*

Invite everyone to think of one value they think is very important in the school-family relationship and to write that value on the paper plate under their chair.

ROUND *Please share the value you have written—a value you think is very important in the school-family relationship—and why that value is important. When you have finished explaining your value, please place your value in the center. I will go first …*

When the round is finished, read all the values and thank everyone for bringing these values to the Circle.

EXPLAIN *In addition to the values you have brought to the Circle, we are suggesting several guidelines for how we can have the conversation.* Offer the following guidelines:

> 1. Respect the talking piece;
> 2. Speak & listen with respect;
> 3. Speak & listen from the heart;
> 4. Be present; and
> 5. Honor privacy.

Write these guidelines down on a board or flip chart.

ROUND *Are these guidelines okay with you? Do you want to add anything to our guidelines to help us have a good conversation?* Add any suggestions to the list and check with the group to see if everyone is okay with the additional guidelines.

EXPLAIN *These values and guidelines create a very strong foundation for our work together on behalf of all of the children. When we see things differently, these values and guidelines will help us listen carefully and find our way through our differences.*

ROUND *Why does family engagement with the school matter?*

ROUND *On this round, I want just the parents to respond. What do you need from the school to support your full engagement in your child's education?* Keep notes on a board or notebook.

ROUND *This time around, everyone is invited to respond. Parents can add more thoughts on what they need, and school staff can respond to what they have heard from the parents.* Continue to keep notes on important ideas.

ROUND *This time around, I want just the school staff to respond. What do you need from the family to support your work with the students?* Continue with notes.

ROUND *This time around, everyone is invited to respond. School staff can add more thoughts on what they need, and parents can respond to what they have heard from school staff.* Continue the notes.

ROUND *Where have you experienced difficulties or challenges around family-school engagement? What are the barriers to family-school engagement?*

Do a second pass on this question if there is a lot of energy or if it feels like there is more to be said.

ROUND *Identify one step you can take that will help reduce one of the barriers around family-school engagement. Keep notes.*

Review the key ideas shared and the actions proposed.

ROUND *Where would you like this conversation to go from here?*

Summarize suggestions; clarify what will happen next.

CHECK-OUT ROUND *What are your closing thoughts about this Circle?*

CLOSING See Appendix 2 or create your own.

Thank everyone for participating in the Circle today!

8.5 Looking at Our Own Relationship to School Circle

PURPOSE To increase awareness of the impact of the parent experience in school; to improve relationships between school and parents; to build relationships among parents.

MATERIALS Talking piece, bell or sound maker, centerpiece items.

PREPARATION Arrange everyone in a circle of chairs with no other furniture.

Welcome to the space of the Circle.

MINDFULNESS MOMENT *Pause, breathe, and listen to the sound.*

OPENING See Appendix 2 or create your own.

INTRODUCE THE TALKING PIECE Explain in detail how it works and the meaning of the particular talking piece you are using.

INTRODUCE "ROUNDS" A round is a pass of the talking piece around the Circle. The keeper poses a question and, as a participant, usually answers first and then passes the talking piece to the person to their left or to their right. On the first round, participants are invited to say their name as well as respond to the question. Remember, it is always okay for a participant to pass.

ROUND *Tell us who you are, and tell us about your involvement in this school.*

ROUND *Name a value that is important to you when you are having a discussion about your children.* Write a list of those values as the participants name them and then place the list in the center.

Review the basic Circle guidelines.

MAIN ACTIVITY Recalling Our Own Experiences in School

EXPLAIN *The Circle helps us access the collective wisdom of us all. Our own life experience is a source of wisdom and insight into the challenges we may face today. We are going to explore our own life experiences in school so we can better help the children.*

ROUND *When you enter a school building as an adult, how does your body react physically? What sensations occur in your body going into a school?*

ROUND *When you were a child in school, what was the best part of your school experience?*

ROUND *Is there anything you would like to add about what went well for you in school?*

ROUND *When you were a child in school, what did not go well? What was hard for you?*

ROUND *Is there anything you would like to add about what did not go well for you in school?*

ROUND *Do you think your child's experience of school is similar to or different from your own?*

ROUND *Do you see any ways to use the wisdom of the experience in this Circle to support your child in school?*

CHECK-OUT ROUND *Do you have anything else you would like to say about our Circle today?*

CLOSING See Appendix 2 or create your own.

Thank everyone for participating in the Circle today!

8.6 Community–School Partnership Circle

PURPOSE To support the development of strong community-school relationships to maximize the success of the child(ren) in school; to strengthen the community by integrating the school into the community.

MATERIALS Talking piece, bell or sound maker, large children's floor puzzle with enough pieces for the number of people you may have in the Circle, paper plates and markers, paper and pens or pencils.

PREPARATION Arrange everyone in a circle of chairs with no other furniture.

Welcome to the space of the Circle.

MINDFULNESS MOMENT Pause, breathe, and listen to the sound.

INTRODUCE "ROUNDS" A round is a pass of the talking piece around the Circle. The keeper poses a question and, as a participant, usually answers first and then passes the talking piece to the person to their left or to their right. On the first round, participants are invited to say their name as well as respond to the question. Remember, it is always okay for a participant to pass.

MAIN ACTIVITY Using the Puzzle Metaphor to Strengthen the School-Community Partnership

OPENING Have pieces of a large floor puzzle in a basket. Pass the basket around, inviting each person to take one piece. Keep passing until all the pieces are taken.

INTRODUCE THE TALKING PIECE Explain in detail how it works and the meaning of the particular talking piece you are using.

ROUND *Look at the pieces of the puzzle you have and tell us what you see.*

Invite everyone to come to the center with their pieces and put the puzzle together.

ROUND *Introduce yourself, tell us how long you have been part of this community, and talk about how it felt to put the puzzle together.*

INVITE EVERYONE *Think of one value you think is very important in the community-school partnership and to write that value on the paper plate that is under your chair.*

ROUND *Please share the value you have written—a value you think is very important in the community-school partnership—and why that value is important. When you have finished, please place your value in the center.*

When the round is finished read all the values. Thank everyone for bringing these values to our work together.

ROUND *How do you see your role in this community? And how do you see your role in the school?*

INVITE PARTICIPANTS *Write down five words that describe how you would like the relationship between the school and the community to be.*

ROUND *Please share the five words you have written down. Record the words on a board or flip chart.*

NOTE *This is our vision for a community-school partnership.*

ROUND *Share an experience, here or in another community, where a school-community partnership significantly benefited students.*

ROUND *What can we learn from those experiences? What conditions supported the effectiveness of that partnership?*

ROUND *What are the strengths of this community that can benefit students?*

ROUND *What are the strengths of this school that can benefit the community?*

ROUND *What is your piece of the puzzle in creating strong community-school partnerships?*

ROUND *How can we weave together our values, our vision of community-school partnerships, and our strengths to serve the well-being of us all?*

Summarize the ideas and next steps raised during the rounds.

CHECK-OUT ROUND *What are your closing thoughts about this Circle?*

SUGGESTED CLOSING *Web activity (see Appendix 2, Section III, page 384).*

Thank everyone for participating in the Circle today!

8.7 Building Bridges to a New Immigrant Community Circle

PURPOSE To build relationships with adults in a new immigrant community to strengthen the ties between school and family; to learn about the culture and circumstances of the immigrant community in order to effectively support their children in school.

BEFORE THE CIRCLE Recruit a few members of the immigrant community to help organize and conduct the Circle. Ask for their advice regarding opening, centerpiece, and talking piece for the Circle. Ask for their advice about how to invite members of the immigrant community to a dialogue with the school. Ask about any cultural protocol that might be incorporated into the welcome and opening of the Circle. Extend the invitation. Arrange for translation if that will be necessary.

MATERIALS talking piece, centerpiece items, bell or sound maker.

PREPARATION Arrange everyone in a circle of chairs with no other furniture.

Welcome to the space of the Circle.

MINDFULNESS MOMENT *Pause, breathe, and listen to the sound.*

OPENING Choose an opening based on conversations with members of the immigrant community.

INTRODUCE "ROUNDS" A round is a pass of the talking piece around the Circle. The keeper poses a question and, as a participant, usually answers first and then passes the talking piece to the person to their left or to their right. On the first round, participants are invited to say their name as well as respond to the question. Remember, it is always okay for a participant to pass.

> **MAIN ACTIVITY** Learning from Immigrant Community Members to Form Respectful Relations

ROUND *Please introduce yourself and tell us about your household—children or other family who live with you.*

ROUND *Name a value that is important to you when you are having a discussion about your children.* Write a list of those values as the participants name them, and then place the list in the center.

Review the basic Circle guidelines.

ROUND *Tell us about the country you come from. What were the good things about living there?*

ROUND *What circumstances made it necessary to leave that country?*

ROUND *What things are difficult to understand in this country?*

ROUND *What was your experience in schools in the country you came from?*

ROUND *What is important for the schools here to know or understand about your children?*

ROUND *What things would you want the school to do to be respectful of your culture?*

ROUND *Do you have an interest in an ongoing dialogue with the school? If so, what would be the best way to do that?*

Summarize any intentions for follow up.

CHECK-OUT ROUND *How do you feel about this Circle?*

CLOSING See Appendix 2 or create your own.

Thank everyone for participating in the Circle today!

8.8 IEP (Individualized Education Program) Circle

> Inclusion is key to the IEP process, both for the student and for planning for the individual's educational programming. Frequently, parents and teachers feel left out by the "special education experts," even though they see the child the most every day. The premise of inclusion in the Circle fits perfectly here—no one feels left out.
>
> — Joan Henke, *Individualized Education Plans Using the Circle Process*

PURPOSE To promote inclusion of all voices for equal participation in developing the IEP and to engage full ownership of the IEP by all key parties.

BEFORE THE CIRCLE Invite parent(s) to bring a talking piece that represents the child to the meeting.

MATERIALS Centerpiece items including some work by the child, bell or sound maker, paper plates and markers, talking piece in case parent(s) forget.

PREPARATION Arrange everyone in a circle of chairs with no other furniture.

Welcome to the space of the Circle.

MINDFULNESS MOMENT *Pause, breathe, and listen to the sound.*

OPENING See Appendix 2 or create your own.

INTRODUCE "ROUNDS" A round is a pass of the talking piece around the Circle. The keeper poses a question and, as a participant, usually answers first and then passes the talking piece to the person to their left or to their right. On the first round, participants are invited to say their name as well as respond to the question. Remember, it is always okay for a participant to pass.

> **MAIN ACTIVITY** Gathering Feedback on How the IEP Can Best Serve the Child's Learning

Explain how the talking piece works.

Ask the parent(s) to explain the talking piece they brought.

ROUND *Please tell us your name, your relationship to (name of child) and your favorite thing about (name of child).*

ASK PARTICIPANTS *Think about a value that is very important to you in your relationship to (name of child). Write that value on the paper plate with the marker.*

ROUND *Please share your value and tell us what it means to you and why it is very important in your relationship with (name of child). After you have shared, please put your value in the center of the Circle.*

Offer basic guidelines to the Circle. Ask if anyone wants any additions.

ROUND *What are (name of child)'s strengths?*

ROUND *What are (name of child)'s areas of improvement since the last IEP meeting?*

ROUND *What specific goals of the IEP do you feel have been achieved?*

ROUND *What do you think are appropriate future goals, and where should they fit in the IEP?*

Continue rounds about the future goals to explore different perspectives and to understand concerns, until participants reach consensus about the goals.

Complete the remaining IEP procedures.

CHECK-OUT ROUND *How do you feel about the Circle today?*

CLOSING *See Appendix 2 or create your own.*

Thank everyone for participating in the Circle today!

Based on Joan Henke, *Individualized Education Plans Using the Circle Process*, available on Jack Mangan's website, Restorative Measures in Schools, http://restorative.tripod.com/.

MODULE 9

Youth-Led and Peer-to-Peer Circles

DEVELOPING YOUTH AS LEADERS OF CIRCLES

Developing leadership skills is woven into every Circle. Every member of the Circle is responsible for the collective creation of the values and guidelines of the Circle, a very important leadership responsibility. Every member of the Circle has responsibility for maintaining a safe and respectful atmosphere in the Circle. Every member *is* the leader when they have the talking piece.

Circles and youth leadership are natural companions. We all need to be leaders in our own lives. Youth have a developmental need to take on more and more leadership in their own lives as they get older. They also have a need to contribute to their families and community. The Circle organically nurtures taking responsibility and looking out for the good of the collective—two very important characteristics of leadership. The Circle also engages collective responsibility for the task of the Circle, so that a "leader" in a Circle is not in control of the Circle and is not directive to others. Circles develop leadership based on "power with" rather than "power over." Youth feel empowered without taking power away from someone else.

As a starting point for sharing more Circle leadership with youth, we can give students the opportunity to make important decisions about parts of the Circle. Students can choose or bring talking pieces. They can choose what will be in the center of the Circle. They can do openings and closings. Students can also decide on important questions for the Circle to discuss. This is true for students of all ages.

It is very important to share leadership with all kinds of students, not just the ones who are well-behaved or high-performing. Circles can channel potentially negative leadership skills into constructive leadership experiences. The opportunity for youth Circle leadership is most impactful on school culture if it is widely available and not related to punishment or reward systems.

Engaging students in leadership roles in the Circle in this way increases ownership of the process and a commitment to engaging constructively in the process. It is helpful to move toward more and more student leadership in the Circle soon after students

> Youth have a developmental need to take on more and more leadership in their own lives as they get older.

> Circles can channel potentially negative leadership skills into constructive leadership experiences.

learn the process. Student leadership will institutionalize the power shift of Circles. Without student leadership there is significant risk that adults will unconsciously slip back into roles of authority or control.

Students can also plan and facilitate Circles. Students could lead most of the Circles in this book, if they have had experience in Circle and been trained in Circle facilitation. Joint training for facilitators with students and staff works very well. Some schools use peer-facilitated Circles to address student conflicts or behavior problems. The trust engendered by adults sharing power at this level with students has a dramatic impact on the school culture. Youth as Circle facilitators become active co-creators with the adults of a restorative school culture.

Additionally, the youths' experience as facilitators embeds the Circle in their skill set, which enhances the likelihood that they will transfer the skills to other parts of their lives. Youth who have led Circles are more likely to use Circles in their family, church, or neighborhood, multiplying the positive impact of the school on the community.

In any school, the young people have a culture among themselves that impacts the overall culture of the school. Youth-led Circles are a powerful way to transform the student-student culture. When students are encouraged by the adults in school to learn to facilitate Circles, they gain the confidence to initiate Circles among their peers, sometimes without adult involvement. They often use their new leadership skills to prevent conflict among peers in less formal ways as well. When young people see their peers in the role of facilitators, all young people feel more competent. Youth learn to trust their own capacity to find solutions to problems and difficulties.

As young people learn to use their voice in Circle, they learn to use their voice outside of Circle as well. As they learn the power of non-violent, dialogue-based conflict resolution, they learn to use those skills outside of Circle. As they learn self-reflection in Circle, they become more able to manage their emotions outside of Circle. Every school and every community needs the wisdom and creativity of the young people. Youth leadership of Circles creates space for that wisdom and creativity to emerge, strengthening the youth themselves and everyone involved in their lives.

While many of the Circles in this book can be facilitated by youth, we have included in Module 9 several model Circles that are designed specifically for youth to lead.

> Youth-led Circles are a powerful way to transform the student-student culture.

What Do Adults Need to Understand about Our Lives? Circle

9.1

PURPOSE To create space for young people to communicate with adults about important issues; to increase adult awareness of what young people experience; and to build relationships.

MATERIALS Talking piece, bell or sound maker, centerpiece items, values and guidelines from previous Circles.

PREPARATION Arrange everyone in a circle of chairs with no other furniture.

PARTICIPANTS Adults and young people; facilitated by young people.

The questions are designed for the young people in the Circle. Adults may just pass and listen, or they may reflect on what they are hearing from the young people.

Welcome to the space of the Circle.

MINDFULNESS MOMENT *Pause, breathe, and listen to the sound.*

OPENING See Appendix 2 or create your own.

Remind the group of the values and guidelines they have created in previous Circles.

INTRODUCE "ROUNDS" A round is a pass of the talking piece around the Circle. The keeper poses a question and, as a participant, usually answers first and then passes the talking piece to the person to their left or to their right. On the first round, participants are invited to say their name as well as respond to the question. Remember, it is always okay for a participant to pass.

ROUND *Introduce yourself and tell us about something you are grateful for in your life.*

> **MAIN ACTIVITY** Youth Expressing What Adults Do and Do Not Understand about Them

ROUND *What are the good things in your life that you want the adults to know about and understand?*

ROUND *What are the hard things in your life that you want the adults to understand?*

ROUND *What are the things adults need to understand about the general culture of you and your friends?*

ROUND *What do you find are the hardest things for adults to "get" about you?*

ROUND *What makes you hopeful about adults?*

Use a second round on any of these questions when there is a lot of energy or it feels like there is more to be said by the participants.

CHECK-OUT ROUND *What can you take from this Circle that is helpful to you?*

CLOSING See Appendix 2 or create your own.

Thank everyone for participating in the Circle today!

Visioning a Good Life Circle

PURPOSE To help participants express their sense of a desirable future and to assist them in recognizing ways to move in that direction.

MATERIALS Talking piece, bell or sound maker, centerpiece items, large roll of paper, magazines, scissors, glue, markers, glitter glue, miscellaneous art supplies.

PREPARATION Arrange everyone in a circle of chairs with no other furniture.

Welcome to the space of the Circle.

MINDFULNESS MOMENT *Pause, breathe, and listen to the sound.*

OPENING *Slowly* read the following visualization:

Take a deep breath—continue to breathe deeply and slowly in a comfortable way. You may close your eyes or use a soft focus on the floor or wall. Notice your breath going in and out. With each out-breath let your body relax a little more. Shoulders relax . . . neck relaxes . . . arms and hands relax . . . legs and feet relax . . . face relaxes. Continue to breathe deeply and slowly in a comfortable way. Notice your breath going in and out. Now imagine we are ten years in the future. You have made good decisions in your life and are living in a way that feels good to you. You are connected to your core self and able to see the core self in others. See yourself in this life. (Pause) Notice the picture that comes to you of what this life is like. Notice the details of your life. Feel the inner peace that is part of your life in the future. Notice any particular parts of this life. (Pause) Now bring your attention back to your breathing. Feel your in-breath and out-breath. Notice your chair and become aware of others in the room with you. Gradually bring your awareness to our space here and this moment in time. Open your eyes when you are ready.

INTRODUCE ROUNDS A "round" is a pass of the talking piece around the Circle. The keeper poses a question and, as a participant, usually answers first and then passes the talking piece to the person to their left or to their right. On the first round, participants are invited to say their name as well as respond to the question. Remember, it is always okay for a participant to pass.

ROUND Introduce yourself and tell us about a positive characteristic you have as a person.

ROUND *Tell us one value you want to guide your life in the future.*

Review the basic Circle guidelines.

MAIN ACTIVITY Drawing a Future Image of Your Life and Reflecting on It

Unroll a long section of the paper (do two if the group is large.) Invite each participant to choose a spot to work on (use both sides of the roll) allowing sufficient space between people not to crowd one another. Invite them to use the art materials—gluing pictures or drawing, etc.—and return to the visualization they did in the opening and create an image of where they would like to be in ten years. Invite them to create images that capture the most important parts of their lives in ten years.

Allow sufficient time for them to work on their images. Call the participants together and have them walk around the paper looking at one another's images. Call them back to the Circle.

ROUND *I invite you to share any feelings or thoughts you have after doing this activity. How did it feel to imagine your future?*

ROUND *What did you notice about similarities and differences in your visions?*

ROUND *Do you know anyone who has the kind of life you visualized? If so, who is that and is that person a role model for you?*

ROUND *What are the benefits or good things of the kind of life you visualized?*

ROUND *Can you identify one change you can make in your life that would move you toward your vision?*

CHECK-OUT ROUND *How was this Circle for you today?*

CLOSING Either create your own closing or read a short quote by Gunilla Norris, "I want to birth a tomorrow that already loves me." Gunilla Norris is a Euro-American psychotherapist and published author of children's books, poetry, and books on spirituality.

Thank everyone for participating in the Circle today!

This activity is based on Boyes-Watson & Pranis, *Heart of Hope*, pp. 298–301.

Circle for Student Focus Groups on a School Issue or Policy

9.3

PURPOSE To engage students' meaningful participation on school issues; to generate students' discussion of an important school issue or policy; and to develop student leadership abilities.

MATERIALS Talking piece, bell or sound maker, centerpiece items.

PREPARATION Arrange everyone in a circle of chairs with no other furniture.

Welcome to the space of the Circle.

MINDFULNESS MOMENT *Pause, breathe, and listen to the sound.*

OPENING See Appendix 2 or create your own.

INTRODUCE "ROUNDS" A round is a pass of the talking piece around the Circle. The keeper poses a question and, as a participant, usually answers first and then passes the talking piece to the person to their left or to their right. On the first round, participants are invited to say their name as well as respond to the question. Remember, it is always okay for a participant to pass.

ROUND *Please introduce yourself and tell us one value you think is important regarding student input into the decisions of the school.*

Review the basic Circle guidelines.

MAIN ACTIVITY Gathering Student Views on a School Issue or Policy

Clarify the issue of concern or the policy question to be addressed in the Circle.

Inform the Circle that, if the Circle is okay with the idea, the information or concerns of the Circle will be shared with school personnel without identifying who said what, so that students will have input on the school's decision-making process. Tell the Circle you will check in with them about this again at the end of the Circle.

Clarify that this Circle will not be making decisions regarding the issue, but students will have the opportunity to share their perspectives.

ROUND *What do you know about (the issue or policy topic)?*

ROUND *Do you have concerns about (the issue or policy topic)? If you do, tell us about your concerns.*

ROUND *What is your greatest fear regarding (the issue or policy topic)?*

ROUND *What needs do you see that the school staff have around (the issue or policy topic)?*

ROUND *What do you think would be a creative and respectful way to handle (this issue or policy topic) that addresses your concerns and the needs of school staff?*

ROUND *Who else has good ideas about (the issue or policy topic)?*

ROUND *Do you have any final comments on the topic?*

Check again to see whether the Circle is okay with sharing key ideas and concerns with the school staff.

CHECK-OUT ROUND *How do you feel about our Circle today?*

CLOSING See Appendix 2 or create your own.

Thank everyone for participating in the Circle today!

Exploring Cultural Responsiveness in the School Circle

9.4

PURPOSE To provide feedback to school staff about the experience of students regarding cultural responsiveness; to create a safe space for students to discuss their concerns about cultural acceptance; to develop youth leadership in Circles.

MATERIALS Talking piece, bell or sound maker, centerpiece items, paper plates, and markers.

PREPARATION Arrange everyone in a circle of chairs with no other furniture.

Welcome to the space of the Circle.

MINDFULNESS MOMENT *Pause, breathe, and listen to the sound.*

OPENING See Appendix 2 or create your own.

INTRODUCE "ROUNDS" A round is a pass of the talking piece around the Circle. The keeper poses a question and, as a participant, usually answers first and then passes the talking piece to the person to their left or to their right. On the first round, participants are invited to say their name as well as respond to the question. Remember, it is always okay for a participant to pass.

CHECK-IN ROUND *What motivated you to get up this morning?*

ASK THE PARTICIPANTS *Think of two values that are important when one person is learning about another person's culture. Write these two values on the paper plate.*

ROUND *Please share the values you wrote on your plate and tell us why they are important. And then place your values in the center.*

Review the basic Circle guidelines.

> **MAIN ACTIVITY Reflecting on Respect for Other Cultures, Their Children, and Their Ways**

ROUND *Is your cultural identity an important part of who you are?*

ROUND *Do you feel your culture is generally respected by other students?*

ROUND *Do you feel your culture is generally respected by school staff?*

ROUND *Can you give us an example of an experience at school that felt very respectful of your culture?*

ROUND *What do you need from school staff to feel that your culture is respected and accepted?*

ROUND *What do you need from other students to feel that your culture is respected and accepted?*

ROUND *What else would you like others to know about what is important to you about how other people react to your culture?*

CHECK-OUT ROUND *What have you learned in this Circle?*

CLOSING See Appendix 2 or create your own.

Thank everyone for participating in the Circle today!

MODULE 10

Circles for Intensive Support

Because schools are expected to serve all children, the myriad challenges within families and communities show up within school. Many of these challenges interfere with learning. Some young people need intensive support to be able to come to school regularly and be successful. The Circle process provides an effective way to create a structure of intensive support. By gathering a group of people to provide support for this young person, the Circle spreads the responsibility so no single person is overwhelmed. The process also takes advantage of the collective wisdom and diverse resources available within the community, remembering to draw from all available resources found among parents, students, and community members as well as staff.

The use of Circle for intensive support will typically involve regular Circle meetings over a period of time. Circles for intensive support might be used to work with students who are chronically truant, pregnant, suffering from mental health issues, homeless, recently incarcerated, or facing other unusual challenges without sufficient support. Though these Circles organize and implement a strong support network, as all Circles do, they also require accountability of every member of the Circle to each other and to the goals of the Circle.

BUILDING A COMMUNITY OF CARE

Using Circle for intensive support begins with interviews with the student and key people in the student's life to understand the challenges he or she faces. Based on that information, the facilitator recruits people to be members of the support Circle. Participants are recruited from the home and community life of the student as well as from the school life of the student. Support Circle participants could include parents, siblings, extended family, pastor, coach, fellow students, favorite teacher, counselor, friends, former babysitter, or youth worker. Anyone who cares about this young person and can commit to an ongoing relationship is a potential participant in the support Circle.

Support Circle members do not have to be model citizens. They need to care about the student and commit to supporting positive outcomes for the student. In the support Circle process, the first work is to build relationships and trust and to develop a vision of success. These early Circles also identify strengths of the student and of the Circle members and create a map of social supports.

Questions for identifying possible support-Circle members:

- Who do you feel safe with? In the community? At school?
- Who would you go to for help when you were younger?
- Who was your favorite teacher in elementary school?
- Who is a role model for you?
- Who turns to you for support, advice, or help?
- Who really listens to you?
- Who knows everything about the situation you are in?
- Who understands you and the challenges you face?
- Who do you want by your side in a new situation?

As the process moves forward, the Circle identifies barriers to success and probes beneath the presenting issues to understand any underlying causes for the barriers. The Circle then creates a plan of action for first steps toward overcoming those barriers. Circles continue meeting regularly to check in on the plan, to problem-solve if the plan is not working, and to expand the plan as the student moves step by step toward the vision of success. Throughout this time, the Circle also continues to deepen the relationships among members.

This module offers model Circles for exploring the strengths within the student's family and community; for mapping the network of social support for a student; for making a plan; for checking in on progress; and for celebration. These Circles are rooted in a positive commitment to the young person and to helping him/her discover his/her unique gifts and talents. The spirit of these Circles is to provide a balance of support and accountability based on a positive vision of that young person and his/her future. Together the community of care within the Circle guides that young person towards developing him/herself as a valuable and contributing member of the community. It begins with a vision but is fulfilled step by step. At each step of the way, the young person is accountable to his or her community of care, just as the community is accountable to fulfilling their commitment to supporting that young person at each and every step. Every step forward is an opportunity for recognition and celebration. It is critical to take the time to appreciate and honor the growth and development of the young person within the Circle.

Intensive Support Circles 10.1 through 10.5 are designed as a sequence to be done in order over an extended period of time for long-term support for making change in the life of an individual student. Intensive Support Circle 10.4—the check-in Circle—may be repeated many times as the Circle implements the plan for change. The support Circle has not finished its work until there is a celebration!

Two additional Circles in this section—10.6 and 10.7—can be used with a group of students to help them identify how to strengthen their own support systems. These Circles are not focused on a single individual and are not part of the sequence.

Intensive Support
Building Relationships Circle

10.1

PURPOSE To build deeper relationships among supporters of the student and to generate a shared commitment to a positive vision for the student.

MATERIALS Talking piece, bell or sound maker, centerpiece items, paper plates, markers, flip chart for guidelines.

BEFORE THE CIRCLE Invite participants to bring an object that represents their dreams and hopes for (name of student) to put in the center of the Circle.

PREPARATION Arrange everyone in a circle of chairs with no other furniture.

KEEPER *Welcome! Thank you so much for being here today! We are beginning our process of building a support structure for (name of student) to help him/her transcend the challenges s/he faces and to enable his/her success in school. Your presence here is a powerful statement of commitment to (name of student). This process is not a quick fix, so our first Circle will focus on getting to know one another and building commitment to a positive vision, so that we have a strong foundation for facing the challenges ahead. In future Circles, we will make specific plans to tackle the challenges. But first, we will weave together a strong container for doing our work.*

MINDFULNESS MOMENT *Pause, breathe, and listen to the sound.*

OPENING See Appendix 2 or create your own.

INTRODUCE "ROUNDS" A round is a pass of the talking piece around the Circle. The keeper poses a question and, as a participant, usually answers first and then passes the talking piece to the person to their left or to their right. On the first round, participants are invited to say their name as well as respond to the question. Remember, it is always okay for a participant to pass.

MAIN ACTIVITY Laying the Foundation for Developing Good Relationships

ROUND *Tell us who are you and tell us how long you have known (name of student) and a bit about your relationship with (name of student).*

ASK PARTICIPANTS *Think of a value that you think would be important for us as a group to guide our work with (name of student). Please write that value down on the paper plate (or paper).*

ROUND When the talking piece comes to you, please share your value and tell us why it is important. Then put your value in the center of our Circle.

EXPLAIN In addition to values, we want to create some agreements about how we work together to support (name of student.) These agreements will be our guidelines that we use each time we meet.

ROUND Are there any agreements that you think would be important to guide us in how we treat one another and how we talk to one another in this process? Record the guideline suggestions on a flip chart.

Read the list of suggested guidelines.

ROUND Are you satisfied with these agreements, and are these something you can commit to trying to practice while you are here in this Circle?

If there are objections to any of the guidelines, pass the talking piece to explore what need that guideline is trying to meet and what need makes it objectionable. Work with the language being used and the underlying needs to search for common ground to create a guideline acceptable to everyone. A guideline around which there is not consensus may be set aside for further conversation in the future, while the remaining guidelines are adopted.

ROUND Please share the object that you brought to represent your hopes and dreams for (name of student), tell us what the object means to you, and then place it in the center of our Circle.

EXPLAIN Life experience is the primary source of wisdom in a Circle. So we will spend some time exploring our own stories. Those stories help us to know one another better, and they offer ideas that may be useful when we begin looking for solutions later in our process.

ROUND Storytelling: Choose one of the suggested questions below or develop one that is most suited to the people within the Circle.

1. Tell us about a time when you were an adolescent and you struggled to fit in.

2. Tell us about a time when you were an adolescent and you did something you were proud of.

3. What strength do you see in (name of student)? Tell us about when you've seen that strength or why you consider (name of student) has that strength.

4. Tell us about a strength you bring to the purpose of this Circle and how that strength helped you in your life.

5. Where can you imagine (name of student) in five years?

ROUND *Where do you get your motivation when you face difficult challenges?*

EXPLAIN *We will talk more about motivation in our next Circle. Please continue to think about motivation and notice what you already know from your own life experience.*

CHECK-OUT ROUND *What are you taking from this Circle that is of use to you?*

CLOSING *See Appendix 2 or create your own.*

Thank everyone for participating in the Circle today!

10.2 Intensive Support
Map of Resources Circle

PURPOSE To build supportive and deeper relationships and to identify the potential web of support for the student.

MATERIALS Talking piece, bell or sound maker, values & guidelines from previous Circle, centerpiece items, and ribbon.

PREPARATION Arrange everyone in a circle of chairs with no other furniture.

Welcome to the space of the Circle.

MINDFULNESS MOMENT *Pause, breathe, and listen to the sound.*

SUGGESTED OPENING Encouragement ribbon exercise (see Appendix 2, Section III, page 386).

INTRODUCE "ROUNDS" A round is a pass of the talking piece around the Circle. The keeper poses a question and, as a participant, usually answers first and then passes the talking piece to the person to their left or to their right. On the first round, participants are invited to say their name as well as respond to the question. Remember, it is always okay for a participant to pass.

CHECK-IN ROUND *How are you doing? Is there anything particular on your mind that you would like to share with the Circle?* If there is anyone new in the Circle, do brief introductions along with the check-in.

Review the values and guidelines created at the first Circle. If there are any new people in the Circle, invite them to add a value and ask if they feel there is anything missing from the guidelines that they would like to add.

> **MAIN ACTIVITY** Identifying a Student's Motivation and His/Her Web of Support

ROUND *What have you thought about since our last Circle about where your motivation comes from? What has your life taught you about motivation?*

ROUND *Share an experience where you thought you could not do something and then you did it?*

On a flip chart, write (the student's name) in the center.

ROUND *Please identify resources or supports for (name of student).* Map these suggested resources around the name of the student and draw a line from the student's name to that resource or source of support.

ROUND *Have we missed any important resources? Can you add anything to our resource map?*

Suspend the talking piece and ask participants to identify connections among the resources and draw lines representing those connections. This image is a web of support.

Ask the student:

> *Who would you call if you were stranded and needed to get home?*
>
> *Who would you call if you had no food in the house?*
>
> *Who would you call if you needed to find an apartment or a job?*
>
> *Who would you call if you needed help with a younger sibling?*
>
> *Who would you call if you needed advice about a problem?*

Add these resources to the map if they were not already identified.

ROUND *What are your thoughts about this web of support? How does it make you feel?*

KEEPER *We have established a foundation of strengths and resources to draw on and have built connections in this Circle. When we meet the next time, we will identify the steps that we all can make. We will also try to identify barriers to success for (name of student) and identify what needs to happen to overcome those barriers.*

CHECK-OUT ROUND *Please share three words that describe how you are feeling at the end of this Circle.*

CLOSING See Appendix 2 or create your own.

Thank everyone for participating in the Circle today!

10.3 Intensive Support
Making a Plan Circle

PURPOSE To develop a plan to address the responsibilities and needs of the student; to identify the supports that will be provided by other Circle members; and to build relationships.

MATERIALS Talking piece, bell or sound maker, centerpiece items, values, guidelines, and map of support from the previous Circle.

PREPARATION Arrange everyone in a circle of chairs with no other furniture.

Welcome to the space of the Circle.

MINDFULNESS MOMENT *Pause, breathe, and listen to the sound.*

OPENING See Appendix 2 or create your own.

INTRODUCE "ROUNDS" A round is a pass of the talking piece around the Circle. The keeper poses a question and, as a participant, usually answers first and then passes the talking piece to the person to their left or to their right. On the first round, participants are invited to say their name as well as respond to the question. Remember, it is always okay for a participant to pass.

Remind the Circle of the values and guidelines they created at the first support Circle.

MAIN ACTIVITY Developing a Plan to Meet the Student's Needs and Responsibilities

ROUND *Please check in, letting us know how you are doing.*

ROUND *Please share a story of something that (name of student) has done well or succeeded in since our last Circle.*

ROUND *Please report briefly on any other activity or action taken since our last Circle regarding (name of student).*

ROUND *What are your greatest concerns regarding success in school for (name of student)? Record ideas on a flip chart.*

ROUND *Please share your reflections on the list of concerns in general and your response to any particular item.*

ROUND *Which of these things on the list are most important and you can offer some help with?*

Display the support map and remind participants of those resources.

ROUND *Who else might be able to offer help for some of these elements?*

ROUND *Based on our discussion of concerns and the possible resources, what elements should be in a practical, doable plan for the next two weeks? And for the next month?* Record the suggestions and the name of the person who would take the lead for that suggestion.

Summarize the suggestions for a plan.

ROUND Pass the talking piece to check for consensus on the ideas in the plan—*including the student.* This may take multiple rounds.

Clarify the plan: only the elements that everyone accepts stay in the plan.

ROUND *What is your responsibility in making this plan work? What do you need from others to fulfill your responsibilities?*

Write up the plan with the responsibilities of (name of student) and the members of the Circle; pass the plan around the Circle for signatures.

Clarify the next steps—who will monitor how the plan is working and when the Circle will meet again to check on progress.

CHECK-OUT ROUND *How do you feel about the work we did today in Circle?*

CLOSING See Appendix 2 or create your own.

Thank everyone for participating in the Circle today!

10.4 Intensive Support
Check-In Circles

After the support Circle creates a plan, the Circle meets on a regular basis—the frequency is determined by the Circle members—to check on the progress in implementing the plan. The check-in Circles may modify the plan to adjust to changing circumstances or new information. The check-in Circles review developments since the last Circle, continue to identify strengths and resources, and decide whether to adjust the plan. The check-in Circles also continue to build relationships in the group and share stories from the lives of Circle members that provide insight into the situation.

PURPOSE To review the progress of the plan for (name of student); to review all the participants' responsibilities; to adjust the plan when necessary; and to build relationships.

MATERIALS Talking piece, bell or sound maker, centerpiece items, values and guidelines of this Circle, support map, and plan.

PREPARATION Arrange everyone in a circle of chairs with no other furniture.

Welcome to the space of the Circle.

MINDFULNESS MOMENT Pause, breathe, and listen to the sound.

OPENING See Appendix 2 or create your own.

INTRODUCE "ROUNDS" A round is a pass of the talking piece around the Circle. The keeper poses a question and, as a participant, usually answers first and then passes the talking piece to the person to their left or to their right. On the first round, participants are invited to say their name as well as respond to the question. Remember, it is always okay for a participant to pass.

Remind Circle members of their own values and guidelines.

> **MAIN ACTIVITY** Gathering Feedback on How the Plan Is Working and Adjusting It

ROUND *Please check in, letting us know how you are doing.*

ROUND *Please share a story of something that (name of student) has done well or succeeded in since our last Circle.*

ROUND *Please report briefly on your actions related to the plan since our last Circle.*

ROUND *Please share your thoughts and your reactions to the reports of the last round.*

ROUND *What seems to be working really well?*

ROUND *Select a storytelling question from Appendix 1, pages 324–25, such as, Share an experience from your life where you made a major change in your habits.*

ROUND *We want to discuss possible adjustments to our plan. Is there anything not working in the plan that we should adjust, or are we ready to take on any new challenges?*

ROUND *What are your thoughts about the ideas suggested in the last round?*

Determine whether there is consensus for any changes in the plan.

ROUND *What is your specific commitment for the next two weeks?*

ROUND *What would you like to say to (name of student) before we close this Circle?*

Clarify next steps and the time of the next intensive support check-in Circle.

CHECK-OUT ROUND *How do you feel about our Circle today?*

CLOSING See Appendix 2 or create your own.

Thank everyone for participating in the Circle today!

10.5 Intensive Support
Celebration Circle

PURPOSE To celebrate milestones of achievement or the completion of the plan; to recognize success; and to strengthen relationships to sustain the success.

BEFORE THE CIRCLE Ask the student to bring a talking piece and to plan an opening and a closing for the Circle.

MATERIALS Talking piece chosen by student, bell or sound maker, centerpiece items, values and guidelines of this Circle.

PREPARATION Arrange everyone in a circle of chairs with no other furniture.

Welcome to the space of the Circle.

MINDFULNESS MOMENT *Pause, breathe, and listen to the sound.*

OPENING See Appendix 2 or create your own.

INTRODUCE "ROUNDS" A round is a pass of the talking piece around the Circle. The keeper poses a question and, as a participant, usually answers first and then passes the talking piece to the person to their left or to their right. On the first round, participants are invited to say their name as well as respond to the question. Remember, it is always okay for a participant to pass.

Remind Circle of their own values and guidelines.

MAIN ACTIVITY Expressing Appreciation for the Work of the Circle

ROUND *Please pick one of our values and tell us about a time when you felt the whole Circle or someone in the Circle demonstrated that value.*

ROUND *Please express your appreciation for something that (name of student) has done.*

ROUND *Please express your appreciation for something that others in the Circle have done to bring us to this point.*

ROUND *Please tell us what you feel good about in your own contribution to the progress of this Circle.*

ROUND *What are your hopes for (name of student)?*

ROUND *What is the gift you have received from being part of this Circle that may help you in another part of your life?*

CHECK-OUT ROUND *How are you feeling right now?*

CLOSING Led by student.

Thank everyone for participating in the Circle today!

10.6 What Went Right in Your Family Circle

PURPOSE To focus attention on the positive aspects of childhood, which are a source of wisdom and strength for shaping a satisfying life.

MATERIALS Talking piece, bell or sound maker, centerpiece items, art materials (construction paper, scissors, glue, markers, stickers, yarn, pipe cleaners, etc.

PREPARATION Arrange everyone in a circle of chairs with no other furniture.

Welcome to the space of the Circle.

MINDFULNESS MOMENT *Pause, breathe, and listen to the sound.*

OPENING See Appendix 2 or create your own.

INTRODUCE "ROUNDS" A round is a pass of the talking piece around the Circle. The keeper poses a question and, as a participant, usually answers first and then passes the talking piece to the person to their left or to their right. On the first round, participants are invited to say their name as well as respond to the question. Remember, it is always okay for a participant to pass.

CHECK-IN ROUND *How are you feeling today?*

VALUES ROUND *Name a value that was important to you as a small child and is still important to you.* Write a list of those values as participants name them and place the list in the center.

Review the basic Circle guidelines.

> **MAIN ACTIVITY Recalling What Went Right in Childhood and the Gifts Gained from It**

EXPLAIN *Author George Vaillant wrote, "What goes right in childhood predicts the future far better than what goes wrong." What went right in your childhood? I invite you to use the art materials to create an image or drawing that represents what went right in your childhood.*

ROUND *I invite you to share your creations about what went right in your childhood and to talk about what the images mean.*

ROUND *What strength or gift do you have from what went right in your childhood?*

ROUND *How do you share that gift with the world?*

CHECK-OUT ROUND *What can you take from today's Circle that is useful to you?*

CLOSING See Appendix 2 or create one of your own.

Thank everyone for coming and being part of the Circle.

This activity is adapted from Boyes-Watson and Pranis, *Heart of Hope,* pp. 164–66.

10.7 Identifying Sources of Support Circle

PURPOSE To help participants identify the people in their lives that they can turn to for different kinds of social support.

MATERIALS Talking piece, centerpiece items, bell or sound maker, blank paper, pencils, colored markers: red, green, and yellow.

PREPARATION Arrange everyone in a circle of chairs with no other furniture.

Welcome to the space of the Circle.

MINDFULNESS MOMENT *Pause, breathe, and listen to the sound.*

OPENING See Appendix 2 or create your own.

INTRODUCE "ROUNDS" A round is a pass of the talking piece around the Circle. The keeper poses a question and, as a participant, usually answers first and then passes the talking piece to the person to their left or to their right. On the first round, participants are invited to say their name as well as respond to the question. Remember, it is always okay for a participant to pass.

CHECK-IN ROUND *Tell us briefly about something good in your life right now.*

VALUES ROUND *Name a value that is important to you in your relationships with people who support you.* Write a list of those values as participants name them and place the list in the center.

Review the basic Circle guidelines.

MAIN ACTIVITY Taking Stock of Our Support Networks

Ask participants to make a list of people in response to each of the following three scenarios, one at a time, on a blank sheet of paper:

1. *Suppose you had an important doctor's appointment, but on the day of the appointment, you found that your car was broken and you had no way of getting to the appointment. List all the people in your life you could call to give you a ride.*

2. *Imagine you just had a fight with your boyfriend or had a terrible day at school or work and you want to be with someone to whom you can vent your frustration or concerns. List all of the people in your life you could call to have a good cry or to talk to about your problems at work.*

> 3. You just found out that the job you were expecting to start next week is no longer available. List all the people you could call to see if they know of a place to get a job.

Give participants another blank sheet and ask them to put their names in the center in large letters. Ask them to map each of these people from the lists onto this sheet. Using the yellow marker, draw an arrow between you and the people you identified in list 1; using a red marker, draw an arrow between you and all the people you identified in list 2; and using a green marker, draw an arrow between you and all the people you identified in list 3.

Put a triangle around people who are members of your family; a box around friends; and a Circle around neighbors and/co-workers. Finally, draw lines between people (whether in triangles, squares, or boxes) who know each other.

EXPLAIN Now everyone has a visual map of their network of social support. We all need different kinds of support: emotional (red), informational (green) and practical (yellow). Look at the map to notice: Where are the gaps? Do you have a lot of emotional support but not much in the way of informational contacts? Where does more of your support come from: friends, family, or neighbors? Are there ways that you can increase the support in your life?

ROUND What have you learned from your map about your support network? Where does most of your support come from?

ROUND What else do you notice about your support network?

ROUND Are there ways to increase different kinds of support in your life?

CHECK-OUT ROUND What are your last thoughts as we end today's Circle?

CLOSING See Appendix 2 or create your own.

Thank everyone for participating in the Circle today!

This activity is adapted from Boyes-Watson and Pranis, *Heart of Hope*, pp. 228–31.

PART III

Using Circles When Things Go Wrong

Restorative Discipline

UNDERSTANDING RESTORATIVE DISCIPLINE

This guide is based on the assumption that building a strong caring community is the foundation for a healthy school. All of the Circles presented thus far in this guide are focused on the creation of a positive school climate in which all members experience a sense of belonging and respect. If schools invest the bulk of their time and energy in building healthy relationships, only a fraction of their time and energy need be spent repairing those relationships when things go wrong.

Restorative discipline is rooted in the core assumption that everyone wants to be in good relationship with others and themselves. Everyone wants to feel respected, to have a sense of dignity, to feel as if they matter to others, and to feel that they are valued. Building strong and positive relationships within a school community is key to using restorative discipline when students and adults make mistakes. Establishing a school culture where all members of the community are cared for and respected forms the foundation. The use of restorative discipline is effective only if there is a whole school approach that rests on the shared aspiration to build a caring school community.

When something goes wrong in a school setting, the question arises: What needs to happen to respond to what went wrong? Restorative discipline says that what happens next is that the parties involved explore ways to understand the harm and to determine how to fix it. The restorative framework emerges from the assumption that wrongdoing must be examined from the perspective of what harm has happened as the result of a specific incident, what needs to be done to repair the harm, and what needs to happen so it does not occur again.

Whether the harm involves breaking a rule, hurting another person, or being disruptive in a classroom, the initial focus is on the specific harm of that event. To understand the specific harm, we must work with those who were harmed: this is absolutely necessary. No one else can define the harm. The institution or third parties, such as the teacher or principal, cannot define the harm. A restorative response attends to those harmed by a specific incident to understand how they were affected. Then the focus is on repair. What are the obligations for repair that emerge from the harm? What can the wrongdoer do to repair the harm to individuals and to the community of the classroom or school? What can the community (friends, classroom) do to repair the harm to the person hurt? What do the students or adults who were affected by the harm need in order to feel safe again in the school?

> The use of restorative discipline is effective only if there is a whole school approach that rests on the shared aspiration to build a caring school community.

Restorative discipline therefore requires working with the person harmed as well as with the person who caused the harm. This is a big shift from traditional discipline, which tends to focus exclusively on the wrongdoer rather than on the one who has been hurt. From a restorative perspective, we have found that, without working with the person harmed, the wrongdoer cannot gain a real understanding of how the behavior has hurt someone else. Without hearing the voice(s) of those harmed, we also have no basis for understanding what could be done to fix the situation for the person(s) harmed. Further, ignoring the needs of the person hurt can lead to further negative dynamics, such as their hurting themselves or hurting others.

After addressing the need to repair the harm of that incident, a restorative response explores what needs to happen so the behavior is not repeated. This requires acknowledging and attending to underlying causes of the behavior, which may involve prior hurts that were never addressed. A restorative response attempts to promote healing for all the hurts—those caused by the current incident and those revealed by the current incident. What changes does the wrongdoer need to make so that the harm will not happen again? What changes does the community (school or classroom) need to make so that the harm does not happen again? What prior hurts need to be healed to go forward in a good way?

The community of those involved in the incident, including classmates, friends, and family, are key participants in this process. The person who was hurt needs the community to help them separate their hurt from who they are as a person, just as the person who did the harm needs the community to help them separate their behavior from who they are as a person.

A restorative response is one of exploration: the answer to the question of what needs to be done is not known at the beginning. Those most affected or involved in the situation of harm do the exploring. Those who facilitate this exploration process assist the key parties in exploring the situation. They pose questions that help participants tell their own story of what happened, how they were impacted, and what they need for the situation to be repaired. Restorative thinking involves the recognition that the educator cannot answer the key questions for the parties involved; only the parties directly involved can answer these key questions, which in turn can lead to a restorative discipline plan.

The restorative questions used in a variety of formal and informal processes are:

- What happened?
- What were you thinking at that time? How did you feel? What have you thought about since?
- Who was affected by what happened?
- What are your strengths?
- What needs to be done to repair the harm
- What needs to be done to prevent it from happening in the future?

ACCOUNTABILITY IN A RESTORATIVE FRAMEWORK

In the restorative framework, accountability means taking responsibility for your actions and taking steps to repair any harm resulting from your actions. Accountability is not imposed from the outside. Accountability arises from within—from the recognition that your actions hurt others. This recognition makes you consequently aware that you have an obligation to repair the harm or make things right. The most powerful way to understand the impact of your actions is to hear directly from those who were hurt by your actions. When appropriate, a face-to-face process is the most meaningful form of accountability.

> **Accountability has five dimensions in a restorative framework:**
>
> 1. Acknowledging that you caused harm with your actions or behavior.
> 2. Understanding how others were affected by your actions.
> 3. Taking steps to repair the harm to those hurt.
> 4. Giving back to the community.
> 5. Making a plan so it does not happen again.

In a face-to-face restorative discipline process, the first two elements of accountability are achieved by the dialogue itself. The remaining three elements are addressed in the discipline plan that emerges from the dialogue.

Before convening a face-to-face process, the facilitator prepares the parties. Preparation may be as simple as a brief verbal check-in with all parties about their willingness to work on repairing the harm. In more serious cases, preparation may involve one-on-one meetings with all affected parties for an in-depth discussion of the incident and related events. Through this more intensive preparation, the facilitator is exploring the degree of harm, underlying related issues, past history of trauma, the capacity to articulate needs and feelings, and any concerns about safety with each of the parties separately. The keeper may ask key parties:

- What do you want to happen?
- What outcome do you want?
- What role do you want to play?

This is the first step in reflection and empowerment. In these meetings, the keeper avoids rescuing, ignoring wishes, or being overly influential. The purpose of preparation meetings is to help the facilitator decide whether to move forward with a face-to-face process, determine who needs to be there, and design the specifics of the process to fit the situation.

A face-to-face restorative process includes the person who caused harm, the person harmed, supporters for each, selected school personnel, sometimes other community members, such as classmates, and a facilitator. Each participant responds to the restorative questions from his/her perspective, so that the group can develop an understanding of the harm and the possibilities for repair. The answers to the restorative questions lead the Circle to formulate the actions that become the discipline plan—the plan for making it right. The collective wisdom of the group, rather than an authority figure, determines the terms of accountability to make things right. These terms of accountability become a written agreement that all participants sign.

Follow up after the agreement is a critical part of the restorative discipline process. The agreement must be monitored to make sure commitments are fulfilled. Problem-solving strategies are engaged if there are problems with the agreement, including the possibility of convening the group again and adjusting the agreement if it is not workable. Finally, when the agreement is finished, some form of celebration is important to honor its successful completion. As Nancy Riestenberg says, "It is not done until you celebrate!!"

Parts of the Restorative Discipline Process

Preparation for a face-to-face meeting

Convening the face-to-face meeting and creating an agreement

Follow up to support completion of the agreement

Celebration!

Restorative discipline shifts from:

telling	to	listening
knowing the answers	to	being curious
institution/third party trying to restore balance	to	those affected trying to restore balance
focus on wrongdoer	to	focus on those harmed and those who caused harm
external coercion	to	internal motivation

MODULE 11

Learning Restorative Discipline

Many people find that restorative approaches align with their personal sense of justice and resonate with practices within families and schools. Yet restorative approaches are not the dominant paradigm for responding to wrongdoing in a culture that has come to rely heavily on imposing punishments and the threat of them as a strategy for responding to and preventing harmful conduct. Many messages within our culture and within schools link discipline with punishment. The shift to restorative thinking and approaches therefore takes time and practice.

This module offers three learning Circles for developing an understanding of restorative discipline among all the members of the school community and the surrounding larger community. To make a shift towards a restorative school, all members of the community must reflect on their own needs when they are harmed and imagine what they would *need* to make things right. They also need to think about what they would need *to do* to make things right when they cause harm. We strongly urge schools to invest time in using the three introductory learning Circles presented in this module so everyone—teachers, students, staff, police liaison officers, bus drivers, food service workers, building engineers, as well as parents, volunteers, and community partners—can learn about restorative discipline. We also urge schools to engage all members of the community in a deep conversation about how they would like to respond to wrongdoing within their community.

> Many messages within our culture and within schools link discipline with punishment. The shift to restorative thinking and approaches therefore takes time and practice.

11.1 Understanding the Restorative Justice Framework for Addressing Harm Circle I

●●●●●●

PURPOSE To build a foundational understanding of restorative justice principles in the school community.

MATERIALS Talking piece, bell or sound maker, centerpiece items, and materials for journaling.

PREPARATION Arrange everyone in a circle of chairs with no other furniture.

Welcome to the space of the Circle.

MINDFULNESS MOMENT *Pause, breathe, and listen to the sound.*

OPENING See Appendix 2 or create your own.

INTRODUCE "ROUNDS" *A round is a pass of the talking piece around the Circle. The keeper poses a question and, as a participant, usually answers first and then passes the talking piece to the person to their left or to their right. On the first round, participants are invited to say their name as well as respond to the question. Remember, it is always okay for a participant to pass.*

CHECK-IN ROUND *Tell us your name and something good your friends would say about you.*

VALUES ROUND *Name a value that is important to you when you face a difficult situation.* Write a list of those values as participants name them and place the list in the center.

Review the basic Circle guidelines.

> **MAIN ACTIVITY** Expressing the Feelings and Needs That a Past Harm Has Caused

EXPLAIN *In the Circle today, we are going to explore the principles of restorative justice by examining our own life experiences. Howard Zehr, an early leader in restorative justice, suggests that the first principle of restorative justice is that it is harm-focused. By that, he means that it is not focused on laws or rules but on the actual human hurt that results from harmful behavior.*

Think of a time when you felt harmed or hurt by another person. We suggest you might prefer to focus on an experience of hurt that does not currently make you feel upset. Remember that experience and notice the feelings that came up for you after that experience.

Allow a little silence for participants to focus on that memory. *Write a list of all the feelings that are associated with that experience of being hurt. Or draw pictures of the feelings you had.* Allow time to write the list or create images.

ROUND *Share the feelings that you wrote on your list or drew. We may all have similar words. That is okay. Say all your words, even if they have already been said. Repetition as the talking piece goes around is good, so that students see the commonality of feelings.* Write responses on the board (write all the words on the board to honor each person's feelings).

Now go back again in your memory to that time when you were hurt and think about what you needed to feel better after that hurt. Write a list of those needs or draw pictures of what you needed. Allow time for participants to write the list or draw images.

ROUND *Share the needs that you wrote on your list or drew. Write responses on the board.*

ROUND *When you listened to everyone's list, what did you notice about the feelings and needs of people harmed?*

ROUND *What do you think it means to say that restorative justice is harm-focused?*

At end of the round explain:

Restorative justice is about putting things right after some harm has happened. In order to put things right, we need to understand how things have gone wrong. The hurts of those harmed are what has gone wrong, so they become the first point of exploration for figuring out how to make things right.

CHECK-OUT ROUND *Would you like to add any comments about our discussion before we close the Circle?*

CLOSING See Appendix 2 or create your own.

Thank everyone for participating in the Circle today!

11.2 Understanding the Restorative Justice Framework for Addressing Harm Circle II

● ● ● ● ● ●

PURPOSE To continue to build a foundational understanding of restorative justice principles in the school community.

MATERIALS Talking piece, bell or sound maker, and centerpiece items.

BEFORE THE CIRCLE Write on the board in large letters: *Accountability = taking responsibility and taking action to repair the harm caused by our behavior.*

PREPARATION Arrange everyone in a circle of chairs with no other furniture.

Welcome to the space of the Circle.

MINDFULNESS MOMENT *Pause, breathe, and listen to the sound.*

OPENING See Appendix 2 or create your own.

INTRODUCE "ROUNDS" A round is a pass of the talking piece around the Circle. The keeper poses a question and, as a participant, usually answers first and then passes the talking piece to the person to their left or to their right. On the first round, participants are invited to say their name as well as respond to the question. Remember, it is always okay for a participant to pass.

CHECK-IN ROUND *I invite you to tell us your name and to tell us how your day is going.*

VALUES ROUND *Name a value that is important to you when you make a mistake and then try to fix it.* Write a list of those values as participants name them and place the list in the center.

Review the basic Circle guidelines.

MAIN ACTIVITY Exploring What "Taking Responsibility" Means

EXPLAIN *In Circle today, we are going to continue to explore the principles of restorative justice by examining our own life experiences. Howard Zehr's second principle of restorative justice is that, when we cause harm, we create the obligation or duty to be accountable for how our behavior affects others. Zehr defines accountability as taking responsibility and taking action to repair the harm caused by our behavior.*

ROUND *What does it mean to you to "take responsibility for your behavior"?*

ROUND *How might taking action to repair the harm of your behavior be different from taking responsibility for the harm of your behavior?*

ROUND *What might be the needs of someone who is trying to take responsibility and repair the harm or make amends?*

ASK PARTICIPANTS *Think of a time when you caused harm and then took responsibility and made it right. Remember that time and notice the feelings you had. Write a list of the feelings or draw pictures of those feelings.* Allow time for remembering and making a list of feelings.

ROUND *What feelings came up for you in remembering a time when you took responsibility and made it right.* List the feelings on the board.

EXPLAIN *Accountability in a restorative justice process is not easy. It is quite difficult to take responsibility—to acknowledge that we caused harm to another person. It takes courage. However, in the process of accountability, we grow and become a better person, more in alignment with our best self. When we take responsibility, we lift a great weight off our own shoulders.*

CHECK-OUT ROUND *Would you like to add any comments about our discussion before we close the Circle?*

CLOSING See Appendix 2 or create your own.

Thank everyone for participating in the Circle today!

11.3 What Will Make It Right? Circle

PURPOSE To increase our understanding of the action-implications of the restorative justice framework by exploring the needs of those hurt and possible actions for making things right after a harm.

MATERIALS Talking piece, bell or sound maker, centerpiece items, and scenario worksheets.

PREPARATION Arrange everyone in a circle of chairs with no other furniture.

Welcome to the space of the Circle.

MINDFULNESS MOMENT *Pause, breathe, and listen to the sound.*

OPENING See Appendix 2 or create your own.

INTRODUCE "ROUNDS" A round is a pass of the talking piece around the Circle. The keeper poses a question and, as a participant, usually answers first and then passes the talking piece to the person to their left or to their right. On the first round, participants are invited to say their name as well as respond to the question. Remember, it is always okay for a participant to pass.

CHECK-IN ROUND *I invite you to tell us your name and share something unexpected that has happened to you recently.*

VALUES ROUND *Name a value that is important to you when you want to have a good relationship with someone.* Write a list of those values as participants name them and place the list in the center.

Review the basic Circle guidelines.

> **MAIN ACTIVITY** Reflecting on Harms and What "Making Things Right" Might Involve

EXPLAIN TO PARTICIPANTS *Our Circle today will explore how to apply the principles of restorative justice in our community when harms happen.*

ROUND *Briefly share an example of an action you did to make things right after you had done something that hurt someone else. We do not need details of the situation—just an example of making things right.*

READ from the worksheet the appropriate scenario for the age of this group.

ROUND *Who was hurt in this situation? What kinds of hurts did they experience?* List responses on the board.

ROUND *Who has responsibility for trying to make things right again?* List responses on the board.

ROUND *Do you think we missed anyone in thinking about who was hurt and who has responsibility? Who else might have been impacted by the situation or might be helpful in finding solutions?* Add any additional information to the lists on the board.

ROUND *What kinds of actions might make things right again?* List responses on the board.

EXPLAIN *When something goes wrong between humans, restorative justice focuses on understanding the hurts and determining how to best repair those hurts or heal those hurts. We are all learning together how to understand the harms of our actions and how best to repair things when we cause harm. Thank you for exploring these ideas together today.*

CHECK-OUT ROUND *Do you have anything else you would like to say about our Circle today?*

CLOSING See Appendix 2 or create your own.

Thank everyone for participating in the Circle today!

Worksheet for 11.3

What Will Make It Right? Circle

SCENARIO 1

Jessica is sitting at a table drawing with colored markers. When she gets up to ask the teacher a question, Kimberly comes to the table, takes a red marker, and makes a large scribble across Jessica's drawing.

SCENARIO 2

Adam is walking down the hallway when Joseph knocks the book he is holding out of his arms to the floor. A group of kids laugh when they see this happen, and as Adam goes to pick it up, Joseph kicks the book down the hall, much to the amusement of the kids who laugh even harder as Adam scrambles to retrieve his book.

SCENARIO 3

Melissa is late to class, noisily dropping her books on her desk and settling in while the teacher is explaining the day's assignment to the class. The teacher asks Melissa to quiet down, and Melissa stands up and shouts, "Screw you!" and storms out of the classroom.

SCENARIO 4

Jake and Jonathan are throwing spitballs back and forth at the back of the classroom whenever the teacher's back is turned to write math problems on the board. They keep the game up through much of the class period, distracting most of the other students who are eager to see if they will get caught. The teacher can hear the class getting increasingly rowdy, but he does not know what is happening until late in the class period when he catches Jake in the act of throwing the spitball.

SCENARIO 5

In the cafeteria, a group of 8th graders are fooling around flipping spoonfuls of mac and cheese across the table at one another. One missile is sent to an adjacent table and soon both tables are hurling mac and cheese at one another. Before long, the entire cafeteria is engaging in a food fight, ignoring instructions of the lunch monitors to stop immediately. When the principal walks in, the floor and walls are covered in food, the adults are red-faced with fury, and several younger children are huddled in the corner crying.

Doing Restorative Discipline in Circle

Schools can use multiple techniques to implement a restorative discipline process. Restorative conferences, restorative mediation, and informal restorative chats are all highly effective ways to address wrongdoing. They are all based on the foundational principles that the six restorative questions raise (discussed in the previous section). This book does not detail those processes, but we do provide resources in Appendix 4 for more information. While we encourage schools to experiment with the use of multiple formats for restorative discipline, we also encourage schools to always maintain a strong Circle practice within the school community focused on building healthy relationships. This section of the guide details the use of the Circle process for restorative discipline.

The six restorative questions listed earlier are the heart of a restorative inquiry. In the Circle, the restorative questions come in the third and fourth quadrants of the Circle process (See the diagram in Part I: The Basics, "Balance in the Process," on page 34.) Before these restorative questions are asked, however, the Circle spends time getting to know one another, developing values and guidelines, and sharing stories or interests from the lives of all the participants. These parts of the process are designed to build empathy and a sense of connection. Building relationships in this way reduces the feelings of isolation or alienation that might make it difficult for parties to hear one another or understand the perspective of one another. After establishing guidelines and building a sense of connection among the participants, the focus of a restorative Circle can turn to addressing the incident of harm.

The restorative questions are designed to help participants explore who has been affected and to understand what needs to be done to repair the harm. The sequence of different kinds of questions is extremely important. It is essential to build empathy and connection before discussing the harm. Then it is important to fully explore the harm before moving to the agreement phase. Though the talking piece always goes in order around the Circle, in a Circle focused on harm, it may be preferable to hand the talking piece to a specific participant to start a particular round. After that person answers, he/she passes it to the next person to go around the Circle for others to respond.

We provide a specific template for a Circle addressing harm that can be adapted to fit the particular incident and participants. Following are numerous sample questions that might be appropriate for the different parts of the restorative discipline Circle based on the Medicine Wheel teaching about balance in the process. Choose the questions that are relevant and meaningful for the situation or create your own modifications. Because the nature of the Circle is the passing of the talking piece all the way around for each question, all of these questions are intended to be answered by everyone in the Circle, unless they choose to pass.

Quadrant 1
MEETING AND GETTING ACQUAINTED

Questions for introducing participants to one another

- Can you introduce yourself and share what you hope will be accomplished in today's Circle?
- Can you introduce yourself and share one value you are bringing to the Circle today?
- Can you introduce yourself and share how long you have been involved with this school community, as well as one thing you appreciate about the community?
- Can you introduce yourself and tell how a friend would describe you?
- Can you introduce yourself and share a positive thing that has happened to you in the last week?
- What value would be important for you in our space today?
- What agreements do we need to have a respectful conversation today?

Quadrant 2
BUILDING RELATIONSHIPS

Questions for building trust and developing empathy

We all have strengths and weaknesses; we all have times when we act badly and times when we act positively.

- Can you share with us a positive experience with (names of persons most affected) and then tell us what strengths you see in (repeat names)?
- Can you share an experience when you were an adolescent and struggled, and what may have helped you at that time?
- Can you share an experience of making a mistake and then fixing it?
- Can you share a strength you bring to the Circle that may help us today?
- Can you share an experience of feeling that you did not fit in?
- Can you share a proud moment in your life?
- Can you tell us about a time when you accomplished something you thought you could never do?
- What are your strengths?
- What are your family's strengths?

Quadrant 3
ADDRESSING ISSUES/EXPLORING HARM

Questions for telling the story of the incident

- What happened?
- What were you feeling/thinking at the time or when you learned about it?
- How were you involved in the incident?
- What was going on in your head when this happened or when you heard about it?
- What have you thought about since it all happened?
- What is going on in this situation?

Questions for exploring the impact of the incident

- How has this affected you?
- Who else do you think has been affected? In what way?
- What has been the worst part of all this for you?
- What is the hardest thing for you about this situation?
- How did your family and friends react when they heard about the incident?
- What has changed for you as a result of this incident?

- Has this situation changed your home life or school life?
- What are the main issues for you?
- What concerns you the most?

The order of these parts of the Circle is designed to help people express strong negative emotions in a respectful way. The first two quadrants build an atmosphere of respect, and the third quadrant invites participants to honestly tell their story, express feelings, and release emotions. *It is the dynamic between the participants within the Circle that will change how people feel about the incident.* As the Circle unfolds, participants' feelings may change as they hear and see the response of others in the Circle. It is important not to rush through this phase of the process: facilitators should pay attention to the "emotional temperature" in the Circle and continue exploring the harm until there is a sense that everyone has said what they need to say.

This is likely to be a highly emotional phase of the Circle, as participants talk about strong feelings generated by the incident. Anger, grief, loss, hurt, shame, embarrassment, defensiveness, sadness, frustration, remorse, and confusion are common emotions to come up for participants during Quadrant 3. Body language and facial expressions too will reflect the emotions that the participants feel. The facilitator has no need to fix or respond to any particular emotion. The expression of feelings is critical to the emotional dynamics of the restorative process.

These questions are designed to facilitate emotional clearance for all parties. Emotional clearance means that parties on all sides of harm feel released from draining emotions and are able to move forward without being trapped in negativity. The goal of emotional clearance or resolution depends on people expressing how they feel in a face-to-face encounter within the structured safety of the Circle.

It is important for all the participants to express their feelings about what has happened and how it has affected them before turning to what needs to be done to repair the harm. If not all the information comes out, wait, count to 10, and pass the talking piece again, or wait and, after a 5 count, ask, "What else?" Keep passing the talking piece until you have heard most of what you expected to hear. As a keeper, you do not fill in information for others. You may speak about your own feelings and your own direct experience, but take care to resist the temptation to relay the experiences of others.

Quadrant 4
MAKING AGREEMENTS/ DEVELOPING PLANS/AFFIRMING A SENSE OF UNITY

Once the phase of exploring the harm has been fully covered, the facilitator should move on to the final phase of Making Agreements. Here, it is important for the facilitator to make notes as people talk about what they would like to see happen. At various points, the facilitator may summarize what has been suggested to see if there is anything else people would like to see happen.

Questions for repairing harm
- What do you need so things can be put right and you can move on from this?
- What needs to happen to make things right?
- What would you like to see happen to fix things?
- What do you want to see happen as a result of this Circle to make it safe for you?
- What else needs to be done to make things better?
- What else would you like to see happen?
- What needs to be done to make sure that this does not happen again?

Questions for making agreements

- Building on our strengths, what could happen now to meet these needs and repair the harm?
- What is each of you willing to do to repair the harm or support others in repairing the harm?
- What else needs to happen so it does not happen again?
- What changes are you committed to making?
- What should our plan look like?
- What should the agreement say?
- Does this seem fair to you?
- Is there anything that anyone feels is unfair?
- Do you agree with this plan?
- Can you sign your name to the agreement?
- Who should be responsible for making sure agreements are kept?
- What should we do if there are problems with the agreement?

THE ROLE OF APOLOGY AND FORGIVENESS

The emotional dynamics of the Circle create conditions in which a wrongdoer is very often moved to express a genuine apology or statement of remorse. This may be expressed or accompanied by nonverbal signals—tears, blushing, stammering, heads down—that convey the authenticity of those feelings. These expressions, however, cannot be forced. Participants may express a desire or need for an apology, but for it to be satisfying emotionally, the wrongdoer must give it voluntarily and authentically. Emotional clearance depends on the emotional interaction between the parties within the Circle itself. Experienced facilitators have learned to trust the process and to let the participants do the work themselves.

Many of these same points can be made about feelings of forgiveness and reconciliation. The same emotional dynamics that may motivate a wrongdoer to express genuine remorse, also may lead to authentic feelings of forgiveness on the part of those who are harmed. Again, none of these feelings can ever be forced, nor should there be any pressure or expectations placed on those who have been harmed to feel this way. These emotional shifts depend on the individuals involved and are part of their own journey. Experienced facilitators must learn to let go and let the participants do the work themselves. An experienced school Circle keeper says, "I am not looking for apology, shame, or blame. I want to know what actions can be done to repair the harm."

MODULE 12

Restorative Discipline and Conflict Circles

Module 12 provides a model Circle format to use when things go wrong in the course of everyday life. As human beings, all of us make mistakes. Part of our growth and development is to understand how our behavior affects others and to learn how to take responsibility and restore the positive quality of the relationship. Restorative discipline seeks to build a stronger community by involving the whole school community in the positive resolution of wrongdoing. The restorative process uses conflict as an opportunity to strengthen positive relationships. When disruptions occur, resolving harm carries important lessons—not only for the wrongdoer but for all members of the community.

> When disruptions occur, resolving harm carries important lessons—not only for the wrongdoer but for all members of the community.

Because this guide is about the Circle, we offer a simple template for asking the restorative questions within the Circle format. Once a Circle practice is established within a community, the use of the Circle format for restorative discipline feels like a natural place to have a meaningful conversation about something that really matters. The values and guidelines already established within the group during community-building Circles are essential resources for restoring and repairing harm when something goes wrong. The first template is a simple format that can be used when disruptions occur in everyday life that involves a clear wrongdoing by one party toward another.

In Module 12, we include six different Circle templates for resolving conflict. One is a Circle to use when there has been a fight or conflict between two parties and both are equally responsible for committing harm to one another. The second Circle is a variation on the first. The third Circle uses silence and journal writing to work through conflict in Circle using restorative principles. Another Circle welcomes a student back after suspension. Two additional Circles deal with common difficulties in the classroom.

12.1 Template for a Restorative Discipline Circle

PURPOSE To talk about and resolve an incident of harm within the classroom or school community.

MATERIALS Talking piece, bell or sound maker, centerpiece items, flip chart for recording guidelines, paper plates, and markers.

PREPARATION Arrange everyone in a circle of chairs with no other furniture.

Welcome to the space of the Circle.

MINDFULNESS MOMENT *Pause, breathe, and listen to the sound.*

OPENING See Appendix 2 for a quote or story or create your own.

EXPLAIN WHY WE ARE HERE *We are in Circle today to work out how to make things right after (briefly summarize the incident being resolved). Our goal in the Circle is to understand how everyone has been impacted by what happened and what things we can do to repair the harm that happened as a result of this incident. We also will try to figure out what we can do to make sure it does not happen again. I want to thank everyone for their willingness to be part of finding a good way forward out of a difficult situation.*

INTRODUCE "ROUNDS" A round is a pass of the talking piece around the Circle. The keeper poses a question and, as a participant, usually answers first and then passes the talking piece to the person to their left or to their right. On the first round, participants are invited to say their name as well as respond to the question. Remember, it is always okay for a participant to pass.

ROUND *When you are at your best, what value defines you?* Ask participants to write the value on a paper plate and to place the paper plate in the center after they have shared their value.

OFFER THE BASIC CIRCLE GUIDELINES Check with the group by asking if there are any additional guidelines that they would like to add for this Circle.

> **MAIN ACTIVITY Engaging the Restorative Process to Form a Plan to Repair the Harm**

ROUND *Can you agree to try to follow these guidelines in our Circle today?*

ROUND *Introduce yourself and tell us one thing you are good at.*

ROUND *Our own life experiences are a source of wisdom for dealing with difficult situations. We will draw on our own stories for guidance. Please tell us about a time when you had to use a lot of courage to do the right thing.*

ROUND *Based on what you know, what happened in this incident?* Start the talking piece with the person harmed and then have it go in order around the Circle.

ROUND *What were your thoughts and feelings when this happened or you first heard about it?*

ROUND *Who has been affected by what happened and how?*

ROUND *What has been the hardest part for you?*

ROUND *What are your thoughts and feelings about the incident now?*

ROUND *What are your strengths? What are your family's strengths?*

ROUND *What do you need so things can be put right and you can move on from this?* Start the talking piece with the person harmed and have it go in order around the Circle from that person.

ROUND *Building on our strengths, what could happen now to meet these needs and repair the harm?* Keep notes about ideas and suggestions.

ROUND *What else needs to happen to make sure it does not happen again?* Keep notes.

ROUND *What should our plan look like?* Start the talking piece with the person who did the harm and continue around the full Circle.

ROUND Summarize agreements. *Do you agree with this plan? Can you sign your name to the agreement?*

ROUND *What can you do to make sure these agreements are followed?*

CHECK-OUT ROUND *Does anyone have anything else they want to say?*

CLOSING Select a quote or story from Appendix 2 or create your own.

Thank everyone for contributing to the Circle.

This activity is based on work by Nancy Riestenberg at the Minnesota Department of Education and is adapted from Kay Pranis, *The Little Book of Circle Processes* and the work of the organization Transforming Conflict (see Appendix 4: Resources, Section I, Websites).

12.2 Template for a Circle about a Conflict

PURPOSE To talk about and resolve an incident of harm within the classroom or school community.

MATERIALS Talking piece, bell or sound maker, centerpiece items, flip chart for recording guidelines, paper plates, and markers (you may also use existing guidelines/value statements).

PREPARATION Arrange everyone in a circle of chairs with no other furniture.

Welcome to the space of the Circle.

MINDFULNESS MOMENT *Pause, breathe, and listen to the sound.*

OPENING See Appendix 2 or create your own.

INTRODUCE "ROUNDS" A round is a pass of the talking piece around the Circle. The keeper poses a question and, as a participant, usually answers first and then passes the talking piece to the person to their left or to their right. On the first round, participants are invited to say their name as well as respond to the question. Remember, it is always okay for a participant to pass.

> **MAIN ACTIVITY** Engaging the Restorative Process to Move Past a Conflict

EXPLAIN WHY WE ARE HERE *We are in Circle today to work out how to make things right between (briefly name the parties to the conflict). Our goal in the Circle is to understand how everyone has been impacted by what happened and what things we can do to repair the harm that happened as a result of this conflict. We also will try to figure out how we can make sure it does not happen again. I want to thank everyone for their willingness to be part of finding a good way forward out of a difficulty.*

ROUND *Introduce yourself and tell us how long you have been at this school or in this community.*

ROUND *What value can you bring that would help us work through this conflict successfully?* Ask participants to write the value on a paper plate and to place the paper plate in the center after they have shared their value.

OFFER THE BASIC CIRCLE GUIDELINES Check with the group to ask if there are any additional guidelines that they would like to add for this Circle.

ROUND *Can you agree to try to follow these guidelines in our Circle today?*

ROUND *Tell us about a person you admire who handles conflict well.*

ROUND *Based on what you know about this situation, what happened?*

ROUND *What has been the hardest part for you?*

ROUND *Have you done anything to make the situation worse?*

ROUND *What can you do to make the situation better?*

ROUND *What do you need to do to repair any harm from this conflict and move past the conflict?*

ROUND *What do you need from others to move past this conflict?*

Summarize ideas that seem broadly supported for moving past the conflict.

ROUND *Can you agree to support these ideas for moving past the conflict?*

ROUND *How will you know if things are getting better?*

If appropriate, write up the agreements and have participants sign them.

CHECK-OUT ROUND *Share some wisdom that you learned from the Circle today.*

CLOSING See Appendix 2 or create your own.

Thank everyone for participating in the Circle today!

This activity is adapted from the work of the Oakland Unified School District.

12.3 Template for a Silent Circle Responding to Conflict Immediately

This Circle is appropriate as an immediate response to a group of middle school or high school students fighting or arguing in the hallway or classroom.

PURPOSE To help students who are in conflict safely reflect on their behavior immediately and then collectively develop options for repairing relationships.

PREPARATION Invite all the students into an empty room/classroom. Ask them to move their chairs into a Circle and to sit down. Provide each student with a pad and pencil or pen.

MINDFULNESS MOMENT *Pause, breathe, and listen to the sound.*

MAIN ACTIVITY Using Journaling to Defuse and Resolve Conflict

Tell students that we will hold a silent Circle. Ask students to please write down the number of the question and their thoughts in response to the question. Words, phrases, anything will do. The questions can be written on a board.

QUESTION 1 *What has been going on these last few weeks that has made you angry or upset?*

Allow time for the students to write. When it seems most are finished, ask:

QUESTION 2 *What did you do to contribute to the problems?*

Allow time for the students to write. When they seem ready, ask:

QUESTION 3 *What can you do to make things better in the next two weeks?*

Allow time for the students to write.

When all the students are finished, collect the pads. Taking each question in turn, read to the students what they have written in response to that question without identifiers.

ROUND After reading everything back to them, pass the talking piece, asking: *Based on your own wisdom and reflections, what commitments can you make out loud to each other?*

Make notes on the commitments. Ask the students whether they want a copy of the commitments. Ask the students whether they need a further Circle.

Thank the students for their thoughtful engagement in the situation.

SUGGESTED CLOSING Lead a short breathing exercise with the students.

This activity is based on Riestenberg, *Circle in the Square*, pp. 170–71.

12.4 Classroom Circle for Responding to Harm without Focusing on the Wrongdoer

This Circle can be used to discuss a harm without putting the person who has caused the harm in the spotlight. It can also be used in a situation where harm happened but the person who caused the harm is unidentified.

PURPOSE To engage the whole classroom in the discussion of harm to increase awareness of how behavior affects others; to strengthen relationships in the classroom by working together to resolve a difficulty.

MATERIALS Talking piece, bell or sound maker, centerpiece items.

PREPARATION Arrange everyone in a circle of chairs with no other furniture.

Welcome to the space of the Circle.

MINDFULNESS MOMENT Pause, breathe, and listen to the sound.

OPENING See Appendix 2 or create your own.

INTRODUCE "ROUNDS" A round is a pass of the talking piece around the Circle. The keeper poses a question and, as a participant, usually answers first and then passes the talking piece to the person to their left or to their right. On the first round, participants are invited to say their name as well as respond to the question. Remember, it is always okay for a participant to pass.

Read the classroom values and guidelines.

MAIN ACTIVITY To Address a Harm within a Positive Frame

EXPLAIN Something sad happened (on the playground or in the hallway or in the classroom, . . .) and we want to work together to make things better. Our goal is not to blame anyone or make anyone feel bad, but we want to understand how everyone has been affected by what happened and what we can do to make this a good classroom for everyone.

ROUND Choose one of our values that you are thinking about today and tell us about a time you saw someone in our classroom show or express that value.

ROUND What do you think we have all done well today?

ROUND *What happened today that did not go well? Or, what happened today that hurt a classmate(s)?*

ROUND *How are you feeling about what happened?*

ROUND *How can we support our classmate(s) who has been hurt?*

ROUND *What can each of us do to make our classroom safe and happy and to take care of each other?*

CHECK-OUT ROUND *Is there anything we need to discuss in another Circle?*

CLOSING See Appendix 2 or create your own.

Thank everyone for participating in the Circle today!

12.5 Welcome Back after Suspension Circle

If a student has been out of school as a result of a disciplinary action, the student needs to reconnect with the school community in a positive way. This may include addressing any unresolved issues that caused the student to be excluded. Participants may include other students who were affected by the situation, parents, school staff, community volunteers, supporters for the student, as well as the student.

PURPOSE To reduce anxiety about the return of the student to the school by sharing perspectives or concerns; to affirm connections with multiple members of the school community for the student; to nurture a sense of unity toward success for everyone.

MATERIALS Talking piece, bell of sound maker, centerpiece items, paper plates, markers.

PREPARATION Arrange everyone in a circle of chairs with no other furniture.

Welcome to the space of the Circle.

MINDFULNESS MOMENT *Pause, breathe, and listen to the sound.*

OPENING See Appendix 2 or create your own.

INTRODUCE "ROUNDS" A round is a pass of the talking piece around the Circle. The keeper poses a question and, as a participant, usually answers first and then passes the talking piece to the person to their left or to their right. On the first round, participants are invited to say their name as well as respond to the question. Remember, it is always okay for a participant to pass.

> **MAIN ACTIVITY Reintegrating the Student in an Affirming Way That Also Addresses What Happened**

ROUND *Introduce yourself and tell us how you know (name of student).*

ROUND *Please think of a value that is important for the well-being of (name of the student) and the school community. Write that value on the paper plate with the marker. When the talking piece comes to you, please share the value you wrote and why that value is important, and then place the paper plate in the center.*

Present basic guidelines for the Circle and check to make sure everyone can accept them.

ROUND *What are the strengths or capacities of (name of student) that s/he can bring to this school?*

ROUND *What strength or gift do each of you bring to support (name of student)'s success in school?*

ROUND *Are there lingering concerns about what happened before (name of student) was sent away that we need to talk about?*

Follow up with another round if concerns have been expressed.

ROUND *Is there any harm that needs to be repaired regarding this situation?*

ROUND *What steps are necessary for (name of student) and the school community to come together in the way that our values describe?*

Follow up with another round if that feels appropriate.

ROUND *What are your hopes or wishes for (name of student), and what can you do in the next two weeks to make those hopes a reality?*

CHECK-OUT ROUND *What are your last thoughts as we close this Circle?*

CLOSING Select a quote or reading from Appendix 2 or create your own.

Thank you to everyone!

12.6 The Class That Ate the Sub Circle

PURPOSE To change the school culture regarding student behavior when a substitute teacher takes a class; to increase awareness among students of the impact of their behavior on the adults who work with them; to engage reflection about accountability for behavior and options for better behavior in the future.

BEFORE THE CIRCLE Invite the substitute teacher back the following day for a Circle with the students. Explain the Circle process and the purpose of this particular Circle.

MATERIALS Talking piece, bell or sound maker, centerpiece items.

PREPARATION Arrange everyone in a circle of chairs with no other furniture.

Welcome to the space of the Circle.

MINDFULNESS MOMENT *Pause, breathe, and listen to the sound.*

OPENING See Appendix 2 or create your own.

Remind the class of the classroom values and guidelines.

INTRODUCE "ROUNDS" A round is a pass of the talking piece around the Circle. The keeper poses a question and, as a participant, usually answers first and then passes the talking piece to the person to their left or to their right. On the first round, participants are invited to say their name as well as respond to the question. Remember, it is always okay for a participant to pass.

> **MAIN ACTIVITY** Talk about How the Class Treated the Substitute Teacher

ROUND *Please say your name and tell us something good about yourself.*

ROUND *Choose a value you would like to demonstrate to (name of the substitute teacher) today in our Circle and tell us why you chose that value.*

Invite the substitute teacher to talk about the experience of being with this class yesterday: What it was like for her/him with them? How did s/he feel at the end of the day? How did s/he interact with others because of her bad day? What was the hardest part of that experience? …

ROUND *What happened yesterday?*

ROUND *What did you do to make things worse or to make them better?*

ROUND *What were you thinking about or what were you trying to do with your behavior?*

Someone was hurt at our school yesterday. A guest left our school feeling (sad, alone, offended, . . .).

ROUND *What will you do differently the next time there is a substitute teacher?*

ROUND *Is there anything else you want to say?*

CHECK-OUT ROUND *How do you feel at the end of this Circle?*

CLOSING See Appendix 2 or create your own.

Thank everyone for participating in the Circle today!

This Circle is adapted from Jack Mangan's website, Restorative Measures in Schools (see Appendix 4: Resources, Section I, Websites).

MODULE 13

Complex and Multi-Process Circles for Serious Incidents of Harm

In a Circle process designed for more serious issues, we invest more time at each and every stage of the process. We invest more time before the Circle in planning and preparation, especially in reaching out to invite and prepare more people to participate. We also invest more time within the Circle to build empathy and connection between all the parties. We are likely to also consider planning a series of Circles—different Circles for different sets of participants for different reasons—that will take place over time. We take this care so that we are sure we are meeting the needs of all stakeholders.

Module 13 provides a framework for a more complex series of Circles in instances of serious harm, wrongdoing, and conflict. In these instances, the behavior may have caused harm that requires substantial healing and is often rooted in deeper cycles of harm and victimization. These kinds of issues include bullying, chronic truancy, weapons offenses, violence, and persistent disrespect and misbehavior. We provide guidance here for Circles that will involve many more participants, including parents, guidance staff, social workers, and administrators as well as students and teachers. These Circles will most likely involve a far greater time investment in preparation and planning; and most of them will be lengthier Circles and/or will consist of a series of Circles.

Because more serious incidents are connected to deeper problems, it is necessary to have a process designed to address both the incident and its underlying issues. We believe the Circle is particularly well suited to this kind of intervention, and we discuss what forms it might take. We also present a framework for using the Circle to address incidents of bullying.

THE IMPORTANCE OF PRE-WORK AND PREPARATION

Preparation or pre-meetings with all parties is essential in response to incidents of serious harm, because different incidents call for crafting different kinds of restorative responses. Facilitators need to understand the full scope, history, and impact of problematic behaviors by meeting with: victims and their families; wrongdoers and their families; staff and other students or witnesses. It is important for these to be face-to-face meetings, particularly with direct stakeholders. And the Circles should be held at a time and place that maximizes the sense of safety and comfort of the affected parties.

In these meetings, the guiding questions are the exact same restorative questions outlined above:

1. What happened?
2. What were you thinking and feeling at the time?
3. How have people been affected?
4. What are your strengths?
5. What is needed to repair the harm?
6. What needs to be done to prevent this from happening in the future?

By engaging all the participants with these questions in pre-meetings, the facilitator will gain important understandings, discover who might have been affected and therefore also needs to be involved, and learn what some of the underlying issues may be that will need to be addressed.

These meetings also afford participants with a valuable opportunity for voicing their own needs and concerns. For victims, the opportunity to be heard and to articulate what they would need to make things right begins with the preparation meeting. This meeting is of inherent restorative value even if no further Circles take place. For wrongdoers and their parents, the opportunity to think about who has been affected and to consider ways to repair the harm may mitigate the tendency to be defensive or to fear that their child will be shamed and labeled. In a restorative response, the demonization of the wrongdoer is avoided: the goal is to promote genuine accountability by giving wrongdoers an opportunity to understand how they have affected others and the chance to make amends for their behavior.

Based on these meetings, facilitators may decide to hold a single restorative Circle if the incident falls toward the milder end of the spectrum without significant recurrence over time. On the other hand, if the incident is complex, the behavior pattern has been chronic, or a child has been subjected to bullying, facilitators may want to consider a series of Circles, as outlined below. It is also possible that a facilitator might suggest additional counseling or other kinds of support for a victim. So, too, additional counseling may be a wise suggestion for a wrongdoer who needs to address underlying issues or needs ongoing support for learning how to relate to others positively.

There is no cookie-cutter formula for how to craft a sensitive and constructive restorative process. The guiding principles are the values of restorative justice: dignity, respect, and care.

> The guiding principles are the values of restorative justice: dignity, respect, and care.

FOLLOW-UP CIRCLES

In a sequence of Circles associated with a serious incident or chronic problem, once agreements are made, it is advisable to follow up with support Circles. These are designed to provide support for ongoing behavioral change and to periodically check in on the progress being made in keeping these agreements. These follow-up Circles can be a subset of the Circle participants who come together as a support group for any party, or they can be the whole group coming back together to check in on whether the agreements made in Circle are being fulfilled. It is extremely important that follow-up not be neglected, since an important element of accountability for everyone is to see the fulfillment of agreements and a genuine change in behavior over time. Follow up is often extremely important to those who have been harmed. It is also true that behavior change may require ongoing support. In Part II, Module 10, we have provided several templates for ongoing intensive support Circles.

CELEBRATION CIRCLES

In Part II, Module 10, we also offer a model Circle for celebrating success. A celebration Circle can be held as a final Circle. Everyone acknowledges the progress that has been made. As a Circle, participants recognize the achievement and what this means for different members of the community. A celebration can also be built into ongoing support Circles: steps of progress can be affirmed and appreciated, at the same time that areas of challenge and difficulty are acknowledged and addressed. It is especially important to all concerned that we do not neglect to acknowledge the good that arises from an incident of harm. This is very often the highest hope that participants have in the wake of harm, and we should take the time to reflect on positive change with joy and appreciation.

MULTI-CIRCLE PROCESSES FOR SERIOUS HARM

As in all restorative processes, the needs of victims are a primary concern. We propose separate support Circles to affirm victims both with the family and with fellow members of the student body. The needs of the wrongdoer—especially to understand the harm they have caused and to be given the opportunity to make amends—are also paramount. We therefore propose separate Circles with the wrongdoer and their family with students and staff to help support his/her accountability and to provide intensive support and assistance in addressing any underlying issues. A multi-Circle process for serious harm likely includes these differently focused Circles:

1. A support Circle for the person harmed and his/her family focuses on fully understanding the impact of the harm; hearing their story; affirming that they are not to blame; and developing a plan of social support for them.

2. A support Circle for the person harmed with members of the school community, students, and staff gives those harmed an opportunity to tell their story; to alleviate shame associated with victimization; and to give the community the opportunity to express their own feelings about the behavior, to take responsibility, and to express support to the person harmed.

3. A responsibility Circle for the wrongdoer and the family with members of the school community, staff, and students seeks to gain a better understanding of the thinking and feelings associated with the behavior; to explore its impact on others; to explore ways to make amends; and to develop a plan for the future. The goal of this Circle is to deepen the wrongdoer's awareness of accountability and to help everyone understand the underlying issues that may need addressing.

4. An accountability Circle brings the two sets of stakeholders together—those harmed and those who did the harm—along with members of the school community, students, and staff. The focus is on repairing harm and making agreements.

5. Ongoing intensive support Circles support longer-term behavioral change. They bring together a community of care for an individual committed to making significant change in behavior.

6. Celebration Circles acknowledge the fulfillment of obligations, the achievement of goals, and the attainment of significant growth and development.

USING CIRCLES FOR INCIDENTS OF BULLYING

It is now widely recognized that the most important anti-bullying effort for schools is to invest time and energy in building a safe and respectful school climate. Most children neither participate in nor become direct targets of bullying behavior. This is very good news. Sustained cruelty by the powerful against the weak is not the norm among children or adults, and the more this fact is made well known within a school community, the more likely such behavior will not be tolerated by both children and adults.

Bullying behavior flourishes in contexts in which there are social rewards for the behavior from peers and few restraints from adults and peers who may disapprove. The work of building a culture of empathy and respect through the regular use of the Circle is a pathway towards creating a climate in which such behavior is neither rewarded nor acceptable. Using Circles on a regular basis is also a way to develop a robust capacity within your community to respond with care and concern for all parties when bullying behavior does occur.

Most of the Circle work presented in this manual is designed to support the building of a culture of prevention. Cultivating emotional intelligence in an environment in which all children and adults are seen, heard and valued is the best defense against bullying. Creating a community where all members know one another and intentionally practice values of respect and consideration increases the likelihood that bystanders will express disapproval of the bullying behavior and thereby neutralize its social value. Circles that focus on talking about difference—particularly sexual orientation, but also ethnicity, race, nationality, family structure, religion, gender norms, and other aspects of identity—promote a culture of acceptance, not just tolerance. All of the Circle work in this guide, regardless of its explicit purpose, quietly but significantly contributes to creating this climate.

The restorative inquiry and response that we have outlined in Part III are just as relevant to the harm of bullying as they are to other kinds of harm, only with some caveats. Like all serious incidents of harm, it is important to take the time to do all four quadrants of the Circle process: making introductions; telling stories; addressing the problem, and making agreements. As we noted above, the more serious the harm, the slower the process should be. Addressing serious harm using Circles requires an experienced keeper, a community grounded in values, and a robust Circle practice. A healthy school climate becomes the foundation of the community. Using Circles to address bullying behavior is not a quick fix. Circles should not be used for bullying unless there is a long-term commitment to inclusion, non-domination, and deep respect for every person in the Circle.

The use of a restorative intervention in the Circle when a pattern of bullying does occur is a very serious form of intervention. It requires deliberate consideration, planning, and a high level of skill and experience with preparation and facilitation. We highly recommend that schools seek out experienced facilitators or commit to in-depth training for school personnel in order to use Circles as a restorative intervention in cases of bullying.

WHAT BULLYING IS AND WHAT BULLYING IS NOT

The first question is what bullying behavior is and how it is different from other kinds of conflict, misconduct, aggression, or teasing behaviors. The classic definition provided by Dan Olweus is helpful. In order for behavior to be classified as bullying, it must meet three criteria:

1. there is an intention to do harm;
2. the behavior is repeated; and
3. there is a power imbalance between the parties.

Mean behavior is not something that should be ignored within a school community, but for the behavior to rise to the level of bullying, it must be part of a pattern of behavior that persists over time. This may involve verbal or physical behavior; it may occur face to face in school or indirectly through phone calls, texting, or more commonly, social media.

SUGGESTED POSSIBLE CIRCLES THAT CAN BE USEFUL IN BULLYING CASES

1. A support Circle for the person harmed and their family to really understand the harm and design a plan of support for the person harmed.
2. A support Circle with the person harmed and peers for community support and accountability and for developing a safety plan for the person harmed.
3. Classroom Circles about bullying in more general terms. (See Model Circle 6.3.)
4. A responsibility Circle for the person doing the harm and the family for a better and shared understanding of the problematic behavior and the underlying issues.
5. An accountability Circle if it is appropriate to bring the parties together to repair harm and make agreements.
6. Ongoing support Circles for the person harmed.
7. Ongoing support Circles for person doing the harm to make changes in behavior patterns.
8. Community Circle(s) to talk about community responsibility for promoting a culture that neither rewards nor accepts bullying by adults.

Bullying behavior, though it manifests as excessive power, is often a symptom of feelings of powerlessness. As discussed at the beginning of this guide, all human beings need to experience healthy personal power. Circles are particularly effective at providing an experience of personal power that is not gained at the expense of someone else's power. As a result, the need to exercise power over others is reduced. Additionally, the deep respect accorded everyone in a Circle reduces the need of the bully to command respect through power.

Chronic behavior patterns are not easily changed, even when there is a desire to do so. By definition, bullying is a form of chronic behavior. Consequently, a commitment to multiple Circles is very important when working with bullying behavior. Broad involvement is also crucial, because bullying depends upon silence or secrecy to continue.

Circles hold enormous potential to transform problems of bullying into opportunities to understand the underlying stress or trauma in the lives of those affected. There is also a potential to do harm if the Circle process is not steeped in values and guided by the Core Assumptions that began this guide. The attitude of the keeper of the Circle is as important as the technique. Adults using Circles to address bullying need to be self aware—aware of their own values, aware of their communication style, aware of their affect and body language, and aware of their own biases and triggers. This is a journey that takes courage and heart. Perhaps every Circle dealing with bullying could begin with reading the Core Assumptions to remind everyone of the good in all of us.

Appendices

APPENDIX 1 Sample Prompting Questions/Topics for Circles

APPENDIX 2 Openings & Closings

APPENDIX 3 Theoretical Essay on Why Circles Are Important in Schools

APPENDIX 4 Resources

  I. Resources on Restorative Justice, the Circle Process, Schools, and Youth
  II. Resources for Circle Openings and Closings

APPENDIX 5 Level Guide to the Circles

APPENDIX 1

Sample Prompting Questions/Topics for Circles

EXPLORING VALUES

- When you are being human, at your best, what qualities describe you? (in a word or short phrase)
- Imagine you are in conflict with a person who is important in your life. What values do you want to guide your conduct as you try to work out that conflict?
- What value would you like to offer for our space together?
- Tell us about your work and what the challenges are.
- What is your passion?
- What do you keep returning to in your life?
- What touches your heart?
- What gives you hope?
- What demonstrates respect?
- What is something you value about your family? Why?
- What is something you value about yourself? Why?
- What is something that you are thankful for? Why?
- Talk about something that you want and something that you need. What is the difference?
- What have you learned about power? What does it mean to you?
- What have you learned about work? What does it mean to you?
- What have you learned about money? What does it mean to you?
- In your experience, what supports healing?
- What sustains you during difficult times?

Michelle Brenneman used this question with 5th graders: "In a good discussion, the people would be...." They wrote their answers on construction paper and placed them in the middle of the Circle. She then did a quick round, asking them if they would commit to acting on these values during their discussion.

GETTING ACQUAINTED

- Share a happy childhood memory.
- Share a funny story from your work (or life).
- If you could be a superhero, what super powers would you choose and why?
- What do you appreciate about your work or main activity?
- How would your best friend describe you?
- What would you not want to change about your life?
- If you could talk to someone from your family who is no longer alive, who would it be and why?
- If you had an unexpected free day, what would you like to do?
- If you were an animal, what animal would you be and why?
- Name two things or people who always make you laugh.
- I like to collect . . .
- Name one male and one female who is a good role model for young people.
- When was the last time you said "yes" and would have liked to say "no?" Why did you say, "yes?"
- If you could have a face-to-face conversation with someone alive today or someone who has passed on, who would it be and why?
- Describe your ideal job.
- Describe your favorite vacation.
- If you could change anything about yourself, what would it be?
- What is one skill or talent you have?
- What are three "gifts" (attributes of yourself) that you bring to the Circle?
- If you were a reporter, what kind of stories would you like to write about?
- Who are some of your heroes? Why are they your heroes?
- What do you think other people see as your best quality? Why?
- What is the silliest thing that ever happened to you?
- What is the best thing that happened to you this past week? What was the most difficult or challenging thing that happened to you this week?

STORYTELLING FROM OUR LIVES TO SHARE WHO WE ARE AND WHAT HAS SHAPED US

These questions are designed to build community, deepen relationships, and develop empathy. Invite participants to share:

- A time when you had to let go of control.
- A time when you were outside your comfort zone.
- An experience in your life when you "made lemonade out of lemons."

- An experience of transformation when, out of a crisis or difficulty, you discovered a gift in your life.
- An experience of causing harm to someone and then dealing with it in a way you felt good about.
- An experience of letting go of anger or resentment.
- A time when you acted on your core values, even though others were not.
- A time from your adolescence when you were in conflict with your parents or caregiver.
- An experience where you discovered that someone was very different from the negative assumptions you first made about that person.
- An experience of feeling that you did not fit in.
- A time in your life when you experienced justice.
- A time in your life when you experienced injustice.
- An embarrassing moment that you can laugh at now.
- Something that scares/scared you. How do/did you deal with it?
- Something that makes/made you angry. How do/did you deal with it?
- A time that was one of your most difficult challenges. How did you deal with it?

TAKING RESPONSIBILITY

- How have we each contributed to this situation, and how can each of us, by taking responsibility, act differently now?
- Does anyone have anything to clear?
- What is unspoken in the group that blocks good relationships or possible success?
- Name one thing about yourself you would like to grow or improve in.
- What do you think other people see as a quality that you need to work on?
- What is the most important lesson in life you have ever learned? What made it so important?

COMMUNITY

- What change would you like to see in your community? What can you do to promote that change?
- What is something you value about your community (culture, school, youth group, etc.)? Why?
- What is your favorite place to go in your community and why?
- Think about the neighborhood that you grew up in. What are some of your earliest memories? What are some of your more recent memories?
- Think of something that you like and something that you do not like about your neighborhood. Why?

- What is one thing about your family (community, school, team, etc.) that you would change if you could?
- If you could change or overhaul two things in our culture or society, what would they be?

EXPLORING RELATIONSHIPS

- What is the most important quality to you in a relationship with someone else? How and why is it important to you?
- Talk about a relationship between people you know that you admire. Why do you admire this relationship?
- Who is someone in your life that you look up to?
- Who is someone in your life that you have learned from? What did you learn from them?
- Who is someone in your life that has helped you to grow? How have you grown? How did they help you to do so?
- Who was a teacher who influenced you in positive ways? In what ways did they influence you?
- How are you different from your father if you are male, or from your mother if you are female?
- Tell us about a time when you felt like you really belonged.
- Tell us about a time when you felt left out.
- In what social setting or situation have you felt the least powerful? What was it that caused you to feel that way?
- What person or persons in your life is your greatest challenge?
- What do you remember that your father or mother figure most often said to you?
- What have you learned about sex, relationships, and responsibility?
- Complete this sentence: Let me introduce you to my father; he's the kind of man who . . . (Do the same with mother.)
- What person or people know you the best? How well do you feel they really know you?
- What do others want from you?
- What do you want from others?
- What is a quality that you've seen in the opposite sex that you'd like to have or have more of in yourself?
- What do you most appreciate about someone who is important to you in your life?

HOPES AND DREAMS

- If you could go anywhere in the world, where would you go? Why?
- Close your eyes and imagine yourself ten years from now. Where are you? What are you doing? Who/what is one person or thing that stands out to you? Describe them. (You can also do this for your family, community, school, or neighborhood.)
- What is it that you do that gives you the most pleasure?
- What is it that you do that gives you the most satisfaction?
- What is one skill or talent you wish you had?
- If you could do anything that you wished in the world, what would that one thing be?
- What did you dream about when you were a young child?
- What do you dream about now?
- What are three things you would do if you could change the world?
- What is a goal you have for yourself? How will you celebrate yourself when you accomplish it?
- What is one obstacle that gets in the way of your reaching your goals? What is your plan to overcome this obstacle?
- If you were totally free, what would that mean? What would it look like?
- What brings you the most joy?
- What are you honestly looking for in your life right now?
- What are you really trying to learn at this point in your life?

TOWARD THE END OF A CIRCLE

- Is there anything you came with that you would like to leave behind?
- What are you taking from this Circle that supports your healing?
- Where do you see yourself moving forward?
- What have you learned?
- What can you take away that is useful to you?
- How will these insights help you in the next two weeks?
- If you were to give a name to this Circle (group), what would you name it?

APPENDIX 2

Openings & Closings

The following is a selection of openings and closings that you may want to use in your Circle processes. Of course, this material is just a springboard for your own research into openings and closings that can meaningfully serve a Circle's subject and focus. We would like to have included more material with humor, for example. Other themes that could be helpful in schools include gratitude, friendship, relationships, trust and trustworthiness, cooperation, and working together. Many wonderful ideas, quotes, and short clips are out there and available on the Web.

The openings and closings to help you get started are organized into five categories:

- I. Readings Organized by Themes
- II. Meditations & Visualizations
- III. Affirmation & Group-Building Exercises
- IV. Movement Exercises
- V. Music & Songs

I. READINGS ORGANIZED BY THEMES

(See the Table of Contents for the list of themes, pages xi–xii.)

CIRCLES

"The Circle is . . ."

The circle is perhaps the most ancient of mystical symbols and the most universal of all dances. It is the earth and the sun in eternal movement, an unbroken line symbolizing continuity and eternity. The circle creates solidarity. Because it takes more than two people to complete a circle, the circle creates community. It is the perfect democracy; there is equality. The circle is charmed because it encloses emptiness—an emptiness constructed by, and charged with, the concentrated energy of our moving, connected bodies. Encircling is the incorporating, the giving and receiving of power. In the process, a higher being is discovered, namely, the group soul.

— Iris J. Stewart, *Sacred Women, Sacred Dance,*
  American teacher of dance and women's studies

The Circle itself as a ceremony

Beyond the opening and closing ceremonies, the Circle itself is a ritual that communicates meaning. Sitting in the round says that everyone is included equally without regard to rank, status, or hierarchy. Shedding titles gives a further message of equality and of looking beyond outer roles to who we are in our hearts. Joining hands expresses community. The opening ceremony invites reflection and a spiritual sense of connectedness. The talking piece cultivates a capacity both to listen and to speak with respect. The guidelines convey shared ownership of the process and responsibility for its outcomes. And the closing ceremony inspires gratitude for the good achieved. Together, these rituals create a secure space where we can share personal stories, express emotions, be honest, take risks, and seek solutions to very difficult issues.

— Kay Pranis, Barry Stuart, & Mark Wedge, *Peacemaking Circles*, 119.
These authors from the U.S., Canada, and First Nations are long-time Circle practitioners and trainers.

". . . Until Circles seem almost invisible—just second nature"

Each Circle is different, and no one can predict what will happen in any given gathering. On one hand, Circles have no fixed formula. On the other hand, definite factors—inner and outer, unseen and seen—help to create their unique dynamics. The more a group comes to know and use Circles, the less obvious some of these factors become. They get woven into a community's way of being together, until they seem almost invisible—just second nature.

— Kay Pranis, Barry Stuart, & Mark Wedge, *Peacemaking Circles*, 7.

"Everything the power of the world does is done in a circle"

Everything the Power of the World does is done in a circle. The sky is round, and I have heard that the earth is round like a ball, and so are all the stars. The wind, in its greatest power, whirls. Birds make their nests in circles, for theirs is the same religion as ours. The sun comes forth and goes down again in a circle. The moon does the same, and both are round. Even the seasons form a great circle in their changing, and always come back again to where they were. The life of a person is a Circle from childhood to childhood, and so it is in everything where power moves.

— Black Elk, from Neihardt, *Black Elk Speaks*, 194–95.
Black Elk was an Oglala Tituwan (Lakota) holy man, 1863–1950.

"The Healing Song"

I heard you singing—
I saw your fire glowing—
And I crept, weary and bedraggled
To your Circle.

You have nourished me.
You have cleansed me.
You have held me in your embrace of acceptance.
You have sung the Healing Song
Until the dull embers in my heart exploded
Consuming the dark emptiness.

You have given me courage
To gallop again into the hills—
To sing the Healing Song
To be Fire in the darkness.

— Mary Skillings, excerpt from "The Healing Song," Euro-American Circle keeper and restorative justice practitioner. Reprinted with permission.

"The whole hoop of the world"

Then I was standing on the highest mountain of them all, and round about beneath me was the whole hoop of the world. And while I stood there, I saw more than I can tell and I understood more than I saw; for I was seeing in a sacred manner the shapes of all things in the spirit, and the shape of all shapes as they must live together like one being. And I saw the sacred hoop of my people was one of many hoops that made one circle, wide as daylight and as starlight, and in the center grew one mighty flowering tree to shelter all the children of one mother and one father. And I saw that it was holy.

— Black Elk, from Neihardt, *Black Elk Speaks*, 43.

"Circle poem"

People in a circle

Share stories, values, dreams

Create a unity

Of life ongoing

Universal wisdom

Wedded with hope

Of a world renewed

And no one left out

> — William Tweed Kennedy, written at a Circle training in Virginia. Reprinted with permission.

The power of collective caring

The beliefs and traditions may vary, and they certainly do vary . . . but their common thread is the power of collective caring, its power to break down or penetrate walls of separation, its power to heal, bring reassurance, and peace, and its power to bind our separate lives into a community of deep and eternal unity.

> — Holly Bridges, Euro-Canadian journalist, author, reporter, and talk show host

A circle of trust: sitting quietly and waiting for the shy soul to show up

Like a wild animal, the soul is tough, resilient, resourceful, savvy, and self-sufficient: it knows how to survive in hard places. I learned about these qualities during my bouts with depression. In that deadly darkness, the faculties I had always depended on collapsed. My intellect was useless; my emotions were dead; my will was impotent; my ego was shattered. But from time to time, deep in the thickets of my inner wilderness, I could sense the presence of something that knew how to stay alive even when the rest of me wanted to die. That something was my tough and tenacious soul.

Yet despite its toughness, the soul is also shy. Just like a wild animal, it seeks safety in the dense underbrush, especially when other people are around. If we want to see a wild animal, we know that the last thing we should do is go crashing through the woods yelling for it to come out. But if we will walk quietly into the woods, sit patiently at the base of a tree, breathe with the earth, and fade into our surroundings, the wild creature we seek might put in an appearance. We may see it only briefly and only out of the corner of an eye—but the sight is a gift we will always treasure as an end in itself.

Unfortunately, *community* in our culture too often means a group of people who go crashing through the woods together, scaring the soul away. In spaces ranging from congregations to classrooms, we preach and teach, assert and argue, claim and proclaim, admonish and advise, and generally behave in ways that drive everything original and wild into hiding. Under these conditions, the intellect, emotions, will and ego may emerge, but not the soul: we scare off all the soulful things, like respectful relationships, goodwill, and hope.

A circle of trust is a group of people who know how to sit quietly "in the woods" with each other and wait for the shy soul to show up . . . In such a space, we are freed to hear our own truth, touch what brings us joy, become self critical about our faults, and take risky steps toward change—knowing that we will be accepted no matter what the outcome.

> — Parker J. Palmer, from *A Hidden Wholeness: The Journey Toward an Undivided Life*, pp. 58–59. Parker Palmer is a Euro-American author, educator, and activist who focuses on education, community, leadership, spirituality, and social change.

UNITY & INTERCONNECTEDNESS

"Whatever we do to the web, we do to ourselves"

You must teach your children that the ground beneath their feet is the ashes of our ancestors. So that they will respect the land, tell your children that the land is rich with the lives of our kin. Teach your children what we have taught our children—that the earth is our mother. Whatever befalls the earth befalls the sons and daughters of the earth. If men spit upon the ground, they spit upon themselves.

This we know: The earth does not belong to man; man belong to the earth. This we know. All things are connected like the blood which unites one family. All things are connected. . . .

Humankind has not woven the web of life. We are but one thread within it. Whatever we do to the web, we do to ourselves. All things are bound together. All things connect.

> — Chief Si'ahl (Seattle), Duwamish, c. 1780–1866
> Text taken from California Indian Education website

"Widening our circle of compassion"

A human being is a part of the whole, called by us 'universe,' a part limited in time and space. He experiences himself, his thoughts and feelings as something separated from the rest, a kind of optical delusion of his consciousness. This delusion is a kind of prison for us, restricting us to our personal desires and to affection for a few persons nearest to us. Our task must be to free ourselves from this prison by widening our circle of compassion to embrace all living creatures and the whole of nature in its beauty.

— Albert Einstein, German-born theoretical physicist, 1879–1955

The wise woman's stone

A wise woman who was traveling in the mountains found a precious stone in a stream. The next day she met another traveler who was hungry, and the wise woman opened her bag to share her food. The hungry traveler saw the precious stone and asked the woman to give it to him. She did so without hesitation. The traveler left, rejoicing in his good fortune. He knew the stone was worth enough to give him security for a lifetime. But a few days later he came back to return the stone to the wise woman. "I've been thinking," he said, "I know how valuable the stone is, but I give it back in the hope that you can give me something even more precious." "Give me what you have within you that enabled you to give me the stone."

— Anonymous

"Considering the interests of others is the best form of self-interest"

I believe that to meet the challenge of our times, human beings will have to develop a greater sense of universal responsibility. Each of us must learn to work not for his or her self, family or nation, but for the benefit of all mankind. Universal responsibility is the real key to human survival. . . .

Whether we like it or not, we have been born on this earth as part of one great family. Rich or poor, educated or uneducated, belonging to one nation, ideology or another, ultimately each of us just a human being like everyone else. Furthermore, each of us has the same right to pursue happiness and avoid suffering. When you recognize that all beings are equal in this respect, you automatically feel empathy and closeness for them. Out of this, in turn, comes a genuine sense of universal responsibility; the wish to actively help others overcome their problems. . . .

The need for a sense of universal responsibility affects every aspect of modern life. Nowadays, significant events in one part of the world eventually affect the entire planet. Therefore, we have to treat each major local problem as a global concern from the moment it begins. We can no longer invoke the national, racial or ideological barriers that separate us without destructive repercussions. In the context of our new interdependence, considering the interests of others is clearly the best form of self-interest.

> — The 14th Dalai Lama of Tibet is a high lama and leader of Tibetan Buddhism and Tibetan people; he is now living in exile in India. Available at: http://www.dalailama.com/messages/environment/global-environment

"Wholeness—all things are interrelated"

Wholeness. All things are interrelated. Everything in the universe is a part of a single whole. Everything is connected in some way to everything else. It is therefore possible to understand something only if we can understand how it is connected to everything else.

> — Bopp, Bopp, Brown, and Lane, Jr., *The Sacred Tree*, 26,
> Co-founders of the Four Worlds International Institute,
> a Native and First Nation group

When the dignity and safety of an individual is assaulted, the dignity and fabric of the group as a whole is diminished.

> — William M. Bukowski and Lorrie K. Sippola, "Groups, Individuals, and Victimization: A View of the Peer System" (*Peer Harassment in School*)

Exploring all the factors that might have contributed to a behavior

Traditional teaching suggests that the principle—or law—of wholeness applies not only to the nonhuman realms, but to the human one as well. When people cause problems, for instance, this law of interconnectedness requires that [we] investigate all the factors that might have contributed to the misbehavior. That investigation must go back much further in time than is the custom in Western courts, and it must encompass a greatly expanded circle of friends, family, employers and other influences. Further, any plan of action must involve not only the individual doing what he or she can with *his or her* problem, but the whole, larger group doing what they can about *their* problem. Disharmony within one individual is seen as everyone's disharmony, for it "infects" all relationships which involve that person. The principle thus requires looking for, and responding to, complex interconnections, not single acts of separate individuals. Anything short of that is seen as a naive response destined to ultimate failure....

"In our teachings," [an Ojibway friend] said, "people heal best when they heal *with* each other."

— Rupert Ross, *Returning to the Teachings: Exploring Aboriginal Justice*, 65–66. Now retired, Euro-Canadian Rupert Ross has traveled remote areas of Canada as a Crown attorney and has learned from Aboriginal people about Indigenous ways of mending harms.

Connected to everyone and everything

We were created to be indispensable, dependent liberators. But such a self-concept will not be achieved easily by most of us. A radical turning around . . . will be required. Dependence, the keystone, is not a state we have been taught to acknowledge as healthy reality. We have too long been admonished to stand on our own, a posture finally and tragically impossible for us. . . . Our deep-seated notions of separateness must be seen as fantasy—deluding and dangerous dreams. To the degree we can see ourselves as connected to everyone and everything in the creation, we can be freed from the terrible burden of having to be right, of having to be adequate. We can fail—or rather we can admit failure, for fail we will. Our questions can become: How do you disagree with me? How do I disagree with you?

How is my understanding partial or erroneous? What do you know that I do not? Together we can tell the truth.

— Caroline A. Westerhoff, "Conflict: The Birthing of the New," in *Conflict Management in Congregations*, 55–56.

LISTENING

"Listening is a magnetic and strange thing"

Listening is a magnetic and strange thing, a creative force. Think how the friends that really listen to us are the ones we move toward, and we want to sit in their radius as though it did us good, like ultraviolet rays.

This is the reason: When we are listened to, it creates us, makes us unfold and expand. Ideas actually begin to grow within us and come to life.

— Brenda Ueland, Euro-American feminist, journalist, and writer, 1891–1985, from "Tell Me More: On the Art of Listening." Online at: http://wickwoodinn.com/spring08notebook/tell_me_more.htm.

Listening looks easy, but it is not simple. Every head is a world.

— Cuban proverb

Hearing is something that happens to us. Listening is something in which we choose to participate.

— James E. Miller, *The Art of Listening in a Healing Way*, 10. Jim Miller is an American writer/photographer, spiritual director, and grief counselor.

Bringing our values to how we listen

To listen in a healing way is to *listen carefully*, paying real attention to all that's being said and not said. You *listen respectfully*, holding both the other person and whatever they have to say with clear regard. You *listen caringly*, allowing a warmth to develop between you if it feels natural, always desiring what is best for the other. You *listen compassionately*, accepting the one you're with just as they are, without comparing them to others or to yourself. And you *listen believingly*, trusting in the healing potential of those who verbally and nonverbally share their lives with you.

— James E. Miller, *The Art of Listening in a Healing Way*, 21.

"Listeners become the sparks of hope . . ."

Within my rich oral-tradition childhood, elders and kin prepared me, guided me and gave me a way to value how life can come into correct relationship when a person will respectfully listen. I believe people can learn to listen. Stories help us to remember joyously, even as the songs, stories, and tellers change. In the heart of every being there is a "listener" who is hungry, thirsty, and possibly crippled. Listeners all want one thing: something to hope for. Something that will satisfy a gnawing hunger, quench a deep thirst, heal and restore life. Even in an immensely dark time, against seemingly impossible odds, hope flickers. It may be a tiny flame, yes, yet a flame can be kindled, making a small fire to come close to and enjoy. Listeners are the lifeblood of an oral tradition. Peoples' songs and stories are potent seed, needing listeners. Listeners become the sparks of hope that will bring fresh fire and make new lives out of ashes.

— Larry Littlebird, Pueblo from Laguna and Santo Domingo Pueblos, author, speaker, trainer, filmmaker, artist, and founding director of HAMAATSA. From *Hunting Sacred, Everything Listens*, 15–16.

"I started listening and being"

I stopped hating and started just being. My whole life, I had been the most defensive person you'd meet, unable to tolerate any criticism. But now I started listening and being.

— Anthony Kiedis, Euro-American musician, lead singer of Red Hot Chili Peppers, from his autobiography, *Scar Tissue*

Being heard is so close to being loved that for the average person, they are almost indistinguishable.

— David Augsburger, Euro-American Anabaptist author, Mennonite minister

A friend asks, "Tell me one word which is significant in any kinds of relationship." Another friend says, "LISTEN!"

— Santosh Kalwar, Nepalese poet, from this collection of poems, *Adventus*

Letting go of any attempt to control the speaker

It's hard to overestimate the importance of one aspect of being a healing listener: you release your own will so you can follow the lead of the other's will as it relates to the communication between you.

You let go of any attempt to control the one who's talking and to shape whatever they're saying. The agenda is theirs, not yours. It is their direction to be followed, their wisdom to be honored, their life to be witnessed, their thoughts and directions to be given form. . . .

Healing listening asks you to stay out of the way so that what is most healing for another has the best possible chance of appearing and then growing.

— James E. Miller, *The Art of Listening in a Healing Way*, 47.

Listening with the heart

When you listen with your heart, you concentrate on what the heart knows best and response to most naturally. You focus on feelings. . . .

A deep place in the other reaches out toward a deep place in you, hoping for a connection. Their heart calls to yours, and when you're at your listening best, your heart responds, "I am here."

Listening with your heart invites you to stay open to another even if their feelings are much different from yours, even if the expression of those feelings is stronger than you expect. In doing so, your heart will lead you to encounters with your own wholeness too. You cannot separate the one from the other.

> — James E. Miller, *The Art of Listening in a Healing Way*, 41.

The Other Way to Listen

Take a horned toad, for example. If you think you're better than a horned toad, you'll never hear its voice, even if you sit in the sun forever.

> — Byrd Baylor, American Southwest author of children's books, excerpt from *The Other Way to Listen*.

"Be Silent and Listen"

The inspiration you seek
Is already inside you,
Be silent and listen.

> — Jalāl al-Dīn Rumi, Persian Sufi poet and mystic, 1207–1273, known in the English-speaking world simply as Rumi

The quieter you become, the more you can hear.

> — Ram Dass, born Richard Alpert, Euro-American spiritual teacher and author

"You dare not hurry healing listening itself"

You dare not hurry healing listening itself. Should you attempt to do so, it will become less healing. The one who's speaking will then not open up naturally and comfortably. They may not touch upon all that is important, and something critical will remain missing. Human growth often requires periods in which change is allowed to unfold as it will, which means that temporarily it may not unfold at all. This all takes time, which takes patience.

> — James E. Miller, *The Art of Listening in a Healing Way*, 63.

SPEAKING FROM THE HEART

Speak from the heart

One Christmas I hiked down into the Grand Canyon, whose bottom lay a vertical mile below the rim. Its walls were layered like a cake, and a foot-high stripe of red or gray rock indicated a million-plus years of erosion by the Colorado river. Think of water—so soft and gentle—gradually carving through the hardest stone to reveal great beauty. Sometimes what seems weakest is actually most powerful.

In the same way, speaking from an open heart can seem so vulnerable yet be the strongest move of all. Naming the truth—in particular the facts of one's experience, which no one can disprove—with simplicity and sincerity, and without contentiousness or blame, has great moral force. You can see the effects writ small and large, from a child telling her parents "I feel bad when you fight" to the profound impact of people describing the atrocities they suffered in Kosovo or Rwanda.

I met recently with a man whose marriage is being smothered by the weight of everything unsaid. What's unnamed is all normal-range stuff—like wishing his wife were less irritable with their children, and more affectionate with him—but there's been a kind of fear about facing it, as if it could blow up the relationship. But not talking is what's actually blowing up their relationship—and in fact, when people do communicate in a heartfelt way, it's dignified and compelling, and it usually evokes support and open-heartedness from others.

— Rick Hanson, Ph.D., Euro-American neuropsychologist and author of *Hardwiring Happiness: The New Brain Science of Contentment, Calm, and Confidence.* Online at: http://www.psychologytoday.com/blog/your-wise-brain/201105/speak-the-heart.

What is speaking from the heart?

What does it mean to speak from the heart? It is a metaphor for speaking with genuine emotion. It is not deliberately inserting emotional material to elicit emotional responses from the audience. It isn't just telling sad stories. Who says the only emotion from the heart is sadness? If your heart is glad, let it be glad! Speaking from the heart is being fully present and in the moment. It is being centered. It is sharing from your essence, in each moment. It is being authentic, being real. It is about sharing your feelings with the audience and inviting them to share with you.

— Craig Senior, Euro-Canadian speech coach and trainer. Online at: http://craigsenior.wordpress.com/2007/12/18/speaking-from-the-heart-vs-using-techniques/.

Never apologize for showing feeling. When you do so, you apologize for truth.

> — Benjamin Disraeli, 1st Earl of Beaconsfield, British conservative politician, twice British Prime Minister, 1804–1881

Out beyond ideas of wrong-doing and right-doing,
there is a field. I'll meet you there.

> — Rumi, Barks with Moyne, translators, *The Essential Rumi*, 36.

STORYTELLING

"The story . . . is a thing that people hunger after"

THE STORY is more than a reminder of humanity or a teacher of tribal ways. It is a thing that people hunger after. Need to remain alive. Like a natural portion of fresh water, clean air, good food. If the American air has gone strange, the water turned murky and the food become filled with unnatural additives, can you imaging how unhealthy the story told has become?

> — Larry Littlebird, from his website: http://www.hamaatsa.org/index.html

"The story makes you what you are"

It's like everyone tells a story about themselves inside their own head. Always. All the time. That story makes you what you are. We build ourselves out of that story.

> — Patrick Rothfuss, Euro-American fantasy author, from *The Name of the Wind*

"Stories go in circles"

Listen, stories go in circles. They don't go in straight lines. So, it helps if you listen in circles because there are stories inside and stories between stories and finding your way through them is as easy and as hard as finding your way home. And part of the finding is the getting lost. And when you're lost, you really start to open up and listen.

> — Corey Fischer et al. *Coming from a Great Distance*, 1978, Jewish-American actor, director, writer

If we can share our story with someone who responds with empathy and understanding, shame can't survive.

> — Brené Brown, Euro-American scholar, author, and speaker

All sorrows can be borne if you put them into a story and tell a story about them.

— Karen Blixen, Danish author, known by her pen name Isak Dinesen, 1885–1962

"Sometimes a person needs a story more than food"

The stories people tell have a way of taking care of them. If stories come to you, care for them. And learn to give them away where they are needed. Sometimes a person needs a story more than food to stay alive. That is why we put these stories in each other's memory. This is how people care for themselves."

— Barry Lopez, from *Crow and Weasel*. Barry Lopez is a Euro-American author, essayist, and fiction writer whose work is known for its humanitarian and environmental concerns.

BELONGING

"We are wired to love, to be loved, and to belong"

A deep sense of love and belonging is an irreducible need of all people. We are biologically, cognitively, physically, and spiritually wired to love, to be loved, and to belong. When those needs are not met, we don't function as we were meant to. We break. We fall apart. We numb. We ache. We hurt others. We get sick.

— Brené Brown

"Belonging starts with self-acceptance"

The truth is: Belonging starts with self-acceptance. Your level of belonging, in fact, can never be greater than your level of self-acceptance, because believing that you're enough is what gives you the courage to be authentic, vulnerable, and imperfect.

— Brené Brown

"Working through the ways that you're different"

I'm not practising, I don't go to church, but what I got from it was a sense of belonging to something bigger. What I really miss is being forced to be in a community with people that aren't the same as you. Then, you really have to work through the ways that you're different.

— Edwin Farnham "Win" Butler, Euro-American lead vocalist and songwriter of the Montreal-based indie rock band Arcade Fire.

Different and belonging

When I was four years old they tried to test my IQ, they showed me this picture of three oranges and a pear. They asked me which one is different and does not belong; they taught me different was wrong.

— Ani DiFranco, American singer, guitarist, poet, and songwriter

RESPECT

"Respect is the main thing"

Johnny Johns, an Elder of the Carcross/Tagish First Nation, said, "Respect is the main thing. If you don't have that, you don't have anything." A Minnesota public defender said the same: "In a Circle, respect comes first. We may not always agree, but we must always have respect." Respect means honoring ourselves by acting in accord with our values, honoring others by recognizing their right to be different, and treating others with dignity. We express respect not only in how we speak and act but also through our emotions and body language. Respect comes from a deep inner place of acknowledging the worth inherent in every aspect of creation.

— Kay Pranis, Barry Stuart, & Mark Wedge, *Peacemaking Circles*, 34–35

SELF-LOVE & DISCOVERING OUR TRUE SELVES

You deserve your love and affection

You can search throughout the entire universe for someone who is more deserving of your love and affection than you are yourself, and that person is not to be found anywhere. You, yourself, as much as anybody in the entire universe, deserve your love and affection.

— Attributed to Gautama/Siddhārtha Buddha, sage of India, c. 563–483 BCE
http://www.goodreads.com/author/quotes/2167493.Gautama_Buddha

Liking yourself

It is rewarding to find someone you like, but it is essential to like yourself. It is quickening to recognize that someone is a good and decent human being, but it is indispensable to view yourself as acceptable. It is a delight to discover people who are worthy of respect and admiration and love, but it is vital to believe yourself worthy of these things.

For you cannot live in someone else. You cannot find yourself in someone else.

You cannot be given a life through someone else. Of all the people you will know in a lifetime, you are the only one you will never leave or lose.

To the question of your life, you are the only answer. To the problems of your life, you are the only solution.

— Jo Coudert, *Advice from a Failure*, Euro-American author

"You can never love anybody if you are unable to love yourself"

One of the best guides to how to be self-loving is to give ourselves the love we are often dreaming about receiving from others. There was a time when I felt lousy about my over-forty body, saw myself as too fat, too this, or too that. Yet I fantasized about finding a lover who would give me the gift of being loved as I am. It is silly, isn't it, that I would dream of someone else offering to me the acceptance and affirmation I was withholding from myself. This was a moment when the maxim "You can never love anybody if you are unable to love yourself" made clear sense. And I add, "Do not expect to receive the love from someone else you do not give yourself."

— bell hooks, African-American author and social activist

"The Masks I Wear," *actually titled* "Please Hear What I Am Not Saying"

Charles C. Finn, Euro-American, wrote this poem in 1966, and it has become a classic. Versions of it have been passed around the world. The original text—as well as the poem's unique story—are available on Charles Finn's website: http://www.poetrybycharlescfinn.com/.

The Invitation

This well-known poem by Oriah, Euro-Canadian storyteller and author, is available on her website, http://oriahmountaindreamer.com/.

"Our deepest fear is that we are powerful beyond measure"

This well-known passage from Marianne Williamson's book, *A Return to Love,* 190, is widely available online. See, for example: https://en.wikiquote.org/wiki/Marianne_Williamson. Marianne Williamson is a Euro-American spiritual teacher, author, and lecturer.

"We are the ones we've been waiting for"

We don't need someone to show us the ropes. We are the ones we've been waiting for. Deep inside us we know the feelings we need to guide us. Our task is to learn to trust our inner knowing.

— Sonia Johnson, Euro-American feminist, social activist and writer, from *Going Out of Our Minds: The Metaphysics of Liberation.*

"More than that..."

Two classes of the Todd County High School on the Sicangu Lakota homeland, the Rosebud Reservation, produced this YouTube video in response to the ABC documentary, "Children of the Plains." http://www.youtube.com/watch?v=FhribaNXr7A

"Keep knocking"

Keep knocking, and the joy inside
will eventually open a window
and look out to see who's there.

— Rumi, Barks with Moyne, translators, *The Essential Rumi,* 101

"You are already that"

Do you know what you are?
You are a manuscript of a divine letter.
You are a mirror reflecting a noble face.
The universe is not outside of you.
Look inside yourself;
everything that you want,
You are already that.

— Rumi, Shahram Shiva, translator, *Hush, Don't Say Anything to God*

"The entire ocean in a drop"

You are not a drop in the ocean.
You are the entire ocean,
In a drop.

— Rumi

LEARNING

"Without education, you're not going anywhere in this world"

My alma mater was books, a good library . . . I could spend the rest of my life reading, just satisfying my curiosity. Without education, you're not going anywhere in this world.

— Malcolm X, African-American Muslim minister and human rights activist, 1925–1965

Neuroplasticity: growing our brains throughout life

- Neuroplasticity refers to the lifelong capacity of the brain to change and rewire itself in response to the stimulation of learning and experience. Neurogenesis is the ability to create new neurons and connections between neurons throughout a lifetime.
- Learning is thought to be "neuro-protective." Through neuroplasticity, learning increases connections between neurons, increases cellular metabolism, and increases the production of nerve growth factor, a substance produced by the body to help maintain and repair neurons.
- There is not one single "attention," but three separate functions of attention: alerting, orienting, and executive attention.
- The fear of failing, the fear of looking not smart, is a key obstacle to learning that I see too often, especially with people who want to protect perceived reputations to such an extent that they do not let themselves try new learning cycles.
- Emotion is the system that tells us how important something is. Attention focuses us on the important and away from the unimportant things. Cognition tells us what to do about it. Cognitive skills are whatever it takes to do those things.
- Exercise increases the brain's volume of gray matter (actual neurons) and white matter (connections between neurons).

- Current recommendations suggest that a brain-healthy life style should include at least balanced nutrition, stress management, physical exercise, and brain exercise.... Sleep and overall health conditions are other factors that also matter.

    — Avaro Fernandez, Dr. Elkhonon Goldberg, and others, *The SharpBrains Guide to Brain Fitness*. Online at: http://sharpbrains.com/blog/2011/12/06/top-10-quotes-on-lifelong-neuroplasticity-neurogenesis-and-brain-fitness-and-a-call-to-ebook-readers/. SharpBrains is a business made up of doctors and businesspeople that explores the practical implications of neuroscience.

Neuroplasticity: positive emotions can be cultivated

Among other things, neuroplasticity means that emotions such as happiness and compassion can be cultivated in much the same way that a person can learn through repetition to play golf and basketball or master a musical instrument, and that such practice changes the activity and physical aspects of specific brain areas.

    — Andrew Weil, *Spontaneous Healing*. Dr. Weil is a Euro-American medical doctor and naturopath who also teaches and writes on holistic health.

"A person can learn a lot from a dog"

A person can learn a lot from a dog, even a loopy one like ours. Marley taught me about living each day with unbridled exuberance and joy, about seizing the moment and following your heart. He taught me to appreciate the simple things—a walk in the woods, a fresh snowfall, a nap in a shaft of winter sunlight. And as he grew old and achy, he taught me about optimism in the face of adversity. Mostly, he taught me about friendship and selflessness and, above all else, unwavering loyalty."

    — John Grogan, *Marley and Me: Life and Love With the World's Worst Dog*. John Grogan is a Euro-American journalist and nonfiction writer.

Interest produces learning more than fear can

I think the big mistake in schools is trying to teach children anything, and by using fear as the basic motivation. Fear of getting failing grades, fear of not staying with your class, etc. Interest can produce learning on a scale compared to fear as a nuclear explosion to a firecracker."

    — Stanley Kubrick, Jewish-American filmmaker, 1928–1999

"Have patience with everything unresolved in your heart"

I beg you . . . to have patience with everything unresolved in your heart and try to love the questions themselves as if they were locked rooms or books written in a very foreign language. Don't search for the answers, which could not be given you now, because you would not be able to live them. And the point is, to live everything. Live the questions now. Perhaps then, someday far in the future, you will gradually, without even noticing it, live your way into the answer.

> — Rainer Maria Rilke, a Bohemian-Austrian poet and novelist, 1875–1926. From Letter Four, Worpswede, near Bremen, 16 July 1903.

Know more today and lessen suffering

For me, I am driven by two main philosophies: know more today about the world than I knew yesterday and lessen the suffering of others. You'd be surprised how far that gets you.

> — Neil deGrasse Tyson, African-American astrophysicist, author, and science communicator

"Let it all mature slowly inside you"

Slowly but surely I have been soaking Rilke up these last few months: the man, his work and his life. And that is probably the only right way with literature, with study, with people or with anything else: to let it all soak in, to let it all mature slowly inside you until it has become a part of yourself. That, too, is a growing process. Everything is a growing process. And in between, emotions and sensations that strike you like lightning. But still the most important thing is the organic process of growing."

> — Etty Hillesum, 1914–1943, was a Jewish-Dutch woman whose letters and diaries, kept between 1941 and 1943, describe life in Amsterdam during the German occupation. She died at Auschwitz. This quote is from *An Interrupted Life: The Diaries, 1941-1943; and Letters from Westerbork*, p. 102.

"Everyone does what they know"

I believe everyone does the best they can. Everyone does what they know. If people act in improper ways is not because of a flaw in their spirit, but due to lack of information and clarity of incentives. That is why I try hard not to judge others, or tell them what to do. I understand that everyone sees a different piece of the puzzle.

> — Carlos Miceli, born in Argentina, describes himself as a lifelong learner with a strong entrepreneurial spirit: http://carlosmiceli.com/philosophies/

James Baldwin on life and learning

James Baldwin was an African-American novelist, essayist, playwright, poet, social critic, and activist for human rights, 1924–1987.

You think your pain and your heartbreak are unprecedented in the history of the world, but then you read. It was books that taught me that the things that tormented me most were the very things that connected me with all the people who were alive, or who had ever been alive.

— From the film, *James Baldwin: The Price of the Ticket*, 1990

American history is longer, larger, more various, more beautiful, and more terrible than anything anyone has ever said about it.

— "A Talk to Teachers," 1963

SELF-DETERMINATION & EMPOWERMENT

People don't resist change. They resist being changed.

— Peter Senge, Euro-American systems scientist who focuses on organizational learning

"The freedom to choose one's attitude, . . . one's own way"

We who lived in concentration camps can remember the people who walked through the huts comforting others, giving away their last piece of bread. They may have been few in number, but they offer sufficient proof that everything can be taken from a person but one thing: the last of human freedoms—to choose one's attitude in any given set of circumstances, to choose one's own way.

— Viktor E. Frankl, *Man's Search for Meaning*, 75. Frankl was an Austrian psychiatrist, Holocaust survivor, and founder of logotherapy, 1905–1997

If you hear a voice within you say "you cannot paint," then by all means paint and that voice will be silenced.

— Vincent Van Gogh, Dutch-born post-Impressionist painter, 1853–1890

Choosing to learn and practice compassion, kindness, and happiness

A dangerous belief in our culture is that we can't change. We've all heard the disempowered statements: "He's just grumpy. He can't change that." or "I will always be anxious. It's the way I was born." While we most certainly have genetic predispositions, the brains of individuals' young and old can change in amazing ways.

Neuroplasticity is a fancy way of saying that our brains can change.... We are empowered creators of our mental states. The erroneous belief that we are "set in stone" can stop people from trying to change and take away their responsibility. In the same way that germ theory altered the way we look at sanitation and hygiene, I think that spreading the knowledge about our brain's ability to change can alter the way our culture approaches emotions, attitudes, and values....

Knowing that our brains can change, we then ask, what do we want in our brains? And as a result, what do we want in our world? Most people of good will yearn for happiness, compassion, and love. Let's start practicing.

Gratitude reflections, compassion priming, and meditation interventions are some strategies found to enhance well-being and increase prosocial behavior. Several studies have shown the positive impact of gratitude journals, which involve self-guided listing of what you are thankful for. Individuals who kept a daily gratitude journal reported higher levels of positive emotions, including feeling attentive, determined, energetic, enthusiastic, excited, interested, joyful, and strong, compared to individuals who kept a journal on daily hassles or ways in which one was better off than others (downward social comparison). In addition, individuals who maintained daily gratitude journals were more likely to offer emotional support to others and help someone with a problem....

In my experience, learning about the concept of neuroplasticity and finding the skills to change my emotional responses has immensely improved my life. Before grasping this, I thought my mind was a black box. I didn't understand why I felt certain things beyond the immediate external circumstances. I had no idea how to change things.... The practice of meditation gave me the set of skills to guide my own transformation. It has been the most life altering skill that I have gained. I shifted from thinking that my emotions and thoughts owned me to feeling like I could play a role in changing my state. This is challenging work and takes patient practice, but as I am experiencing the fruits of these skills, peaceful relationships, a joyful outlook on life, and a safe harbor within myself during difficult times, I am determined to work even harder.

— Joanna Holsten, "Neuroplasticity: Changing Our Belief about Change," from her blog, *Let's Live Nice* at: http://www.letslivenice.com/2012/01/neuroplasticity.html

CHANGING THE WORLD... STARTING WITH OURSELVES

Bringing about world peace by the inner transformation of individuals

Although attempting to bring about world peace through the internal transformation of individuals is difficult, it is the only way. Wherever I go, I express this, and I am encouraged that people from many different walks of life receive it well. Peace must first be developed within an individual. And I believe that love, compassion, and altruism are the fundamental basis for peace. Once these qualities are developed within an individual, he or she is then able to create an atmosphere of peace and harmony. This atmosphere can be expanded and extended from the individual to the family, from the family to the community and eventually to the whole world.

— H. H. The Dalai Lama, Foreword to Thich Nhat Hanh, *Peace Is Every Step*, vii.

"The Art of Peace begins with you"

The Art of Peace begins with you. Work on yourself and your appointed task in the Art of Peace. Everyone has a spirit that can be refined, a body that can be trained in some manner, a suitable path to follow. You are here for no other purpose than to realize your inner divinity and manifest your innate enlightenment. Foster peace in your own life and then apply the Art of Peace to all you encounter.

— Morihei Ueshiba, Japanese martial arts, founder of Aikido, 1883–1969

"A great workshop inside me"

Sometimes it is as if there were a great workshop inside me where hard labouring is being done, much hammering and who knows what else. And sometimes it is as if I were made of granite inside, a chunk of rock ceaselessly lashed and hollowed by the powerful currents. A granite cave being hollowed out more and more, and having contours and shapes cut into it. Perhaps the shapes will lie ready inside me one day with sharply defined outlines, and all I will have to do then is to copy what I find in myself.

— Etty Hillesum, 10th of June 1942, *An Interrupted Life: The Diaries*

"One moral duty: to reclaim large areas of peace in ourselves"

Ultimately, we have just one moral duty: to reclaim large areas of peace in ourselves, more and more peace, and to reflect it toward others. And the more peace there is in us, the more peace there will also be in our troubled world.

— Etty Hillesum, 29 September 1943, *An Interrupted Life: The Diaries*

Our struggle

We're all lovers and we're all destroyers. We're all frightened and at the same time we all want terribly to trust. This is part of our struggle. We have to help what is the most beautiful to emerge in us and to divert the powers of darkness and violence. I learn to be able to say, "This is my fragility. I must learn about it and use it in a constructive way."

— Jean Vanier, Canadian Catholic theologian and humanitarian

All this is, is trying to come home to our humanity and to help others come home to their humanity.

— Anonymous

That it's not about doing good for others, but learning how to be good with others.

— Rhidian Brook, *More Than Eyes Can See.* Novelist, screenwriter, and broadcaster

Mary Oliver's poetry

Mary Oliver is a Euro-American poet who draws heavily on images from the natural world. Her poems can be read from her books as well as online. Consider, for example, the following poems, all of which can be found online at: http://peacefulrivers.homestead.com/maryoliver.html.

"The Journey"
"Wild Geese"
"Song of the Builders" from **Why I Wake Early** (2004)

"Take time to live—It is what life is for"
by Stanislaus Kennedy

Sister Stanislaus Kennedy, "Sister Stan," is an Irish member of the Sisters of Charity. An author of many books, she describes herself as a visionary and social innovator. One of the easiest places to find this poem online is on a Facebook page: https://www.facebook.com/danceofenergyconscioushealing/posts/405636492870174.

I am only one, but still I am one. I cannot do everything, but still I can do something. And because I cannot do everything, I will not refuse to do something that I can do.

— Edward Everett Hale, Euro-American author and Unitarian clergyman, 1822–1909

INCLUSION & EXCLUSION

What Is Inclusion?

Across this country a definition of inclusion is offered. It is generally accepted that "Inclusion" means inviting those who have been historically locked out to "come in". This well-intentioned meaning must be strengthened. A weakness of this definition is evident. Who has the authority or right to "invite" others in? And how did the "inviters" get in? Finally, who is doing the excluding? It is time we both recognize and accept that we are all born "in"! No one has the right to invite others in! It definitely becomes our responsibility as a society to remove all barriers which uphold exclusion since none of us have the authority to "invite" others "in"!

So what is inclusion? Inclusion is recognizing our universal "oneness" and interdependence. Inclusion is recognizing that we are "one" even though we are not the "same". The act of inclusion means fighting against exclusion and all of the social diseases exclusion gives birth to - i.e. racism, sexism, handicapism, etc. Fighting for inclusion also involves assuring that all support systems are available to those who need such support. Providing and maintaining support systems is a civic responsibility, not a favor. We were all born "in".

— Shafik Asante, African-American community activist and organizer, fighter for social justice, former leader of New African Voices in Philadelphia, Pennsylvania, 1948–1997. From "What Is Inclusion?" Online at: http://www.inclusion.com/inclusion.html

"Outwitted"

He drew a circle that shut me out
Heretic, rebel, a thing to flout
But love and I had the wit to win
We drew a circle that took him in.

— Edwin Markham, Euro-American poet, 1852–1940

POWER

"Becoming mindful of our own will to power"

Since racism is about power, it always behooves those of us in subordinate groups to be mindful of our own will to power, otherwise we risk asserting power in harmful ways in any situation where we are in the one-up position. Martin Luther King understood this. In his wise sermon, "Loving Your Enemies," he contends: "There will be no permanent solution to the race problem until oppressed men develop the capacity to love their enemies... For more than three centuries American Negroes have been battered by the iron rod of oppression, frustrated by day and bewildered by night by unbearable injustice, and burdened with the ugly weight of discrimination. Forced to live with these shameful conditions, we are tempted to become bitter and to retaliate with a corresponding hate. But if this happens, the new order we seek will be little more than a duplicate of the old order." The will to dominate knows no color. Every citizen in a dominator culture has been socialized to believe that domination is the foundation of all human relations.

— bell hooks, *Teaching Community*, 75

Naming the culture of power

Why don't white people see white benefits? Whenever one group of people has benefits at the expense of another group, the privileged group creates a culture that places its members at the center and other groups at the margins. People in the in-group are accepted as the norm, so if you are in that group it can be very hard to see the benefits you receive.

Since I'm male and I live in a culture in which men have more social, political, and economic power than women, I often don't notice that women are treated differently than I am. I'm inside a male culture of power. I expect to be treated with respect, to be listened to, and to have my opinions valued. I expect to be welcomed. I expect to see people like me in positions of authority. I expect to find books and newspapers that are written by people like me, that reflect my perspective, and that show me in central roles. I don't necessarily notice that the women around me are treated less respectfully, ignored, or silenced; that they are not visible in positions of authority nor welcomed in certain spaces; and that they are charged more for a variety of goods and services and not always safe in situations where I feel perfectly comfortable.

> — Paul Kivel, "The Culture of Power," *Uprooting Racism*, 38. Paul Kivel is a Euro-American social justice educator, activist, writer, and leader in violence prevention.

ANTI-BULLYING

Bully/victim problems concern our basic values and principles

Bully/victim problems in school really concern some of our basic values and principles. For a long time, I have argued that it is a fundamental democratic right for a child to feel safe in school and to be spared the oppression and repeated, intentional humiliation implied in bullying. No student should be afraid of going to school for fear of being harassed or degraded, and no parent should need to worry about such things happening to his or her child.

> — Dr. Dan Olweus in "Sweden," *The Nature of School Bullying: A Cross-National Perspective*. Dr. Olweus is a Norwegian professor of psychology who has for decades researched both the phenomena and the prevention of bullying in schools.

I realized that bullying never has to do with you. It's the bully who's insecure.

> — Shay Mitchell, Canadian actress and model

"They are all in pain"

Bullying is killing our kids. Being different is killing our kids, and the kids who are bullying are dying inside. We have to save our kids whether they are bullied or they are bullying. They are all in pain.

> — Catherine Ann "Cat" Cora, Euro-American chef

"Standing up for him, I learned to stand up for myself"

I was bullied quite a lot when I was growing up in my Peking Opera School. I allowed myself to be bullied because I was scared and didn't know how to defend myself. I was bullied until I prevented a new student from being bullied. By standing up for him, I learned to stand up for myself.

> — Jackie Chan, a Hong Kong actor, choreographer, comedian, director, producer, martial artist, screenwriter, singer, and stunt performer

DEALING WITH CONFLICTS, HURTS, & HARMS

Not everything that is faced can be changed, but nothing can be changed until it is faced.

> — James Baldwin, "As Much Truth As One Can Bear," *New York Times Book Review*

I imagine one of the reasons people cling to their hates so stubbornly is because they sense, once hate is gone, they will be forced to deal with pain.

> — James Baldwin, *The Fire Next Time*, 1963

A "talking out" principle

Navajo traditional justice relies on a "talking out" principle so there is group discussion of a given problem and it can be "talked out" by way of getting to the nature of a given problem, identifying who got hurt and how, and how the injury affects people. If you can talk out the nature of the hurt, then solutions should present themselves.

> — Hon. Robert Yazzie, Diné, Chief Justice Emeritus of the Navajo Nation. In "Whose Criminal Justice System? New Conceptions of Indigenous Justice."

Setting free every other person to be who she or he is intended

To be who we are . . . we must be actively engaged in the setting free of every other person to be who she or he is intended: someone different from who we are, someone who will see the world from another perspective, someone who will not agree with us. Anything short of such liberation is suppressive and destructive and ultimately death producing. . . .

Conflict is not just inevitable, as we are prone to say wisely and with a sigh of resignation. Instead it is . . . a gift. . . . Conflict doesn't sometimes provide us with energy, insight, and new possibility as reluctant by-products; newness cannot come without conflict. It is not a price to be paid and endured, but a condition to be sought and welcomed and nurtured. . . .

To manage conflict then would be to allow it, not to suppress it; to open our doors and windows to its fresh wind. Following this line of thought to its ultimate conclusion, violence and war become not conflict run amuck, conflict out of all bounds, but the final outcome of conflict quelled. *They result when we will not allow the other to be different, when we deny our life-giving dependence on the different one with all our might and means.* [Italics added]

> — Caroline A. Westerhoff, "Conflict: The Birthing of the New." Carolyn Westerhoff, Euro-American, is the retired canon for ministry in the Episcopal Diocese of Atlanta, Georgia.

"How do we reclaim a proper relationship to the world?"

Where do we start? How do we reclaim a proper relationship to the world? It is said that in the Babemba tribe of South Africa, when a person acts irresponsibly or unjustly, he is placed in the center of the village, alone and unfettered. All work ceases, and every man, woman, and child in the village gathers in a large circle around the accused individual. Then each person in the tribe speaks to the accused, one at a time, about all the good things the person in the center of the circle has done in his lifetime. Every incident, every experience that can be recalled with any detail and accuracy is recounted. All this positive attributes, good deeds, strengths, and kindnesses are recited carefully and at length. The tribal ceremony often lasts several days. At the end, the tribal circle is broken, a joyous celebration takes place, and the person is symbolically and literally welcomed back into the tribe.

> — Alice Walker, from *Sent by Earth: A Message from the Grandmother Spirit after the Attacks on the World Trade Center and Pentagon.* Alice Walker is a Pulitzer Prize-winning, internationally celebrated, African-American novelist, poet, and activist.

RACE

"Racism springs from the lie"

Racism springs from the lie that certain human beings are less than fully human. It's a self-centered falsehood that corrupts our minds into believing we are right to treat others as we would not want to be treated.

— Alveda King, African-American civil rights activist, minister, and author

Greater genetic variations within so-called "racial" populations than between them

[G]reater genetic variation exists *within* the populations typically labeled Black and White than *between* these populations. This finding refutes the supposition that racial divisions reflect fundamental genetic differences. Rather, the notion that humankind can be divided along White, Black, and Yellow lines reveals the social rather than the scientific origin of race.

— Ian F. Haney López, Latino law professor, from "The Social Construction of Race," 166.

James Baldwin on race, racial progress, and poverty

To be a Negro in this country and to be relatively conscious is to be in a rage almost all the time.

— Interview for *The New Negro* (Ahmann, 1961)

The American idea of racial progress is measured by how fast I become white.

— "On Language, Race, and the Black Writer," *The Cross of Redemption*

Anyone who has struggled with poverty knows how extremely expensive it is to be poor.

— *Nobody Knows My Name*, 1961

"The name dates back to when the Native American population was being exterminated"

[T]he name is a textbook definition—it's a—the textbook definition of the word is a racial slur, and it's a disparaging name towards Native American people. And, you know, in my community, we don't call each other by the "R" word.... It's just not something that we do. We have other names, like Native American, American Indian, or even Indian, but we never call each other by the "R" word.

And so, the name itself actually dates back to the time when the Native American population was being exterminated, and bounty hunters were hired to kill Native American people. And so, one could make a great living off of just killing Native American people. And there was a tier effect that was paid out. The highest paid was for a Native American man and then a woman and then a child. And so, based off of that, there were news clippings and flyers and stuff that were posted up, asking people to go out to kill Indians and bring back the red skin. So, in order to show that they made their kill, they had to bring back a scalp or their skin. That's where the "Redskin" word has been kind of passed down. So, in our community, we do not use that word.

— Amanda Blackhorse, Diné, social worker and member of the Navajo Nation, and plaintiff in *Blackhorse et al. v. Pro-Football Inc.*, speaking on *Democracy Now!* 19 June 2014

James Baldwin on being black

You were born where you were born and faced the future that you faced because you were black and for no other reason. The limits of your ambition were, thus, expected to be set forever. You were born into a society which spelled out with brutal clarity, and in as many ways as possible, that you were a worthless human being. You were not expected to aspire to excellence: you were expected to make peace with mediocrity. Wherever you have turned, James, in your short time on this earth, you have been told where you could go and what you could do (and how you could do it) and where you could live and whom you could marry. I know your countrymen do not agree with me about this, and I hear them saying "You exaggerate." They do not know Harlem, and I do. So do you. Take no one's word for anything, including mine—but trust your experience. Know whence you came.

— *The Fire Next Time*, 1963

Transforming ourselves from fearful caterpillars into courageous butterflies

Race is the great taboo in our society. We are afraid to talk about it. White folks fear their unspoken views will be deemed racist. People of color are filled with sorrow and rage at unrighted wrongs. Drowning in silence, we are brothers and sisters drowning each other. Once we decide to transform ourselves from fearful caterpillars into courageous butterflies, we will be able to bridge the racial gulf and move forward together towards a bright and colorful future.

— Eva Paterson, African-American civil rights activist, CEO and co-founder of Equal Justice Society

LOVE

"If they can learn to hate, they can be taught to love"

No one is born hating another person because of the colour of his skin, or his background, or his religion. People must learn to hate, and if they can learn to hate, they can be taught to love, for love comes more naturally to the human heart than its opposite.

— Nelson Mandela, born into the Madiba clan, Former President of South Africa, anti-apartheid revolutionary, 1918–2013

"Love takes off masks"

Love takes off masks that we fear we cannot live without and know we cannot live within. I use the word "love" here not merely in the personal sense but as a state of being, or a state of grace—not in the infantile American sense of being made happy but in the tough and universal sense of quest and daring and growth.

— James Baldwin, from *The Fire Next Time*, 1963

Hatred paralyzes life; love releases it. Hatred confuses life; love harmonizes it. Hatred darkens life; love illumines it.

— Rev. Dr. Martin Luther King, Jr., African-American minister, civil rights activist, and author, recipient of the 1964 Nobel Peace Prize, 1929–1968

bell hooks on love

bell hooks is an African-American author, feminist, and social activist. These quotes are from her book, *All About Love: New Visions*.

[T]he wounded child inside many males is a boy who, when he first spoke his truths, was silenced by paternal sadism, by a patriarchal world that did not want him to claim his true feelings. The wounded child inside many females is a girl who was taught from early childhood that she must become something other than herself, deny her true feelings, in order to attract and please others. When men and women punish each other for truth telling, we reinforce the notion that lies are better. To be loving we willingly hear the other's truth, and most important, we affirm the value of truth telling. Lies may make people feel better, but they do not help them to know love.

All too often women believe it is a sign of commitment, an expression of love, to endure unkindness or cruelty, to forgive and forget. In actuality, when we love rightly we know that the healthy, loving response to cruelty and abuse is putting ourselves out of harm's way.

Everything moves. Except love—hold on to love. Do what love requires.

> — Sister Helen Prejean, *Dead Man Walking*, 244. Helen Prejean is a Roman Catholic nun and a leading American advocate for the abolition of the death penalty.

All life is a manifestation of the spirit, the manifestation of love. And the Art of Peace is the purest form of that principle. Universal love functions in many forms; each manifestation should be allowed free expression. The Art of Peace is true democracy.

> — Morihei Ueshiba, Japanese martial arts, founder of Aikido, 1883–1969

FORGIVENESS

The power to forgive is the power to love

We must develop and maintain the capacity to forgive. He who is devoid of the power to forgive is devoid of the power to love. There is some good in the worst of us and some evil in the best of us. When we discover this, we are less prone to hate our enemies.

> — Rev. Dr. Martin Luther King, Jr.

Forgiveness is not an occasional act: it is an attitude.

> — Martin Luther King, Jr.

What forgiveness does for us

Regardless of our unique story, forgiveness holds the promise that we will find the peace that we all really want. It promises our release from the hold that another's attitudes and actions have over us. It reawakens us to the truth of our own goodness and lovableness. It holds the sure promise that we will be able to increasingly unburden ourselves from emotional turmoil and move on feeling better and better about ourselves and about life.

> — Robin Casarjian, *Forgiveness: A Bold Choice for a Peaceful Heart*, 10. Euro-American speaker and writer on emotional literacy and forgiveness and founder and director of the Lionheart Foundation

What forgiveness is not

Forgiveness is *not* condoning negative, inappropriate behavior—your own or someone else's.... Forgiveness is *not* pretending everything is just fine when you feel it isn't.... Forgiveness is *not* assuming an attitude of superiority or self-righteousness.... Forgiveness does *not* mean you will or must change your behavior.... Forgiveness does *not* require that you verbally communicate directly to the person you have forgiven....

> — Robin Casarjian, *Forgiveness*, pp. 12–14

"We restore a relationship that would otherwise be lost forever"

Forgiving is love's revolution against love's unfairness. When we forgive, we ignore the normal laws that strap us to the natural law of getting even and, by the alchemy of love, we release ourselves from our own painful pasts.

We fly over a dues-paying morality in order to create a new future out of the past's unfairness. We free ourselves from the wrong that is locked into our private histories; we unshackle our spirits from malice; and, maybe, if we are lucky, we also restore a relationship that would otherwise be lost forever.

> — Lewis B. Smedes, a Euro-American Christian author, ethicist, and theologian, 1921–2002

Forgiveness is a decision

Forgiveness is a decision to see beyond the limits of another's personality. It is a decision to see beyond fears, idiosyncrasies, neuroses, and mistakes—to see pure essence, unconditioned by personal history, [to see a person who] has limitless potential and is always worthy of respect and love.

— Casarjian, *Forgiveness*, p. 23

SUPPORT FOR ONE ANOTHER

I always try to believe the best of everybody—it saves so much trouble.

— Rudyard Kipling, English short-story writer, poet, and novelist, 1865–1936

"Providing support systems is a civic responsibility"

Fighting for inclusion also involves assuring that all support systems are available to those who need such support. Providing and maintaining support systems is a civic responsibility, not a favor.

— Shafik Asante, "What Is Inclusion?"

People won't remember what you did. People won't remember what you said. But people will always remember the way you made them feel.

— Maya Angelou, celebrated African-American author and poet, 1928–2014

Few things can help an individual more than to place responsibility on him and to let him know that you trust him.

— Booker T. Washington, African American educator, author, orator, and advisor to U.S. presidents, 1856–1915

We all take different paths in life, but no matter where we go, we take a little of each other everywhere.

— Tim McGraw, Euro-American country music singer, songwriter, and actor

"Our offering is . . . simply a peaceful manner"

There are times when our offering is not necessarily some tangible gift or helpful act, but rather simply a peaceful manner. If we are clear and present, if we are quiet and centered, then others may be nourished simply by our lack of agitation. Our world is so agitated that to be in the presence of a single person who is at peace can feel remarkably healing, a great blessing. If we are still, others will come when they need to remember who they are.

— Wayne Muller, Euro-American minister and therapist, from his book, *How, Then, Shall We Live?*

"Walk beside me"

Don't walk in front of me. I may not follow.
Don't walk behind me. I may not lead.
Just walk beside me and be my friend.

— Excerpt from a Jewish children's song

Be kind, for everyone you meet is fighting a great battle.

— Philo of Alexandria, Hellenistic Jewish philosopher, 20 BCE–c. 50 CE.

"Struggle makes their wings strong enough to fly"

I hate to see others suffer. I see that as a weakness in me, because it probably indicates that I'm afraid their pain will recall all the pain that lives in me. So I have been guilty of trying to take everyone's tears away, to stop crying and heal their wounds—prematurely. I wonder how many butterflies I've killed by tearing off their cocoons too soon and denying them the struggle that makes their wings strong enough to fly.

— Margaret Wold, *The Critical Moment: How Personal Crisis Can Enrich a Woman's Life*, American author.

Presence: the gift of connection

Presence is a way of being available in a situation with the wholeness of one's unique individual being. It is the acknowledgment of a sacred quality operating within us that can intentionally connect with the sacred quality in others. This process results in an exchange of authentic meaningful awareness and essence linking that can offer integration and balance in the healing relationship.

At the spiritual level, to be fully present with another person is to communicate the energy of unconditional love, or what some would call unconditional positive regard. It is a letting go of external judgments and completely accepting people where they are at that moment, believing they are doing the best that they can in the situation, and bringing into it their own individual patterns and beliefs.

When one is surrounded with unconditional love, which requires the intention of presence by the other person, one is empowered to access their own innate healing abilities.

> — Attributed to McKivergin and Day, 1998. Found in Mark Umbreit, "Peacemaking and Spirituality: A Journey Toward Healing & Strength," Saint Paul, MN: Center for Restorative Justice & Peacemaking, 2000.

I wish I could show you when you are lonely or in darkness the astonishing light of your own being.

> — Hafez (also written Hafiz), Persian poet born in Shiraz, Iran, whose collected works are considered the pinnacle of Persian literature, c. 1325–c. 1390 C.E.

CHILDREN & ANCESTORS

"Your children are not your children"

Your children are not your children.
They are the sons and daughters of Life's longing for itself.
They come through you but not from you,
And though they are with you, yet they belong not to you.
You may give them your love but not your thoughts,
For they have their own thoughts.
You may house their bodies but not their souls,
For their souls dwell in the house of tomorrow, which you cannot visit, not even in
    your dreams.
You may strive to be like them, but seek not to make them like you.
For life goes not backward nor tarries with yesterday.
You are the bows from which your children as living arrows are sent forth.
The archer sees the mark upon the path of the infinite, and He bends you with
    His might that His arrows may go swift and far.
Let your bending in the archer's hand be for gladness;
For even as He loves the arrow that flies, so He loves also the bow that is stable.

> — Kahlil Gibran, Lebanese artist, poet, and writer, 1883–1931. *The Prophet* was first published in 1923.

"And how are the children?"

Among the most accomplished and fabled tribes of Africa, no tribe was considered to have warriors more fearsome or more intelligent than the mighty Masai. It is perhaps surprising then to learn the traditional greeting that passed between Masai warriors. "Kasserian ingera," one would always say to another. It means, "And how are the children?"

It is still the traditional greeting among the Masai, acknowledging the high value that the Masai always place on their children's well-being. Even warriors with no children of their own would always give the traditional answer, "All the children are well." Meaning, of course, that peace and safety prevail, the priorities of protecting the young, the powerless are in place, that Masai people have not forgotten its reason for being, its proper functions and responsibilities. "All the children are well" means that life is good. It means that the daily struggles of existence, even among poor people, do not preclude proper caring for its young

I wonder how it might affect our consciousness of our own children's welfare if, in our culture, we took to greeting each other with this same daily question. "And how are the children?" I wonder if we heard that question and passed it along to each other a dozen times a day, if it would begin to make a difference in the reality of how children are thought of or cared for in this country?

I wonder if every adult among us, parent and non-parent alike, felt an equal weight for the daily care and protection of all the children in our town, in our state, in our country. I wonder if we could truly say without any hesitation, "The children are well, yes, all the children are well."

What would it be like? If the President began every press conference, every public appearance, by answering the question, "And how are the children, Mr. President?" If every governor of every state had to answer the same question at every press conference, "And how are the children, Governor? Are they all well?" Wouldn't it be interesting to hear their answers?

> — Rev. Dr. Patrick T. O'Neill, Euro-American Unitarian minister, from a sermon first given in 1991 at First Parish in Framingham, Massachusetts

"Mother to Son" by Langston Hughes

This poem is from *The Collected Poems of Langston Hughes,* 30, and is also widely available online. Langston Hughes was an African-American poet, social activist, novelist, playwright, and columnist, 1902–1967. See online at: http://www.poetryfoundation.org/poem/177021.

"All children are created whole"

We find these joys to be self evident: That all children are created whole, endowed with innate intelligence, with dignity and wonder, worthy of respect … We commit ourselves to peaceful ways and vow to keep from harm or neglect these, our most vulnerable citizens.

> — Raffi Cavoukian, better known as Raffi. Egyptian-born Canadian singer-songwriter, author, essayist, and lecturer of Armenian descent.

"The line stretches all the way back"

To acknowledge our ancestors means we are aware that we did not make ourselves, that the line stretches all the way back, perhaps to God; or to Gods. We remember them because it is an easy thing to forget: that we are not the first to suffer, rebel, fight, love and die. The grace with which we embrace life, in spite of the pain, the sorrows, is always a measure of what has gone before.

> — Alice Walker

"Ancestors and future generations are present in us"

We are aware that all generations of our ancestors and all future generations are present in us.

We are aware of the expectations that our ancestors, our children, and their children have of us.

We are aware that our joy, peace, freedom, and harmony are the joy, peace, freedom, and harmony of our ancestors, our children, and their children.

We are aware that understanding is the very foundation of love.

We are aware that blaming and arguing never help us and only create a wider gap between us; that only understanding, trust, and love can help us change and grow.

> — Thich Nhat Hanh, Vietnamese Zen Buddhist monk, teacher, poet, and peace activist, from *Teachings on Love*, 98. Reprinted from *Teachings on Love* (1998, 2007 rev.ed.) by Thich Nhat Hanh with permission of Parallax Press, Berkeley, California www.parallax.org.

WORKING TOGETHER FOR A BETTER WORLD

"If you have come here to help me..."

If you have come here to help me, you are wasting our time. But if you have come because your liberation is bound up with mine, then let us work together.

> — Aboriginal activists group, Queensland, 1970s, in which Lilla Watson, Indigenous Australian, Murri community, Gangulu artist, activist, and academic, participated.

"Call Me by My True Names" by Thich Nhat Hanh

This famous poem by Thich Nhat Hanh conveys the essence of "interbeing," the inner connectedness of all things, and what this truth implies for how we work together for a better world. Published in his book, *Peace Is Every Step: The Path of Mindfulness in Everyday Life*, the poem is also widely available online, for example: http://www.quietspaces.com/poemHanh.html.

A Hopi Elder speaks

This could be a good time! There is a river flowing now very fast. It is so great and swift, that there are those who will be afraid. They will try to hold on to the shore. They will feel they are being torn apart and will suffer greatly.

Know that the river has its destination. The elders say that we must let go of the shore, push off into the middle of the river, keep our eyes open, and our heads above water. And I say, see who is there with you and celebrate. At this time in history, we are to take nothing personally, least of all ourselves. For the moment that we do, our spiritual growth and journey come to a halt.

The time for the lone wolf is over. Gather yourselves! Banish the word 'struggle' from your attitude and your vocabulary. All that we do now must be done in a sacred manner and in celebration.

We are the ones we have been waiting for.

> — Attributed to an unnamed Hopi elder, Hopi Nation, Oraibi, Arizona, June 2000

"I Dream a World" by Langston Hughes

This poem is from *The Collected Poems of Langston Hughes,* 311, and is also widely available online. See: http://www.learningfromlyrics.org/Langstones.html.

"There is no power greater than a community discovering what it cares about . . ."

This poem by Margaret Wheatley, excerpted from *Turning to One Another*, page 145, is available online at: http://tamarackcommunity.ca/downloads/clife/Faith/margaret_wheatly.pdf. Margaret Wheatley is a Euro-American writer and management consultant who studies organizational behavior.

"We can really transform the world"

I think we can really transform the world in all sorts of ways. There could be a new movement growing up, rising from the ground, reaching for the light and growing strong, just like a tree.

> — Peter Gabriel, "Peter Gabriel: Fight Injustice with Raw Video," *TED Talk*, February 2006. English singer-songwriter, musician, and humanitarian activist.

"Small acts can quietly become a power"

We don't have to engage in grand, heroic actions to participate in the process of change. Small acts, when multiplied by millions of people, can quietly become a power no government can suppress, a power that can transform the world. . . .

And if we do act, in however small a way, we don't have to wait for some grand utopian future. The future is an infinite succession of presents, and to live now as we think human beings should live, in defiance of all that is bad around us, is itself a marvelous victory.

> — Howard Zinn, *A Power Governments Cannot Suppress*, 270. Euro-American historian, author, playwright, and social activist, 1922–2010.

You cannot change the world by fighting against it. You must build a new model that makes the old one obsolete.

> — R. Buckminster Fuller, Euro-American neo-futuristic architect, systems theorist, author, designer, and inventor, 1895–1983.

"Who packed your parachute?"

Captain Charlie Plumb, Euro-American, was a U.S. Navy jet pilot in Vietnam. After 75 combat missions, his plane was destroyed by a surface-to-air missile. Plumb ejected and parachuted into enemy hands. He was captured and spent six years in a communist Vietnamese prison, where he was tortured. Charlie Plumb describes meeting—decades later—the man who packed his parachute:

Recently, I was sitting in a restaurant in Kansas City. A man about two tables away kept looking at me. I didn't recognize him. A few minutes into our meal he stood up and walked over to my table, looked down at me, pointed his finger in my face and said, "You're Captain Plumb."

I looked up and I said, "Yes sir, I'm Captain Plumb."

He said, "You flew jet fighters in Vietnam. You were on the aircraft carrier Kitty Hawk. You were shot down. You parachuted into enemy hands and spent six years as a prisoner of war."

I said, "How in the world did you know all that?"

He replied, "Because, I packed your parachute."

I was speechless. I staggered to my feet and held out a very grateful hand of thanks. This guy came up with just the proper words. He grabbed my hand, he pumped my arm and said, "I guess it worked."

"Yes sir, indeed it did", I said, "and I must tell you I've said a lot of prayers of thanks for your nimble fingers, but I never thought I'd have the opportunity to express my gratitude in person."

He said, "Were all the panels there?"

"Well sir, I must shoot straight with you," I said, "of the eighteen panels that were supposed to be in that parachute, I had fifteen good ones. Three were torn, but it wasn't your fault, it was mine. I jumped out of that jet fighter at a high rate of speed, close to the ground. That's what tore the panels in the chute. It wasn't the way you packed it."

"Let me ask you a question," I said, "do you keep track of all the parachutes you pack?"

"No" he responded, "it's enough gratification for me just to know that I've served."

I didn't get much sleep that night. I kept thinking about that man. I kept wondering what he might have looked like in a Navy uniform—a Dixie cup hat, a bib in the back and bell bottom trousers. I wondered how many times I might have passed him on board the Kitty Hawk. I wondered how many times I might have seen him and not even said "good morning", "how are you", or anything because, you see, I was a fighter pilot and he was just a sailor. How many hours did he spend on that long wooden table in the bowels of that ship weaving the shrouds and folding the silks of those chutes? I could have cared less . . . until one day my parachute came along and he packed it for me.

So the philosophical question here is this: How's your parachute packing coming along? Who looks to you for strength in times of need? And perhaps, more importantly, who are the special people in your life who provide you the encouragement you need when the chips are down? Perhaps it's time right now to give those people a call and thank them for packing your chute.

— *Reprinted with permission from Charlie Plumb, charlieplumb.com.*

We will surely get to our destination if we join hands.

— Aung San Suu Kyi, Burmese leader and 1991 Nobel Peace Prize Laureate

"You have to have a sense of humor"

"You have to have a sense of humor. Otherwise, you will end up crying into your grave. You will die of a broken heart," [Archbishop Desmond] Tutu told us. He told stories and giggled . . . a lot. "I am old, and sometimes, I repeat stories," he said. He launched into a fabulous story of himself and Mandela. "You are all Africans," he would say, referring to the origins of mankind, and then he giggled more. . . .

"Climate change is the moral struggle that will define humanity this century. I hope you will find yourself on the right side of this struggle—the one which will say no to the pipelines and the carbon. . . ."

In the broader philosophical world view," he also said, ". . . the ability to be magnanimous is essential. . . .

Then he asked the rhetorical question which puts the onus on each of us. "Who can stop this? We can stop this. We can. You, you and I can stop this." . . . "And it is not just that we can stop it. We have a responsibility to do so," he said. . . .

Then, for his finale, [quoting Rev. Dr. Martin Luther King, Jr.]: ". . . If we do not learn to live together as brothers, we will perish together as fools."

— From Winona LaDuke, "LaDuke: His Giggles Illuminated His Wisdom." Winona LaDuke is executive director of Honor the Earth, and Ojibwe writer and economist on Minnesota's White Earth Reservation. Desmond Mpilo Tutu is a South African social rights activist, a retired Anglican bishop, and famous opponent of apartheid.

HOPE

"Hope is a state of mind"

Hope is a state of mind, not of the world or a particular situation
Hope is a choice we make
We can keep it alive within us, or we can let it die
It is a dimension of the soul
It is an orientation of the heart
It is a motivation of the spirit
Hope transcends the world and situations that are immediately experienced.
It is anchored somewhere beyond its horizons
Hope is deep and powerful in its greatest sense
It is not the same as joy when things go well and lead to success
It is the ability to work for something
Because it is good and worthwhile
Hope is the vitality that keeps life moving
It is the courage to be
Hope grows the spirit bigger than the problems we face
Hope is the quality that helps you to go on in spite of it all
I can light my way with hope through joy and hardship and sorrow
Embracing both joy and sorrow is to be at peace with and experience life in all of its fullness.

— Carlos De Pina, 13 years old, blended this piece directly from writings of former Czechoslovakia President Vaclav Havel and Rev. Dr. Martin Luther King, Jr.

"Hope is one of the best antidotes to violence"

I believe that hope is one of the best contraceptives to teen pregnancy and one of the best antidotes to violence. Children need to have a sense of an achievable future in order to make good choices. They also need good choices, [as well as] families, communities, and a nation that values and protect them enough to give them the time, attention, and necessities they need to succeed. Parents are the most important people in the lives of children, but parents need jobs and the support of their community to fulfill their responsibilities to their families.

— Marian Wright Edelman, *Guide My Feet*, eBook version. Marian Wright Edelman is a lawyer and African-American activist for racial justice and the rights of children, president and founder of the Children's Defense Fund.

"Hope keeps life moving"

If you lose hope, somehow you lose the vitality that keeps life moving, you lose that courage to be, that quality that helps you go on in spite of it all."

— Rev. Dr. Martin Luther King, Jr.

HEALTHY SEXUALITY

Sex is not a game
I am not a toy
Sex means that we care
Sex means that we share
Our bodies, our hearts and
Our joy!

— Poem by Migdalia, age 17

HAPPINESS

We can be extremely happy just sitting and breathing in and out. We don't have to do or achieve anything. We enjoy the miracle of simply being here.

— Thich Nhat Hanh

A reason to be happy

To the European, it is a characteristic of the American culture that, again and again, one is commanded and ordered to "be happy." But happiness cannot be pursued; it must ensue. One must have a reason to "be happy." Once the reason is found, however, one becomes happy automatically. As we see, a human being is not one in pursuit of happiness but rather in search of a reason to become happy, last but not least, through actualizing the potential meaning inherent and dormant in a given situation.

— Viktor E. Frankl, *Man's Search for Meaning*

STRENGTH & RESILIENCE

What does life expect from us?

It did not really matter what we expected from life, but rather what life expected from us. We needed to stop asking about the meaning of life, and instead to think of ourselves as those who were being questioned by life—daily and hourly. Our answer must consist, not in talk and meditation, but in right action and in right conduct. Life ultimately means taking the responsibility to find the right answer to its problems and to fulfill the tasks which it constantly sets for each individual."

— Viktor E. Frankl, *Man's Search for Meaning*

Death is not the greatest loss in life. The greatest loss is what dies inside while still alive. Never surrender.

— Tupac Shakur, African American rapper and actor, 1971–1996

Tupac Shakur's poetry:

"The Rose That Grew from Concrete"
"And Tomorrow"
These and other poems by Tupak Shakur are available online at: http://www.2pac2k.de/poems.html

You need to spend time crawling alone through shadows to truly appreciate what it is to stand in the sun.

— Shaun Hick, New Zealand storyteller and author

"Impossible is just a big word"

Impossible is just a big word thrown around by small men who find it easier to live in the world they've been given than to explore the power they have to change it. Impossible is not a fact. It's an opinion. Impossible is not a declaration. It's a dare. Impossible is potential. Impossible is temporary. Impossible is nothing.

— Muhammad Ali, African-American former professional boxer and activist for racial justice and principles over expedience

"I Have Learned"

I HAVE LEARNED: From losing so much, I learned to win.
Tears drew the smile I carry.
I know the ground so much, that I only see the sky.
I have touched bottom so many times, that every time I go low,
I already know that tomorrow I will rise.
I am so in awe of the nature of humanity,
That I have learned to BE MYSELF.
I had to deeply feel loneliness to learn to be with myself
And to know that I am good company.

I LEARNED: That no one encounters another by accident...
People enter your life for a reason.

When you begin to discern their reason for being with you,
you will know what to do with that person.
When someone is in your life for a reason,
it is generally to fill a need that you have demonstrated you have.
They show up to help you through a difficulty,
Providing guidance and support.
Physical, emotional, or spiritual support.
They may be a gift from God... actually, they are!!
When people part ways, we must understand that those needs have been met,
Our desires have been fulfilled,
And their jobs are done.
Every human being has some unique experience.
They may show you things you have never done...
Relationships worth lifetimes...
Lifetimes worth of life lessons,
The small things that can help you build a solid emotional foundation.
Our task is to accept the lesson
And to put in practice what you have learned from everything,
To know that you have grown as a human being.

— Jennifer Lopez Olivero, written for a Circle training in Boston

"The Guest House"
by Rumi, Barks with Moyne, translators

From *The Essential Rumi*, 109, also widely available on the Internet, for example: http://www.gratefulness.org/poetry/guest_house.htm.

PERSEVERANCE

Fall seven times, stand up eight.

— Japanese Proverb

Anyone who has never made a mistake has never tried anything new.

— Albert Einstein

"I have failed over and over..."

I've missed more than 9000 shots in my career. I've lost almost 300 games. 26 times I've been trusted to take the game winning shot and missed. I've failed over and over and over again in my life. And that is why I succeed.

— Michael Jordan, African-American former professional basketball player

LIFE'S TRIALS

Yamiley Mathurin is a young woman convicted and doing time at Suffolk County's House of Corrections, Boston, Massachusetts. Some of her poetry has been published in *Not Beyond Hope: Artwork, Poetry, and Prose Presented by the Inmates of the South Bay House of Correction and Detainees of the Nashua Street Jail*, Boston, MA: Suffolk County Sheriff's Department, Fall 2013. Her poems are available online at: http://www.scsdma.org/news/notbeyondhope/13fallNBH.pdf.

We like two of her poems in particular:
"Life Exchange"
"Forever"

II. MEDITATIONS & VISUALIZATIONS

BASIC MEDITATION

Read the following basic meditation at a relaxed, leisurely pace.

Find a place where you're sitting comfortably. If you feel okay doing so, close your eyes. If you don't want to, then just find a place in front of you where you can gently focus, maybe on the table, floor, or the wall across from where you are sitting.

Now, take four deep breaths. Feel your chest rise and fall as you take the air in and let it out. Each time you breathe in, imagine taking in a calm, peaceful feeling. As you breathe out, let all the stress leave your body. Let your shoulders relax and soften. Let your eyes relax and soften.

Meditation is simply paying attention to your breathing. One place in your body to follow your breathing is your nose. Notice how the air feels as it comes in through your nostrils. Perhaps the air is cooler as you breathe in but slightly warmer as you exhale. Follow the breath completely as you breathe out.

Another place to become aware of your breathing is in your belly. It sometimes helps to gently place your hands across your stomach—almost like you're holding a basketball. Notice how your belly expands or gets bigger as you take a breath in and the air fills your lungs. As you breathe out, you'll feel your chest and belly sink—just like letting the air out of a basketball. Let your breath come in and go out naturally. You don't have to "try" and take deep regular breaths. Just let your body's natural breathing rhythm happen. Your job is not to change your breath; it's just to pay attention to what's going on already.

As you meditate, your mind will naturally wander. This is just how the brain works. Each time this happens, your job is simply to bring your attention gently back to your breathing. If you hear a sound, just say "sound" to yourself and return to your breathing. Your mind might wander many times as you meditate. That's okay. Each time you notice it happening, gently turn your attention back to the breath.

When you are ready, slowly open your eyes and bring your awareness back to the room and all of us sitting here.

BIG SKY MEDITATION

Find a place where you're sitting comfortably. If you feel okay doing so, close your eyes. If you don't want to, then just find a place in front of you where you can gently focus, maybe on the table, floor, or the wall across from where you are sitting.

Now, take four deep breaths. Feel your chest rise and fall as you take the air in and let it out. Each time you breathe in, imagine taking in a calm, peaceful feeling. As you breathe out, let all the stress leave your body. Let your shoulders relax and soften. Let your eyes relax and soften.

After you have focused on your breathing for a little while, imagine a big, blue sky. Try picturing a wide-open space that seems to go on forever with nothing else in sight. The emptiness is calm and peaceful. There are no trees, houses, or people. There are no sounds to interrupt the silence of the big sky. For miles and miles, there is nothing but wide-open blue sky. Now imagine that your mind is just like that sky—large, peaceful, and calm.

Sometimes a small cloud appears overhead and floats through the big sky. Although you can see it, it is just a tiny object compared to the vastness of the big sky. The cloud makes its way across the open space above, until it gets smaller and fainter and then vanishes. As you meditate, think of yourself as the big sky. Thoughts may pop into your head—just like a little cloud—but they don't stay forever. Soon they disappear just as they arrived.

But no matter what, the endless, calm sky is still there. You may notice sounds as you meditate. No problem, just another small cloud soon to fade away. Thoughts, memories, or great ideas might come up, but this is no big deal. Just tell yourself, "Hey, another small cloud in the big sky," and return your focus to your breathing and to the peace and calm of the big sky.

Occasionally we lose our perspective on the big sky. We look up expecting to see a calm, wide-open space but see thunderheads and darkness instead. But this is just an illusion. Above the clouds the same big sky is there—blue, endless, and filled with light.

The clouds may cover the big sky temporarily, but above it all, the perfect calm of the big sky is there. As you go through your day, you can take some time to remember the big sky that surrounds you. If something upsetting or annoying happens, you can picture the clear, calm, expansive big sky and stay with this image until you feel ready to handle whatever situation is in front of you.

Now bring your awareness back to this room. If you had your eyes closed, you may open them when you are ready. Look around and notice the room and who is here. Welcome, everyone.

— Casarjian and Casarjian, *Power Source Facilitator's Manual*, pp. 17–18.

MOUNTAIN MEDITATION

Find a place where you're sitting comfortably. If you feel okay doing so, close your eyes. If you don't want to, then just find a place in front of you where you can gently focus, maybe on the table, floor, or the wall across from where you are sitting.

Now, take four deep breaths. Feel your chest rise and fall as you take the air in and let it out. Each time you breathe in, imagine taking in a calm, peaceful feeling. As you breathe out, let all the stress leave your body. Let your shoulders relax and soften. Let your eyes relax and soften.

Meditation is simply paying attention to your breathing. One place in your body to follow your breathing is your nose. Notice how the air feels as it comes in through your nostrils. Perhaps the air is cooler as you breathe in but slightly warmer as you exhale. Follow the breath completely as you breathe out.

When you are ready, imagine that you have become a large mountain sitting far away from civilization. From a distance, you rise like a giant, almost scraping against the sky. Perhaps you are a mountain whose top is covered in deep layers of ice and snow. Or maybe you are found in the deep region of the rain forest, and dense trees, bushes, and plant life grow on your surface. Maybe you are a desert mountain whose sides are made of sand and rock. Whatever you look like as a mountain, know that you are ancient and magnificent. You are deeply rooted beneath the earth so that nothing can move you from where you stand. For thousands of years you have rested there as calmly and peacefully as the stars above you. You have no company, yet you are not lonely.

Over time, many changes have happened on and around the mountain. Day turns to night, but still you stand. The temperature changes as the seasons move from summer to winter, but none of this affects you. Storms come and go. Animals make their homes on you. They are constantly on the move looking for food and shelter, but still you stand as firmly and powerfully as the day you were created. The creatures who make their home on you see only the ground before them, but you rise high above the earth. You see for miles.

No matter what happens around the mountain, you remain as you have always been. Your strength comes from being who you are—something that remains constant from day to day, year to year.

As you go through your day, imagine that you are this great mountain. Minor annoyances or small problems might come up, but they do not have the power to shake the mountain. No matter what happens, keep it in perspective. See it like the mountain would.

> — Mountain Meditation is adapted from Jon Kabat-Zinn's "Mountain Meditation." See Appendix 4: Resources, Section II, Websites, Kabat-Zinn for a link to free audio and transcript versions of this and other of Jon Kabat-Zinn's meditations.

PRESENT MOMENT, WONDERFUL MOMENT MEDITATION

In our busy society, it's a great fortune to be able to sit and breathe consciously from time to time...

There are many exercises we can use to help us breathe consciously. Besides the short breathing in and out exercises, there are four-line *gathas*, or practice poems, that we can recite silently as we breathe:

> Breathing in, I calm my body
> Breathing out, I smile
> Dwelling in the present moment,
> I know this is a wonderful moment!

"Breathing in, I calm my body." Reciting this line is like drinking a glass of cool water on a hot day—you can feel the coolness permeate your body. When I breathe in and recite this line, I actually feel my breath calming my body and mind.

"Breathing out, I smile." A smile can relax hundreds of muscles in your face. A smile shows that you are in charge of yourself.

"Dwelling in the present moment." While I sit here, I don't think of anything else. I sit here, and I know exactly where I am.

"I know this is a wonderful moment." It is a joy to sit, stable and at ease, and return to our breathing, our relaxed smiles, and our true nature. Our appointment with life is in the present moment. If we don't have peace and joy right now, how can we have peace and joy tomorrow, or after tomorrow? What is preventing us from being happy right now? As we follow our breathing we can say, simply:

> Calming,
> Smiling,
> Present moment,
> Wonderful moment."

While we practice conscious breathing, our thinking slows down, and we can give our minds and bodies a real rest. When we continue breathing in and out this way for a few minutes, we become quite refreshed.

— Thich Nhat Hanh, *Making Space*, from Chapter Two. Reprinted from *Making Space: Creating a Home Meditation Practice* (2012) by Thich Nhat Hanh with permission of Parallax Press, Berkeley, California, www.parallax.org.

SANCTUARY: A PLACE OF ACCEPTANCE FOR WHO YOU ARE

Sit comfortably. If you feel okay doing so, close your eyes. If you don't, then just find a place in front of you where you can gently focus—maybe on the table, floor, or the wall across from where you are sitting.

Now, take four deep breaths. Feel your chest rise and fall as you take the air in and let it out. Each time your breathe in, imagine taking in a calm, peaceful feeling. As you breathe out, let all the stress leave your body. Let your shoulders relax and soften. Let your eyes relax and soften. As you meditate, your mind will naturally wander. Each time you notice this happening, gently turn your attention back to the breath.

You can relax now. Imagine being in your own special place. It can be a place inside or outside. Place anything in it you want: a comfy chair, a soft bed, a lamp that shines with a cozy glow or a lake, a beach, a river, a meadow, trees, flowers, birds . . . anything you want.

Now imagine a wall around this space. This wall keeps this special place totally safe for you. It brings you comfort and protects all you need to be your best self. You can make the wall as tall or as low as you want. The gate is locked and you hold the key.

You are free to come and go as you please. You are free to allow visitors in or be by yourself. You hold the key.

Enjoy the feeling of comfort and security in this place. Notice and enjoy the light in your special place as well as the quiet and soft sounds. If you want to add anything or change anything, it is yours to do so. You can keep all fears, worries, and concerns away. Focus on what is good in your space. It is your sanctuary.

Look around you and see all the beauty in your sanctuary. Know that you can return to this place you are in right now any time that you wish. It is a beautiful place, a place of comfort, a place where you can truly be your best self.

For now, it is time to take your key and walk towards the gate. As you walk out and lock the gate behind you, you can trust that this sanctuary will stay just as you left it until you want to come again.

Now, wiggle around a little bit. When you are ready open your eyes, stretch and come back to the Circle.

SITTING IN SILENCE

Invite participants to sit in silence. As they sit in silence, ask them to notice without speaking what they hear outside themselves. Pause. Ask them to notice what they hear inside themselves. Pause. Ask them to notice what they feel in their body while sitting in silence. Pause. Ask them what word comes to mind for them to describe how it feels to sit in silence. Pass the talking piece, inviting them each to share the word that describes the silence for them.

INNER STRENGTH VISUALIZATION

Take three of four deep, relaxing breaths. As you breathe out each time, picture all of the noise and problems in your life going out of your body with each breath. All that is left behind is the quiet, calm, and peacefulness of your core self. [Pause]

Imagine that this calm energy is at the center of your body near your heart. It is like a bright light glowing deep inside of you. As you breathe out, feel the light getting brighter. Each time you breathe in and out, that light gets stronger, like the sun's light growing. All of the troubles you have had to face in your life can't put the light out. In fact, all of those struggles made you wiser and more powerful. These troubles have made the light more brilliant and stronger.

The next time you are faced with a difficult situation or a painful problem, remind yourself of this light that is always within you. Let this peaceful energy help calm you and guide you in making positive decisions. Think of how your life up to now has made these powerful qualities in you even stronger. See these strengths as part of your wisdom and power. See yourself deal with the challenges in your life using the strength you already possess.

— Casarjian, *Power Source Facilitator's Manual*, p. 86.

A GOOD LIFE VISUALIZATION

Take a deep breath. Continue to breathe deeply and slowly in a comfortable way. You may close your eyes or use a soft focus on the floor or wall. Notice your breath going in and out. With each out-breath, let your body relax a little more. Shoulders relax—neck relaxes—arms and hands relax—face relaxes. Continue to breathe deeply and slowly in a comfortable way. Notice your breath going in and out. Now imagine we are ten years in the future. You have made good decisions in your life and are living in a way that feels good to you. You are connected to your core self and able to see the core self in others. See yourself in this life. [Pause] Notice the picture that comes to you of what this life is like. Notice the details of your life. Feel the inner peace that is a part of your life in the future. Notice any particular parts of this life. [Pause] Now bring your attention back to your breathing. Feel your in-breath and out-breath. Notice your chair, become aware of others in the room with you. Gradually bring your awareness to our space here in this moment in time. Open your eyes when you are ready.

FAMILY CONNECTIONS VISUALIZATION

I invite you all to take a deep breath and exhale slowly. Continue to breathe deeply and slowly as I speak. Close your eyes if that is comfortable. Imagine around us a circle of your ancestors—grandparents, great grandparents, great great grandparents—who care deeply about you. Imagine them looking at us with love and pride . . . They surround us, hold a circle of protection and love. . . . Feel their support and their complete acceptance of you as you are. . . . See the light in their eyes as they look at you with unconditional love... Bring your attention back to your breath. Breath deeply and slowly three more times. . . . Return your awareness to this room and our space together, bringing with you the love given by your ancestors. Breathe deeply, knowing that they can see the core goodness in you.

Remain silent for a few moments.

RELAXATION EXERCISE

Take a deep breath, and close your eyes if you are comfortable doing so. Otherwise, focus softly on the floor or wall in front of you. We want to defocus our eyes and focus on our ears. Continue breathing deeply and exhaling slowly. Listen to your breath as it goes in and out. Breathe in and out slowly listening [pause], listening [pause], listening [pause] to your breath. Hold the rest of your body still and relaxed. Relax your shoulders and neck. As you breathe out, relax your legs and feet. Now listen to your heartbeat, feel the rhythm of your heartbeat. As you relax, feel your heartbeat slow down slightly. Listen (pause), listen (pause), listen (pause),to your heart. Breathe deeply, relaxing your shoulders, arms and back even more. [Pause] Now listen to your head. What's happening in your head? Listen [pause], listen [pause], listen [pause]). Turn your attention back to your breath and listen to your breath as you breathe in and out. Now refocus your eyes and bring your attention to our space together. Notice who is sitting next to you on your left [pause]. Notice who is sitting on your right, [pause]. Notice yourself inside and outside. Welcome to our Circle!

III. AFFIRMATION & GROUP-BUILDING EXERCISES

GUIDELINES WEB ACTIVITY

Stand in a circle. One person holds a ball of yarn to begin. He/she hangs on to the string at the end and makes a commitment to practice living one of the guidelines. He/she tosses the ball of yarn to someone else in the Circle. Each person makes his/her commitment and tosses the ball to someone else in the Circle who has not yet had a turn. The activity continues until everyone in the Circle has made a commitment.

The exercise creates a web of connectedness based on shared guidelines.

MAKING THE WORLD A BETTER PLACE FOR SOMEONE

Invite participants to think of someone for whom they would like to make the world a better place. Ask them to write down this person's name on a piece of paper and to place it in the center of the circle. Invite them to close their eyes if they are comfortable or to just focus softly on the floor. Invite them to take several deep breaths in silence, using the following script: "Inhale deeply, exhale slowly. [Repeat this four times slowly.] Picture the person whose name you put in the circle. [Pause.] Imagine that person smiling and happy. [Pause.] Feel yourself as a source of support and strength for that person. Feel the strong energy in your body to make the world a good place for that person. Inhale deeply, exhale slowly. [Repeat this two times slowly.]

Open your eyes and return your focus to this space. Thank everyone for sharing the people they have named. Suggest that the good energy of our Circle surrounds these special people and that together we can make the world a better place. When things are difficult, we can remember those we want to make the world better for and that may help us keep going.

SELF-AFFIRMATIONS

Pass a roll of toilet paper around the circle, inviting participants to take as many sheets as they wish from the roll before passing it to the next person. Ask them to separate and stack the sheets they tore off the roll. Pass the talking piece asking each participant to make a positive statement about him or herself for each piece of toilet paper they have. Encourage them to do statements about their physical being, their mental being, their emotional being, and their spiritual being. We suggest that the keeper go first to model the activity.

PASS THE STRENGTHS ON AND ON

Pass out index cards. Ask each person to write one "strength" word or statement on the card. It can be a strength they have or want to have, or it can be a strength they admire in someone else. Examples of cards are: Courageous. Strong. Compassionate. Patient. I am Determined. When I set my mind to something, I persist. I am a Survivor. Emotionally Aware. I have Empathy for others. I understand others who are having a hard time.

One person starts by reading his or her card aloud and passing it on to the person next to them to keep. That person then reads their original card and passes it on to the person next to them to keep. That person then reads their original card and passes it on, and so on all the way around the circle. Each person then has their original strength inside of them and one on a card to hold that someone else has shared with them. Depending on the size of the Circle, you can hold repeat rounds.

GRATITUDE

Passing the talking piece, invite each person to take a deep breath as they hold the talking piece and then in a word or phrase say something they are feeling gratitude for.

MEDICINE WHEEL SELF-LOVE COLLAGE

Invite each participant to create a Medicine Wheel Self Love Collage. Cut enough circles from construction paper for each person in the group to have one of their own. Ask participants to use a marker to divide the circle into four quadrants. Explain that each quadrant represents one of four aspects of self: your mental (intellectual) self, your physical self, your emotional self, and your spiritual self. Participants should label each quadrant, starting with mental in the upper right quadrant. Ask people to close their eyes for a minute and to take ten deep and peaceful breaths. Think about the ways they care for themselves in each of these aspects of self.

Then have people decorate each quadrant in a way that is meaningful expression of who they are. These collages can be shared during the check-in round.

RESPECT

Invite participants to create an acrostic on R-E-S-P-E-C-T with each letter representing a word that is important and meaningful to them with regard to respect. Participants can use markers and glitter pens to make their creations. Passing the talking piece, invite them to share the words in their acrostic and then to place it in the center of the circle.

ROLE-MODEL RIBBON EXERCISE

Have a piece of ribbon about one yard long on each chair. Ask the group to stand and take the ribbon from their chair (it is okay to sit if someone has difficulty standing throughout the opening). Invite the Circle members to think of someone who has helped them or been a role model for them. What is the gift to them from that person? Explain that we will go clockwise in the circle with each person having an opportunity to name the person and the gift and then tie their ribbon to the ribbon of the person to their left. At the end, the ribbon will be tied all the way around. When the ribbon is tied all the way around, thank everyone for sharing these important people in their lives and reflect that their gifts are always with us. Have everyone step forward and drape the ribbon around the center of the circle.

EMBODIED VALUES

Ask participants to look at the values on the paper plates in the center and to think of someone they know who embodies many of those values. Invite them to write the name of that person on the piece of paper at their seat. Passing the talking piece, invite participants to say the name of the person they wrote down and to put the piece of paper in the center of the circle. The keeper leads to model the response.

ENCOURAGEMENT RIBBON EXERCISE

Distribute one piece of ribbon to each person. Turn to the person to your left. While tying your ribbon to that person's ribbon, give some words of encouragement to that person. When you have finished, invite the person to your left to turn to the person to his/her left, tie the ribbon to the next person's ribbon, and say something encouraging to that person. Repeat around the circle, until the ribbon is tied all the way around, and each person has both given and received encouragement.

THE TALKING PIECE: THE IMPORTANCE OF LISTENING AND SPEAKING

Describe the function of the talking piece in a Circle and explain that the opening ceremony for this Circle will be creating a talking piece together. Use a stick or piece of driftwood 12–15 inches long and a basket of materials such as yarn, pieces of leather, feathers, beads, shells, buttons, etc. Explain that as the stick and basket are passed, each person will have an opportunity to add something to the talking piece and to say what they think is important about speaking and listening to one another.

CIRCLE ENERGY

Invite everyone to stand and hold their hands out to the persons on each side, left hand palm up and right hand palm down. Then have them join hands. Invite them to inhale slowly and exhale slowly. As they continue to breathe deeply, invite them to think of their left hand receiving energy and their right hand giving energy. Invite them to feel the energy going around the circle from hand to hand. Invite them to feel the power of connected purpose. Invite them to imagine (those impacted by the purpose of this Circle) in the center of the circle, protected by the power of their Circle of caring. Hold this image for a moment. Thank everyone for coming and being part of this Circle. When they are ready, invite them to release their hands.

AFFIRMING OTHERS IN THE CIRCLE

Invite participants to stand. Give the ball of yarn to a participant. Ask that participant to share a positive experience with someone else in the Circle and toss the ball of yarn to that person, while holding onto the end of the yarn. The second person now shares a positive experience with someone else in the Circle and tosses the yarn, while holding the end s/he has. Continue as each person speaks about someone who has not yet been named and shares a positive experience. With each sharing, the yarn is tossed to that person with the tosser holding onto the end s/he has. When finished, there should be a crisscross of yarn including everyone in the Circle. Gently lower the web of yarn onto the floor and place the centerpiece items on top of the web.

CREATING A GROUP STORY

One person begins with, "Once upon a time there was a team . . . " and completes the sentence. Each person adds one meaningful sentence that builds on the sentence that came before it. The story should travel around the Circle once—twice for smaller groups—with the last person in the Circle contributing the final sentence and then saying, " . . . and that for now is The End"!

CIRCLE OF PEOPLE

Invite participants to stand and join hands forming a circle. Note the circle they have formed. Going clockwise around the circle, ask each participant to say a word or phrase that comes to mind for them when they think of a circle of people. Thank everyone for those images and invite them to sit.

WE ARE KITCHEN IMPLEMENTS

Gather a basket of cooking implements from the kitchen. Pass the basket around the circle inviting each person to take one implement from the basket. Going around the circle clockwise, ask each person to say some way in which they are like the implement they took out of the basket.

I CAN CHOOSE...

Distribute a sheet with the affirmation below. Ask participants to fill in the blank space in the first line with a fear based-emotion or negative feeling. Passing the talking piece, invite each participant to read the poem he or she has created by filling in the blank. The keeper goes first to model how it works.

I can choose _____.
(Fill in the blank with the name of a fear-based emotion or negative reaction, i.e. anger, frustration, anxiety ...)

or I can choose peace

(or love or patience or compassion or understanding).

Which one I choose is up to me.

Today I will let go and be my self,

calm, clear, and aware

There is another way of looking at the world.

IV. MOVEMENT EXERCISES

NAME, MOTION, & REMEMBER

Everyone stands in a circle (as they are able). The first person says his/her name and makes a movement. The next person in the circle repeats the first person's name and motion before showing his/her own. The third person repeats the names and motions of the first two before showing his/her own. Keep going around the circle until everyone has had a turn. If someone needs help, it is okay to ask for it and have the Circle participants help out. Finally, the person who went first has to repeat everyone's name and motion.

NAME WAVE

The first person begins by stating his/her name and doing a motion. One by one around the circle, the other members say that name and do the motion, like a wave. The wave ends with the person who started it. The next person in the circle says their name and does a motion. The name and motion move around the circle in a wave. Continue around the circle with each person saying their name and doing a motion until everyone has introduced themselves. The keeper does it first to model the activity and to create a practice round.

RAINSTORM ACTIVITY

The keeper starts by slapping his/her hands alternately on his/her thighs. The next person joins in the motion, and then the next and the next all around the circle. When the motion returns to the keeper, the keeper stops slapping his/her thighs and begins to alternately stomp feet. The next person follows the keeper's change. One by one around the circle, each person follows the change of movement of the person before them. When the movement returns to the keeper, the keeper stops stomping his/her feet and starts rubbing his/her hands up and down in front of his/her chest. This movement is followed one by one around the circle. The keeper once again does the thigh slapping motion. When that motion comes back to the keeper, then the keeper sits still. One by one, each person in the circle follows the person before them in stopping, until all are quiet.

GROUP JUGGLE

Invite everyone to stand in a circle in an open space, if that is available, at their chairs if not. Ask everyone to put one hand in the air. Give a small stuffed animal to the person next to you and ask that person to call the name of someone in the group and throw the stuffed animal to that person. That person, in turn calls a name and throws it to the named person. This continues until everyone has been called and had the stuffed animal thrown to them. Once a person has been called, he/she takes his/her hand down so others know not to throw it to him/her. Each person must pay attention to whom they throw the stuffed animal, because they will repeat the same pattern again and again.

The first time around, a pattern is created: each person is thrown the stuffed animal only once. The last person to get it throws it back to the person who started it. Ask the group to repeat the pattern, but do it faster. Remind them that it is important to call the name before throwing it. After it has been thrown to a few people into the pattern, throw a new stuffed animal to the starting person. In a little bit, add another and another, until there are 4–7 animals all flying around the group. Keep them going around continuously for a while.

At some point call "Halt, everyone stop where you are." Then ask them to reverse the pattern. That is, tell them to throw to the one who originally threw to them. Allow this to go on for a bit, and then collect the animals as they come back to the starting person next to you. Have everyone return to their seats.

You can do a pass of the talking piece for people to share their thoughts on how this felt, but it is not essential. You may comment on the busyness of our lives and the many things we juggle. This activity brings in humor and tends to break up the stiffness people often feel coming into a new setting. It also begins weaving the group together as a community.

SHOWING EMOTIONS WITH OUR BODIES

Invite everyone to stand and stretch their arms high in the air while inhaling. Then lower their arms, exhaling. Invite them to show sadness with their bodies (no talking). Hold that for a moment. Invite them to release sadness and then to show curiosity with their bodies (no talking). Invite them to release curiosity and then to show anger with their bodies. Invite them to release anger and then to show excitement with their bodies. Invite them to release excitement and then to show contentment with their bodies. Invite them to shake their bodies all over with a deep, releasing exhalation, shaking out any negative feelings.

HUMAN SCULPTURE

Explain that we are going to make a human sculpture. Ask for someone who is willing to start the sculpture. Invite that person into the center of the circle to take a position and hold the position until the sculpture is finished. One by one going clockwise around the circle from the person who started the sculpture ask each participant to come to the center and arrange themselves in the human sculpture and then hold that position until it is finished. When the sculpture is finished, ask participants to take a deep breath and notice their creation as something more than the collection of their individual identities. Invite them to take another deep breath and then to return to their chairs in the circle.

(Re)place the centerpiece items in the center of the circle.

BODY STRETCH & SHAKE

Have everyone stand. Invite everyone to stretch their arms very high and then swing their arms down bending over at the waist, then slowly come up, one vertebra at a time, until they are standing straight, then shake their bodies all over energetically. When the energy dissipates, invite them to relax their bodies and take a deep breath.

YOGA, TAI CHI, OR QIGONG

If someone in the Circle is a practitioner of one of these disciplines, invite that person to lead the group in movement for an opening or a closing.

V. MUSIC & SONGS

(to be performed, played, sung and/or read)

DRUMMING CIRCLE

Invite everyone to take a drum or percussion instrument. They can also use their hands by clapping or slapping their legs. Invite everyone to create whatever beat they wish with their instrument simultaneously. It may be coordinated, or it may be each person doing his/her own thing. Allow the activity to go on until it seems to end of its own accord.

Songs can be played on smart phones or lyrics downloaded from the Internet to be read. Following are the titles of songs that might be used for openings or closings.

SONGS ABOUT MUTUAL SUPPORT & CREATING A BETTER WORLD

"Lean on Me" by Bill Withers, 1972

"Love Invincible" by Michael Franti & Spearhead, American band, 2003

From "Feel No Pain" as performed by Sade, 1992:

> *Help them to strive*
>
> *Help them to move on*
>
> *Help them to have some future*
>
> *Help them to live life*
>
> *Help them to smile*

African-American spiritual, "I've Got Peace Like A River"

"With My Own Two Hands" by Jack Johnson and Ben Harper, 2002

"If Everyone Cared" by Nickelback, 2005

"Candles in the Sun" by Miguel, 2012

"Man in the Mirror" by Michael Jackson, 1987

"Hold On (A Change is Comin')" by Sounds of Blackness, 1997

SONGS ABOUT RESILIENCE & SELF-CONFIDENCE

"Beautiful" by Christina Aguilera, 2002

"Born This Way" by Lady Gaga, 2011

"Firework" by Katy Perry, 2010

SONGS RELATED TO SEXUAL EDUCATION

"Let's Talk about Sex" by Salt-n-Pepa, 1991

SONGS ABOUT FAMILY-LIFE CHALLENGES

"Kathleen (Hard For Me to Love)" by Jayy Perry, 2012
"Family Portrait" by P!nk, 2001

SONGS ABOUT HISTORICAL, CULTURAL TRAUMA AND HEALING

"Motherless Child" by Sweet Honey In The Rock, composed by Carol Maillard from a traditional African-American spiritual, 2001
"We Are" by Sweet Honey In The Rock, written by Dr. Ysaye Barnwell, 1993

OTHER SINGER-SONGWRITERS TO CONSIDER:

Miriam Makeba: see http://www.oldies.com/artist-songs/Miriam-Makeba.html
Buffy Sainte-Marie: see http://www.lyricsmode.com/lyrics/b/buffy_sainte_marie/
Sweet Honey In The Rock: see http://www.lyrics.com/sweethoneyintherock)

APPENDIX 3

Theoretical Essay on Why Circles Are Important in Schools

This section of *Circle Forward* explains the theoretical underpinnings for why we believe that Circles are important for building a healthy school community.

EDUCATING THE WHOLE CHILD

One of the foundational assumptions of this guide is that human beings are integrated wholes. All parts of our beings—mind, spirit, emotion, and physical self—are involved in learning. These parts of ourselves are integrated with one another and therefore are present in all that we do. Our physical state affects how we think and feel; how we think and feel affects us physically; our sense of purpose and meaning—the spiritual side of human beings—influences feelings and thoughts; and how we feel about others and ourselves affects memory, cognition, and perception.

The whole-child movement in modern education has its roots in the 19th-century philosophy of education espoused by John Dewey. This philosophy embraces the core assumption that schools need to attend to all dimensions of human development in order for optimal learning and social development to take place (Dewey, 1956).

It is hardly surprising that children who are not adequately nourished or well rested are unable to learn. School breakfast programs for low-income children increase attendance and school participation (Brown et al., 2011; Murphy et al., 1998; Murphy, 2007). It is also well established that physical activity has a positive effect on mental and emotional well-being. The epidemic of childhood obesity and the high rates of adolescent mental illnesses are warning signs that the sedentary nature of modern life in and out of school is adversely affecting the health of children (Ogden et al., 2006). Nutrition programs at school, recess, after-school sports, dance, and music programs are not distractions from the all-important academic curriculum but essential ingredients in the developmental process of the entire child that supports academic achievement (Basch, 2010).

The idea that intelligence consists of multiple domains or aptitudes, including social and emotional intelligence, resonates with the whole-child approach to education. Howard Gardner's (1983; 2000) concept of multiple intelligences challenges the idea of the single cognitive capacity known as "intelligence." Instead, he argues there are distinct types of intelligence, including spatial, interpersonal, bodily/kinesthetic, and musical. These are in addition to the traditionally valued verbal and quantitative capacities that standard IQ tests measure and that the traditional academic curriculum values most highly.

In his path-breaking book, Daniel Goleman (1995) introduced the idea of emotional intelligence to refer to a range of abilities distinct from the cognitive abilities that are essential for all kinds of achievements. These qualities include the ability: to regulate one's moods and control impulses; to empathize with others; to motivate oneself; and to work hard for rewards far into the future. It also refers to the ability to persist despite obstacles and frustrations. These qualities, according to Goleman, are necessary companions to what we think of as intellect, and they are competencies that can be taught and developed, much as we develop the cognitive skills of reading, writing, and arithmetic.

The field of social emotional learning or SEL has developed to refer to educational processes that help adults and children acquire what Goleman identified as fundamental emotional skills (CASEL, 2008). These skills include recognizing and managing one's own emotions; reading and responding to emotions in others; developing empathy and concern for others; making responsible decisions; and establishing and maintaining positive, healthy relationships.

More recently, the concept of "character education" has been re-tooled from its earlier emphasis on civics and morality to refer to the set of emotional competencies similar to those Goleman identified (Tough, 2012). Research is showing that these qualities have more impact on successful learning and academic achievement than raw intelligence. Often thought of as inherited personality traits, these are attitudes such as optimism, enthusiasm, curiosity, grit, gratitude, and self-control. People who tend to see the "glass half full" are more resilient, motivated, and resourceful; they are able to ask for help and deal constructively with setbacks and frustrations, which helps them persist in the achievement of their goals. More than IQ, these qualities predict success—not only academic success throughout high school and college and beyond, but even more importantly, success in facing challenges throughout one's life.

While the field of psychology has historically focused its attention on the study of negative emotions—depression, anxiety, fear, aggression and so forth—it was not until the 1990s that positive psychology emerged. Martin Seligman, who championed this approach, sought a greater understanding of the role that positive emotions play within a successful life. In his first book, *Learned Optimism* (1991), Seligman demonstrated how important these qualities are to the goal of living a happy, healthy, and satisfied life. More significantly, Seligman demonstrated that these characteristics are not immutable genetic endowments but acquired traits: habitual ways of thinking and acting that can be cultivated. The qualities identified by educators and positive psychologists as most predictive of achievement are: self-control, zest, social intelligence, gratitude, optimism, and curiosity. Research demonstrates that, more than IQ, these are the individual qualities that predict long-term success (Tough, 2012).

EDUCATING THE WHOLE CHILD MEANS CARING FOR THE WHOLE CHILD

Another core assumption in our guide is that human beings—indeed, all of life—is interconnected. We develop our character traits—like optimism, grit, and focus—in dynamic ongoing relationships with others within our environment. We tend to think of these traits as inborn traits inhering within individuals. However, they are now more accurately understood to be qualities that are nurtured and developed in relationship with others—families, schools, peers, and communities. We can see this most obviously in the bond between a nurturing caregiver and a helpless infant: the responsiveness of the caregiver shapes a core psychological sense of trust in others and the world (Bowlby, 1983; 1986). Parents who are tuned into the cues and moods of their infants create confident and outgoing children willing to explore their environment, secure in the knowledge that they are cared for and loved. Conversely, offspring with inattentive caregivers cope with adverse and sometimes lasting psychological consequences of that primal sense of insecurity (Karen, 1998).

James Coleman's study in the 1960s helped us understand the enormous advantage children bring to school from a home environment that nurtures them (Coleman, 1966). His argument was that no amount of financial capital invested in low-income schools could offset the human capital generated within the home. More recent research suggests that the gifts that come from healthy home environments matter even more than we originally imagined. On the negative side, the liabilities of unhealthy relationships also undermine learning (Cole et al., 2005).

The breakthrough insight, however, is that all of these qualities—from the executive functions of the prefrontal cortex, to the emotional capacity for empathy and awareness, to the attitudinal habits of persistence, attention, optimism and grit, to the cognitive abilities measured by standardized tests—are subject to change under the right circumstances (Jensen and Snider, 2013). This means that within the context of certain kinds of relationships, all children can develop and grow their capacity for these qualities. The folk wisdom that "kids don't care what you know until they know you care" turns out to be expressing a profound truth about the importance of relationships in the intellectual, moral, and social development of children. Not surprisingly it turns out that the quality of the relationships within schools matters just as much as the quality of the parental relationship (Bloom, 1995; Glasser 1992).

Nel Noddings (2005) emphasizes that in order for a caring relationship to exist, it must be mutual. That is, the one who is being cared for must feel that they are cared for and give feedback to the carer that signals their sense of gratitude and appreciation for that care. Without that feedback, carers—teachers or parents—burn out, because they depend on that positive feedback to nurture their own dedication to the well-being of another person. On the other side of the relationship, it is essential that students actually perceive that a teacher cares about them. If they don't perceive themselves as cared for, they are not receiving the benefit of that relationship. The relational quality of the interaction means that both sides must participate for the relationship to be meaningful.

William Glasser's choice theory (1992) states that, as human beings, we are agents of choice. This is the insight related to another of our core assumptions: all human beings are powerful. No one can make someone else do anything. True, we can overpower them with coercion or threaten them so they choose to comply out of fear of reprisals, but individuals can, and often do, choose to resist control, even to their own detriment. In the end, we always exercise choice about how we behave. All teachers are familiar with the hard truth that it is not possible to force a student to learn: ultimately, learning is something that each student must choose to do.

Glasser believes that children will choose to learn only from teachers whom they have assessed to be part of their "quality" world. By this, he means those they trust—teachers they feel recognize and respect them. Students choose to learn from these teachers, because they see them as meeting their needs. Part of helping students mature into successful adults is helping them believe that hard work—which may not feel all that good today or be meeting one's immediate needs—will ultimately meet their needs in the future. This is the key to all the "character" traits discussed above: the ability to delay gratification, to persist, to work towards one's goals, to ask for and get assistance, and so forth. These qualities of character develop within the context of "quality" relationships: the autonomous young person trusts that adults are on their team, so to speak, and are there to help them get where they are choosing to go.

The qualities of "character" that are so critical to academic achievement—especially throughout the span of the educational career to the completion of college—can be taught and practiced within the school environment. As students become more self-aware about their own learning, they develop greater self-discipline, more motivation to persist in the face of obstacles, and strategies for dealing with challenges that translate into better grades and higher test scores. The part of the brain that carries out these executive functions—the prefrontal cortex—gains strength as students engage in planning and problem solving. These activities develop their capacity for the higher degrees of self-control and emotional regulation that studying and long-term goal setting require (Tough, 2012).

School programming designed to teach social and emotional literacy increases the ability of youth at all ages—kindergarten to high school—to engage in meta-thinking about their own feelings and to be more aware of the emotions of others (Zins et al., 2004.) The skill set of emotional awareness taught through systematic classroom instruction is, in turn, associated with significant changes in behavior. Foremost is a decline in the disruptive and problem behaviors associated with disciplinary incidents. In addition, research finds measurable and significant gains in academic achievement.

In more old-fashioned language, we would probably refer to this as a process of maturation, becoming responsible and responsive to others, or more simply, growing up. The important point is that growing up is not an internal biological process that automatically unfolds under some biological clock. As human beings, we develop and mature through our relationships with others—parents, teachers, and peers. It is in and through these "quality" relationships that the human being develops. In a sense, we are open systems continually shaped by our relationships within our environment. However, not just any type of relationships will support healthy development; our development depends specifically on those that are "caring relationships."

THE WHOLE-SCHOOL APPROACH: THE IMPORTANCE OF SCHOOL CLIMATE AND CONNECTEDNESS

We come full circle in recognizing that individual change is possible but only within the context of certain kinds of relationships. The good news about the role of relationships—teacher-student relationships, peer relationships, and relationships within the wider school and community culture—is the potential to intervene and foster the development of a whole range of human capacities relevant to learning, human development, and ultimately successful living. Because we are in relationship with each other and our environment all our lives, we continue to be open to the positive impacts of healthy relationships.

School connectedness refers to the level of attachment or bond that a student has with his or her school (Osterman, 2002). Sociologists have established that students with more positive attachments to teachers, those who have invested greater effort into school, and those who are involved in more school activities and believe in the rules of the school are less likely to engage in deviant activities (Hirschi, 1969; Welsh et al., 1999). Social control theory (Gottfredson and Hirschi, 1990) identifies attachment to the school community as one of the key preventative factors in reducing a range of problem behaviors, including drug use, aggression, crime, and truancy. The more a student cares about school and believes teachers care about them, the more time they invest in school and internalize the norms and values of the school.

And, of course, the converse is also true: students who do not believe that the adults at school care about them are detached from the school community and more likely to engage in a range of problem behaviors, including ultimately dropping out. Research has confirmed that a common reason students identify for why they left school is their feeling that "no adults in the school cared about me" (Yazzie-Mintz, 2010).

A sense of belonging is one of the basic needs for everyone and especially for young people. Schools that are able to foster a sense of belonging to the school community enhance positive outcomes for students and teachers alike. Schools in which members of the staff experience a shared sense of purpose, collaboration, and support and where staff believe that others care about them personally have higher levels of teacher satisfaction, parental satisfaction, positive student-staff relationships, and academic achievement among students. These schools also experience lower levels of teacher absenteeism, staff turnover, and a whole range of student problem behaviors.

School climate is a term that often refers to the non-academic culture of the school—how students treat each other in the hallways, on the bus, or on the playground. It encompasses the peer culture—how students treat each other—and the quality of the relationships between the teachers and the students. Schools that intentionally have a strong sense of community are places where students experience stronger bonds with the school. The culture among the adults shapes the culture among the students and has a real impact on the individual students and their behavior: a positive school climate can reduce negative behavior and increase pro-social and academic behaviors.

Physical and emotional safety is a necessary foundation for learning. When danger is present, the neo-cortex shuts down. On national surveys, about 28% of students report having been bullied on school grounds within the past year; and about 4% of students report having stayed away from school within the past thirty days because they were afraid to come to school (U.S. DOE, 2013). Adults are often aware of the insults and teasing taking place in the hallways or on the playground but feel powerless to intervene constructively. Within the classroom, an unsafe emotional climate impairs learning: students who fear the laughter or eye-rolls of fellow students are unlikely to concentrate on learning and are very unlikely to risk participation.

As Parker Palmer (1998) notes, the kind of relationships a teacher nurtures within the individual classroom is a matter of intention. If teachers want to see respectful peer relationships, they must take steps to support and cultivate those kinds of relationships. Similarly, at the school-wide level, the quality of the school climate is a matter of intentional steps to develop positive relationships among all members of the community. In some school communities, teachers who want to care and students who want to be cared for are unable to form and sustain these relationships, because the structure of the school makes it difficult to interact in meaningful ways. Even if the intention and desire to be in good relationships exist at the individual level, the wider school structure must support and encourage trusting positive relationships for them to develop.

CARING FOR THE WHOLE CHILD ALSO INVOLVES DISCIPLINING THE CHILD

The word "discipline" comes from the Latin "to teach and to train" (Stutzman Amstutz and Mullet, 2005). The process of discipline and the process of learning are one and the same. The process of disciplining has far more in common with teaching than with the impersonal imposition of sanctions through the criminal legal system. Like all learning, the capacity to discipline a child lies in the quality of the caring relationship between the child and the adult.

According to Glasser, the two most basic and sometimes contradictory needs for all human beings are the need for belonging and the need for power. In a sense, both of these needs pull against one another: the need for power—to assert oneself and to feel that one is in charge of one's own choices—is in tension with the need for order and belonging to a group.

This tension is often called a paradox, and it is one of the most important realities to come to terms with when understanding human relationships. Physicist Niels Bohr explains the distinction between contradictory facts and contradictory truths (Rozental, 1967). When it comes to factual truth, two facts cannot both be true at the same time. If one is true, the other is false. But facts are different from profound truths about the human condition. Here opposites are simultaneously and powerfully true. Part of the human condition is to accept both sides of the coin as essential parts of the whole reality. Bohr says, "The opposite of a true statement is a false statement, but the opposite of a profound truth can be another profound truth."

When it comes to human nature, the paradox arises from two profound truths about us. On one hand, we are social beings, highly attached and influenced and impacted by our relationship with others. On the other hand, we are also autonomous beings who resist being dominated by those who deny our basic sense of dignity and whom we do not trust. Both of these are equally true about the human condition. All parents are familiar with the power struggles that emerge in the early childhood: even a small child will resist coercion in the effort to assert their innate need for autonomy. Any experienced teacher will recognize the capacity of students to resist learning despite all coercive efforts to control their behavior.

In hierarchical environments, we face an enormous temptation to forget this paradox and to treat other people as if they are inanimate objects that we truly can control. We mistakenly believe that, with the right balance of rewards and punishments, we are in control of others when in reality they remain human beings with choice and autonomy. The use of rewards and punishments means teachers often achieve the veneer of compliance—a superficial kind of control that relies on constant vigilance by adults. Rules may be followed, but only if students perceive a likelihood of getting caught if they break them. A control-based model of relationship does not help students internalize the values underlying the rules, yet this is the level of self-discipline and self-control needed for higher learning and life-long achievement.

This form of control relationship between adults and students ultimately comes at an extremely high cost: it harms the quality of the relationship with the student. Acts of punishment tend to undermine the bond between the giver and receiver, reducing trust and therefore the capacity for learning. Sometimes punishment is an expression of power, fueled by the emotions of anger, hurt, or frustration. In the end, coercive relationships are never caring relationships, and caring relationships are the only relationships that afford the trust and connection that promote maturation and growth. The limits of punishment as an effective strategy for changing student behavior can be seen with the consequences of the widespread implementation of zero-tolerance policies over the last two decades in many schools across the country.

THE UNINTENDED HARMS OF ZERO TOLERANCE

The origins of zero tolerance policies in schools lie in the federal Gun Free School Act passed by Congress in 1995. This Act required that all states receiving federal funding to enact legislation requiring mandatory expulsion for not less than one year for any student who brings a firearm to school. Within a short period, the meaning of zero tolerance expanded far beyond the federally mandated policies regarding guns. It has come to refer to a wide range of "predetermined consequences or punishments for specified offenses." School districts modeled their disciplinary policies after the zero tolerance model for alcohol, drugs, tobacco, fighting, bad language, and sexual harassment, as well as other infractions. They instituted mandatory suspensions or expulsions for a wide range of student misbehavior.

Schools have clearly adopted the zero-tolerance approach to all kinds of student misconduct far beyond what was required by state law. For example, in a statewide study of Texas schools (Fabelo et al., 2011)—the second largest public school system in the country—researchers found that over half (54%) of all students had been subject at least once to an in-school suspension, while almost one third (31%) of all students had experienced an out-of-school suspension for at least three days. Yet only 3% of all of these disciplinary actions were for conduct that the state law had mandated these sanctions. In addition to punitive exclusions, schools have also increasingly turned to other measures more reminiscent of the prisons than schools. Police officers, metal detectors, canine units, security cameras, armed guards, lockdown drills, and SWAT sweeps of the lockers are the new normal in many schools.

An unintended consequence of these policies has been higher rates of exclusion of minority students. In Texas, African-American males and females are subject to significantly higher rates of suspensions, followed by Latinos and then whites (Fabelo et al., 2011). This find holds true in other states and cities where studies have been conducted, including New York, Massachusetts, Illinois, Colorado, California,

Minnesota, and Florida (Advancement Project, 2005; Fenning and Rose, 2007; Skiba et al., 2006).

The reality that students of color are more likely to be subject to exclusionary discipline than white students is compounded by another negative consequence of zero tolerance policies. The phrase "school to prison pipeline" captures the harsh reality that students who are suspended and expelled are far more likely to become involved with the criminal justice system. Nationwide, a student who is suspended or expelled is three times more likely to be involved with the juvenile justice system the following year, compared to similar students with similar characteristics who have not been exposed to these practices (Fabelo et al., 2011).

The final criticism of zero tolerance policies is that research shows no evidence that schools with zero tolerance polices are safer due to these policies (Skiba, 2000; Skiba et al., 2006). Contrary to expectations, schools with high levels of in-school and out-of-school suspensions have seen an increase in troublesome behaviors among students, including higher drug use, poor academic achievement, long-term disaffection and alienation, and higher levels of withdrawal and avoidance behaviors by school staff.

Suspension and expulsion are attractive responses to student misbehavior for schools, because they offer an immediate, albeit short-term, "solution" to the problem. If you cannot persuade a student to cease the troublesome behavior, then at least it is possible to make the student go away. The hidden costs of this approach, however, eventually become apparent. In most districts, the costs per hour for expulsion proceedings are somewhere between $50 and $500 per hour (Riestenberg, 2003).

Far more troubling is that the "problem," namely, young people in need of adult supervision and guidance, are kicked out of school into communities where they are most likely to come under the influence of those who are less likely to help them get their needs met in ways that are healthy and positive. As agents of choice, young people will continue to seek to meet their needs—in particular, their need for belonging, power, and respect. Many schools use suspensions as wake-up calls to parents, hoping that exclusion from school will strengthen parental supervision and engagement to support cooperative behavior in school. No doubt this occasionally happens. But for the most part, exclusionary discipline takes students who are already marginally attached to the culture of the school and pushes them into alternate social networks to satisfy these needs. The result is an unintended strengthening of attachment to oppositional subcultures and an attenuation of bonds to schools and parents alike (Gottfredson, 2001).

This style of discipline also leaves other students who have been affected by the misbehavior on the sidelines with no official response to their needs. Students who have been victimized by other students are rarely included in any process that is designed to address their needs for emotional or physical safety or social support. Furthermore, there is little attempt to involve the wider school community. In the wake of an incident, rumors often abound, but the wider school community has no opportunity to learn positive lessons. Instead, students are often resentful of the punishment without really understanding what happened and who was affected.

One of the most important findings from the statewide survey of Texas schools is that rates of zero-tolerance style discipline varied enormously from school to school (Fabelo et al., 2011). Some schools had higher rates than expected, given their demographic characteristics, while others had lower rates. In fact, 27% of the schools had much lower rates than predicted by their school characteristics. This suggests that schools operating in the same resource environment and statutory regulatory environment have significant discretion in how they conduct the process of discipline within their school community. As the alarm has risen about the disproportionate impact of zero-tolerance polices on students of color and the rise in dropouts, schools have been seeking alternate ways to respond to student misconduct—ways that do not resort to the highly destructive over-reliance on punitive exclusions.

DISCIPLINING WITH RESPECT: RESTORATIVE PRACTICES IN SCHOOLS

Many schools have not adopted a zero-tolerance approach and do not rely heavily on detentions, suspensions, and expulsion to manage student misbehavior. Studies show that these schools have better behavioral outcomes compared to similar schools with a punishment-centered discipline system.

Disciplining students is an intrinsic part of the relationship between students and teachers, yet few teachers are formally trained in any particular approach to discipline. Traditionally, administrators set school-wide rules, and teachers develop their own personal approaches to managing behavior in the classroom. Teachers who are successful in managing student behavior may have a wide variety of styles. These range from what appears to be highly authoritarian to styles that are more democratic and collaborative. A common element is that these teachers rely less on coercion—the use of punishments and rewards to achieve compliance—and more on the quality of relationship between themselves and the students. Whatever the outward appearance, adults who are effective at disciplining have developed relationships that are based on a sense of trust and caring.

> What we must realize is that there is a very fine distinction between coercion, which is never caring, and a coercive style of teaching that is, at its core, very caring. If the [students] see the [teacher] as caring, then they can accept whatever he does, no matter how coercive it may seem on the surface (Glasser, 1992: 39).

The power to discipline students—that is, to help them understand why a specific behavior is wrong and to help them choose better behavior in the future—depends on the quality of the relationship between the students and the adults. When students believe that adults care about them, the conditions for learning are possible, and positive discipline is about learning to do the right thing (Nelson, 2006).

Restorative discipline is a response to wrongdoing that focuses on repairing the harm caused by the misbehavior (Morrison, 2007). It is a victim-centered response because it focuses on meeting the needs of those who have been hurt, as well as on using the incident as a "teachable moment" for the one who has done harm. Punitive discipline focuses heavily on dealing with the person who broke the rules; restorative discipline focuses on meeting the needs both of those who have been harmed by the misbehavior and of the one who committed harm.

In a restorative environment, people who harm others are held accountable to the person they hurt as well as to the wider community. In restorative discipline, restoring positive relationships (or forming them for the first time) is a key goal of the response. Rather than focusing on the violation of rules, a restorative response engages in a structured face-to-face dialogue about the impact of the behavior on others and the harm that has resulted. This dialogue—which can be facilitated within the Circle structure or other formats, including one-on-one conversations—allows people to explore fully the context of behavior. Through the dialogue, people gain a deep understanding of why the behavior occurred and what can be done positively to put things right.

Those who have been negatively impacted by an incident are encouraged to express their feelings and to articulate what they need to have the harm repaired. Those who are hurt are offered support by the community. Those who have done harm are given the chance to understand how their behavior has affected others and to make things right in the future. The ultimate outcome is that relationships that have been damaged by wrongdoing are repaired and strengthened. Everyone contributes to a fuller understanding of what happened, who has been affected, and what can be done both to repair harm and to prevent similar harms from happening in the future. Consequences are understood as obligations to take part in putting things right. These obligations are determined by the needs of the situation and are tailored so that they make sense to those directly involved.

Restorative discipline is rooted in the core assumption that everyone wants to be in good relationship with others and themselves. Everyone wants to feel respected, to have a sense of dignity, to feel as if they matter to others, and to feel valued. Building strong and positive relationships within a school community is key to learning and to responding with positive discipline when students and adults make mistakes. We lay the foundation for this by establishing a school culture in which all members of the community are cared for and respected. Using restorative discipline is effective only if a whole-school approach has been established and laid a foundation for a caring school community. As Nancy Riestenberg (2012) points out, "One cannot effectively teach without relationship, and relationships themselves teach."

Positive Behavioral Intervention and Supports (PBIS), Discipline with Dignity, Developmental Design, and Responsive Classroom are similar approaches to discipline. Each of these approaches clearly articulate the values that matter to the school community. They also articulate systematically the specific behaviors that embody those values. And they place far greater emphasis on encouraging and rewarding positive behavior than on prohibiting negative behaviors. As a result, all members of the school community know what behavior is desired and expected of them.

A whole-school approach clearly states the expectations for behavior. Moreover, a restorative school that is rooted in respectful and caring relationships emphasizes the importance of involving students in developing the shared values of the community and the expectations that go with them.

THE PROBLEM OF BULLYING

Bullying is a specific type of aggression defined by repeated and unprovoked attacks by a more powerful aggressor against a less powerful victim (Olweus, 1993; Rigby, 2002). A whole-school approach has been seen as particularly important in addressing chronic victimization through bullying behavior. The vast majority of bullying takes place within the context of peer groups with little adult involvement. Research shows that the behavior is sustained by its efficacy in establishing status among peers (Bazelon, 2013). As bystanders, the community of students can either support the behavior by laughing, teasing, or refusing to intervene, or they can reject the behavior by speaking out or turning to adults. Research demonstrates that whole-school efforts are most effective. When administrators, teachers, and students work together to create an anti-bullying school environment, victimization goes down (Vreeman and Carroll, 2007).

A restorative response to bullying begins with establishing the foundation of a positive school climate—a climate that promotes positive relationships and problematizes disrespectful interpersonal behavior. By contrast, a school climate that tolerates bullying within the school culture supports serious bullying behavior rooted in individual psychological factors, such as low self-esteem, a need for approval, and a need to exert power over others. Restorative practices, especially Circles, help to build a school climate that does not tolerate bullying-like interactions, and this has preventative effects. The more cohesion and trust there is among students and teachers, the more willing members of the community are to take action for the common good, and the less bullying occurs within that social context (Williams and Guerra, 2011).

Restorative interventions to respond to incidents of bullying are effective for another reason: they focus concern on victims. Most traditional discipline targets the wrongdoer, either with a punitive response or some kind of counseling or intervention, while victims' needs and concerns are often left unattended. In a restorative response, understanding and attending to victims' needs are a primary concern. Much effort is placed on marshaling school resources to meet their needs for reassurance, support, safety, and dignity. At the same time, the needs of the wrongdoer—their need for support, respect, understanding, and concern—are an equally fundamental component of the restorative intervention. In a restorative process, the behavior is clearly condemned—not the individual. Every effort is made to support the individual in developing more healthy patterns—mentally, emotionally, and behaviorally.

ADDRESSING TRAUMA IN SCHOOLS

We know that not all children come to school with the emotional and cognitive benefits of a secure and healthy home environment. Our understanding of the effects of adverse childhood events helps us to understand that the behavior of the distracted, hyper-aroused, defiant, or aggressive child is often the result of traumatic relationships: the child's basic need for caring, trust, and stability have gone unmet (Cole et al., 2005). The child's behavior is often unconscious or a habitual coping strategy that has emerged within an unhealthy relationship. This behavior is extremely challenging in the classroom.

Research confirms that events that disrupt the quality of the parent-child attachment in early years of infancy and childhood may have psychological consequences that last a lifetime. ACE or "adverse childhood experiences" refers to a wide range of events—divorce, abuse, incarceration, addiction, mental illness—that negatively impact the parent-child relationship. Research shows a stunningly high correlation between ACEs and a wide range of negative adult outcomes, such as suicide, smoking, drug use, alcoholism, and incarceration, as well as an elevated likelihood of numerous physical ailments, such as cancer, heart disease, liver disease, and obesity (Edwards et al., 2005).

Stress is the factor that mediates this correlation, or, to be more accurate, feeling stressed is our physiological response. Designed as an alert system to deal with imminent danger, the body's response to stress leads to a series of physiological changes known as "fight or flight." Faced with danger, our bodies prepare to run or confront an enemy. Yet the modern sources of stress are typically not acute dangers. Instead, many children face chronic sources of anxiety and insecurity: never knowing if dinner will be made, hearing parents yelling and fighting, moving from house to house or from one foster home to another, hearing gunshots in the neighborhood, or being afraid of walking to the corner store or playground. These are the chronic stresses of neglect and dysfunction.

According to researchers, the prefrontal cortex region is the seat of the brain's executive functions, such as self-control, working memory, and emotional regulation. Planning, reflecting, and choosing how to react are all parts of the executive function that is critical to all the behaviors necessary for academic achievement. This is a kind of meta-thinking—thinking about thinking and also thinking about feeling—that is essential for being able to control one's temper, delay gratification, deal with setbacks, and make and follow through on plans. This part of the brain continues to develop throughout adolescence and into early adulthood, which helps to explain the notorious impulsivity of adolescence.

Many children come to the school environment without the protective positive psychological qualities that develop within warm, supportive home environments. This is obvious in kindergarten and preschool. Children who grow up in stressful environments find it harder to sit still, to concentrate, to handle disappointments and frustrations, and to listen and follow directions. While they may also lack vocabulary and reading skills, the biggest liability for their success in school is behavioral: from day one, these are the "problem children," and they often continue this behavior throughout their school career.

Within some communities, so many children have not been cared for within healthy relationships that some degree of trauma has become "normal." Sandra Bloom (1995) points out that there is a distinction between what is "normal" and what is "healthy." Increasingly, whole communities and families can be engulfed in negative patterns of relationships that are passed on from generation to generation. The stresses caused by poverty, crime, violence, drug addiction, and discrimination, which are endemic within poor communities, have only grown greater as economic conditions have worsened.

The good news is that schools are well positioned to be a place that offers healthy relationships by intentionally cultivating healthy relationships within the school environment (Macy et al., 2003). The teacher's response to problem behavior can either escalate the trauma and contribute to its reenactment or can offer the child an opportunity to overcome it. So, too, the type of relationships that are developed within the school have the potential either to further the damage done by parents, who are themselves damaged too, or to provide the child with alternate adult relationships that model a positive way to be in the world.

> The school can further the damage already done by damaged—and damaging—parents. Or alternatively, the school can provide another option for the child, a choice, another hope-sustaining way of viewing themselves and other people. The children we call resilient, the ones who survive and transcend traumatic home environments, are the children who are provided with choices that they are able to use advantageously (Bloom, 1995:5).

Some children may need expert or specialized treatment. However, the real potential to heal trauma lies within the daily, routine interactions and the ordinary relationships between children and others within the school community, most importantly, with and among teachers and peers (Macy et al., 2003). Trauma is a fragmenting experience. The school community can be an oasis of calm, caring, and continuity in a child's life, that is, if that community is itself stable, supportive, and built on a foundation of positive enduring relationships.

Teachers and other adults who interact with hurt children have an enormous opportunity to effect major change. Traumatized children do not necessarily require psychiatrists; they require adults who can extend the vital relational skills that good parents provide and a system that provides the safety and security for these relationships to be sustained. With sufficient will and commitment, any school can create its own orchestral suite and by doing so, can play the music of healing (Bloom, 1995:19).

A safe and supportive school climate is good for all children, but it is healing for those who have had little experience of emotional and physical safety in their lives. Schools can serve as sanctuaries for children whose homes and neighborhoods are chaotic and unsafe. A whole-child approach gives a child with painful emotional experiences an opportunity to gain some tools to understand and control his/her emotions and a safe space to practice emotional awareness and emotional literacy. If adults within the school community are intentional about listening to all children and meeting the children's needs for love, support, competency, and belonging, then children without reliable parents may find a new network of trustworthy relationships to help them grow and mature.

We have a tendency in our culture to respond to problem behavior either by demonizing (a child who misbehaves is bad) or by medicalizing (a child who misbehaves is sick). In both instances, this way of thinking locates the source of the problem within the child and fails to understand the relational nature of behavior. Research by Dr. Martin Tieicher of Harvard and others indicates that trauma and toxic stress become hardwired into our biology. (Teicher, 2002). All children create neural pathways in response to their environment and their interactions with adults, particularly their primary caregivers. If the environment is high stress or experiences in the home are traumatic, if stress for any reason is continuous and unsupported, that is *toxic*, and those conditions will have an effect on the brain as it develops.

The past experience of trauma should never, however, be seen as having created a damaged or bad person: rather, the brain has created pathways for behaviors that help the person cope in a high-stress environment. Those behaviors may not be useful, though, in a more regulated environment, like a school. Hyper-vigilance, impulsivity, competitiveness, being quick tempered, or conversely, being depressed, withdrawn, and numb may help a child survive in a violent home or community, in a refugee camp, after a natural disaster, or in a war zone, but those same behaviors can cause disruption or lead to violations of rules in a school. (Mead, Beauchine, & Shannon, 2010).

The challenge for adults is to support children, increasing their resilience by providing care, concern, and compassion. Dr. Gordon Hodas describes what is needed in a school or program to help support children who have experienced trauma. He writes:

> [E]ach adult working with any child or adolescent [should] *presume* that the child has been trauma exposed ... providing unconditional respect to the child and being careful not to challenge him/her in ways that produce shame and humiliation. Such an approach has no down side, since children who have been exposed to trauma require it, and other, more fortunate children deserve and can also benefit from this fundamentally humanistic commitment. (Hodas, 2006, p. 40).

Regular Circle practice encourages resilience and can help students develop new neural pathways for the behaviors needed to manage school as well as to develop caring relationships. Regardless of whether you make a mistake or you help other students out, in a restorative school, you are supported, not sent away. Resilience is often defined as the ability to bounce back in the face of adversity. Children who are resilient despite adverse circumstances have had the benefit of positive relationships—through family and other capable adult caregivers, through effective teachers and schools, and through pro-social peers and community resources (Masten & Obradović, 2006). Somewhere in their lives, caring competent adults and peers have had the time and the interest to help children develop other responses, skills, and practices. Through the continual "serve and return" interactions of care, compassion, and relationship, new neural pathways for new, more relationship-oriented behaviors can develop.

One of the core assumptions of this guide is that all people possess a healthy core self that is capable of choosing to be in good relationship with others. Children, more easily than adults, can learn new skills and come to trust others if the relationships that surround them are positive and healthy. Our core assumption is that we are shaped through our relationships with one another. Although the children who have experienced trauma are deeply affected by that experience, they are still open to being positively impacted by other relationships. In a whole-school approach, the healing impact of good relationships falls not only to the teacher but also to the entire community, including other children and adults.

We advocate a holistic response to trauma by cultivating safe, supportive, and trusting relationships. While we do not disagree that some individuals may require specialized treatment from therapeutic professionals, we believe that the most profound healing can be promoted through a whole-school approach to a caring environment.

THE ADDED BENEFIT OF MINDFULNESS

The practice of mindfulness—an intentional effort to focus on the present moment, often by focusing awareness on the breath, and the attendant practices of meditation—is now widely known and practiced within the Western world. However, only relatively recently has Western science studied how these practices impact physical health, cognition, behavior, mental health, and wellness (Kabat-Zinn, 1996). The use of these practices for children within schools, juvenile detention facilities, and other settings is in its infancy, both in practice and research.

Early research, however, shows positive outcomes. Even with relatively short interventions, mindfulness studies indicate that the practices increase attentiveness, reduce behavioral issues, and improve mental health (Black et al., 2013). These findings are particularly relevant for groups of students who may have been exposed to high levels of stress and trauma. Increasing the capacity of the child or adolescent to focus on the breath decreases emotional reactivity and the triggering associated with traumatic environments. At the same time, it increases focus, attentiveness, and self-control. Building brief mindfulness practices into the routine of the school day strengthens the capacity of all students and teachers to manage stress.

As we characterized Circles from the outset, the Circle itself is a mindfulness practice. By focusing the attention of all participants within the Circle itself, the Circle focuses attention on the present moment. In addition, in this guide, we have incorporated a "mindfulness moment" into all the Circle lesson plans. We strongly recommend that teachers use Circles on a regular basis and consider how to build a routine mindfulness practice into the daily rhythm of the school.

REFERENCES

Advancement Project. (2005). *Education on lockdown: The schoolhouse to jailhouse track.* Washington D.C.: Advancement Project.

Aronson, J., Fried, C. B., & Good, C. (2002). Reducing the effects of stereotype threat on African American college students by shaping theories of intelligence. *Journal of Experimental Social Psychology*, 38(2), 113–25.

Basch, C. E. (2010). Healthier students are better learners: A missing link in school reforms to close the achievement gap. *Equity Matters Research Review*, No. 6. New York: Teachers College, Columbia University. Retrieved from http://www.equitycampaign.org/i/a/document/12557_EquityMattersVol6_Web03082010.pdf.

Bazelon, E. (2013). *Sticks and stones: Defeating the culture of bullying and rediscovering the power of character and empathy.* New York: Random House Publishing Group.

Black, D. S., & Fernando, R. (2013). Mindfulness training and classroom behavior among lower-income and ethnic minority elementary school children. *Journal of Child and Family Studies*, June 2013.

Bloom, S. L. (1995). Creating sanctuary in the school. *Journal for a Just and Caring Education*, October, 1995, I(4), 403–433.

Bond, L., Butler, H., Thomas, L., Carlin, J., Glover, S., Bowes, G., & Patton, G. (2007). Social and school connectedness in early secondary school as predictors of late teenage substance use, mental health, and academic outcomes. *Journal of Adolescent Health*, April 2007, 40(4), 357.e9–18. Epub February 5, 2007.

Bowlby, J. (1983). *Attachment and loss, Vol. I: Attachment.* New York: Basic Books.

———.(1986). *Attachment and loss, Vol. II/III: Separation.* New York: Basic Books.

Brown, L., Beardslee, W. H., & Prothrow-Stith, D. (2011). *Impact of school breakfast on children's health and learning: An analysis of the scientific research.* Commissioned by the Sodexo Foundation. Available online: http://www.sodexofoundation.org/hunger_us/Images/Impact%20of%20School%20Breakfast%20Study_tcm150-212606.PDF.

Brown, T. (2007). Lost and turned out: Academic, social, and emotional experiences of students excluded from school. *Urban Education,* (42)5, 432–55.

Carlson, S. A., Fulton, J. E., Lee, S. M., Maynard, L. M., Brown, D. R., Kohl, H. W., III, & Dietz, W. H. (2008). Physical education and academic achievement in elementary school: Data from the early childhood longitudinal study. *American Journal of Public Health,* April 2008, 98(4), 721–27.

Casarjian, B., & Leonard, N. (2013). Mindfulness training improves attentional task performance in incarcerated youth: A group randomized controlled intervention trial. *Frontiers in Psychology,* November 8, 2013, 4:792.

CASEL: Collaborative for Academic, Social and Emotional Learning. (2008). Social and emotional learning (SEL) and student benefits: Implications for the safe schools/healthy students core elements. Chicago. Retrieved from http://www.casel.org/downloads/EDC_CASELSEL ResearchBrief.pdf.

Coe, D. P., Pivarnik, J. M., Womack, C. J., Reeves, M. J., & Malina, R. M. (2006). Effect of physical education and activity levels on academic achievement in children. *Medicine & Science in Sports & Exercise,* August 2006, 38(8), 1515–19.

Cole, S., O'Brien, J., Gadd, M., Ristuccia, J., Wallace, D., & Gregory, M. (2005). *Helping traumatized children learn: Supportive school environments for children traumatized by family violence: A report and policy agenda.* Boston, MA: Massachusetts Advocates for Children.

Coleman, J. S. (1966). *Equality of educational opportunity study (EEOS).* Washington, DC: U.S. Department of Health, Education, and Welfare.

Curwin, R., Mendler, A., & Mendler, B. (2008). *Discipline with dignity: New challenge and new solutions,* 3rd Edition. Alexandria VA: ASCD.

Deary, I. J., Whalley, L. J., Batty, G. D., & Starr, J. M. (2006). Physical fitness and lifetime cognitive change. *Neurology,* October 10, 2006, 67(7), 1195–1200.

Dewey, J. (1956b [1899]). *The school and society.* Chicago: The University of Chicago Press.

———.(1966 [1916]). *Democracy and education: An introduction to the philosophy of education.* New York: The Free Press.

Duckworth, A. L., & Seligman, M. E. P. (2005). Self-discipline outdoes IQ in predicting academic performance of adolescents. *Psychological Science,* 16(12). Available online at: http://www.sas.upenn.edu/~duckwort/images/PsychologicalScienceDec2005.pdf.

Durlak, J. A., Weissberg, R. P., Dymnicki, A. B., Taylor, R. D., & Schellinger, K. B. (2011). The impact of enhancing students' social and emotional learning: A meta-analysis of school-based universal interventions. *Child Development*, 82, 405–432.

Dweck, C. (2008). *Mindset: The new psychology of success*. New York: Ballantine Books.

Eccles, J. S., Early, D., Fraser, K., Belansky, E., & McCarthy, K. (1997). The relation of connection, regulation, and support for autonomy to adolescents' functioning. *Journal of Adolescent Research*, 12(2), 263–86.

Edwards, V. J., Anda, R. F., Dube, S. R., Dong, M., Chapman, D. F., Felitti, V. J. (2005). The wide-ranging health consequences of adverse childhood experiences. In K. Kendall-Tackett & S. Giacomoni, (Eds.), *Victimization of children and youth: Patterns of abuse, response strategies*. Kingston, NJ: Civic Research Institute, 21–1 to 21–6.

Fabelo, T., Thompson, M. D., Plotkin, M., Carmichael, D., Marchbanks, M. P., & Booth, E. A. (2011). *Breaking schools' rules: A statewide study on how school discipline relates to students' success and juvenile justice involvement*. New York: Council of State Governments Justice Center and The Public Policy Research Institute, Texas A&M University.

Felitti, V., Anda, F., Nordenberg, D., Williamson, D., Spitz, A., Edwards, V., Koss, M., & Marks, J. (1998). Relationship of childhood abuse and household dysfunction to many of the leading causes of death in adults: The adverse childhood experiences (ACE) study. *American Journal of Preventative Medicine*, May 1998, 14(4), 245–58.

Fenning, P., & Rose, J. (2007). Overrepresentation of African American students in exclusionary discipline: The role of school policy. *Urban Education*, 42, 536–59.

Gardner, H. (1983). *Frames of mind: The theory of multiple intelligences*. New York: Basic Books.

———.(2000). *Intelligence reframed: Multiple intelligences for the 21st century*. New York: Basic Books.

———.(2006). *Five minds for the future*. Boston MA: Harvard Business School Press.

Glasser, W. (1992). *The quality school*. New York: Harper Collins.

Goleman, D. (1995). *Emotional intelligence: What it is and why it matters more than IQ*. New York: Bantam Books.

Gottfredson, D. C. (2001). *Schools and delinquency*. New York: Cambridge University Press.

Gottfredson, M. R., & Hirschi, T. (1990). *A general theory of crime*. Stanford, CA: Stanford University Press.

Hirschi, T. (1969). *Causes of delinquency*. Berkeley: University of California Press.

Hodas, G. R. (2006). Responding to childhood trauma: The promise and practice of trauma informed care. Harrisburg, PA: Pennsylvania Office of Mental Health and Substance Abuse Services.

Jensen, E., & Snider, C. (2013). *Turnaround tools for the teenage brain: Helping underperforming students become lifelong learners*. San Francisco, CA: Jossey-Bass.

Kabat-Zinn, J. (1996). Mindfulness meditation: What it is, what it isn't, and its role in health care and medicine. In Haruki, Y., Ishii, Y., & Suzuki, M. (Eds.) *Comparative and psychological study on meditation*. Delft, Netherlands: Eburon, 161–70.

Karen, R. (1998). *Becoming attached: First relationships and how they shape our capacity to love*. New York: Oxford University Press.

Klatt, M., Harpster, K., Browne, E., White, S., & Case-Smith, J. (2013). Feasibility and preliminary outcomes for Move-into-Learning: An arts-based mindfulness classroom intervention. *Journal of Positive Psychology*, 8(3), 233–41.

Klem, A. M., & Connell, J. P. (2004). Relationships matter: Linking teacher support to student engagement and achievement. *Journal of School Health*, 74, 262–73.

Luster T., Small, S., & Lower, R. (2002). The correlates of abuse and witnessing abuse among adolescents. *Journal of Interpersonal Violence*, 17(12), 1323–40.

Macy, R. D., Johnson, D. J., Gross, S. I., & Brighton, P. (2003). Healing in familiar settings: Support for children and youth in the classroom and community. *New Directions for Youth Development*, Summer, 2003(98), 51–79.

Masten, A. S., & Obradović, J. (2006). Competence and resilience in development. *Annals of the New York Academy of Sciences*, 1094: 13–27. doi: 10.1196/annals.1376.003

Mead, H. K., Beauchine, T. P., & Shannon, K. E. (2010). Neurobiological adaptations to violence across development. *Development and Psychopathology*, February 2010, 22(1), 1–22.

Morrison, B. (2002). Bullying and victimization in schools: A restorative justice approach. *Trends and Issues in Crime and Criminal Justice*, (219), 1–6. Canberra, AU: Australian Institute of Criminology. Retrieved from http://www.aic.gov.au/publications/current%20series/tandi.aspx.

———.(2007). *Restoring safe school communities: A whole school response to bullying, violence and alienation*. Annandale, NSW, AU: Federation Press.

Murphy, J. M. (2007). Breakfast and learning: An updated review. *Current Nutrition and Food Science*, 3(1), 3–36.

Murphy, J. M., Pagano, M. E., Nachmani, J., Sperling, P., Kane, S., & Kleinman, R. E. (1998). The relationship of school breakfast to psychosocial and academic functioning: Cross-sectional and longitudinal observations in an inner-city school sample. *Archives of Pediatrics & Adolescent Medicine*, 152(9), 899–907.

Noddings, N. (2005). *The challenge to care in schools: An alternative approach to education*. New York: Teachers College Press.

Ogden, C. L., Carroll, M. D., Curtin, L. R., McDowell, M. A., Tabak, C. J., & Flegal, K. M. (2006). Prevalence of overweight and obesity in the United States, 1999–2004. *Journal of the American Medical Association*, 295(13), 1549–55.

Olweus, D. (1993). *Bullying at school: What we know and what we can do*. Oxford, UK: Blackwell.

Osterman, K. F. (2000). Students' need for belonging in the school community. *Review of Educational Research,* 70(3), 323–67.

Parker, P. J. (1998). *The courage to teach: Exploring the inner landscape of a teacher's life.* San Francisco, CA: Jossey-Bass.

Payton, J. W., Weissberg, R. P., Durlak, J. A., Dymnicki, A. B., Taylor, R. D., Schellinger, K. B., & Pachan, M. (2008). *Positive impact of social and emotional learning for kindergarten to eighth-grade students: Findings from three scientific reviews (Executive Summary).* Chicago, IL: Collaborative for Academic, Social, and Emotional Learning (CASEL). Available online: http://www.casel.org/library/2013/11/1/the-positive-impact-of-social-and-emotional-learning-for-kindergarten-to-eighth-grade-students.

Peterson, C., & Seligman, M. (2004). *Character strengths and virtues: A handbook and classification.* Oxford: Oxford University Press.

Riestenberg, N. (2003). *Zero and no: Some definitions.* Roseville, MN: Minnesota Department of Education, 2003.

———.(2012). *Circle in the square: Building community and repairing harm in school.* St. Paul, MN: Living Justice Press.

Rigby, K. (2002). *New perspectives on bullying.* London, UK: Jessica Kingsley.

Rozental, S. (1967). *Niels Bohr: His life and work as seen by his friends and colleagues.* New York: Wiley.

Seligman, M. (1991). *Learned optimism: How to change your mind and your life.* New York: A. A. Knopf.

Skiba, R. J. (2000). *Zero tolerance, zero evidence: An analysis of school disciplinary practice.* Indiana Education Policy Center, *Policy Research Report #SRS2.* August, 2000. Online: http://www.indiana.edu/~safeschl/ztze.pdf.

Skiba, R., Reynolds, C., Graham, S., Sheras, P., Conoley, J., & Garcia-Vazquez, E. (2006). *Are zero tolerance policies effective in the schools? An evidentiary review and recommendations: A report by the American Psychological Association Zero Tolerance Task Force.* Washington D.C.: American Psychological Association.

Stearns, E., & Glennie, E. (2006). When and why dropouts leave high school. *Youth Society,* (38), 29.

Stewart, E. (2003). School social bonds, school climate and school misbehavior: A multi-level analysis. *Justice Quarterly,* 20(3).

Stinchcomb, J. B., Bazemore G., & Riestenberg, N. (2006). Beyond zero tolerance: Restoring justice in secondary schools. *Youth Violence and Juvenile Justice,* April 2006, 4(2), 123–47. Available online at: https://www.ncjrs.gov/App/Publications/abstract.aspx?ID=234985.

Stutzman Amstutz, L., and Mullet, J. H. (2005). *The little book of restorative discipline for schools: Teaching responsibility; creating caring climates.* Intercourse, PA: Good Books.

Sumner, M. D., Silverman, C., & Frampton, M. L. (2010). *School-based restorative justice as an alternative to zero-tolerance policies: Lessons from West Oakland.* Berkeley, CA: Thelton E. Henderson Center for Social Justice.

Teicher, M.H. (2002). Scars that won't heal: The neurobiology of child abuse. *Scientific American,* V2009, 286(3): 54–61.

Tough, P. (2012). *How children succeed: Grit, curiosity and the hidden power of character.* Boston: Houghton, Mifflin, Harcourt.

U.S. Department of Education, National Center for Education Statistics (NCES). (2013). *Indicators of school crime and safety: 2012.* NCES, 2013–036.

Vreeman, R. C., and Carroll, A. E. (2007). A systematic review of school-based interventions to prevent bullying. *Archives of Pediatric and Adolescent Medicine* 2007, 161(1), 78–88.

Welsh, W. N., Greene, J. R., & Jenkins, P. H. (1999). School disorder: The influence of individual, institutional, and community factors. *Criminology,* 37, 601–643.

Williams, K., & Guerra, N. (2011). Perceptions of collective efficacy and bullying perpetration in schools. *Social Problems,* 58(1), 126–43.

Wisner, B. L. (2013). An exploratory study of mindfulness meditation for alternative school students: Perceived benefits for improving school climate and student functioning. *Mindfulness,* (2013), 1–13.

Yazzie-Mintz, E. (2010). *Charting the path from engagement to achievement: A report on the 2009 high school survey of student engagement.* Bloomington, IN: Center for Evaluation & Education Policy.

Youth Transition Network. (2006). *Too big to be seen: The invisible dropout crisis in Boston and America.* Boston: Youth Transition Partners.

Zins, J. E., Weissberg, R. P., Wang, M. C., & Walberg. H. J. (Eds.). (2004). *Building academic success on social and emotional learning: What does the research say?* New York: Teachers College Press.

APPENDIX 4

Resources

I. RESOURCES ON RESTORATIVE JUSTICE, THE CIRCLE PROCESS, SCHOOLS, AND YOUTH

Books: Print and online

Armstrong, Margaret, and David Vinegrad. *Working in Circles in Primary and Secondary Classrooms*. Victoria, AU: Inyahead Press, 2013. This book is an excellent resource for elementary-age use of Circles.

Boyes-Watson, Carolyn. *Peacemaking Circles and Urban Youth: Bringing Justice Home*. Saint Paul, MN: Living Justice Press, 2008.

Boyes-Watson, Carolyn, and Kay Pranis. *Heart of Hope: A Guide for Using Peacemaking Circles to Develop Emotional Literacy, Promote Healing, and Build Healthy Relationships*. Boston, MA: Center for Restorative Justice at Suffolk University and Saint Paul, MN: Living Justice Press, 2010.

Casarjian, Bethany. *The Power Source Facilitator's Manual*. Boston, MA: Lionheart Foundation, 2003.

Claassen, Ron, & Roxanne Claassen. *Discipline That Restores: Strategies to Create Respect, Cooperation, and Responsibility in the Classroom*. South Carolina: Booksurge Publishing, 2008.

Coloroso, Barbara. *The Bully, the Bullied, and the Bystander: From Preschool to High School—How Parents and Teachers Can Help Break the Cycle of Violence*. New York: Quill, HarperCollins, 2003.

Holtham, Jeannette. *Taking Restorative Justice to Schools: A Doorway to Discipline*. Colorado Springs, CO: Homestead Press, 2009.

Hopkins, Belinda. *Just Schools: A Whole-School Approach to Restorative Justice*. London: Jessica Kingsley Publishers, 2004.

Kaba, Mariame, J. Cyriac Mathew, and Nathan Haines. *Something Is Wrong Curriculum: Exploring the Roots of Youth Violence*. Chicago, IL: Project NIA, n.d.. Online: http://www.project-nia.org/docs/Something_Is_Wrong-Curriculum.pdf.

Katz, Judith H. *White Awareness: Handbook for Anti-Racism Training*. Norman, OK: University of Oklahoma Press, 1978, Second Edition, 2003.

Minnesota Department of Children, Families and Learning. *Respecting Everyone's Ability to Resolve Problems: Restorative Measures.* Roseville, MN: Minnesota Department of Children, Families and Learning, 1996.

Nelson, Jane. *Positive Discipline.* New York: Ballantine Books, 2006.

Pittsburgh Action Against Rape: Jayne Anderson, Gail Brown, Julie Evans, Larry Miller, & Jamie Posey Woodson. *Teens and Primary Prevention of Sexual Violence: Where to Start!* n.d. Online at: http://www.pcar.org/sites/default/files/file/TA/teen_primary_prevention_sexual_assault.pdf.

Pranis, Kay. *The Little Book of Circle Processes: A New/Old Approach to Peacemaking.* Intercourse, PA: Good Books, 2005.

Pranis, Kay, Barry Stuart, and Mark Wedge. *Peacemaking Circles: From Crime to Community.* Saint Paul, MN: Living Justice Press, 2003.

Riestenberg, Nancy. *Circle in the Square: Building Community and Repairing Harm in School.* Saint Paul, MN: Living Justice Press, 2012.

Roffey, Sue. *Circle Time for Emotional Literacy.* Thousand Oaks, CA: Sage Publications, 2006. This book is an excellent resource for elementary-age use of Circles.

Stutzman Amstutz, Lorraine, and Judy H. Mullet. *The Little Book of Restorative Discipline for Schools: Teaching Responsibility; Creating Communities.* Intercourse, PA: Good Books, 2005.

Thalhuber, Patricia, and Susan Thompson. *Building a Home for the Heart: Using Metaphors in Value-Centered Circles.* Saint Paul, MN: Living Justice Press, 2007.

Thorsborne, Margaret, and Peta Blood. *Implementing Restorative Practices in Schools: A Practical Guide to Transforming School Communities.* London, UK: Jessica Kingsley Publishers, 2013.

Thorsborne, Margaret, and David Vinegrad. *Restorative Practice in Classrooms: Rethinking Behaviour Management.* Buderim, Queensland: Margaret Thorsborne and Associates, 2002; London: Speechmark Publishing LTD, New Edition 2008.

———.*Restorative Practice in Schools: Rethinking Behaviour Management.* London: Speechmark Publishing Ltd, New Edition 2008.

Wachtel, T., B. Costello, and J. Wachtel. *The Restorative Practices Handbook for Teachers, Disciplinarians and Administrators.* Bethelhem, PA: International Institute of Restorative Practices, 2009.

Watchel, T. and L. Mirsky. *Safe Saner Schools: Restorative Practices in Education.* Bethlehem, Pa.: International Institute for Restorative Practices, 2008.

Wise, Tim. *White Like Me: Reflections on Race from a Privileged Son.* Brooklyn, NY: Soft Skull Press, 2005.

Zehr, Howard. *Changing Lenses: A New Focus for Crime and Justice.* Scottdale, PA and Waterloo, ON: Herald Press, 1990, 3rd edition, 2005.

———.*The Little Book of Restorative Justice.* In the series *The Little Books of Justice & Peacebuilding.* Intercourse, PA: Good Books, 2002.

Articles and handouts: Print and online

Ashley, Jessica, and Kimberly Burke. *Implementing Restorative Justice: A Guide For Schools*. Illinois Criminal Justice Information Authority, 2009. Retrieved from: http://www.healthiersf.org/RestorativePractices/Resources/documents/RP%20Community%20Resources%20and%20Articles/Implementation%20Community%20Resources/SCHOOL%20BARJ%20GUIDEBOOOK.pdf.

Bane, Rosanne. "Seven Levels of Writing Feedback." *The Bane of Your Resistance*. Online at: http://baneofyourresistance.com/2013/04/16/seven-levels-of-writing-feedback/.

Blomberg, Neil. "Effective School Discipline for Misbehavior: In School vs. Out of School Suspension." *Department of Education and Human Services, Villanova University*, (n.d.). Retrieved from: http://www.healthiersf.org/RestorativePractices/Resources/documents/suspension%20ineffective.pdf.

Blood, Peta, and Margaret Thorsborne. "The Challenge of Culture Change: Embedding Restorative Practice in Schools." Paper presented at the Sixth International Conference on Conferencing, Circles and other Restorative Practices: "Building a Global Alliance for Restorative Practices and Family Empowerment." Sydney, Australia, March 2005. Retrieved from: http://www.thorsborne.com.au/conference_papers/Challenge_of_Culture_Change.pdf.

Boyes-Watson, Carolyn, and Kay Pranis. "Science Cannot Fix This: The Limitations of Evidence-Based Practice." *Contemporary Justice Review: Issues in Criminal, Social, and Restorative Justice*, DOI:10.1080/10282580.2012.707421, 2012: 1–11. To link to this article: http://dx.doi.org/10.1080/10282580.2012.707421

Hamre, Bridget K., and Robert C. Pianta. "Early Teacher-Child Relationships and the Trajectory of Children's School Outcomes Through Eighth Grade." *Child Development*, Vol. 72, No. 2 (Mar. – Apr., 2001): 625–38. Retrieved from: http://www.healthiersf.org/RestorativePractices/Resources/documents/RP%20Community%20Resources%20and%20Articles/Power%20of%20Relationships/Early%20Teacher-Child%20Relationships%20and%20the%20Hamre%202001.pdf.

Henke, Joan. *Individualized Education Plans Using the Circle Process*. Available online at http://restorative.tripod.com/page0026.html.

IIRP Graduate School. "Improving School Climate: Findings from Schools Implementing Restorative Practices." Bethlehem, PA: International Institute for Restorative Practices, 2009. Retrieved from: http://www.iirp.edu/pdf/IIRP-Improving-School-Climate.pdf

Las Caras Lindas (LCL) Youth LEAD Institute (YLI), *LEAD Core Program Curriculum*, 2006, revised 2013. http://www.tandemspring.com/wp-content/uploads/LCL-Core-Program-Curriculum_Full-2013.pdf.

Losen, Daniel J., and Russell J. Skiba. "Suspended Education: Urban Middle Schools in Crisis." (n.d.). Retrieved from: http://www.healthiersf.org/RestorativePractices/Resources/documents/RP%20Community%20Resources%20and%20Articles/Out%20of%20School%20Suspensions%20and%20Disproportionality/Suspended-Education_FINAL-2.pdf.

Minnesota Department of Education: "Stages of Implementation." (n.d.) Retrieved from:http://www.healthiersf.org/RestorativePractices/Resources/documents/RP%20Community%20Resources%20and%20Articles/Implementation%20Community%20Resources/016267%20Brief.%20Stages%20of%20Implementation-%20Minnesota.pdf.

Morrison, Brenda, Margaret Thorsborne, and Peta Blood. "Practicing Restorative Justice in School Communities: The Challenge of Culture Change." *Public Organization Review: A Global Journal*, 5(4) (2005): 335–57.

Oakland Unified School District: Family, School, and Community Partnerships Department. "Whole School Restorative Justice." (n.d.) Retrieved from: http://www.ousd.k12.ca.us/cms/lib07/CA01001176/Centricity/Domain/134/Whole%20School%20Restorative%20Justice%20info%20sheet%20FINAL.pdf

Pranis, Kay. "The Practice and Efficacy of Restorative Justice." *Journal of Religion and Spirituality in Social Work*, 23 (1/2), 2004: 133–57.

———."Restorative Values." In D. Van Ness & G. Johnstone (eds.), *Handbook of Restorative Justice*. Portland, OR: Willan, 2007, 59–75.

Riestenberg, Nancy. "Applying the Framework: Positive Youth Development and Restorative Practices." (n.d.) Retrieved from IIRP.edu website: http://www.iirp.edu/pdf/beth06_riestenberg.pdf

Pennsylvania Action Against Rape. *Teens and Primary Prevention of Sexual Violence: Where to Start!* Retrieved from: http://www.pcar.org/sites/default/files/file/TA/teen_primary_prevention_sexual_assault.pdf

Vaandering, Dorothy, and Mark VanderVennen. "Putting Restorative Justice into Practice." *Restorative Justice in Education Monthly Dialog*, September 2013, Volume 5:1. Retrieved from: http://www.ocsta.org/wp-content/uploads/2013/09/Sept-2013-r.pdf.

Warren, Cathy. "Evaluative Review: Lewisham Restorative Approaches Partnership." *CW Associates*, 2005. Retrieved from http://www.healthiersf.org/RestorativePractices/Resources/documents/RP%20Community%20Resources%20and%20Articles/Implementation%20Community%20Resources/RP%20school%20comparisons.pdf.

Websites

Barron County Restorative Justice Programs: Truancy Prevention Programs: http://www.bcrjp.org/students-and-schools/truancy-prevention

Center for Justice and Peacebuilding, Eastern Mennonite University, Harrisonburg, Virginia: http://www.emu.edu/cjp/.

Center for Restorative Justice at Suffolk University: http://www.suffolk.edu/college/centers/14521.php

IIRP: School Based Restorative Zones: http://zones.iirp.edu/

Living Justice Press: www.livingjusticepress.org

Mikva Challenge: http://www.mikvachallenge.org/

Minnesota Department of Education: Restorative Measures: http://education.state.mn.us/MDE/StuSuc/SafeSch/RestorMeas/index.html

Morningside Center for Teaching Social Responsibility: http://www.morningsidecenter.org/, see especially their web pages on Restorative Circles: http://www.morningsidecenter.org/node/760/

Oakland Men's Project: http://paulkivel.com/

Oakland Unified School District: http://www.ousd.k12.ca.us/restorativejustice http://www.ousd.k12.ca.us/cms/lib07/CA01001176/Centricity/Domain/134/Whole%20School%20Restorative%20Justice%20info%20sheet%20FINAL.pdf

Positive Discipline: http://www.positivediscipline.com/

Power Source: The Lionheart Foundation: Emotional Literacy Programs for Prisoners, At Risk Youth, and Teen Parents: http://lionheart.org/

Project NIA: Building Peaceful Communities: http://www.project-nia.org/

Restorative Justice for Oakland Youth: http://rjoyoakland.org/

Restorative Measures in Schools—Jack Mangan: http://restorative.tripod.com/

Safer Saner Schools: http://www.safersanerschools.org/

San Francisco United School District (SFUSD): http://www.sfusd.edu/en/programs/restorative-practices.html http://www.healthiersf.org/RestorativePractices/

Sensibilities Prevention Services, Cordelia Anderson: http://www.cordeliaanderson.com/

STAR (Strategies for Trauma Awareness and Resilience) at Center for Justice and Peacebuilding Program, Eastern Mennonite University, Harrisonburg, Virginia: http://www.emu.edu/cjp/star/.

Teens and Primary Prevention of Sexual Violence: Where to Start! http://www.pcar.org/sites/default/files/file/TA/teen_primary_prevention_sexual_assault.pdf

Transforming Conflict: National Centre for Restorative Approaches in Youth Settings. www.transformingconflict.org

II. RESOURCES FOR CIRCLE OPENINGS AND CLOSINGS

Books and printed material

Baldwin, James. *James Baldwin: Collected Essays: Notes of a Native Son / Nobody Knows My Name / The Fire Next Time / No Name in the Street / The Devil Finds Work / Other Essays*. Toni Morrison, editor. Library of America, 1998.

Barks, Coleman, with John Moyne, translators. *The Essential Rumi*. San Francisco, CA: HarperSanFrancisco, 1995.

Baylor, Byrd, and Peter Parnall. The Other Way to Listen. New York: Aladdin, 1997 Reprint edition.

Bopp, Judie, Michael Bopp, Lee Brown, and Phil Lane, Jr. *The Sacred Tree: Reflections on Native American Spirituality*. Lethbridge, AB, Canada: Four Worlds International Institute, 1984.

Brown, Brené. *Daring Greatly: How the Courage to Be Vulnerable Transforms the Way We Live, Love, Parent, and Lead*. New York: Gotham Books, Penguin, 2012.

———. *The Gifts of Imperfection: Let Go of Who You Think You're Supposed to Be and Embrace Who You Are*. Center City, MN: Hazelden, 2010.

Casarjian, Robin. *Forgiveness: A Bold Choice for a Peaceful Heart*. New York: Bantam, 1992.

Clark, Dan. *Puppies For Sale*. Available online at: http://danclarkspeak.com/story-of-the-day/.

Coudert, Jo. *Advice from a Failure*. Bloomington, IN: iUniverse, 2003.

Edelman, Marian Wright. *Guide My Feet: Prayers and Meditations for Our Children*. New York: Harper Paperbacks, 2000.

Fernandez, Avaro, Dr. Elkhonon Goldberg, Dr. Misha Pavel, Gloria Cavanaugh, Dr. Sandra Bond Chapman, and Dr. Pascale Michelon. *The SharpBrains Guide to Brain Fitness: How to Optimize Brain Health and Performance at Any Age*. San Francisco, CA: SharpBrains Incorporated, 2nd Edition, 2013.

Frankl, Viktor E. *Man's Search for Meaning*. Boston, MA: Beacon Press, 2006 edition, originally published in 1946.

Gabriel, Peter. "Peter Gabriel: Fight Injustice with Raw Video." *TED Talk*, February 2006. Transcript at: http://www.ted.com/talks/peter_gabriel_fights_injustice_with_video/transcript

Gibran, Kahlil. *The Prophet*. Ware, Hertfordshire, England: Wordsworth Editions Limited, 1996.

Hillesum, Etty. *Etty Hillesum: An Interrupted Life: The Diaries, 1941–1943; and Letters from Westerbork*. New York: Picador/Macmillan, 1996.

hooks, bell. *Teaching Community: A Pedagogy of Hope*. New York: Routledge, 2003.

———. *All about Love: New Visions*. New York: William Morrow, 2001.

Hughes, Langston, *The Collected Poems of Langston Hughes*, Arnold Rampersad, editor. New York: Alfred A. Knopf, 1994.

Johnson, Sonia. *Going Out of Our Minds: The Metaphysics of Liberation*. Berkeley, CA: Crossing Press, 1987.

Kalwar, Santosh. *Adventus: Collected Poems*. lulu.com, 2011.

Kivel, Paul. *Uprooting Racism: How White People Can Work for Social Justice*. Gabriola Island, BC: New Society Publishers, 2002.

LaDuke, Winona. "LaDuke: His Giggles Illuminated His Wisdom." *Inforum*, 7 June 2014. Online at: http://www.inforum.com/content/laduke-his-giggles-illuminated-his-wisdom.

Littlebird, Larry. *Hunting Sacred, Everything Listens: A Pueblo Indian Man's Oral Tradition Legacy*. Santa Fe, NM: Western Edge Press, 2001.

López, Ian F. Haney. "The Social Construction of Race," in *Critical Race Theory: The Cutting Edge, Second Edition*, Richard Delgado & Jean Stefancic, editors. Philadelphia, PA: Temple University Press, 2000.

Miller, James E. *The Art of Listening in a Healing Way*. Fort Wayne, IN: Willowgreen Publishing, 2003.

Neihardt, John G. *Black Elk Speaks: Being the Life Story of a Holy Man of the Oglala Sioux*. Lincoln, NE: University of Nebraska Press, 1979.

Oliver, Mary. *Dream Work*. New York: The Atlantic Monthly Press, 1986.

Olsen, W., and W. A. Sommers. *A Trainer's Companion: Stories to Stimulate Reflection, Conversation and Action*. Baytown, TX: AhaProcess, 2004.

Oriah. *The Invitation*. San Francisco: HarperOne, 2006, originally published 1999.

Palmer, Parker. *A Hidden Wholeness: The Journey Toward an Undivided Life*. San Francisco, CA: Jossey-Bass, 2009.

Pranis, Kay, Barry Stuart, and Mark Wedge. *Peacemaking Circles: From Crime to Community*. Saint Paul, MN: Living Justice Press, 2003.

Ross, Rupert. *Returning to the Teachings: Exploring Aboriginal Justice*. Toronto, ON: Penguin Canada, 1996, 2006.

Shannon, Maggie Oman, ed. *Prayers for Healing: 365 Blessings, Poems, & Meditations from Around the World*. Newburyport, MA: Conari Press, 2000.

Shiva, Shahram. *Hush, Don't Say Anything to God: Passionate Poems of Rumi*. Fremont, CA: Jain Publishing Company, 1999.

Stewart, Iris J. *Sacred Women, Sacred Dance: Awakening Spirituality Through Movement and Ritual*. Rochester, VT: Inner Traditions, 2000.

Thich Nhat Hanh. *Teachings on Love*. Berkeley, CA: Parallax Press, 2013.

———. *Making Space: Creating a Home Meditation Practice*. Berkeley, CA: Parallax Press, 2011.

———. *Peace Is Every Step: The Path of Mindfulness in Everyday Life*. New York: Bantam, 1992.

Walker, Alice. *Revolutionary Petunias*. Fort Washington, PA: Harvest Book, an imprint of Harcourt, Brace, 1973.

———.*Sent by Earth: A Message from the Grandmother Spirit after the Attacks on the World Trade Center and Pentagon*. New York: Seven Stories Press, 2001.

Weil, Andrew. *Spontaneous Healing: How to Discover and Embrace Your Body's Natural Ability to Maintain and Heal Itself*. New York: Ballantine Books, 2000.

Westerhoff, Caroline A. "Conflict: The Birthing of the New." In *Conflict Management in Congregations,* ed. David B. Lott. Bethesda, MD: The Alban Institute, 2001, 54–61. The article was originally published in *Action Information* 12, no. 3 (May/June 1986): 1–5.

Wheatley, Margaret J. *Turning to One Another: Simple Conversations to Restore Hope to the Future*. San Francisco, CA: Berrett-Koehler Publishers, 2002, Second Edition 2009.

Williamson, Marianne. *A Return to Love: Reflections on the Principles of "A Course in Miracles."* San Francisco: HarperOne, 1996.

Wold, Margaret. *The Critical Moment: How Personal Crisis Can Enrich a Woman's Life*. Minneapolis, MN: Augsburg, 1978.

Yazzie, Hon. Robert. "Whose Criminal Justice System? New Conceptions of Indigenous Justice." In *Justice as Healing: A Newsletter on Aboriginal Concepts of Justice,* 2014, Vol. 19, No. 2. Saskatoon, SK: Native Law Centre, 2014.

Zinn, Howard. *A Power Governments Cannot Suppress*. San Francisco, CA: City Lights Publishers, 2006.

Websites

Albert Einstein Site Online—Albert Einstein Quotes: http://www.alberteinsteinsite.com/quotes/einsteinquotes.html

California Indian Education website: http://www.californiaindianeducation.org/famous_indian_chiefs/chief_seattle/

Dalai Lama: http://www.dalailama.com/messages/environment/global-environment

Gratitude HD—Moving Art: http://www.youtube.com/watch?v=nj2ofrX7jAk&feature=youtu.be

Inclusion Press, "What Is Inclusion?": http://www.inclusion.com/inclusion.html

Kabat-Zinn, Jon. Palouse Mindfulness: Stress Reduction and Wellness. http://palousemindfulness.com/index.html.

Littlebird, Larry. HAMAATSA. http://www.hamaatsa.org/index.html. This site has a wealth of resources, including short video clips that offer Indigenous wisdom and perspectives.

More than that . . . : http://www.youtube.com/watch?v=FhribaNXr7A

Rosanne Bane. *The Bane of Your Resistance*: http://baneofyourresistance.com/2013/04/16/seven-levels-of-writing-feedback/

Williamson, Marianne. http://www.marianne.com/

APPENDIX 5

A Level Guide to the Circles

Most of the Circles in this book can be adapted to the age of the participants by changing the language, though some in Module 6 are obviously suited for older students. That said, we offer this guide for the level of the Circles "as is"—as they are written and presented here, perhaps with only minor adjustments. The x's in parentheses signify Circles that may be relevant but would need to be adapted for the age group.

For elementary school teachers, wonderful additional resources exist. We point to Jack Mangan's work on Restorative Measures in Schools, http://restorative.tripod.com/, as well as to Marg Armstrong's website, Just Practices, http://www.justpractices.com.au/, especially under "Resources": "Circle Time Resources."

Circle Subject	Elemen. School	Middle School	High School	Page No.
1.2 Introducing Circles in Schools	x	x	x	49
1.3 Introducing the Talking Piece	x	x	x	51
1.4 Circle for Making a Talking Piece	x	x	x	52
1.5 Practicing the Use of the Talking Piece Circle	x	x	x	54
1.6 Building Our Circle Skills Circle	x	x	x	56
2.1 Creating a Safe and Happy Classroom Circle	x			59
2.2 Circle for Designing Our Classroom Community to Meet Our Needs	x	x	x	60
2.3 Exploring Our Values-in-Action Circles	x	x	x	62
2.4 Coming to Consensus on Classroom Agreements (Guidelines) Circle	x	x	x	63
2.5 Checking-In with Guidelines Circle (I): Setting Our Intentions	x	x	x	65
2.6 Checking-In with Guidelines Circle II: Taking the Temperature on Classroom Climate	x	x	x	66
2.7 Understanding and Living with School Rules Circle	x	x	x	68
3.1 Finding Out What Students Already Know Circle	x	x	x	71
3.2 Checking for Understanding Circle	x	x	x	72
3.3 Building Vocabulary Circle	x	x	x	73
3.4 Sharing Student Writing in a "Read-Around" Circle		x	x	75
3.5 Practicing a Foreign Language Circle: Beginner to Intermediate		x	x	79
3.6 Sharing Reflections Circle		x	x	81
3.7 Using Storybooks to Teach Values Circle (also easily adapted to higher levels)	x	(x)	(x)	83
3.8 Talking About Homework/Studying Circle	x	x	x	85

Circle Subject	Elemen. School	Middle School	High School	Page No.
3.9 Three-Minute Focus Circle	x	x	x	87
4.1 Check-In Circle: Practices for Building Relationships	x	x	x	91
4.2 Celebration Circle	x	x	x	92
4.3 Showing Gratitude and Appreciation Circle	x	x	x	94
4.4 Sticking Together Circle	x	x	x	96
4.5 What Is Friendship? Circle	x	x	x	97
4.6 Picturing My Future Circle	x	x	x	99
4.7 What Does Success Mean? Circle		x	x	100
4.8 Relationship Building Circle	x	x	x	101
4.9 Exploring Dimensions of Our Identity Circle	x	x	x	103
4.10 The Gender Box Circle	(x)	x	x	106
4.11 Elements of a Healthy Relationship Circle	(x)	x	x	109
4.12 Choosing Trustworthy Friends	(x)	x	x	111
4.13 Sports Team-Building: Relationship Circle		x	x	113
4.14 Sports Team-Building: Deepening Relationships Circle		x	x	115
4.15 Reflecting on Winning and Losing Circle		x	x	116
4.16 Reflection after a Game Circle		x	x	118
4.17 Welcome Back after Classroom Absence Circle	x	x	x	119
5.1 Listening to the Silence Circle	x	x	x	123
5.2 Who and What Makes Us Feel Good? Circle	x	x	x	125
5.3 Dealing with Inside and Outside Hurts Circle	x	x	x	126
5.4 What Triggers Your Anger? Circle	x	x	x	128
5.5 What Are You Worried About? Circle	x	x	x	129
5.6 Daily Emotional Weather Report Circle	(x)	x	x	131
5.7 Who Am I Really? Circle		x	x	135
5.8 Safe Space Circle	x	x	x	138
5.9 Managing Mountains Circle	x	x	x	140
6.1 What Motivates You? Circle		x	x	145
6.2 Being Left Out Circle	x	x	x	147
6.3 Let's Talk about Bullying Circle	x	x	x	148
6.4 The Impact of Gossip Circle	x	x	x	149
6.5 Bereavement Circle	x	x	x	151
6.6 Responding to Community Trauma Circle	x	x	x	153
6.7 Dealing with Losses Circle	(x)	x	x	155
6.8 Masking Grief Circle	x	x	x	160
6.9 Understanding Trauma Circle	(x)	x	x	163
6.10 Witnessing Violence Circle	(x)	x	x	165
6.11 Roots of Youth Violence Circle	(x)	x	x	169
6.12 The Impact of Social Hierarchies on Me Circle		x	x	172
6.13 Talking about Structural Inequality: Privilege and Oppression Circle			x	175

Circle Subject	Elemen. School	Middle School	High School	Page No.
6.14 What Do We Know about Race? Circle		x	x	179
6.15 What Difference Does Race Make? Circle		x	x	182
6.16 Exploring Our Feelings about Race Circle		x	x	184
6.17 Exploring White Privilege Circle			x	186
6.18 Exploring the Impact of Social Inequality Circle			x	190
6.19 Thinking about Gender and Violence Circle			x	193
6.20 Thinking about Gender Inequality Circle			x	196
6.21 Thinking and Talking about OUR Boundaries Circle (For Girls)	(x)	x	x	198
6.22 Sexual Harassment and Bystander Circle	(x)	x	x	200
6.23 Love and Marriage Circle		x	x	203
6.24 When We're Different or At-Odds with Society Circle	(x)	x	x	205
7.7 Student and Teacher Class Assessment Circle	x	x	x	220
7.10 Exploring Our Core Assumptions Circle		x	x	226
9.1 What Do Adults Need to Understand about Our Lives? Circle	x	x	x	257
9.2 Visioning a Good Life Circle	x	x	x	259
9.3 Circle for Student Focus Groups on a School Issue or Policy		x	x	261
9.4 Exploring Cultural Responsiveness in the School Circle		x	x	263
10.1 Intensive Support: Building Relationships Circle	(x)	x	x	267
10.2 Intensive Support: Map of Resources Circle	(x)	x	x	270
10.3 Intensive Support: Making a Plan Circle	(x)	x	x	272
10.4 Intensive Support: Check-In Circles	(x)	x	x	274
10.5 Intensive Support: Celebration Circle	x	x	x	276
10.6 What Went Right in Your Family Circle	(x)	x	x	278
10.7 Identifying Sources of Support Circle	(x)	x	x	280
11.1 Understanding the Restorative Justice Framework for Addressing Harm Circle I	(x)	x	x	290
11.2 Understanding the Restorative Justice Framework for Addressing Harm Circle II	(x)	x	x	292
11.3 What Will Make It Right? Circle	(x)	x	x	294
12.1 Template for a Restorative Discipline Circle	x	x	x	302
12.2 Template for a Circle about a Conflict	x	x	x	304
12.3 Template for a Silent Circle Responding to Conflict Immediately		x	x	306
12.4 Classroom Circle for Responding to Harm without Focusing on the Wrongdoer	x	x	x	308
12.5 Welcome Back after Suspension Circle	(x)	x	x	310
12.6 The Class That Ate the Sub Circle	x	x	x	312

About the Authors

CAROLYN BOYES-WATSON and **KAY PRANIS** have been collaborating to generate resources and literature on restorative justice, the Circle process, and restorative practices in schools for a number of years. Their coauthored works include:

- *Heart of Hope Resource Guide: A Guide for Using Peacemaking Circles to Develop Emotional Literacy, Promote Healing, and Build Healthy Relationships* (Center for Restorative Justice at Suffolk University and Living Justice Press, 2010).

- "Science Cannot Fix This: The Limitations of Evidence-Based Practice," *Contemporary Justice Review: Issues in Criminal, Social, and Restorative Justice,* July 2012, pp. 265–75. DOI:10.1080/10282580.2012.707421. Online at: http://www.tandfonline.com/doi/abs/10.1080/10282580.2012.707421#.U6riN6gysjU.

CAROLYN BOYES-WATSON, PH.D.

Carolyn Boyes-Watson is the founding director of Suffolk University's Center for Restorative Justice and Professor of Sociology at Suffolk University where she has been on the faculty since 1993. She holds a bachelor's degree from the University of Pennsylvania and a Ph.D. in sociology from Harvard University. Carolyn has authored and coauthored a number of articles and books about the criminal justice system, juvenile justice system, and restorative justice. Of particular interest is *Peacemaking Circles and Urban Youth: Bringing Justice Home* (Living Justice Press, 2008) and *Heart of Hope,* co-authored with Kay Pranis.

KAY PRANIS

Kay Pranis is an international leader in restorative justice, specializing in peacemaking Circles. She served as the Restorative Justice Planner for the Minnesota Department of Corrections from 1994 to 2003 and worked six years before that as the director of research services at the Citizen's Council on Crime and Justice. She has written and presented papers on peacemaking Circles and restorative justice in the United States, Canada, Australia, Brazil, and Japan. Since 1998, Kay has conducted Circle trainings in a diverse range of communities—from schools to prisons to workplaces to churches, from rural farm towns in Minnesota to Chicago's South Side. Kay has written a number of articles and books on restorative justice and the peacemaking including:

- *Peacemaking Circles: From Crime to Community* with Barry Stuart and Mark Wedge (Living Justice Press, 2003).

- *Doing Democracy with Circles: Engaging Communities in Public Planning* with Jennifer Ball and Wayne Caldwell (Living Justice Press, 2010).

- *The Little Book of Circle Processes: A New/Old Approach to Peacemaking* (Good Books, 2005).

Institute for Restorative Initiatives (IRIS)

The Institute for Restorative Initiatives (IRIS) was founded in 2013 to promote collaborative partnerships with schools, juvenile justice agencies and youth-serving organizations. IRIS assists schools, agencies, and systems to implement restorative approaches within their organizations through training, professional development, coaching, and evaluation.

http://www.instituteforrestorativeinitiatives.org/

ABOUT THE CENTER FOR RESTORATIVE JUSTICE SUFFOLK UNIVERSITY

The Center for Restorative Justice (CRJ) at Suffolk University was founded by Carolyn Boyes-Watson in 1997. CRJ's mission is to serve as a bridge between the academy, professionals, and communities through public education, training, technical assistance, research, evaluation, and scholarship. As a community-engaged academic center, CRJ fosters restorative approaches to resolving conflict and harm in justice systems, schools, and communities.

http://www.suffolk.edu/college/centers/14521.php

OTHER BOOKS ON CIRCLES & EDUCATION FROM LIVING JUSTICE PRESS

A 501(c)(3) tax-exempt, nonprofit publisher on restorative justice

Circle in the Square: Building Community and Repairing Harm in School by Nancy Riestenberg, ISBN 978-0-9721886-7-8, paperback, 192 pages, index; eBook ISBN: 978-1-937141-08-0.

Heart of Hope Resource Guide: A Guide for Using Peacemaking Circles to Develop Emotional Literacy, Promote Healing, and Build Healthy Relationships by Carolyn Boyes-Watson & Kay Pranis. ISBN 978-0-615-37988-3, spiral bound, 352 pages. Co-published with the Center for Restorative Justice at Suffolk University, 2010.

Peacemaking Circles: From Crime to Community by Kay Pranis, Barry Stuart, and Mark Wedge, ISBN 0-9721886-0-6, paperback, 271 pages, index; eBook ISBN: 978-1-937141-01-1.

Peacemaking Circles and Urban Youth: Bringing Justice Home by Carolyn Boyes-Watson, ISBN 978-0-9721886-4-7, paperback, 296 pages, index; eBook ISBN: 978-1-937141-05-9.

Building a Home for the Heart: Using Metaphors in Value-Centered Circles by Pat Thalhuber, B.V.M., and Susan Thompson, foreword by Kay Pranis, illustrated by Loretta Draths, ISBN 978-0-9721886-3-0, paperback, 224 pages, index; eBook ISBN: 978-1-937141-04-2.

Doing Democracy with Circles: Engaging Communities in Public Planning by Jennifer Ball, Wayne Caldwell, and Kay Pranis, ISBN 978-0-9721886-6-1, paperback, 208 pages, index; eBook ISBN: 978-1-937141-07-3.

A Call for Indigenous Education: Returning to Our Communal Ways by Gregory A. Cajete, ISBN 978-1-1937141-17-2, paperback, approx. 220 pages, index; eBook ISBN: 978-1-937141-18-9.

20% discount on orders of 10 books or more—call or email us. Print and eBooks are available from LJP's website as well as other places online and can be ordered through most bookstores.

Order by phone, fax, mail, or online at:

2093 Juliet Avenue, St. Paul, MN 55105
Tel. (651) 695-1008 / Fax. (651) 695-8564 / E-mail: ljpress@aol.com
Website: www.livingjusticepress.org

BOOKS ON ADDRESSING HARMS BETWEEN PEOPLES FROM LIVING JUSTICE PRESS

A 501(c)(3) tax-exempt, nonprofit publisher on restorative justice

Justice As Healing: Indigenous Ways, edited by Wanda D. McCaslin, ISBN 0-9721886-1-4, paperback, 459 pages, index; eBook ISBN: 978-1-937141-02-8.

What Does Justice Look Like? The Struggle for Liberation in Dakota Homeland, by Waziyatawin, ISBN 0-9721886-5-7, paperback, 200 pages, index; eBook ISBN: 978-1-937141-06-6.

In the Footsteps of Our Ancestors: The Dakota Commemorative Marches of the 21st Century, edited by Waziyatawin Angela Wilson, ISBN 0-9721886-2-2, oversize paperback, 316 pages, over 100 photographs, color photo insert, index; eBook ISBN: 978-1-937141-03-5.

He Sapa Woihanble: Black Hills Dream, edited by Craig Howe, Lydia Whirlwind Soldier, and Lanniko L. Lee, ISBN 978-0-9721886-9-2, paperback, 240 pages, index; eBook ISBN: 978-1-937141-09-7.

From the River's Edge, by Elizabeth Cook-Lynn, ISBN 978-1-937141-12-7, paperback, 148 pages; eBook ISBN 978-1-937141-13-4.

Indigenous Nations' Rights in the Balance: An Analysis of the Declaration on the Rights of Indigenous Peoples, by Charmaine White Face, ISBN 978-0-9721886-8-5; paperback, 158 pages; index; eBook ISBN: 978-1-937141-11-0.

Harm-Dependent No More: Who Are We—Winners and Losers or Relatives? by Denise C. Breton, ISBN 978-1-937141-00-4, index; eBook ISBN: 978-1-937141-10-3. Forthcoming.

20% discount on orders of 10 books or more—call or email us. Print and eBooks are available from LJP's website as well as other places online and can be ordered through most bookstores.

Order by phone, fax, mail, or online at:

2093 Juliet Avenue, St. Paul, MN 55105
Tel. (651) 695-1008 / Fax. (651) 695-8564 / E-mail: ljpress@aol.com
Website: www.livingjusticepress.org

Notes